# *Drawing Close to God*
# *365 Days*
# *of*
# *Daily Devotionals & Prayer*

*By: Nicole Atkinson*

ISBN: 1718716354
ISBN-13: 978-1718716353

# DEDICATION

This book is dedicated to my loving husband. Mr. Jamar Atkinson who has always supported me in all of my dreams and aspirations. You are my number 1 fan and I love you forever. To my beautiful children Jamiya, Janel, Janae, and Jace thank you for always supporting mommy and allowing me to teach you in the admonition of the Lord. To my family and friends thank you for being true endorsers of everything I put my mind too. I love you all!!!!!

# Table of Contents

# January 1

*Ask of Me, and I will give You the nations as Your inheritance, and the uttermost parts of the earth as Your possession.* (Psalm 2:8)

What better way to fulfill our passion than to ask God for a vision. God gives willingly to His children who seek His face. Since He is the ruler of the earth it only seems fitting for us to honor Him by seeking His divine plan for our life. At the beginning of each year most people make resolutions. Everyone has high hopes of achieving their new goals, forgetting the past and aiming for an improved future. This is the life God desires for us to have in every season. He doesn't require us to wait for a new year. He wants us to continuously move forward with His divine plan for our lives. Principles for accomplishing God's plans for our life require us to serve Him with reverent awe and allow Him to instruct our daily pursuits. When we dedicate time to fellowship with God, He is able to reveal Himself to us. Our success is tied to our obedience to God's voice. His plans are already established. If we are willing and obedient He is more than prepared to make known to us His design for our lives. We are able to ask God for anything. He anticipates us coming to receive our inheritance. He has it prepared for us and is ready to release it. Every dream, every desire that God has implanted in our spirit has the potential to be manifested this year. Seek His face with reverence and long for His greatness, believing the promise and we will receive what we ask for.

**The Promise of God is Yea and Amen!**

Prayer: Hallelujah Lord, we made it by Your grace and mercy alone. Lord, we rejoice in Your goodness, loving kindness and grace, which You give new each day. We count this year as blessed. You know the end from the beginning and we stand in agreement with Your Word for our lives. You know the thoughts and plans You have for us. Thoughts of peace and not of evil to give us an expected end. We expect this year to be greater than ever before. This is the year where we will worship You like never before. We will honor You like never before. We will sit in Your presence and labor at Your feet until You move in our lives. Open our eyes that we may render our hearts to You. We offer up a sacrifice of praise. Give us the vision and we will write it and make it plain. Yes is our response to Your voice. Develop us this year; establish everything we set out to do. In Jesus' name we praise You, Amen.

# January 2

*Making the very most of your time on earth, recognizing and taking advantage of each opportunity and using it with wisdom and diligence, because the days are filled with evil.* (Ephesians 5:16)

I bet you are extremely busy with the cares of the world on your shoulder. Personal goals, family obligations and careers all fight for our attention, making it hard to obtain a consistent balance. We live in such a fast-paced society that nearly everyone is busy trying to accomplish a million things at once. This is great, but without seeking God and His plan it is all worthless.

Our lives should be filtered before God. We have to make a constant effort to bring our plans to Him and ask for clear direction. Having a false balance is an abomination to God (Proverbs 11:1); meaning God is not pleased when we have too many things going on and we aren't proficient in doing what He called us to do. We are to make the most of our time by not wasting it on things that are contrary to God's purpose. Instead, we are to use every opportunity to walk as the light of the earth and bring glory to God. Time is precious, and the days are filled with evil. There is a constant battle between our flesh and God's Spirit within us. Wisdom from God and diligence (constant effort) to accomplish good work will be the deciding factor in how we choose to utilize our time. Giving God first place and being obedient is a sure way to relieve pressure and rest in the peace of God.

**Spend 10 minutes in silence before God with no distractions, just an expectation of God's Spirit.**

Prayer: "Thank You Father for salvation. Because of You we have another opportunity at life. Not just any life but a perfect life in Christ Jesus. We will follow Christ's example and live righteous, putting the needs of others before our own; aiming to please You in our conduct and character. Set us apart for Your holy work. Renew our mind continuously so we can do only what is pleasing in Your sight. Our love for You could never compare to the way You love us. We are forever thankful and give our life to be used by You. Remove everything that tries to keep us in bondage. We are free in Christ Jesus. We give you glory. In Jesus' name we pray, Amen."

# January 3

*The Lord said to him, "Take off your sandals, because the place where you are now standing is holy ground."* (Acts 7:33)

Father, please forgive us for taking Your presence for granted. To think about the majestic being of God we must understand and realize His presence warrants respect and honor. We are all guilty of falling short of giving God the proper honor. Thankfully, God is merciful and has granted us grace. He knew our hearts would be tainted by the cares of the world that cause us to sometimes put Him on the back burner. This is not our desire but so often it is our reality. So today we ask for forgiveness. We ask for another chance to come before the throne of grace and give God the respect and honor He desires. We put God first by seeking His face and worshipping in His presence; not asking for anything, just enjoying His company. Lord, turn our intellect off and fill us with Your Spirit as we bask in Your presence. This place of holies is the best place any of us could ever experience. Complete surrender in God's face for Him to reveal His beauty.

**Here I am to Worship!**

**What areas in your life do you need to offer to God in Worship? (Romans 12:1)**

Prayer: Lord, we thank You for another day on earth where we can experience the beauty of Your presence. Make us aware of Your surroundings. Help us not to take Your love for granted. Help not to be so busy we put other things before You. You are holy and require that we be holy. Open our mind to know and understand Your majestic beauty. Don't let us wait until we see You face to face to honor You. We honor You now. We love You now. We worship You now. We expect to see Your goodness in the land of the living. All praise belongs to You and we give it to You. In Jesus' name we pray Amen.

# January 4

*A few days later, Jesus went out to a mountain to pray. He stayed there all night praying to God. The next morning he called his followers. He chose twelve of them and called them apostles. These are the ones he chose:* (Luke 6:12-13)

Making a decision in life without hearing from God is like walking down a busy street wearing a blindfold. Advice from friends and family is great and can provide some insight; yet it is incomparable with hearing clear direction from God. Before Jesus made any decisions He sought God. He only did what He saw the Father doing. We find comfort in knowing that everything God does is perfect. Jesus was about to pick the men who would closely follow Him and whom He would entrust with carrying out the gospel. God uniquely created each of us with greatness, leaving the only way for us to tap into our full potential and plans for our life to the act of fellowship with Him on a continuous basis. The more we pray the more God reveals Himself to us. In getting to know Him, we learn who we are and the reason for our existence. This is an awesome principle for kingdom living. Get in God's face and receive guidance before every decision. This way you know for sure success is guaranteed. Don't grow anxious if you don't hear from God immediately after-all the bible says Jesus stayed in God's face all night.

**The more you pray!**

**Are you willing to sacrifice time for a lifetime of blessings?**

Prayer: God give us a heart to pray. In your presence is the fullness of joy. You know all things. Give us a heart to seek You in every decision we make. Show us Your plan for our life. Give us business plans, financial instruction, and guidance on how to love and honor You. Prayer is the gateway to heaven. We come boldly to hear what heaven is saying. Your will be done in earth as it is in heaven. In Jesus' name we pray Amen!

# January 5

*And he said to them, "The harvest is plentiful, but the laborers are few. Therefore pray earnestly to the Lord of the harvest to send out laborers into his harvest."* (Luke 10:2)

Who told you about Jesus? Whether it was a friend, family members or a plain ole tug on your heart, we found ourselves surrendering our all to Him. It doesn't stop there; God has called us fishers of men. Our very lives should draw people to want to know Him. I get that we live in a world where it's easy to talk about sex and drugs, but at the mention of the name of Jesus people shy away. The reason is we have become so comfortable seeing these images on TV, billboards, and magazines that they become a normal part of our conversations. Wrong answer, instead Jesus should be the focal point. My pastor always says three things should always reflect Jesus in our lives and that is our conduct, conversation, and our character. Once we have these things intact we will be able to minister without bible thumping people over the head. Our lifestyle will exemplify kingdom standards. God's harvest is plentiful, meaning there is room in His kingdom to bring the lost in and give them eternal life. We are commissioned as labors to deny ourselves and spread the gospel. After all, it should be our desire for others to experience the joy we have found in Jesus.

**Give someone Jesus!**

Prayer: Lord give us the mindset to labor for Your kingdom. Your harvest is plentiful but the laborers are few. We pray now that our heart is concerned about the condition of the world. We are bold as lions, declaring the wonder working power of Your hands. We call ever unbeliever saved and every backslider restored. The lost know You. The sick are healed. The broken are at peace. You reign Supreme. Show us Your power in the transformation of lives. All glory belongs to You. In Jesus' name we pray, Amen.

# January 6

*As the Scriptures say, "Who can know what is on the Lord's mind? Who is able to give him advice?" But we have been given Christ's way of thinking.* (1 Corinthians 2:16)

Let us not forget the many gifts of God; one being His awesome Spirit. As we know, the Spirit searches the heart of God and comes to give those who love God clear direction and revelation. God is wisdom and apart from Him we are wasting our time on earth. If we utilize the gifts of God and allow His Spirit to speak to us concerning the things of God, we will tap into God's spiritual blessings. The bible says we have been blessed in the spiritual realm with ALL spiritual blessings. Hallelujah! Every blessing God is going to give us is already prepared. We have to seek His face and allow His Spirit to guide us in all truth. Scripture also states no eye has seen no ear heard or entered into the heart of man the things which God has prepared for him. These revelations only come by God's Spirit within us (2 Corinthians 2:9-10). Walking around as if we can do life without God is causing us to miss out on our divine purpose. Just think about wanting to give someone you love a perfect gift. You have it all prepared, and you're excited to give it to him or her. You wait day and night for them to come receive it and they never come. God exclusively took his time to create His perfect plan for us. Walking in the Spirit allows us to become aware of God's presence moment by moment. I'll let you in on a little secret, honoring God is two-fold; you reap benefits as well.

**You are God alone!**

Prayer: God, thank You for giving us Your Spirit. Teach us what is on Your heart. Show us how to accomplish those things You have prepared for us long ago. Give us wisdom concerning everything in our lives. Help us to have a heart that desires the things You desire. You get all the glory. In Jesus' name we pray, Amen.

# January 7

*"Of course I will go with you," Deborah answered. "But because of your attitude, you will not be honored when Sisera is defeated."* (Judges 4:9)

My, my, my, how many times has our attitude gotten us in trouble? One of the hardest things to do is to maintain a right attitude, especially when people or life throw us punches. God teaches us how the matter of the heart determines one's attitude. So if we want to have a right attitude we have to deal with the issues of our heart. For out of the heart flow the issues of life (Proverbs 4:23). Here in scripture we discover how a man's attitude changed the very outcome of his situation. During a trial is not the time to examine our heart, because it might be too late. Daily, we must surrender our heart to God and bind His Word around our neck and allow it to influence our actions. Whatever our hearts are filled with will overflow through our attitude. It's our choice to make room for joy, peace, understanding and the ability to let things go in order for our attitude to reflect the Spirit of God. The good thing is, God doesn't leave us to do this on our own. Spending time with Him will heal broken areas, transform our thinking and give us proper perspective. We were never created to carry the weight of the world on our shoulders. God has always commanded us to cast our cares on Him. As we do this on a consistent basis, God develops our faith and we are able to get through challenges with a right attitude because we are aware of God's presence within us. We will be tested and will have to make a choice on whether our attitude will produce righteousness or be the work of our flesh.

**Check your heart!**

Prayer: Heavenly Father, create in us a clean heart and renew a right Spirit within us. Examine our motives. Get to the deepest place in our heart and uproot EVERYTHING that is not like You. We need to have a right attitude so we can accomplish Your good work here on the earth. Father, have Your way in and through us; starting with transforming our mind and conditioning our heart to

ALWAYS reflect the kingdom. In Jesus' name we pray Amen.

## January 8

*Continue steadfastly in prayer, being watchful in it with thanksgiving.* (Colossians 4:2 ESV)
*Devote yourselves to prayer with an alert mind and a thankful heart.* (Colossians 4:2 NLT)

God has put it on my heart to rejoice. Its time to remove complaining from our thought pattern and be thankful. I think it is amazing how this verse says to continue in steadfast prayer (steadfast: firmly fixed in place; immovable) with an alert mind and thankful heart. We should be continuously praying for things to take place in our lives. If we are not pleased with the way things are developing, Paul encourages us to pray about it. This verse teaches us to consciously think about everything we do by having an "alert mind." Being aware of what we think helps us in the process of building our future through our choices. What we do today are the seeds for our future tomorrow. To be in right standing with God we have to devote ourselves to prayer. This is personal communication with Him through His son Jesus. We have to focus our minds to be alert, while teaching our hearts to be thankful no matter what our current circumstances are. I heard a pastor say one time that our emotions aren't that smart. What he meant is, if we tell our emotions to be sad by constantly thinking about what is not working for us, it will manifest in complaining and a negative attitude. The same process works if we demand our emotions to fall in line with God's command to rejoice and again I say rejoice (Philippians 4:4). Paul was on to something and wanted to share his revelation with others. He knew that it is during prayer, times of communion with God, where we have all of our needs met. Just think about how comforting it feels when you talk to someone you love. You pour out your heart to them and they comfort you, give you guidance and words of encouragement. God will communicate with you, He will guide you on the right path. We must do everything with a thankful spirit. Thanking God at all times through the good and the bad. He loves you.

**I command my spirit to be thankful!**

Prayer: God, the most gracious and Almighty. I love you and praise you. Thank you, Thank you, thank you for allowing me to see another day. Thank you that my family is healthy and we are all able to open our mouths and give you praise. Lord, if we have fallen short in any way in which our spirits were not thankful or grateful for your mercy, please forgive us. Lord, you alone consume our hearts and minds. God. make them alert. Grant us the desire to seek you in prayer at all times about everything, big or small. You are a God who hears every word. Lord, if someone can't speak the words that are on their heart on mind, we understand you know what is best for their lives. God, work your merciful powers in our lives to make us holy and acceptable to you. If there is anything we need let us come before the throne of grace, boldly asking our Father to supply our every need. Thank you Jesus for being our friend and guide in every season. We are forever thankful. Bless your saints all this week and forever, In Jesus' Holy Name, Amen.

# January 9

*For what is our hope or joy or crown of boasting before our Lord Jesus at his coming? Is it not you? For you are our glory and joy.* (1 Thessalonians 2:19-20)

My motivation in life is to see all men become believers and see themselves as the joy and glory of God. Yes, God created all of mankind, but He has given us a choice. Some choose life while others choose death. Like Paul, our daily prayer must be to see the lost and confused awakened by the power of the Most High. It must be our desire to see the unsaved brought into the light of Christ.

Just like God, we must desire that no one perish but choose to have everlasting life. Our mission as God's ambassadors should be to pray and live in such a manner that we draw people toward accepting and following Christ. Sometimes this will require us to speak boldly to our neighbors about the love of Christ, or that we remain silent and allow our life to exude God's presence.

Whatever the case we must have a passion and be eager to get the message of Christ to a dying world; for this is our purpose and charge in the earth. God created us with the command to love Him with all our heart, and with all our soul and with all our mind and strength, then love our neighbor as ourselves (Mark 12:30-31).

I don't know about you, but I want the VERY best for myself, in that I want the best for others as well. In the world we live in, we are being taught to be self-sufficient, to always work on making ourselves better. God commands us to love Him, and through loving Him we are to love others as ourselves. We are all one, in one body, which is in Christ Jesus. We enjoy our inheritance as kingdom citizens. It is our duty to offer this opportunity to others as it has been so graciously given to us.

**Love others as yourself!**

~The reward of ministry is to see lives saved and changed by spreading the gospel ~ Tyndale

Prayer: Father in heaven, give us a motivation to seek out the lost. Help us to remember that we were once lost, and you sought us out through Your love. We will speak the truth in love, telling the world about Your goodness. Soften hearts today to receive the gift of life. Don't allow us to be discouraged when we plant and water, knowing that only You have power to give the increase. Allow us to be conscious of our decisions so our life will not hinder how people view Your kingdom. You are perfect in all Your ways. In Jesus' name we pray, Amen.

# January 10

*His mother saith unto the servants, Whatsoever he saith unto you, do it.* (John 2:5)

What has God told you to do? God has given each of us a plan for our life. First, we have to realize that our life is now hidden in Christ. The plan He orchestrated for us is one He carefully thought out and created long ago. It is God's original intent for us to have intimate fellowship with Him. Through this relationship we understand our identity, which is the image of God in the earth. We have been given the greatest honor in being used by God to fulfill His purpose. When we think about what God requires of us, we have to be willing to constantly seek His face by coming in His presence and receiving everything He has for us to do. It's comparable to starting a new job. In the beginning we require clear instructions on what the job requires and our boss expects from us. After being on the job awhile, we become comfortable conforming to the bylaws of our company. We accomplish the job we are being paid for. It is our intent to receive a reward (paycheck), so we seek to do what the head (CEO) requires of their employees. In the kingdom, God is our CEO. He has the blueprint for our jobs while on earth. We have to seek God and become comfortable with Him as our head, leading and guiding us. We can look at His Word to see what He wants us to do. Spending intimate time with Him and then being led by His Spirit will give us our daily tasks. Knowing God is perfect and the desires of our heart come from Him anyway only builds our ability to trust Him. We must remember God is not impressed by our daily activities that portray a façade of following Him. He is looking for a heart that is willing and obedient and does exactly what He says.

**Jeremiah 7:23 but I gave them this command:**
**Obey me, and I will be your God and you will be my people.**
**Listen to the heart of heaven!**

Prayer: Lord, thank You for forgiving us of all of our mistakes. This is a new day and we have a new hunger and thirst after righteousness. Use us for Your glory. Speak so that we may obey. As we search Your Word, give us revelation. Help us to receive everything You are pouring into our lives. We will be willing and obedient to walk in the Spirit and do all that You command of us, even when it doesn't feel comfortable. Our aim is to please You. Clear out all distractions. Give us our daily bread that it may be well with us. In Jesus' name we pray, Amen.

# January 11

*Whoever says he abides in him ought to walk in the same way in which he walked.* (1 John 2:6)

**How did Jesus walk?**

**He was humble:** *I am come that they might have life, and that they might have it more abundantly.* (John 10:10b)

**He forgave:** *Jesus said, "Father, forgive them, for they do not know what they are doing."* (Luke 23:34)

**He didn't judge**: *When they kept on questioning him, he straightened up and said to them, "Let any one of you who is without sin be the first to throw a stone at her."* (John 8:7)

**He loved:** *As the Father has loved me, so have I loved you. Abide in my love.* (John 15:9)

**He prayed:** *One of those days Jesus went out to a mountainside to pray, and spent the night praying to God.* (Luke 6:12)

**He cared:** *But Jesus said to them, "They do not need to go away; you give them something to eat!" They replied, "We have nothing here except five loaves and two fish." He said, "Bring them here to Me."* (Matthew 14:16-18)

**Set aside time for God:** *"But why did you need to search?" he asked. "Didn't you know that I must be in my Father's house?"* (Luke 2:49)

**Only did what God did:** *Then answered Jesus and said unto them, Verily, verily, I say unto you, The Son can do nothing of himself, but what he seeth the Father do: for what things soever he doeth, these also doeth the Son likewise.* (John 5:19)

**He ministered –** *He began to teach them, saying, "Those who know there is nothing good in themselves are happy, because the holy nation of heaven is theirs.* (Matthew 5:2-3)

**He was bold:** *Jesus entered the temple courts and drove out all who were buying and selling there. He overturned the tables of the money changers and the benches of those selling doves.* (Matthew 21:12)

**He was silent:** *But Jesus remained silent and gave no answer. Again the high priest asked him, "Are you the Messiah, the Son of the Blessed One?"* (Mark 14:61)

**He was an example:** *Jesus answered and said unto them, Go and shew John again those things which ye do hear and see: The blind receive their sight, and the lame walk, the lepers are cleansed, and the deaf hear, the dead are raised up, and the poor have the gospel preached to them.* (Matthew 11:4-5)

**He was human:** *The Word became flesh and made his dwelling among us. We have seen his glory, the glory of the one and only Son, who came from the Father, full of grace and truth.* (John 1:14)

**He spoke the Word:** *Jesus answered, "It is written: 'Man shall not live on bread alone, but on every word that comes from the mouth of God.'"*(Matthew 4:4)

**He fasted:** *After fasting forty days and forty nights, he was hungry.* (Matthew 4:2)

**He believed:** *I have glorified thee on the earth: I have finished the work which thou gavest me to do.* (John 17:4)

**He was not influenced by the world but influenced the world:** *But he continued, "You are from below; I am from above. You are of this world; I am not of this world.* (John 8:23)

**He put God first:** *Very early in the morning, while it was still dark, Jesus got up, left the house and went off to a solitary place, where he prayed.* (Mark 1:35)

**God help us today to be more like You!**

# January 12

*And now I have told you before it takes place, so that when it does take place you may believe.* (John 14:29)

We shall expect great things from God. We should not leave life up to chance when we have a Father (God), A High Priest (Jesus), and an Advocate (Holy Spirit), all willing and waiting to reveal things to us. Our level of intimacy with God should be so grand that He reveals His plans (vision) to us during our communion with Him. Then we come into alignment with everything He has promised us, and this becomes a cycle of our intimate relationship. As we accomplish God's plans and continuously seek His face, He will reveal things to us we are not able to know with our natural senses. Jesus proclaimed this is a benefit of being God's children (Mark 4:11). When the promise He revealed to us in secret is manifested, it will be a testimony to us by first expanding our faith, because we believed God at His Word and second, it will be a testimony to others of the goodness of God. The bible tells us in Luke 12:32 that it is God's good pleasure to give us His kingdom. Also, God will not withhold any good thing from those who walk uprightly (Psalm 84:11). God doesn't want us to spend quality time with Him to be selfish or to take up the majority of our life. He requires first place because He is the author and finisher who longs for us to get this thing called life right. He knows how to get us to the expected end, and by being in His presence it allows Him to establish our steps. His instructions for our life help us obtain His endless treasures.

**Can you wait patiently for God to act - Tyndale**

Prayer: Lord, You are marvelous. What is man that You are mindful of him? God, we love You. Thank You for showing us the plan before we see the plan in the natural realm. Help us to seek Your first in all things. Knowing that Your purpose is the greatest gift life can offer. Help us to develop faith by hearing Your Word on a daily basis. Let us find the joy in spending quality time with You. In Your presence is the fullness of joy and at your right hand are pleasures forever more. In Jesus' name we pray, Amen.

*Call to Me and I will answer you, and tell you [and even show you] great and mighty things, [things which have been confined and hidden], which you do not know and understand and cannot distinguish.* (Jeremiah 33:3)

# January 13

*Above all, keep loving one another earnestly, since love covers a multitude of sins.* (1 Peter 4:8)

I have never seen love offend anyone. The reason God placed so much emphasis on us loving one another is because He knows it works. Have you ever had a bad day and then somehow you receive a message from someone expressing how much they appreciate you or they offer you words of encouragement? These acts of love are what God longs for us to give out and receive on a daily basis. Everyone, no matter what walk of life they come from, can respond to love. Love is gentle, it cares about others beyond thinking only about self. If we are careful to be kind and see people from God's perspective then more love can be expressed throughout the world. When the bible states love covers a multitude of sin it is not insisting that we condone sin, but that through the power of Christ we show love to draw people away from sin. Just like when Jesus called our name, He didn't twist our arm to come into His fold. He simple extended His love and grace and gave us hope by showing us how much we mean to Him and we responded to His perfect love. He didn't remind us of all the times we messed up. He said son/ daughter I have a better way for you. Life that is eternal, and through that we accepted His loving kindness. The bible says to keep loving one another earnestly, which means it's a continuous action. Have you ever stopped for a second to think about how someone else feels when the pressures of life are on their shoulder? Love can heal that. We oftentimes only want to love when we feel someone is worthy of love. God has not instructed us to love in this manner. He teaches us to love without conditions, let it flow naturally and see lives changed.

**True love will never keep you away!**

Prayer: God, open our heart to show love to one another the way You show love to us. Help us to see beyond our natural eye and to move past our emotions and to be patient and kind, to forsake envy, jealousy, and all evil intent, and to deny pride. Show us how to love one another with the love that flows from Your throne of grace that the world may see You through us displaying Your attributes. In all things we will do them unto Christ our Savior and Lord. In Jesus' name we pray Amen.

# January 14

*And they went out and preached everywhere, while the Lord worked with them and confirmed the message by accompanying signs.* (Mark 16:20)

I heard a man of God ask the congregation where the largest church in the world was. People began to disclose churches that had over 900,000 members, yet that wasn't the answer. The answer was on our jobs or our place of influence. It was every believer who, after they left the four walls on Sunday, really demonstrated through their life that we are the church of God. Even if you don't work a conventional 9-5 job, wherever you go on a daily basis is where your congregation is. God tells us to preach the gospel everywhere- homes, schools, stores, workplaces, etc. Many times people shy away from this out of fear of rejection (*trick from the enemy*). The bible never said go out and do it in our own strength, but what it says is allow the Lord to work through us. We oftentimes fail in this area because we omit seeking the Lord concerning His will for others because we're too busy petitioning things for ourselves. When we seek God's kingdom first, He promised to take care of our needs. Our daily prayer must be "God use me today for Your glory." God will pour His message in us and send us where He needs us to speak and move on His behalf. We have to keep our ear to heaven and be in constant communication with the Holy Spirit in order to be used by God. We are God's fellow workers, He has built His purpose in us to go out and to make disciples - lovers of the gospel throughout all the earth.

**Here I am, use me Lord!**

Prayer: God, open heaven today and send a Word. We belong to You. You dwell on the inside of us. Use us for Your glory. Give us the confidence to be kingdom builders, set apart for holy use. Everything was created by You and for Your perfect plan. Send us out with boldness to proclaim the gospel. We are unashamed. Remove fear, doubt and low self-esteem. You go before us and make our paths straight. We are Your vessels on assignment. Shake us in our inner core so we no longer operate out of fear and are only concerned with ourselves. Put the welfare of the lost at the forefront of our mind that we make speak Your Word at all times. We call multitudes of believers to Your kingdom in Jesus' name we pray. Amen

*And more than ever believers were added to the Lord, multitudes of both men and women,* (Acts 5:14)

## January 15

*For the time will come when people will not put up with sound doctrine. Instead, to suit their own desires, they will gather around them a great number of teachers to say what their itching ears want to hear.* (2 Timothy 4:3)

The word of God is truth, it is full of power. Jesus spoke the word of God throughout His life. He then gave His life to grant us freedom. Knowing the scripture for ourselves is very important to successful daily living. Jesus sent the Holy Spirit so we would be able to comprehend the heart of God, and to help us spread the word of God to others.

Standing for God often may seem like a difficult task, since many people are easily influenced by the attraction of the world. Shame and embarrassment should be the last thing we feel as we witness to people. I am guilty of this also. Sometimes I don't want to write daily devotions, not because my heart is not in it; I don't want to make anyone upset or have them feel guilt, shame or condemnation, or blame me for trying to tell them what to do. I brought this care to God and He simple said "daughter Your purpose is not about you." It is about His Kingdom, people need to know the truth. His word IS power that leads to salvation. "For I am not ashamed of the gospel, because it is the power of God that brings salvation to everyone who believes (Romans 1:16). As God's faithful servants, our wisdom comes from the truth of God. Before we teach the word of God to others we have to know the Word of God for ourselves. We have to be able to accept God's Word as truth and apply it to our life. It is not beneficial if we only accept the Word of God when it suits our lifestyle. God didn't save us so we could continue living life to please the desires of our flesh. He offers us salvation to purify us, to rejoin us in His glory. The truth of God edifies our souls, renews our mind, and changes our heart. This process does not come easy. But with the help of God, Jesus and the Holy Spirit we are made white as snow, pure and holy.

***Thy word is very pure: therefore thy servant loveth it.* (Psalm 119:140)**

**If God be for us, who can be against us!**

Prayer: All Glory and Honor to your throne Lord. Lord, purify our hearts, open our minds, fill us with Your wisdom. Change our heart to accept your Word as truth. Not some of Your Word but all of Your Word. We are ready to be purified in Your righteousness, let it be the desire of our heart to search Your Word day and night. Let it be our goal to be more like You second by second. Thank You for Your grace and mercy for being patient with us this far. Let Your Word be embedded in our heart. Allow Your joy to esteem out of our pores. Let Your love overshadow our heart and be present in all that we do. Grant us our daily bread to continue in the work of building Your kingdom. Help us in all areas of our life to always put You first as Lord and Savior, in Jesus' name we pray, Amen.

# January 16

*But my God shall supply all your need according to his riches in glory by Christ Jesus.* (Philippians 4:19)

There is no desire so complex or extraordinary in which our God is not capable of manifesting. It is God's good pleasure to give us the kingdom (All things). "Do not be afraid, little flock, for your Father has been pleased to give you the kingdom" (Luke 12:32). In God we have obtained access to everything we need to be nourished – physically, emotionally, spiritually, mentally, financially etc. God knows what we need and His hand is open for us to receive it. The thing that intrigued me in this particular scripture was Paul used the singular form for the word "need." Surely we have more than one need in life. God, being so brilliant, encompasses all that we need in His splendid nature. In Luke 10:42 the bible tells us, "but one thing is needful." That thing being Jesus Christ himself. Psalm 16:11 tells us that in God's presence is the fullness of joy and at His right hand are pleasures forevermore. The one thing we need in life for ALL things to be added to us is God Himself. As we desire more of God and seek after His kingdom and His righteousness, we receive everything. God doesn't have to go searching for resources- He is the source. It PLEASES Him to give to His children every single thing we need and want according to His marvelous plan for our life. Being in God's kingdom we come to understand God's plans for us far exceeds anything we can ever imagine for ourselves.

**God has it all under control!**

Prayer: God, praise and glory to Your holy name. One thing I ask from you LORD, this only do I seek: that I may dwell in the house of the LORD all the days of my life, to gaze on the beauty of the LORD and to seek him in his temple (Psalm 27:4). God, You are what we need and desire. We seek to develop a more intimate relationship with You today. We will do our part in seeking Your throne of grace; petitioning heaven to be present in our daily routines. All things belong to You and You are a good Father who gives good gifts to His children. Our arms are open wide to receive Your blessings. Favor is upon us. We walk in righteousness. You are our Shepherd and we shall not want. Shift our focus to kingdom building. Knowing that as we walk in faith You take care of everything which concerns us. In Jesus' name we pray, Amen.

# January 17

*And God said, Let us make man in our image, after our likeness: and let them have dominion over the fish of the sea, and over the fowl of the air, and over the cattle, and over all the earth, and over every creeping thing that creepeth upon the earth.* (Genesis 1:26)

We are positioned in God. Every living thing is birthed from the Word of God and comes directly from His heart. Our place originated in His presence. God, Jesus, and the Holy Spirit were taking counsel, looking over the earth they had created and thought to make you and me after their own image. They deemed us important enough to want to share their nature in the earth to take possession of all they had created. Before Adam became a living soul, God commanded the way in which man should be. He said we were to be His. He told us we were similar in nature to Him and blessed us to have dominion over everything He created. God spoke this to our Spirit FIRST, before we were ever born. Our spirit is waiting for us to catch up with what God has already ordained for us. That is why we are constantly reminded to walk in the Spirit (walk by faith and not by sight 2 Corinthians 5:7). Call those things that be not as though they were (Romans 4:17). These are all indicators to help us align with the way we were created. All things that pertain to life and godliness are in the Spirit realm, waiting for the proper time to manifest in our life. Our job is to be in constant communication with the Trinity (God, Jesus and Holy Spirit) and to follow instructions and receive what God has already been promised.

**Before I formed you in the womb I knew you!**
**(Jeremiah 1:5)**

Prayer: God, You are Holy. The earth and the fullness thereof belong to You. Today we believe and receive everything You have prepared for us. We are Your children, Your righteousness, Your creation. We declare we have dominion over this earth, over our life, over our finances, our careers, and over our ministry. We yield to the governing of the Holy Spirit to walk as kingdom citizens and make right choices. We will represent You well in the earth. God be magnified in us. All glory and power belongs to you. In Jesus' name we pray, Amen.

# January 18

*But whoever listens to me (Wisdom) will live securely and in confident trust And will be at ease, without fear or dread of evil.* (Proverbs 1:33 AMP)

God is such a loving God. When He made creation He designed us with free will. He decided to give us the option of choice. He went a step further to always give us the option to choose His way, His help and His love. The choice that He gives offers us a life of freedom. The ability to bask in His holy presence and receive the best life has to offer. God has given us knowledge of the benefits we receive as a result of a life directed by His wisdom. He says that WHOEVER listens to His wisdom will live securely, in confident trust, and be at ease without fear or dread of evil. Wow! What a way to live life. God's wisdom instructs us in the path that God has already traveled. God knows the end from the beginning and guides us along the journey so we can experience every plan He has written for us in the Lamb book of life. I often say one of the greatest tragedies for our life would be to get to heaven and see all that God had for us but we missed it because we failed to adhere to His plan while on earth. God doesn't desire anyone He created to miss their destiny. So He tells us every day, if we submit ourselves to Him and LISTEN to His voice, we will receive EVERYTHING we need that pertains to life and godliness. The thing I love about God is He knows all and will never cause us to miss anything He has prepared. God is perfect in all His ways, and we are promised this life of perfect fellowship when we put our confidence in Him and allow His wisdom to carry us through life on a daily- moment-by-moment basis.

**God lead me and I will follow!**

Prayer: God, You are so good. Your goodness and mercy are everlasting. Wisdom is what we long for. Our ears are open to Your commands. Order our steps this day and forever to walk the narrow path of righteousness. Your voice is the only voice we will follow. Your plans far exceed anything we could think of for ourselves. Reveal our purpose; stir up Your dreams inside of us. Awaken every dormant spirit within Your people that we may run this race with endurance. Wisdom is principle thing; the wisest thing we can do in this life (Proverbs 4:7). Thank You for freely giving it to us. Speak into every situation in our life and we will obey Your every command. In Jesus' name we pray, Amen.

# January 19

*But put ye on the Lord Jesus Christ, and make not provision for the flesh, to fulfil the lusts thereof.* (Romans 13:14)

We have a sinful nature and a righteous nature. Through the works of Christ we have died to our sinful nature through believing in our hearts and confessing with our tongues that Jesus is Lord. Since the works of Christ are already complete, we have to make a daily choice whether or not to accept and walk in our righteous nature. There is a constant battle between our spirit and the lusts of the flesh. The more time we spend with God, the more His nature is revealed and evilness is denounced. We know sin leads to death, but being in Christ we have everlasting life. We don't have time to give way to the evil desires of our heart; instead we are to live like Jesus Christ in total submission to God by forsaking unrighteousness and not living to satisfy our corrupt flesh. Living according to God's nature is the state God predestined us to function in (Let us make man in our image Genesis 1:26). God's Word and Spirit gives a clear depiction as to what we should be doing and what we are to refrain from doing. The bible teaches we are to take precautions to ensure we make no room for the flesh to rule in our lives. After all, Jesus died for us and our sinful nature is destroyed. Whenever we stray from God it is a choice. Paul is teaching us that in order to walk in the spirit, we have to starve the desires of the flesh and seek only the things of God. This may sound easy, but it requires great self-discipline. Self-control is one of the gifts of God's Spirit. He is there to guide us every step of the way to aid us away from succumbing to the desires of our flesh. This takes action on our part. We are to be aware of how we spend time, what we allow in our soul, and how we conduct ourselves. We have been given the way to escape the snares of the enemy. Now its up to us to make the choice today to live like Christ in God.

**God I choose You!**

Prayer: Lord God Almighty, thank You for being so great.

Forgive us of all of our sins. Lead us by Your Holy Spirit. Fill us with Your wisdom to walk in the righteousness You have freely given to us. As Your Spirit speaks, Lord,' we will listen. We will only pursue those things that pertain to life and godliness. Kingdom of Heaven fall in the earth today. Transform lives and renew minds. We put on the full armor of God and walk in close fellowship with You all the days of our life. Your voice is what we long to hear and we will obey Your commands. Thank You for giving us the strength and power to trample over every evil force that is in the earth. Nothing by no means shall harm us. In Jesus' name we pray, Amen.

# January 20

*Yet I will rejoice in the Lord, I will joy in the God of my salvation.* (Habakkuk 3:18)

God wrote the end of our story before the first day we graced the face of the earth. Now He spends His days trying to remove the blinders from our eyes in order for us to see our destiny through His awesome plans. The enemy's trick is for us to be focused on our natural state instead of our ordained future in an attempt to cause us to miss the move of God. We must understand and begin to operate from a position of victory. Oftentimes we equate our position in the kingdom with what is taking place in our life. God is saying "No, my child, your position is already secure, everything I have you have; now walk in it." Habakkuk consulted with the Lord in regard to the terrible things that were taking place during his time. Destruction was all around him. He complained that it seemed as if the people of God were being punished while the people of the world were getting ahead in life and enjoying themselves. Sound familiar? God told him not to look at what was going on around him but to trust in His holy plan which is perfect and pleasing. In that instant, Habakkuk had to renew his mind and come into agreement with God. He determined in his heart that no matter what took place he would rejoice in the Lord. The scripture says, "Yet I will rejoice in the Lord, I will joy in the God of my salvation." The word YET means "at the same time." Hallelujah! So during the same time you are suffering you can rejoice. While your heart is breaking you can rejoice. When the odds seem stacked against you, you can rejoice. We are not rejoicing as it pertains to our situation, but as we trust our God- the One whom we have a covenant with; the One who will never leave us nor forsake us.

**God I trust You!**

Prayer: Lord, You are so great. Take the scales off of our eyes this day. Help us to rejoice in all things. Lord, no matter what it looks like we will put our trust in You. You know the end from the beginning and it all points to victory. We are a royal priesthood, a chosen generation, the apple of Your eye. You love us with an everlasting love. Nothing is too hard for You. We cast our cares at Your feet and set our mind on our kingdom assignment. Put a new song in our heart. A song of worship, gratitude and thanksgiving. You are God and there is no other. In Jesus' name we pray, Amen.

# January 21

*And when he heard of Jesus,* (Luke 7:3)

Our life is a living example. Before the people in the bible saw Jesus they heard of Him. The scriptures spoke of a King who would come and save the world. Now, Jesus is on the scene and the tales of Him coming are surpassed by His extraordinary acts of power and deliverance. People were witnessing miracles, and His glory was being spread throughout the land. When we first heard of Jesus what were our thoughts? Did we inquire about the One who could save us from the lust of the world, one who could give us eternal life? We too came into the fold by believing in the Jesus we heard about. Now we are totally convinced Jesus is who He says He is. His power continues to be manifested over and over in our lives. We owe Him everything for calling us out of darkness and placing us in the Kingdom. In turn, we have to display His light so that our life speaks of the true and living King. The holy Messiah, Alpha and Omega, the bright and Morning Star. So we must ask ourselves the question: Who do people see when they see us? Can they see a life saved by a High Priest who came and gave His life so that we may live? Do they see the miracle working power of His grace and mercy being manifested? These are the things the world is watching for. In the scripture we find that many believed and some chose not to believe. But what we discover is none could deny the power of Christ. They would marvel and inquire how a man could do such powerful things. The earth needs to hear of Jesus today. As we look around, help is needed. As ambassadors, we are God's workmanship in the earth. We are to let our light shine so that others may hear of the Savior Jesus. When people see Jesus being reflected from our being, they will say they heard of Jesus and inquired of His love and will come to accept Him as Lord and Savior.

**Jesus is Savior!**

Prayer: God, You alone are Worthy. Our life is Yours. We thank You for teaching us who You are. You love us so much You proclaim Your glory day-after-day. Open hearts and minds to receive Your unfailing love. Our lives are examples of Who You are. We are Your ambassadors in the earth. Fill us with the Holy Spirit. Help us to shine the light in this dark world that people may see You through us and be drawn to You. Knock on hearts today, soften them so they may receive Your invitation and walk in open fellowship with You forever. In Jesus' name we pray, Amen.

# January 22

*And He came up and touched the coffin; and the bearers came to a halt. And He said, "Young man, I say to you, arise!"* (Luke 7:14)

Jesus is the way the truth and the life. In Him all things are alive. If we take inventory of our current situations, we may see some things that are dead- no longer in a state of producing life. Jesus is here to breathe life in our situations so it can produce fruit. God doesn't want us to have dead-end jobs, relationships, finances, or dreams. Everything in our life should be fruitful and full of life. Since we are confident Jesus is our head, we should see tangible evidence of Jesus' "life" working through us. When Jesus touched the coffin the young man was already dead, all Jesus did was speak the Word "arise." Allow Jesus to raise every dead situation in Your life. Begin to speak to Your circumstance in the name of Jesus and watch Jesus bring back to life the very thing you lost control of. Jesus is all-powerful and it is His desire to see His children whole. When Jesus touched the coffin, the bearers came to a halt- they stopped in their tracks. When Jesus shows up all power comes as well. There are some things God needs to halt, bring to a complete stop in our lives, so that He can take proper position and work through us. If we find that we have been trying to live life apart from God we are not in right standing. God is not selfish or looking to boost His ego in requiring us to put Him first in our daily pursuits. He requires this position because He knows all, is all and wants us to fulfill our kingdom purpose. We will only be able to walk out this life in our fullest potential when we allow God in.

**Touch us today Jesus!**

Prayer: Lord, You sit high but You look low. You know every situation and see all that Your people are going through. Today we give You every dead situation and accept Your power to change it for our good. Speak the Word and transform us by renewing our mind. You promised not to withhold any good thing from us. In

You we live, move and have our being. Thank You for being our Source in every situation. In Jesus' name we pray, Amen.

# January 23

*Hear ye the word of the Lord.* (Jeremiah 2:4)

O to hear from God. How awesome it is? We hear all sorts of sounds in the world we live in. Many things we hear are of no benefit to us. If we aren't careful to guard our hearing from certain obscenity (vulgar TV, radio, music, people), we will allow our soul to be inhabited by harmful forces that come to hinder us, not propel us. If we understand that faith comes by hearing, and hearing by the Word of God, we see the power associated with letting words rest in our soul. Words from God grant us the ability to stand on a firm foundation and to have a great expectation for the things we believe in to come to fruition, although we can't see them at the present moment. Our ability to hear goes deeper than just enjoying the sounds of our surroundings. What we hear has the power to change our emotions. When we receive good news, our attitude is filled with joy. Hearing our favorite song on the radio sparks feelings of refreshment. On the other end hearing can also cause pain. When someone says something hurtful, our emotions change to feelings of being hurt or angry. Our hearing is associated with our hearts, and depending on what we hear, it has the ability to condition our state of being. Thanks be to God that the words we hear from Him breathe life. Hearing from God is one of the sweetest sounds we will ever hear. Not only do we obtain power, we are able to tap into the spirit realm. Our hearing of God's word ignites our faith. After hearing the word, we are willing to confess that faith is the substance of things hoped for, the evidence of things not seen (Hebrews 11:1). When we hear from God we obtain instruction, guidance, encouragement, correction, and self-fulfillment. Hearing from God is the only sound we will hear that is consistent in its approach to make us better as individuals. Others may encourage us one time and may even be nice for a while; but God is the only one whose words always come to edify our souls to be in alignment with Him and make us whole.

**I hear the sound**

Prayer: God, You are amazing. To think about Your attributes would take a lifetime. Thank You for the many things You do in the lives of Your people. Lord, I declare today that Your voice will be the loudest voice of influence in the lives of Your people. We will not fall victim to lies and deceit from outside forces. We will believe what Your word says. We confess what Your word says about us and our life in Christ Jesus. We are fearfully and wonderfully made. Let the sound of heaven ring loud in our ear. Help us to hear the sweetness of Your voice, which has power to restore. God, You are everything. In Jesus' name we pray, Amen.

# January 24

*Casting all your care upon him; for he careth for you.* (1 Peter 5:7)

What a blessing to have God as the head of our life. We can boldly come before Him on a daily basis, giving Him the cares of our heart and receive His grace and strength for the day ahead. Distractions only have one purpose in our life and that is to take our eyes off of the will of God. Just think about it, everything God desires goes along with His perfect plan of us having an abundant life; a life without falling victim to challenges, just totally focused on enjoying the gifts from heaven. Our adversary the devil wants us to be bottled down with worry, fear, hardships, pain, anger etc. In order to keep us from looking at and accepting the freedom of God, the Bible tells us God is our Help. Whatever need we have, be it emotional, physical, spiritual, or financial, God has the remedy. Our job is to bring it before Him in prayer and then to get out of the way and allow God to be God. God's wisdom knows how to calm a disastrous storm and how to silence the enemy. In our own strength we will only make matters worse. God is able to take on our burdens because nothing is too hard for Him. The bible teaches countless stories of men and women of great faith who were faced with such adversity that, in some instances, it threatened their life. Instead of fear they trusted God. This is the manner in which God has called us to live our life. He says, I love you so much. I did not create you to be destroyed by the work of the enemy or by the challenges of life. He has given us hope. We can come to God, who is our refuge and seek His help at all times. Give God every issue, every concern, and live in the freedom of His grace.

**Thank You for caring!**

Prayer: God, You are Alpha and Omega. You see every storm before it comes. Open the minds of Your people to be clever when the enemy comes in to steal our joy. We cast all of our cares on You because we know You care and You are willing and able to make a way of escape. You promised us an abundant life and the abundant life is what we will live. We will not worry, complain, or find fault in Your perfect plan. Let prayer be our response to every negative influence that tries to infiltrate our domain. All glory and praise belongs to You. In Jesus' name we pray, Amen.

# January 25

*As in water face answereth to face, so the heart of man to man.* (Proverbs 27:19)

The wisdom of God teaches us we are not able to hide what is in our heart. Just as we see our reflection when we look in the mirror, our heart is revealed through our actions. The scriptures states, "face answers to face and so the manner of man answers to the heart." By definition answer means to respond/react. No matter how we try to put up a façade; what is in our heart will be displayed. God wants us to know this and teaches us to guard our heart with all diligence, because out of it flows the issues of life (Proverbs 4:23). The heart is a very important component. It is the very place where we determine what orchestrates our thoughts and behavior. We have made the conscious choice to invite God to live in us so we have to rid our heart/soul of things that keep us from having a God-influenced heart. Our behavior and mannerisms stem from what's in our heart. It may require that we do a constant heart check to ensure our heart is well-focused on the right things in order to produce what is pleasing to God. Not only that, it will be pleasing to us as well. The heart is so powerful that we are not able to control our thoughts and speech if our heart is not right. Whatever we are putting in our heart will come out. Things get in our heart through many ways, including what we watch on television, what we listen to, what we read, thoughts that linger too long, the people we hang around, and anything we give our energy to has the potential to influence us. Our actions follow the commands of the heart. What we can do is ensure we are being filled with things that benefit us to remain clear of all unnecessary debris. It's time once again to give our heart to God.

**What's in Your heart?**

Prayer: Lord God Almighty, examine our hearts. Lord, speak to us clearly so we know what You would have us to do. Tell us what things are not good for us. Lead us so we only focus on things that produce righteous fruit. Renew mindsets right now in the name of

Jesus. Remove all bitterness, anger, hurt, malice, evilness, and deceit. Replace it with Your love. Call us to a higher standard of living. You live on the inside of us. Help us not to fill our hearts with filth where you have no room to work in and through us. Our hearts belong to You. Cleanse us from all unrighteousness and make us aware of the beauty we have in You. We are Your beloved children. Thank You that it's never too late. Change the way we speak, change the way we view things. Help us not to offend or be offended, but to put on love in all situations. As You reside in us, our mannerism will respond to Your love and we will be a walking example in the earth. In Jesus' name we pray, Amen

# January 26

*And other fell on good ground, and sprang up, and bare fruit an hundredfold. And when he had said these things,* ***he cried****, He that hath ears to hear, let him hear.* (Luke 8:8 *emphasis added*)

The Word of God is so important that as Jesus was proclaiming it, He was filled with compassion. His compassion stemmed from His understanding of what the Word of God possesses. God's Word is filled with power and the ability to produce a bountiful harvest in the lives of His children who heed and obey the voice of God. Jesus cried out to His followers, ensuring they heard and understood the principle of His Word being a seed. If we plant a seed it will not grow unless it has the proper nutrients and light source. God has given us His Word, and like the parable, Jesus proclaims if we are not careful it can fall on bad soil. We can receive the Word and then allow the circumstances of life to strip us from believing what God says is true, or we can be so caught up in the world we let it go in one ear and out the other. I know this is not the case for you. You want to receive your fruit and ensure it bears a hundredfold harvest. That means you want it to produce to the maximum potential according to God's promises. Well, the choice is up to us. God's Word is a seed, He always provides light and nutrients for it to grow and harvest in our lives. Faith is the way we receive everything God already has for us. Search His Word, stand believing and wait for the manifestation. Whatever it is, God has a seed for every situation and His purpose (perfect) plan will surely grow in your life.

**Sow and you will reap!**

Prayer: God, You alone are holy. Thank You for being righteous. Lord, remove every distraction from Your people. Help us to have fertile ground, a heart welcoming of Your Word in order to produce heavenly fruit. We have ears to hear what heaven is saying. We walk in purpose. Every Word spoken by You will produce a hundredfold in our life. This pertains to our spiritual walk, our physical body, our career, finances, relationships, and all things that pertain to life and godliness. It all belongs to You. In Jesus' name we pray, Amen.

# January 27

*For this is the love of God, that we keep his commandments: and his commandments are not grievous.* (1 John 5:3)

God has done everything to get His Word to us. We have multiple avenues to receive God in the world today. Smart phones, computers, Internet, church, books, and many other resources. Therefore, we are defiantly without excuse when it comes to knowing God's Word, reading God's Word, and living God's Word. Why do you think it's so important for God to speak to us on a daily basis? The answer is simple, because of love. God created us in love. His commands for our life draw us closer to Him, where we are able to experience the great pleasure of what eternity will be like here and now. God's commands lead us on the narrow path of righteousness- keeping us in right standing with Him. We also know God's commands are NOT grievous. Bless God! The world would have us think it's more fun to live apart from God, but this is far from the truth. "But what fruit were you getting at that time from the things of which you are now ashamed? For the end of those things is death" (Romans 6:21). God teaches us anything not done in faith is sin. When we fail to follow God's commands, we are following our own self guided ambition and this is not pleasing to God. God wants us to receive the joy that His way of life produces and save us from the heartache of doing life on our own. Accept love today!

**But word is very nigh unto thee, in thy mouth, and in thy heart, that thou mayest do it. (Deuteronomy 30:14)**

**In that I command thee this day to love the Lord thy God, to walk in his ways, and to keep his commandments and his statutes and his judgments, that thou mayest live and multiply: and the Lord thy God shall bless thee in the land whither thou goest to possess it. (Deuteronomy 30:16)**

**I want to do Your Will!**

Prayer: Father God in heaven, we accept Your love today. Your commands breathe life and bring us into our destiny. You are the Creator of all things, Your plans are perfect and pleasing. We are no longer slaves to sin, but have been born into the kingdom of Jesus Christ. No longer will we walk in darkness. Speak Lord, and give us a listening ear and a heart to obey. In Jesus' name, Amen.

# January 28

*And the LORD was with Joseph, and he was a prosperous man; and he was in the house of his master the Egyptian.* (Genesis 39:2)

The life of Joseph is an explicit example of the love of God. Joseph found himself in a strange land, away from family and all that was familiar to him. One would think this would be the darkest period in his life. Instead of wallowing in sorrow Joseph remained steadfast in the Lord. In return, God favored Joseph because he trusted the Lord. God is willing and available to do the same thing for us. Every person will experience hardships in their life. The test of life is how we deal with times of trouble. We can fall victim to our circumstances or fall into the hands of God. When we go through difficult times, our mannerism and outlook on life should remain in God. In Joseph's darkest moments God prospered him. He had no lack; although he would have liked things to be different, he accepted the purpose of God for his life. Instead of looking at the problem, we have to focus on God. Nothing that happens in life is sent to destroy us. God wants us to see the blessing not the storm; to know He is more powerful than anything sent to harm us. The devil's only purpose is to deter us from God's destiny. Deter in Hebrew means to refuse; forbid; to break; discourage; make of none effect. This is what happens when our focus is on the challenges instead of God. God is speaking to us through our situations, and He is telling us to give it to Him and allow Him to help us. In the midst of chaos we prosper, because God's grace is sufficient, and when we are weak, God is strong.

**God's grace is enough!**

Prayer: God, we bless You. Lord, you are so amazing. We see how you helped Joseph in the darkest moment of His life. God, we place our life in Your hand. God, lead us at all times. Give us a new mindset. We take authority over every thought and negative force that tries to enter our pathway. You have created us for purpose. You love us with an everlasting love. You cover us and keep us in perfect peace because our mind is stayed on You. Thank

You for Your saving grace. In Jesus' name we pray Amen.

# January 29

*Nor do people light a lamp and put it under a basket, but on a stand, and it gives light to all in the house.* (Matthew 5:15)

God has called us the salt and light of the earth. There is power associated with being God's vessels. As we allow God's Spirit to work through us, God's light is able to shine brightly. His light is so bright it gives light to an entire house. Lets look at our natural house. If we are the only ones in our house who serve God, His work in us can draw our entire house to Him. Light gives us the ability to see things the way God sees them. It guides us in His ways, which are perfect and pleasing. As we walk in our nature of being God's light in the earth, we have the ability to show the world who God is and what He desires. We are able to do things according to God's plan. Light causes us to be stirred up for righteousness. If we show the world the light of God, others will be drawn to Him because of the evidence of God's great power manifesting through us. God will only lead us on a path of freedom; a path He predestined before time began. As we allow God's light to shine on our life we are able to fulfill God's divine purpose. The more we give way to God, the more He is able to show us His perfect plan. Light exposes the beauty of God. He wants to pour His beauty on the entire earth. In order for our light to shine, we must walk in the Spirit. This entails we give way to the Spirit controlling our entire being, to include our tongue, thoughts, and actions. In order for our light to shine, the world must see Jesus when they look at us. A reflection of compassion, non-judgmental, but meeting people where they are. Giving the world the message of hope and truly living it in our daily lives. Allow your light to shine so others may see your good work and glorify YOUR Father, who is in heaven (Matthew 5:16).

**Apart from the Father we can do nothing!**

Prayer: God, we hear Your heart today. You are in heaven and have given us power and authority in the earth. Help us to use our life to be all You created us to be. You desire for us to shine brightly, drawing all men to the beauty of Your grace. Let our lives be a living example. We say, "yes" to being Your ambassadors in the earth. Tame our tongue and control our actions so when people see us they see You. Remove the spirit of laziness and being complacent. We will not hide who we are in Christ. Instead, we will use every aspect of our being to glorify Your name. Your will be done in earth as it is in heaven. In Jesus' name we pray, Amen. God we love You.

# January 30

*But while he thought on these things, behold, the angel of the Lord appeared unto him in a dream, saying, Joseph, thou son of David, fear not to take unto thee Mary thy wife: for that which is conceived in her is of the Holy Ghost.* (Matthew 1:20)

The character of Joseph, stepfather of Jesus, is an important one to examine. Joseph was happy and content, he had a beautiful fiancé he planned to marry and then she ends up pregnant. At the onset of this devastating blow, he decided to weigh his options whether to stay or to put Mary away in secret. It was his first instinct to privately break off the engagement in order not to cause her embarrassment. Instead of reacting rashly, he did what people so often forget to do- he took time out to THINK. As he thought about the situation of his pregnant fiancé, a woman he had not been intimate with, God stepped in and imparted wisdom, understanding, and revelation. Joseph took the time to examine what was taking place, and in that time God stepped in and give him clarity. Often we miss fulfilling God's purpose due to us being too anxious to take the time to stop, think, and allow God the opportunity to deposit His step-by-step plans in us. When we are faced with adverse situations or things that by no means make sense, we have to use our brain and think. We need to allow God to process His plan in us so we understand what He is trying to work through us. The angel of the Lord gave clear instructions and calmed Joseph's inner turmoil. Joseph then went a step further; he not only took time out to think and hear from the Lord, he acted upon God's instructions. Once we hear from God, we can trust that His plans will come to fruition.

**Think, after all it's FREE!**

Prayer: God, Your divine purpose is what we were created for. You know every aspect of our lives. Cause us to dream and hear Your instructions. Give us clarity, insight and purpose. Help us not to walk aimlessly, but to know with certainty what You have designed for us to accomplish. Show us step-by-step everything

You required us to do in order to fulfill Your will for mankind. Let Your purpose be our heart's desire. In all things we give thanks. In Jesus' name we pray, Amen.

# January 31

*Give thanks to the Lord, for he is good; his love endures forever.* (Psalm 118:1)

Each day we can take a moment of our time to consider the precious gifts given to us by our Father. Gratitude is the attitude of heaven and should be reflected in our character, moment-by-moment. Day by day we are blessed with opportunities to share in the goodness of God. Make it a habit to celebrate the good things in life; give thanks on all occasions. As we know, the great things of God go beyond material items. We may not be at a point in our lives where we feel totally satisfied, yet we can still thank God for the ability to strive for excellence. God gives grace in abundance. Everything we need from God is available to us in great measure if we only believe. We are the only thing standing in the way of the goodness of God. If we make ourselves available for God to penetrate His love through us, we are able to share in His everlasting joy. Always give thanks for being united with the Alpha and Omega. Give thanks for an opportunity to get it right with God. Walk in the love of God, which He continuously pours out. When our attitude or the pressures of life try to shift our focus we have to make a conscious effort to stop and just open our mouth and begin to praise. Praise changes us from the inside out. I heard someone say one time, our emotions are not that smart. This is evident, as we can be happy, sad and cry within the same five-minute time span. So if we know our emotions aren't that smart, we have the power to tell our emotions how to respond.

**When the cares of my heart are many, your consolations cheer my soul. (Psalm 94:19 ESV)**

**I choose to give thanks!**

Prayer: Who on earth can keep us from you? There is no god like our God, you are the holy one. With all reverence and praise, we come before you this day. Our hearts are made new today by your grace. Bestow upon us the gifts of your kingdom, that we may endure this life by our hope in your unfailing love. Nothing by any means can separate us from the love of God. We are honored to be Your children. As Your mercy and grace abound each day let us remember the love of Christ, which gave us our inheritance in the kingdom. Be our guide as we walk through the path of life to acknowledge you as head of our lives. In all that we do, we pray that we are thankful for each opportunity. Bless us with a spirit of discernment, wisdom, strength, and knowledge to focus on your kingdom and righteousness. By Your grace, we are living and receive chance after chance. No longer will we walk in confusion; we come seeking after Your plan, which is pleasing and perfect. Help us to grow and develop in Your perfect image, that your name may be glorified in the earth as it is in heaven. Lord, we know forever to be a long time, let us use every opportunity to make you smile. We love you! In Jesus' name we pray, Amen.

# February 1

*Nevertheless when it shall turn to the LORD, the veil shall be taken away.* (2 Corinthians 3:16)

How often do we place God in a box? We let Him in our lives only to help us with those things we feel comfortable with. We give God half of what is on our heart, thinking we can handle the rest in our own strength. We downplay His majesty and power because we are so dependent on ourselves. The world has influenced our mind to only rely on inward strength, when with God it is the total opposite.

God requires His children to turn from all understanding of self-dependence and put all our trust in Him. There should be no boundaries in what we let the Lord have precedence over in our lives. God alone is all-powerful and glorious. We walk about in chains of depression, hardships, anger, anxiety, confusion, and worry because we still have the veil over our hearts and minds. The veil is a representation of separation from God and not allowing Him to have full reign in our lives. In the Old Testament the children of Israel put the veil over their minds and hearts. They became dull to the knowledge and understanding of the great power of God (2 Corinthians 3:14).

The veil hides you from the presence of God. Once we accept Christ the veil is stripped off. The veil not only separates us from God, it keeps us from our true identity, the very purpose in which we were created to possess. Operating outside the will of God is not the real you. Only when you come to Christ are you transformed into the person God designed you to be. Now that we are in Christ we no longer have to walk around bound to our old selves. In Christ we are free. We are the ones who put the veil on each morning by not exercising our freedom in Christ. From the moment we accepted Christ, the veil was lifted off. We were given the free gift of eternal life and freedom. We are open for God's glory to work and abound in us. Take the veil off and let the glory of God fill your being.

**God I give you all!**

Prayer: God, we give you glory. You are so powerful and worthy of all the praise. God, we thank You for being so loving and kind. We thank You for first revealing Yourself to us. God, we have hope in You, we have peace in You and we have power to walk about in freedom because of Your grace. God, we thank You for Your Spirit of holiness. We honor You this day with our whole heart. God, there are some who have not allowed the veil to come completely off, we ask that You touch our mind and heart to know that where the Spirit of the Lord is there is freedom. Help us to take the limits off of Your power and Your glory. Let Your glory fill us like never before. Help our hearts and minds to gain wisdom concerning Your greatness. Let us operate in our true being, which is created in the image of Your glory. We bless Your name today. In Jesus' name we pray, Amen.

# February 2

*Pursue love, and earnestly desire the spiritual gifts, especially that you may prophesy.* (1 Corinthians 14:1)

Pursue, by definition, means to follow or to continue/proceed along a path. God wants us to follow and continue along the path of love. We are to earnestly desire to first love Him, then our neighbors as ourselves. God's nature is love. We know this as the bible informs us how God first loved us. Now He desires us to sincerely yearn for the spiritual gift He has freely given us, which is love (Galatians 5:22). In our society we throw the meaning of love around as a cliché- one day we love, the next day after someone offends us suddenly they are no longer worthy of our love. This is not the love God wants us to pursue or display. He wants us to long for, desire, be unable to live without the love He pours out. Love that cares, love that forgives, love that puts the needs of others before our own, love that binds together, the love of God flowing from heaven. You ask, well how do I get this love, since my heart is filled with pain or no one has shown me how to love. We have to receive it from God. Accept it and then it will begin to develop in us. First Corinthians 16:14 tells us, "Let all that you do be done in love." As we go about our day we have to keep watch over our love meter, constantly checking to ensure we are continuing on the path of doing all things in love. This may require us to check our hearts at the door and ask God for forgiveness when we fall short. Our eyes must remain focused on God, who bestows His love on us each day as we operate in the gift of love.

Prayer: Lord, You are love. Everything about You radiates love. Forgive us this day for not always operating in love; for allowing our selfish ways to blind us of the gift You have given us. Help us to walk in the spirit of love at all times. A pure love that comes from Your throne of grace. A love that is not based upon conditions but based upon the love You have freely given us. Allow love to be our natural language. Help us to please You by displaying love to one another. Thank You for showering us with Your love. In Jesus' name we pray, Amen.

# February 3

*When the dew fell upon the camp in the night, the manna fell with it.* (Numbers 11:9)

God will supply all of your needs. The children of Israel were in the wilderness and were unable to make food for themselves. But being God's seed, He was obligated to supply what they needed. EVERY DAY as the dew fell upon the earth, God provided each family with enough manna to satisfy their need for physical nourishment. God created us, so He is surely able to give us what we need to sustain us through life. The children of Israel didn't have to work for it; the manna arrived every morning as part of their daily supply. (Hallelujah). Don't you know when you wake up that God has a stock of blessings readily available for each of His children. The problem is, sometimes we are too preoccupied to even notice or too greedy to appreciate what God so graciously gives. Don't be like the children of Israel who complained about what God gave them as not being enough. Instead, wake up every morning and thank God for all He gives, which is more than enough. Then be sensitive to His Spirit to recognize all of the blessings He has bestowed upon Your life, the big and the small, and live the abundant life. After all, it is promised to YOU!!!

Prayer: God, You are our Shepherd, we SHALL not want. Thank You for a supplying us with everything we need physically and spiritually. You bless us according to Your divine plan for our life, and Your plan far exceeds anything we can accomplish on our own. Continue to bless the work of our hands and make us fruitful so we can multiply Your goodness in the earth. All the nations shall call us blessed; we are the seed of Abraham. Remove all complaints from our lips- only let them be filled with thanksgiving. Satisfy our soul with Your holy presence. In word and deed we will bless You forever. In Jesus' name we pray, Amen.

# February 4

*Now Jacob's well was there. Jesus therefore, being wearied with his journey, sat thus on the well: and it was about the sixth hour.* (John 4:6)

Physically, you will grow weary with the journey of life. Time will seem unmanageable and the pressures of life will cause you to lose sight of God's purpose. Although Jesus, like you and me, grew tired from the physical demands of life, He never took His eyes off of God's purpose. Here we find our King sitting by the well, exhausted from the journey of traveling. Instead of complaining about all He had yet to complete, He looked to God for His assignment. There is something special about putting all of your faith in God. When you become physically tired He will carry you in the spirit. Jesus was on assignment to tell a lost town about the Hope of Glory- The Father. Not allowing His natural state to keep Him from accomplishing the work of the kingdom, He pressed on and completed what God predestined Him to do and He was successful. God calls us to action. What we see and feel as physically weak is God's perfect opportunity to show us His strength and power. He was in such a state of fatigue that His disciples begged Him to eat and His response was, "My meat is to do the will of Him that sent me, and to finish His work" (John 4:34). This important principle teaches us so many things- one is we must always FINISH what God has called us to do.

**Your greatest success comes from following Christ!**

Prayer: God of all things created, we bless Your holy name. Thank You for creating us with purpose. Lord, we look to You today to feed us our daily bread. Show us the assignment You have for us to complete in the earth. All that we do- we do to bring You glory. Your name will be magnified. Touch our hearts and shift our minds to focus on Your kingdom assignment. We bind up laziness, excuses, fear, doubt, shame, and anything which tries to hinder us from progressing in Your kingdom. We put our hands to the plow and will not look back. We will run this race with endurance. All glory belongs to You. In Jesus' name we pray, Amen.

# February 5

*Mercy, peace and love be yours in abundance.* (Jude 1:2)

God's loving grace is given to us freely each day. One of the best gifts we could ever ask for is for our souls to prosper. God stands at the gate to our hearts, and is available each day, casting His love all over us. In His love we feel the fullness of His joy. All around us we can see the glory of His righteousness. Look at the things He has created in the earth, they all come together according to His perfect plan. Look at the stars in the sky. The sun and moon all serve a purpose. God's purpose for His creation surpasses anything we could ever think of.

Our God so graciously gives us mercy each day. In our darkest moments, we can call upon His name and walk into His arms full of love. When our lives seem to shift from left to right, and confusion clouds our head, one Word from God will cause peace to silence every circumstance so it shall never rise again.

Love from God keeps us functioning each day. It feels our spirit with a boast of confidence, knowing we belong to an everlasting Kingdom. Set up to give us the greatest desires of God's heart, which are plans for the expansion of His Kingdom. Our testament of faith shall exemplify the love showered upon us from heaven. We, in return, shall sow seeds into others, drawing them into the everlasting kingdom.

His love comes in abundance, and is showered upon us for the greater works of His master plan; a plan including you and I operating in our fullest potential, completely satisfied and humbled under His grace. "But you, dear friends, carefully build yourselves up in this most holy faith by praying in the Holy Spirit, staying right at the center of God's love, keeping your arms open and outstretched, ready for the mercy of our Master, Jesus Christ. This is the unending life, the real life!" (Jude20-21)

**God says "seek me while I may be found, what is it that**

**hinders you from me?"**

Prayer: God, we bless Your holy name. We shout praises to Your kingdom. We come with our arms stretched wide, standing in great expectation for Your glory to fall upon us. In your presence alone is total satisfaction. Cover us in the garments of praise. Pour Your oil of joy all over Your people today. Wash us clean from the depths of our inner souls. Build our faith in Your unfailing love. Take the scales from our eyes where we can't see the fullness of Your hand in our lives, show us Your glory. Let there be nothing that stands in the way of us getting to everything You have for our lives to be prosperous. God, we don't come for material gain. Lord, we come humbly to Your throne for our souls. Help our souls to prosper in your love. Let us reach a level of spiritual maturity, which is beneficial to our lives and the lives of those around us. Keep us in the palm of Your hand. Your Words says nothing can separate us from Your love; we stand today basking in Your grace. We love You with all of our heart, mind and soul. In Jesus' name we pray, Amen.

# February 6

*And straightway he called them: and they left their father Zebedee in the ship with the hired servants, and went after him.* (Mark 1:20)

Jesus stepped on the scene as James and John were fishing in a boat with their father. Jesus called them and IMMEDIATELY they left and chose to follow Jesus and became His disciples. They had never seen Jesus before. They had only heard about all of His powerful works and stories of a promise of a soon coming King. As soon as they saw Jesus they knew He was the best thing life could offer. They didn't hesitate, their natural response was to follow Jesus and accomplish God's plan for their life. When God knocked on the door of our heart we too answered the call to follow Jesus. As we continue following after God, we experience all sorts of distractions in life that fight for our attention. Like James and John, we have to forsake ALL and follow Jesus with our whole heart. With a single focus, our eyes fixated on the King, knowing He leads us in our divine purpose; our heart shall instantly pursue the things of God without hesitation. Having this kind of attitude will only enhance our life and the life of others around us. It will propel us to our place of destiny and allow us to hear God's daily plans for our life.

**And be not conformed to this world, but be ye transformed by the renewing of your mind, that ye may prove what is that good and acceptable and perfect will of God. (Romans 12:2)**

Prayer: Lord, You are good and Your mercy endures forever. God, we give You our heart, mind and soul today. Take rule in our life. You have called us for a specific work to walk in close fellowship with You. Let our hearts be intertwined with Yours so our natural response to Your voice is, "Yes, I will obey." Your plans bring us life; your purpose brings glory to Your name. With honor we will bless You. Each day we will seek Your kingdom and Your righteousness on a daily basis. In You we find safety and peace. You are our refuge. All glory belongs to You. In Jesus' name we pray, Amen.

# February 7

*But seek ye first the kingdom of God, and his righteousness; and all these things shall be added unto you.* (Matthew 6:33)

The thing we need to understand about God is that He loves us. The only concern God wants us to have in this life is how to fulfill His divine purpose. God's plans for our life encompasses everything we need in order to be spiritually, emotionally, physically, and financially prosperous. God has it all under control. We often waste countless hours, days, months, and even years worrying about things God never intended for us to be concerned over. After all, He did say cast ALL of your cares on me, because He cares for you. He knows how EVERY single day of our life will pan out before the day even begins. Hence, the reason He teaches us to seek first the kingdom of God. We are kingdom citizens. God is trying to hand-deliver His plan to us, all we have to do is receive it. Every day is another opportunity to sit before God and receive His guidance on the course of our lives. God will not withhold any good thing from us or lead us the wrong way. Actually, His path is perfect and pleasing- apart from Him we are only wasting time. I often say I would hate to get to heaven and see the Lamb's book of life and all that God had prepared for me, but I missed out on because my focus (worrying) was on something else. God is everything, has everything, and wants to give it all to us.

**Blessed be the God and Father of our Lord Jesus Christ, who hath blessed us with all spiritual blessings in heavenly places in Christ: (Ephesians 1:3)**

Prayer: God, You are so amazing. Life is perfect because of You. This day we commit our will to Yours. Your plans are perfect and pleasing. You have ordained every day for us. Thank You for leading us on the narrow path of righteousness for Your name's sake. You guide us in all truth. Your plans are to prosper us and give us hope and a future. In all that we do, we will seek first Your kingdom and Your righteousness. All glory belongs to You. In Jesus' name we pray, Amen.

# February 8

*But as for me I will come into thy house of mercy and in fear will I worship toward thy holy temple.* (Psalm 5:7)

The thing I love about worship is it is an intimate act of dedication to the Lord. NO one can force us to worship and no one can hinder us from worshipping. It is a heart connection that we make with His Spirit. We worship in spirit and in truth. We are allowing the Holy Spirit to take control and lead our intimate time with God. In God's secret place we gain knowledge of Truth (His Word) and begin to grow in awareness of His splendor. Each experience draws us back to enjoy our quiet time alone. As we spend time in worship we are able to take God at His Word and trust Him. We are able to confess His Word and meditate on it throughout the day, filling our mind with His goodness. When we filter out all the distractions taking place around us and think about God, we are able to join in with the angels who cry "Holy, Holy, Holy." God's presence brings solace and peace. His Spirit is fulfilling. We obtain everything we need to enjoy a satisfied life. God doesn't force us to come into His presence. We should be bold, like the psalmist who said, "but as for me I WILL come into thy house." We are coming to the place of mercy, the place of refuge and power. To worship a Holy God who is full of grace.

Prayer: God, as we enter into Your presence we come with a heart of thanksgiving. God, You alone are the best life has to offer. We take time out on purpose to honor Your. We respect You and seek Your will for our life. We don't come with our hand out, we come with our heart in tune with Your perfect plan. Thank You for Your love that keeps us every day. Fill the earth with Your goodness. Help us to recognize it and to always make worship a priority in our life. In Your presence is the fullness of joy. We will dwell in the secret place of the most High and rest under Your shadow. In Jesus' name we pray, Amen.

# February 9

*But I am the Lord, and I can look into a person's heart. I can test a person's mind and decide what each one should have.* (Jeremiah 17:10)

We can hide what's in our heart and on the forefront of our mind from each other, but this is not the case when it comes to God. For God can see us in our rarest form, we are bare before Him. He sees the hidden places of our heart and understands the deep thoughts embedded in our mind. There He examines us on a daily basis to see if we are following through His Holy Spirit or with the works of our flesh. God teaches us how to deny our flesh and rely on Him through renewing our minds in order for our hearts to be pure. There are benefits associated with yielding to the mind of Christ and having the Word of God hidden in our heart. When are minds are in Christ, we are able to know what pleases God. When we please God, it shows Him we are trustworthy of the purpose He placed in each of us. As we allow His Word to be hidden in our heart we are able to reflect His nature on earth and show love to all those we come in contact with. Not only does our mind and heart cause us to be better individuals, standing in right place with God, but God has a promise associated with it. He says He decides what each person should have based on the condition of our heart and the state of our mind.

Prayer: God, You are worthy of all praise. Holy and righteous You are. Examine our hearts and minds today. Create in us a clean heart and renew a right spirit within us. God, only in You are we able to think clearly and have a heart pleasing for You to use us for kingdom business. Purify every ounce of our being that is not like You. Lord, we know in You there is righteousness and life evermore. Thank You for showing us how to walk in faith. We have the mind of Christ and are filled with Your Spirit. Forgive us of all our sins so we can stand in right fellowship with You. We will keep guard over our heart, knowing the issues of life flow from it. We place our life in Your hands. We bless You forever, In Jesus' name we pray, Amen.

# February 10

*For he spake, and it was done; he commanded, and it stood fast.* (Psalm 33:9)

God's Words are power and are guaranteed to accomplish the very thing He desires. Anything that flows from the mouth of God will be established. God loves us so much He gave us principles to follow to grasp the nature of His Word. In Genesis, God spoke things into existence and everything came to be. At the command of His voice everything submits and forms just as He conceives the thought in His mind. Not only does God show us this principle through the power of His Word over and over in the Bible, He also calls us a little higher and tells us to trust in His Word so we can see the manifestation right now in our life. In Jeremiah 1:12 it says, "for I am watching to see that my word is fulfilled." God wants us to speak what He speaks. He is waiting in anticipation for us to believe in His Word, speak His Word and receive His promises. We can learn what God speaks by reading the Bible and seeing just what God is saying about our life, our future, our generation, and the world around us. Whatever we are purposed to do in life there is surely a word to be spoken to ensure we walk in right standing with Him. After all, when God speaks it happens. Everything is submissive to His voice. God has given us power to use His word on a daily basis to come into alignment with His promises and purpose for our lives.

Prayer: God of all the earth, we reverence You. There is no greater love than what You give. We humble ourselves before Your throne. Thank You for teaching us the principles of standing firm in our faith and speaking Your Word into the atmosphere. Align our tongue with Your promises. Your Word is power; it reveals Your loving-kindness and mercy for Your children. Help us to believe and operate in total trust. We will speak what You speak. We commit ourselves to studying Your Word in order to come into alignment with Your heart. We bless You now and forever, Amen.

# February 11

*And I appoint unto you a kingdom, as my Father hath appointed unto me;* (Luke 22:29)

God sent Jesus to the earth to give us eternal life. Jesus came doing only what He saw His Father accomplish in Heaven. He spoke heaven's language. God appointed Jesus to come and make disciples and Jesus appoints us. Jesus did all that the Father instructed Him; He was obedient unto death. Jesus is the perfect example in showing us how to allow God to be glorified in the earth. Through Jesus, God's name was spread throughout the entire earth. Jesus has commissioned us to continue the work of the kingdom. Not only has He given us an assignment, we also have power and authority in the earth to rule. "The heavens are the LORD's heavens, but the earth he has given to the children of man" (Psalm 115:16). Everything we have has been given to us. We have the responsibility as kingdom citizens to rule the earth. Kingdom is an area of territorial rule. We have dominion in the earth. Our success is dependent upon our connection with God. As we turn to Jesus and follow His commands, we will prosper in everything we do. Our assignment is to be living examples so God's name is magnified. No need to worry about how we will accomplish such a task, Jesus laid the foundation for us. In John 17 He prays to God to be with us as He was with Jesus. God loves us so much He didn't leave any aspect of our life uncovered. As we walk with Christ, God bestows His glory upon us so we are equipped to fulfill the work of the kingdom.

Prayer: God, You are wonderful. There is no greater love in all the earth. You fill us with joy. Gladness flows from Your courts. You are the perfect gift. We are completely satisfied in You. Lord, help us to glorify You on earth and accomplish all that You have assigned for us to do. Lead us on Your righteous path. Give us Your heart. Let us love through You. We submit ourselves to You. God, Your plans far exceed anything we could imagine. In You we find peace and obtain eternal life. You are our good thing. In You we will sing praise FOREVER. In Jesus' name we pray, Amen.

# February 12

*If ye love me, keep my commandments.* (John 14:15)

In a world where everyone is searching for love, one glimpse at God will satisfy our entire being. God's love comes with no strings attached because He is love. His love never fails and cannot be retracted. Now God wants to know if we can love Him? Our love for Him is shown through our obedience to His commands. He has given us everything we need and desire. As we lose ourselves in God, we experience exuberant joy. Obeying God becomes a natural response. The more we experience His love, the more enticed we are to respond. We do not serve God for the benefits, but serve God because He is the reward of our compliance. Showing respect to God's commands lets Him know He can trust us. Listening to God opens our heart to receive the goodness His nature is filled with. As we say "yes" to God, He finds pleasure in dwelling in us. At every turn we will see God in our life. He will mold and shape us into His dynamic vessel where His name is glorified. Our adoration for God is two-fold; we please God and receive gratification through His loving embrace. There is no greater feeling than to know we are loved and appreciated. God feels the same way. He is esteemed when He sees His creation committed to uplifting His name.

Prayer: Lord, we lift up Your name and give You glory. We love and adhere to Your commands. Our soul longs for You all day long. You are our portion. Our hope is in You. You are the bright and morning star. Our life is dependent upon Your grace. We recognize You as Lord in our life. Thank You for showering us with Your love and care. You are the best Father, none can compare. Show us areas where we fail to obey Your commandments. Help us to stay on track. With long life You satisfy us. We sing praise to Your name. In Jesus' name we pray, Amen.

# February 13

*Jesus came and told his disciples, "I have been given all authority in heaven and on earth. Therefore, go and make disciples of all the nations, baptizing them in the name of the Father and the Son and the Holy Spirit. Teach these new disciples to obey all the commands I have given you. And be sure of this: I am with you always, even to the end of the age."* (Matthew 28:18-20)

Our lives are a living example of the goodness of heaven. As we obey our Father, we are able to show the world the proper way to function according to God's standards. When we live our lives pure before God, we are lights shinning in the world. God is being shown through us. As children of God, we are under His authority. We willingly release control of our own lives and follow His principles. As He teaches us, it will manifest in our behavior and we will teach others about God's goodness. We shouldn't keep the goodness of God to ourselves. Fear of being rejected or an outcast can be subsided when we allow the Holy Spirit to equip us. There are people in the world who are dying from a lack of knowledge; it could very well be our assignment to minister to them. Diligence, commitment, and constant communication with God prepares us for a time such as this. It's so important to discover God's will for our lives. Everyone has a place in God's kingdom; we are all many parts that form one body. "For as the body is one, and hath many members, and all the members of that one body, being many, are one body: so also is Christ. (1 Corinthians 12:12)

Prayer: Our Father which art in heaven, Hallowed be thy name. Thy kingdom come, Thy will be done in earth, as it is in heaven. Give us this day our daily bread. God, we are under Your authority. All power and majesty is in Your hand. Teach us to follow the narrow path of righteousness all the days of our life. Help us to know Your voice and never follow the voice of another. Be the strongest force of influence in our life. Train us as Your disciples. Let our life be a living example of Your glory. When You prepare us to speak and minister to the lost, don't allow fear to keep us from trusting You. This is Your life; we say have Your way. In Jesus' name, we pray, Amen

# February 14

*The Lord has done great things for us; we are glad.* (Psalm 126:3)

Every day of our life is written in the Lamb's book. Our steps have been marked and ordered by the LORD. From the second He contemplated forming us, He saw our entire life from birth until our last day on earth. His destiny for our lives is complete in Him, and our path is filled with His love. As we stop and think about the marvelous things we have been privileged to experience, we can sit in awe! God has more in store for those who love Him. Walking in His divine purpose only reveals more and more of His good plan for our life. The things God has prepared for us are sure to blow our mind and bring us to our knees in adoration. God's plans are perfect and pleasing. He works in our lives on a consistent basis. Being in constant fellowship with God only further reveals all the good God has done for us before the foundation of the earth. As we continue to embark upon God's loving grace we are filled with gladness, knowing our God has made provision for every day of our lives. We are blessed!

Prayer: Lord, You have done great things for us and we are glad. You are the King of the earth. You make our hearts sing praise to You. We render honor and thanksgiving before Your throne of grace. Thank You for always being our Rock. All things are because of You. We acknowledge You in all that we do. Help us to be aware and follow Your Holy Spirit. Cause us to rejoice in You. In all things we will give thanks. Give us a continuous awareness of Your presence. We know you are near. In Jesus' name we pray, Amen.

# February 15

*"O house of Israel, can I not do with you as this potter has done?" declares the Lord. "Behold, like the clay in the potter's hand, so are you in my hand, O house of Israel."* (Jeremiah 18:6)

The word of the Lord instructed Jeremiah to go to the potter's house to see how the potter made his pottery. In the midst of making a pot the clay had a flaw. In that instance, the potter did not throw the clay away instead he reused it and made something that seemed good to him. God used this illustration to show Jeremiah and us how He operates through us. He is the Master potter and we are the clay. He created us as His masterpiece, but when we make wrong decisions, God is right there to cause our bad to work together for something good. If we repent and turn back to God, He will make our mistakes work for kingdom benefit. What a God we serve! "And we know that all things work together for good to them that love God, to them who are the called according to his purpose" (Romans 8:28). God is not in the business of seeing His people broken. It saddens God to see us toil in despair. If we would relinquish ourselves to God and allow Him to mold us into His perfect work, all that He created us for will manifest. Even when we get off course, He will be right there to restore us back to our proper position in Him through our repentance. It is God's desire to be our potter, the one who molds and shapes us for His glorious work. He looks at us with adoration and is pleased with His wonderful masterpiece.

Prayer: Heavenly Father, we honor You with praise and thanksgiving. Shape and mold us into Your perfect work. Use us for the work of the kingdom. You created all things. We belong to You. Let Your will be known to us. Let us respond to You with love and adoration. Forgive us for trying to do things on our own. You know the thoughts and plans that You have for us. We find joy and pleasure in Your law for our lives. Help us to submit to the governing of the Holy Spirit. We surrender before You; work in us according to Your perfect plan. All glory is given unto You. In Jesus' name we pray, Amen.

# February 16

*Do not quench the Spirit.* (1 Thessalonians 5:19)

It is the Holy Spirit's job to live, pray, operate, love, and work the power of God through us. Hear what God is saying: It's not so much about being self-centered. We are trying so hard to concentrate on personal gain and self-righteousness, when God is trying to show the world His face through us. However, instead we are more focused on feelings. We worry about who loves us and place more emphasis on gaining status quo from other humans. God says, "I love You, you have everything you need and then some in Me. You gave me your life as a living sacrifice, now let Me work through you." People are dying to hear from heaven. Through you and me, we can bring hope to the lost. Through you and me, we can shine as the light of the world. In you and me, we are able to showcase God's love for mankind. Through you and me, God can use us to exhibit His power. Through us, we can show grace and mercy. This is the reason God taught us to forgive and to love one another. Not so we could feel a sense of entitlement, but so we could be love in the world to a generation longing for God's affections. Love is the greatest commandment because it's how God formed us. It's how God communes with us and it's the one thing everyone longs for and can respond to. God's love, shown through us, can shift the atmosphere in the earth. It's time to wake up and allow God's Spirit to work through us to reach the world. Heaven is waiting and earth is in dire need.

Prayer: Father God in heaven, we hear Your voice and heed Your commands. Release Your Spirit in us to reign in the earth. Let Your power work through us. Give us a new kingdom mindset to sit in Your presence and to obey Your every command. Teach us the ways of heaven so Your glory can fill this earth. God, through us You can change the world. We are ready for You to be in every aspect of our lives. God, we need You. All praise is rendered to You. In Jesus' name we pray, Amen.

# February 17

*Then one of them, when he saw that he was healed, turned back, praising God with a loud voice; and he fell on his face at Jesus' feet, giving him thanks. Now he was a Samaritan.* (Luke 17:15-16)

Saying thank you is an act of appreciation. We are acknowledging how grateful we are for what we have been given. In Christ we have been given all things. There is no longer a separation between God and us. He has an open door policy where we are welcome to receive the blessings of heaven. As we breath in-and-out we experience the gift of life. It would take a lifetime to express the gratitude due towards God for all that He does on a continuous basis. Thanksgiving becomes the natural response as we admire God for who He is. We are a living sacrifice to God because of His great love toward us. We always turn and acknowledge God for being in our lives. Thanksgiving is our native language and will always flow from our lips. God is pleased to see our hearts filled with appreciation. Everything God did was so we could be in close proximity with Him to experience His great love openly. Every day we will turn back and say "Thank You."

Prayer: Lord God Almighty, You are more than enough. You fill us to capacity. Our hearts overflow with Your love. In Your mighty grace You have given us all things. There is nothing You desire to keep away from us. Our lips our fixed to give You praise at all times in all things. There is no greater love than what You show us on a daily basis. You are with us every second, we acknowledge You for who You are. You are EVERYTHING. We will never be able to thank You for all that You have done, but with every ounce of our being we will continuously sing of Your love. God, we are forever thankful for who You are to all things created. We will remember we love You. In Jesus' name we pray, Amen.

# February 20

*Then Jacob woke up from his sleep and exclaimed, "Certainly, the Lord is in this place, and I didn't know it!" Filled with awe, he said, "How awe-inspiring this place is! Certainly, this is the house of God and the gateway to heaven!"* (Genesis 28:16-17)

God is always present. If we are not careful, at times we can allow issues of life to hinder us from acknowledging God is in our midst. When we turn our attention toward God we will experience His awesome glory. The experience of God's presence is so satisfying, often it cannot be put into words. He is All-powerful and bestows His greatness into His creation. As we yield ourselves to God and allow Him to enter into our hearts, our lives will never be the same. In God, we partake in heaven on earth. God's virtue develops our spirit to stand in agreement with Him. As we position ourselves to receive God for who He is, we will see God in everything we do. God longs to show Himself in our lives. As we allow the scales to fall off our eyes and release our heart to God, we recognize God is trying to get the kingdom of heaven to us. When we accept God's invitation, we are giving God permission to give us the best life has to offer. Jesus is life and in Him we have all things. Cherishing God and living in His presence is the greatest thing we can ever do. On a daily basis we will set God before us and experience Him on a deeper, more intimate level. The more time we spend with God through relinquishing ourselves to Him, the more we become aware of the fact that He is near at all times. God is refreshing, His presence is holy and contagious- causing those who experience Him to want more and more of Him. God is everything!

Prayer: Lord, You live in this place. We acknowledge You as holy. You rule this earth and all things created. Abide in us. Teach us how to relinquish ourselves to experience You more and more. Two days are never the same with You. You do new things every day. Your love is amazing and unexplainable. You give us more than we could ever ask for. We are forever thankful. This is the place of Bethel where You live. You are able to use us for Your glory. Open the gates of heaven and show us Your visions. Take us to the higher place in You. No longer will we praise You half-heartedly, we want all of You so we give You all of us. Shine Your light on this earth. You are worthy of all honors in Jesus' name we pray, Amen.

# February 21

*Be dressed in readiness, and keep your lamps lit.* (Luke 12:35)

Our life on earth is the practice round for what our life will be like in heaven. The way we act now should line up with how we will act as we spend every waking moment in the presence of God. In actuality, we are always in God's presence. We don't like to think about it like that because if we did we would be eager to pursue the things of God. God gives us day after day to sit with Him and allow Him to develop His attributes in us. It is our heart's desire to grow in God in order to reflect His nature in the earth. At the return of Jesus, we should not be surprised but EXCITED to join with our Savior. We will have spent every day of our life preparing for Christ's return. Our mannerism and mindset are in alignment with Christ in heaven. At all times we are ready for whatever comes our way. We build ourselves up to be able to stand firm by acknowledging God in all things and having an intimate (personal) relationship with Him. As we grow in God, He continues to lead us on the righteous path, and when Jesus returns it will not shock us because we would have been walking in our kingdom nature already. Our light (Jesus) is inside of us; as we relinquish ourselves to His Sovereignty everything flows together.

Prayer: God, we worship You in spirit and truth. You are all things at all times. There is no one greater than You. Prepare us while we still have time. You have given us this life to enjoy. Thank You for setting us free. Show us how to walk in freedom. Teach us how to exhibit Your attributes in everything we do. Transform us from the inside out. When men see us let them see You. We will be watchmen at the door, always alert and giving glory to Your holy name. You are the King of our life, rule in us. We will forever reverence You. We love You. In Jesus' name we pray, Amen.

# February 22

*But he that is greatest among you shall be your servant.* (Matthew 23:11)

In this particular passage Jesus is teaching the people how to be leaders. He describes how the Scribes and Pharisees sit in the seats of authority, executing law but failing to lead by example. Jesus tells us not to be this way. A leader is one you will find serving. They serve the people God has entrusted to them by adhering to all the commands of heaven. Leaders spend time with God so they can be transformed, then they align their actions with God's word and lead their flock by example. Our greatest model of a leader is Jesus. He came to earth and served the people in every capacity. He lived His life in accordance to God's commands and was obedient, even until the point of death. His legacy teaches us how to govern our lives in accordance with God's original intent for mankind. We are all leaders (servants). Jesus boldly tells the people not to get caught up in the TITLE of leader but to know the true meaning which is to become a servant. We have been given the awesome opportunity to supply the needs of those we are serving. In our serving, we are able to display God's virtue. When you think of leaders, they are one's who sacrifice their time to ensure the welfare of others is taken care of. Jesus did this for us and has given us the blueprint to be great leaders. As we serve God, serving others will come natural.

Prayer: Lord, You are God of all the earth. You are so amazing. You sit high but You look low. You see the affairs of men. Nothing is hidden in Your sight. Search us inwardly and teach us how to serve You first and mankind second. Help us to esteem others above ourselves. You said the greatest commandment is to love You with all our heart, mind and soul, and the second is to love our neighbor as thyself. Lord, we love You. In Jesus' name we pray, Amen.

# February 23

*Instead, seek his kingdom, and these things will be added to you.* (Luke 12:31)

The word instead is defined as replacing one thing for another. God teaches us instead of WORRYING about the cares of life, we can find solace in seeking Him. To seek God involves discovering our purpose and finding ways to exude God's greatness in the earth. To seek God's kingdom invites God to put His hand in our affairs. Choosing to prioritize other things in place of God cannot guarantee our end result. After we have sought God's kingdom, we are assured without a wavering doubt God HAS added all things to us. God's principles ALWAYS work- we seek, He adds, plain and simple. Benefits of seeking God include honorable relationships, wisdom in parenting, life purpose, monetary increase, and the ability to live life according to God's fullest potential. Staying focused on God propels us to a level of contentment. God's presence is a reward. His glory is appealing day-after-day in God we yearn for more of Him. Our time seeking God and experiencing Him is well spent. As we realize how incredible God is and truly believe it, worry will diminish. I've tried worrying and it didn't produce anything favorable. I've also tried God and His promises are established every time. God wants us to trust Him. He is practically begging us to acknowledge Him so He can release into the earth what He has lingering in the Spirit realm- His Presence (All Things).

**Fear not, little flock; for it is your Father's good pleasure to give you the kingdom. (Luke 12:32)**

Prayer: Lord, we honor You. You alone deserve our worship. Forgive us for not seeking You first in all things at all times. God, You know EVERYTHING. It is a foolish mistake on our part to exclude You from our affairs. Lord, we invite You into every aspect of our life. We take the limits off. Speak to us directly concerning Your plans. We will be intentional about hearing from heaven. In our quiet time with You, fill us with Your wisdom, knowledge and understanding. You have the key to every situation. Thank You for providing us with tools to overcome in this world. We are victorious. We surrender our worry and cast our cares at Your feet. God, reign in our life. You are welcome here. Blessings to You in heaven forever. God, we love You. In Jesus' name we pray, Amen.

# February 24

*Blessed is the man that trusteth in the Lord, and whose hope the Lord is.* (Jeremiah 17:7)

When we trust God, He welcomes us into His presence and reveals His strategic plan for each step of our life. We are not alienated from obstacles and opposition in life, yet we have an earnest expectation to receive the promises God has made concerning His children. Trusting God causes all things in our life to come under His commands. The beauty of God shows us that before He creates anything, He carefully thinks about every aspect. He ensures we have everything we need for every single day of our life. We know this is true because He has given us so many promises in His Word. Within our area of freedom we have two options, either to trust God or to trust things in the world. If we decide to trust in things other than God, we step out of the realm of promise. God's covenant works only by His commands, which are perfect. He tries to make it simple for us; our job is to trust and receive. We make it hard when we choose not to trust God and deceive ourselves (miss out on His promises). Resolving to put total faith in God renders a blessed life. God's word of promise has no other option but to manifest, as we walk in agreement with Him. Standing in alignment with God enables us to receive the shower of blessings God is pouring down from heaven. The bible says when we trust God, we shall be like a tree PLANTED by the waters. These waters flow from the throne of heaven, waters that satisfy our every need and make us to know gladness. God is in the midst, and when God shows up everything falls into place. We can stay in that blessed place by rendering our hearts to God, trusting Him every step of the way.

**There is a river whose streams make glad the city of God, The holy dwelling places of the Most High. (Psalm 46:4)**

Prayer: Lord, You are Sovereign. We exalt Your name on High. You are in the midst of Your holy city. Dwell here in our hearts. Fill us with Your Holy Spirit. Open our ears to hear and our eyes to see the splendor of Your glory. Live in us. You have full control- we submit our mind, heart, and soul to You. Nothing in earth is more important than knowing You. We long to sit in Your presence to hear what is taking place in heaven. Shine Your light on us once again so that we will know you more intimately. With every ounce of our being we worship You. In Jesus' name we pray, Amen.

## February 25

*But the angel of the Lord said to him, "Why do you ask my name, seeing it is wonderful?"* (Judges 13:18 ESV)

Who is God to You? When we discover God for ourselves, we will obtain a pure satisfaction beyond anything we can experience on earth. No one can satisfy us the way God does. After all, He created us to have that special place in our heart where only He can reside. When we let Him abide in us and experience His supreme presence, we come into the knowledge of how wonderful He truly is. His love overwhelms our spirit and produces pleasure in us that we can't fathom. It is in God that we find our delight. His hand is stretched toward us, comforting us with the sheerness of His holy presence. In God we have found that good thing. At every turn our lives are fulfilled, knowing we belong to the King of Kings. In life we will not have to wonder what our future will hold. We have solid confidence in God. On a daily basis we rise, giving glory to God who is pleasing in all His ways. No longer do we waiver in faith, attempting to figure out what God will do for us. We know full well who God is and everything about Him is brilliant. Confusion is not on our minds, we are convinced God is our redeemer and instead of questioning His strategies, we surrender our worship.

Prayer: God, we love You. God, we know who You are. You are Alpha and Omega. You are Wonderful, Counselor, and Prince of Peace. You are ruler of all things. There is no one greater than You. In all that we do we will acknowledge You. You are the lover of our souls. Shine Your light on us. Lord, in You and You alone do we have our strength. You shine Your light in us. We are forever grateful. Continue to knock on the door of our heart. You get all the glory. In Jesus' name we pray, Amen.

## February 26

*Come now, and let us reason together, saith the Lord: though your sins be as scarlet, they shall be as white as snow; though they be red like crimson, they shall be as wool.* (Isaiah 1:18)

How considerate of God to ask us to engage in conversation with Him. He has invited us to discuss the manner in which we conduct our lives. In fellowship with Him, He tells us that although we were born with a sinful nature, if we surrender ourselves to Him He will wash our sins away. When we commit sin, it contaminates the way God created us to be. Although we have received forgiveness through Jesus, we have to make a conscious choice EVERY DAY to obey God. I know we don't continue in sin intentionally, but sometimes our flesh gets the best of us. This is where our loving Father steps in to talk to us about our behavior and the course of our life. When we fellowship with God, He teaches us how to keep our mind focused on things that benefit the kingdom and develop character in us at the same time. Our heart and mind will be so entangled in the attributes of God that when temptation comes, we'll be able to recognize it and possess the strength to resist it. God doesn't find joy in punishing those who commit sin; it's a part of His righteous judgment. "It is a fearful thing to fall into the hands of the living God (Hebrews 10:31). God longs to wash us clean and usher us into a life of intimate communion with Him. God is pleading with us to stand firm in faith and to adhere to His commands and live a blessed life.

Prayer: Lord, You are Mighty. There is no one greater than You. Forgive us of all of our sins. God, the way we speak, think and act, transform our thinking and help us to be obedient. Touch our minds to come into agreement with each of Your commands. "For if we sin wilfully after that we have received the knowledge of the truth, there remaineth no more sacrifice for sins" (Hebrews 10:26). Thank You for washing us clean in Jesus. We will not forget the sacrifice He made for us. We come boldly before Your throne, submitting our entire being to You. Work in us to reflect Your glory in the earth. Your name be praised now and forever, in Jesus' name we pray, Amen.

## February 27

*O Lord, I know that the way of man is not in himself: it is not in man that walketh to direct his steps.* (Jeremiah 10:23)

If we could have our way, we would plan out the rest of our lives. How we'll spend tomorrow, next week, we'd even plan how we desire to leave this earth. God teaches us that in all our planning, we cannot formulate a strategy grand enough to fulfill our purpose. God is the one who created the stars and the universe, everything living along with the land and water. Before we came into the knowledge of Christ we were content with leading our own life toward destruction. We were actually masters at doing things to satisfy our flesh. Now that we are in Christ, our hope is in God. Our desires have changed and we long to accomplish what God created us for. Not to mention that God is perfect and His ways have been tried and proven to work for our good. It is considered a great blessing to have God leading us and directing our steps. In life, we have free will so we will have to make a choice whether or not we surrender our steps to God, but just know that without God we are walking round and round in circles, accomplishing nothing. Only in God is where we will walk the narrow path straight into His arms of eternity. And I'll let you in on a little secret, when we surrender our plans to God- His thought out plans far exceed anything we could have ever considered, and He satisfies our innerbeing.

Prayer: Lord, You are Mighty. Your grace and mercy keep us day-by-day. Thank You for considering us as Your servants. Forgive us for trying to do things on our own. In all of our ways we will acknowledge You. You know the end from the beginning. All things are under Your control. We dare not deceive ourselves by thinking we'll get ahead in life without You. We honor You in all things. Take control of our life. Order our steps now and forever. Lord, You are greatly to be praised. In Jesus' name we pray, Amen.

# February 28

*The Lord says: "These people come near to me with their mouth and honor me with their lips, but their hearts are far from me. Their worship of me is based on merely human rules they have been taught.* (Isaiah 29:13 NIV)

We worship God in Spirit and in truth. There is no other way to worship Him except through the guidance of His Spirit. Once we accepted Jesus in our life He gave us His Spirit. Now, to worship we have to come into an awareness of His Spirit that is already present inside of us. This means we have to ignore distractions and determine in our heart to give total reverence to God. We surrender all to Him and allow Him to minister to and through us. In return, God shows us the way to function and operate in our daily activities by developing our character in Him. Our love for God will be built on His foundation and our worship will be authentic. Worship cannot be taught, there is no class on how to love God. It is an experience each of us has to partake in one on one with God, Jesus, and the Holy Ghost. In this place of renouncing ourselves, we learn how to speak well of God and honor Him with every ounce of our being. God pours out His Spirit upon His children, and the spirit within us has to fight to overpower our flesh so we can honor God. It's a choice we have to make on a daily basis. We don't fight this battle alone. Jesus finished the battle for us. In our daily pursuit to remain obedient to God, we have to lean on God's Spirit to direct us. If we think about the greatness of God and serve God with our heart we prosper every time.

**And he said to him, "You shall love the Lord your God with all your heart and with all your soul and with all your mind. (Matthew 22:37)**

Prayer: Lord, You are Holy. Forgive us for playing church. Examine us and strip us from any falsehood. You deserve pure worship. We invite You in to live and reside in us. We make a choice to surrender all to You. Keep teaching us and leading us on the narrow path of righteousness. You said if we seek You, You will be found. We come knocking, thank You for opening the door. Your love, grace and compassion builds us up continually. Thank You for never giving up on us. We will honor You in all that we do. In Jesus' name we pray, Amen.

# March 1

*But may all who seek you rejoice and be glad in you; may those who long for your saving help always say, "The Lord is great."* (Psalm 70:4 NIV)

God is a good God. Yes, times in life may overcloud our mind and prompt us to believe God has forgotten about us, but this is not the truth. It is impossible for God not to care for His beloved. Once we master the thought that God is for us, we will be able to overcome thoughts of abandonment. If we find ourselves in constant pursuit of the LORD, joy will be on our lips and our souls will be glad. In God's presence we find nothing but greatness. His grace is being poured out in immeasurable amounts. In the face of adversity we must make the choice to stand in the comfort of the secret place of the Most High while resting under His shadow. God gives need to every care we will ever face in the world. If we stretch out our arm to grab hold of God's unfailing hand we will find refuge. God is always near and those who pursue Him will rejoice and be glad proclaiming, "The LORD is great."

Prayer: Father, You are Lord of all things created. You are a great God. You lead us on the righteous path where we find comfort in Your saving grace. You are in us and we are victorious through Christ Jesus. Nothing can separate us from Your love. We rejoice at the thought of You. Your praise is continuously on our lips. We will make known Your works in all the earth. Thoughts of Your love keep our minds clear from destruction. There is no greater love than to seek after You. You are Abba- Father. We love and appreciate You for who You are in our lives. In Jesus' name we pray, Amen.

# March 2

*It is a good thing to give thanks unto the Lord, and to sing praises unto thy name, O Most High:* (Psalm 92:1)

Every day we are faced with the jungle of life. We enter into a world of choices. Many things fight for our attention. Come here Nicole, Do this Nicole, Watch this Nicole. Daily, the choice is left up to us on what to decide. Giving God praise every morning, thanking Him for being Lord in our life is guaranteed to produce favorable outcomes. Singing praises to God will come before Him like a sweet aroma. God desires our thanksgiving and approves of our songs of praise. As we come in His presence, the sweetness of His splendor creates new songs of praise within us. As we offer our lips to speak well of His glory, God becomes excited to extend Himself in fellowship. As we replay the goodness of God over and over in our thoughts, we are reminded of the blessings we have obtained in being called His children. Spending time with God on a daily basis will create new songs of praise to radiate from our lips. It is honorable to thank God in EVERYTHING and for EVERYTHING. There are many reasons to give thanks. One, life could always be worse, and two, God alone deserves great honor. He is the Holy One who sits high, yet He looks low in order to intertwine Himself in the concerns of man. In devoting ourselves in thanksgiving to our Father, we have chosen the righteous path. A path where we have open access to experience God, Jesus, and the Holy Spirit intimately, day-by-day.

Prayer: God, You are awesome. You deserve honor and praise. We choose to worship and offer thanksgiving before Your throne. We invite You into the affairs of Your people to rule and abide within us. Guide us into the way of peace. Thank You for being a light in darkness. You rescued us from the evil in this world. Thanksgiving will always be found on our lips. Regardless of what life throws our way, we know You are God and we have victory in Christ Jesus. We are seated in heavenly places at Your right hand. Nothing can compare to Your glory. Now and forever, we sing praises to You. In Jesus' name we pray, Amen.

# March 3

*For there is nothing covered, that shall not be revealed; neither hid, that shall not be known.* (Luke 12:2)

In all things, Jesus gave His disciples warning on how to live a righteous life before the Father. Whenever we find ourselves doing things contrary to the will of God we are able to come before the throne of grace and repent. Oftentimes we like to put emphasis on the big sins that are noticeable to the eye when pointing the finger on what we are doing wrong; when God looks at every action and every word that comes out of our mouth and the condition of our heart. Nothing is hidden before God. He has called us to be His consecrated children; sanctified, set aside for His use. God's Holy Spirit will let us know when we have allowed any form of ungodliness to sneak into our lives. Jesus told His disciples to beware of leaven, which is a small substance that causes the yeast in bread to rise (Matthew 16:6). All it takes is a small amount to have a big effect on the process of bread expanding. This same development takes place when we allow a little piece of sin to enter our lives. The little lie will produce, and if we don't deal with it, it will grow and it might overtake us. The gossip will cause division. The horrible attitude will cause strife. The married women flirting on the job will create a lustful heart. The shopper going over their budget will create debt. The little things in life matter and God is watching. Be alert and remain in God's word. This will work as a defense mechanism. Staying in tune with the Holy Spirit will give us warning, correction and guidance to keep us from diversions as we journey on the narrow path of righteousness.

Prayer: Lord, You are good and Your mercy endures forever. You are a great God! You see all that takes place in the earth. Thank You for leading us on the narrow path of righteousness. Help us to keep watch and to pray about everything. We will make a choice to be led by the Holy Spirit. Convict us when we make ungodly decisions. You live in us. Shine Your glory through us to draw all men to You. Lead us not into temptation and deliver us from evil. All glory belongs to You. In Jesus' name we pray, Amen.

# March 4

*If ye then, being evil, know how to give good gifts unto your children, how much more shall your Father which is in heaven give good things to them that ask him?* (Matthew 7:11)

If its in our ability to provide for our loved ones, we will ensure all their needs and wants are met. Our heavenly Father has a supply that can never run out and He is willing and able to provide it to us. This doesn't pertain only to material things, God wants to give us peace and every spiritual attribute to help us live life to our maximum potential. All we have to do is ASK. God sits in heaven, waiting in expectation for us to seek His face and release the supplications of our heart. Jesus tells us to continue asking, seeking and knocking, and God will respond. It gives God great pleasure to work in the lives of His children. Our minds have to be regenerated to comprehend who we are praying to. We are asking God Almighty, the One who created the universe by calling all things into existence by His Words. The One who shaped the foundations of the earth, and at His voice everything obeys His command. As we begin to recognize the power of God, we will come boldly before the throne of grace and ask our Father for whatever is on our hearts; knowing He has already answered and will release that which we ask for. Why do we ask if God already knows what we want and need? Good question!!! God wants us to see ourselves as blessed, walking in our inheritance and staying connected to the vine. If we don't want the abundant life for ourselves, God will not force us to have it. We have to be intentional about staying in alignment with God and longing for what He has already planned for us, which is hope and an expected end.

Prayer: Lord, You are Alpha and Omega. Your name is above all names. Transform us by renewing our minds so we can test and approve Your perfect will for our lives (Romans 12:2). Your plans for us are perfect and we come seeking Your hand of righteousness. We ask for the desires of our heart in accordance with Your will. We believe we have what we say in Jesus' name.

You have stored up for us blessings upon blessings that we don't even have room to receive. Your blessings overtake us. We are the righteousness of Your holy kingdom. Hallelujah! We say thank You. Your name be lifted high in all the earth. In Jesus' name we pray, Amen.

# March 5

*The Lord your God is in your midst, a mighty one who will save; he will rejoice over you with gladness; he will quiet you by his love; he will exult over you with loud singing.* (Zephaniah 3:17)

Many of us try to disqualify ourselves from the kingdom of God by thinking we are not worthy of God's grace. God gives grace because of who He is. As we spend time with God He reveals exactly what He thinks of us. He is not delighted to cast judgment on the world. It is a part of His nature because He cannot co-exist with sin. God, being a loving Father, has set us free from sin, and with repentance He forgets our mistakes as if they never occurred. He doesn't remember them anymore. Instead of us always thinking of ways we have disappointed God, we can come before God and see how much He really loves us. Thinking that God is constantly mad at us is a trick from the enemy. He loves us so much that He looks down from heaven in awe. When we turn to acknowledge Him, His heart is filled with joy and gladness. He sings songs for us in heaven. Songs soothe the spirit and speak about the goodness of His creation. God is thrilled to have each of us as His own. God is in the midst of us and rejoices at our acceptance of who He is. God is trying to get us to look at Him so we can see ourselves as created in His image and adore His presence. Our daily communion with God is like having a birthday party every day. The primary focus is on us as we focus on Him! God prepares all the arrangements and entertainment, all we have to do is show up and experience everything He has already prepared.

Prayer: Father, we exalt Your name on High. Your name is honored in all the earth. "What is man that You are mindful of him, And the son of man that You visit him?" (Psalm 8:4-5). You are elated to live in us. It brings You great pleasure to walk in fellowship with us. Open our hearts and minds to live in the spirit realm, where You show us our true identity. Your love is everlasting and is always searching for us. Thank You for inviting us in to be with You. We will render proper praise and thanksgiving to You. You are holy and righteous. We sing praises to Your name forever. In Jesus' name we pray, Amen.

# March 6

*The LORD is my portion, saith my soul; therefore will I hope in him.* (Lamentations 3:24)

Lord, thank You! God is our portion, therefore we are not consumed. His mercies are new every morning. All that we need resides in His holy presence. It is considered a blessing to wait in the Lord. Anxiety and fear seem to arise when we are unable to determine the outcome of a situation. In God we have security. God's plans for us are already established, and if we abide in Him we will see them manifest. Every aspect of our life is summed up in the Lord being our portion. The obstacles of our day can become stepping stones as we allow God to be our guide. God is always present and able to provide for us through every moment. God becomes our portion when we make a conscious effort to think about His goodness, making a choice to feed ourselves with His awesome word. Then our belief in Him will grow and when situations arise, we will rely on God being our Father. God wants to be our portion; He longs to extend His hand of mercy toward His people. Make a choice to grab His hand and wait patiently as He delivers us day-by-day.

Prayer: Mighty God, we are forever grateful for Your unfailing love. "Wherefore seeing we also are compassed about with so great a cloud of witnesses, let us lay aside every weight, and the sin which doth so easily beset us, and let us run with patience the race that is set before us" (Hebrews 12:1). You are our portion and we are satisfied in You. Lead us on the narrow path of righteousness for Your name's sake. We take the limits off of You. Run rampant in this earth, showing us Your glory. Allow Your Holy Spirit to saturate the earth, God we need You. You know the end from the beginning. Fulfill Your plan in us and through us. We surrender our plans for Yours. We trust and rely on You. Jesus, we love You now and forever. In Jesus' name we pray, Amen.

# March 7

*If thou hast run with the footmen, and they have wearied thee, then how canst thou contend with horses? and if in the land of peace, wherein thou trustedst, they wearied thee, then how wilt thou do in the swelling of Jordan?* (Jeremiah 12:5 KJV)

How long is the question many of us ask God whenever we face hardships or uncomfortable situations. Lord, how long will my children disobey? Lord, how long will I be unemployed? Lord, how long will my enemies prevail? Lord, how long do I have to be single? The list goes on and on. We are all guilty of growing weary in well-doing. God is teaching us our only command is to put our trust in Him through casting all of our cares on Him. Faith and trust in God is the antidote for Him answering our cries of desperation. It is possible for God to deliver us in the blink of an eye and then we go on our merry way. But if we allow unbelief, doubt, and fear to always cripple us, we will be right back at His feet complaining, asking why me. Instead, the command God gave Joshua still reigns, " Have not I commanded thee? Be strong and of good courage; be not afraid, neither be thou dismayed: for the LORD thy God is with thee withersoever thou goest" (Joshua 1:9). God's love for us expands beyond our human intellect. He never created us to watch us fail. He will stretch us in order to develop us into our fullest potential, the very way He sees us. Every time we have to wait in God for something, our strength, trust and dependence is expanded. God told Jeremiah, if you couldn't contend with men on foot how will you be able to keep up with horses. In other words, if we fail to believe God for employment how can we believe God to destroy the plans of terrorists? In every lesson, God prepares us for greater works to be done for the kingdom. The obstacles we face today get us ready for the assignment that's coming tomorrow. Nothing we accomplish in God will be wasted. Run this race with endurance, trusting God beyond our natural ability to see only what God promised in His word.

Prayer: God, You are so amazing. Heaven and earth respond at

Your command, surely You can handle what we are facing. Lord, give us strength for some of the things we are experiencing are difficult. Thank You for being right by our side. We cast our cares on You. You can handle everything. We will focus on Your word and all that You have promised us. You told us not to WORRY about anything. You are our Shepherd and we shall not want. You have given us power, love, and a sound mind. Peace is ours in abundance. Wisdom is ours in abundance. Holy Spirit, order our steps in the Lord. Thank You for shinning Your light on us. Hallelujah! Lord, we love You. In Jesus' name we pray, Amen.

# March 8

*I have been crucified with Christ and I no longer live, but Christ lives in me. The life I now live in the body, I live by faith in the Son of God, who loved me and gave himself for me.* (Galatians 2:20)

I once heard someone say the shortest thing we will ever have to do is live this life. Eternity is forever. The decisions we make today will determine where our soul will rest forever. Since we have made the awesome choice to invite Jesus in to reside inside of us we can rejoice. Yet, it doesn't stop there. Now we have to allow Jesus to settle in us by living our lives in submission to Him. It is no longer us who calls all the shots but Christ who resides on the inside of us. This renunciation of control produces life. As we put total reliance on Jesus and operate in faith, we are able to fulfill God's work on the earth. Thinking about God's love and how He searches for ways to draw us closer to Him every day makes living in Christ jubilant. Remembering what Christ went through so we can experience a genuine relationship with God makes it easy for us to allow Christ to rule in us. Our attitude should exhibit our gratitude for Christ loving us. And Christ will stimulate our actions because we live in Him.

Prayer: Father, You are lovely. We will sing of Your praises forever. Your love will flow from our lips at all times. There is no fault found in You. You seek out new ways to bestow Your love on us day after day. Thank You for thinking of us. Thank You for sending Jesus for us. Thank You for giving us Your Holy Spirit. We die to selves daily. Forgive us for our sins that we have committed against You. Open our heart to the truth of Your word. Saturate us with Your Holy Spirit. Give us wisdom in all that we do. Your name is blessed FOREVER! In Jesus' name we pray, Amen.

# March 9

*And my tongue shall declare Your righteousness And Your praise all day long.* (Psalm 35:28 NASB)

There is no greater love than the love of God. He looks down from His throne in awe. His love for us surpasses our understanding. The love we experience in human relationships fail to compare to the depths of God's adoration for us. When we accept the truth and understand how God loves us beyond all of our mistakes, no matter how far we try to run from Him, His love still remains. God granted us freedom under His grace. We are free to live and enjoy life as we commune with Him. Our relationship with God shouldn't be robotic where we force ourselves to spend time with Him. It is not a matter of checking the box. Oftentimes we become complacent and think our grace and blessings are tied up in whether or not we spend time with God. Our desire to be in God's presence then becomes a burden. Loving God is a gift. The more time we spend with Him, the more time we will want to spend with Him. The mere fact that we were born proves we are blessed. A relationship with God reveals the greatness of who God is and who we truly are in Him. Living apart from God, we aren't being our authentic self. As we come into His presence and experience firsthand how much God loves us, our lips will be filled with praise. It will become our natural response to talk about the goodness of God. When we read the Word of God, it is a time of delight and understanding. It will be hard for us to conceal all that God is disclosing to us through His word. Our tongues will confess the goodness of God all day long because of His great mercy and grace.

Prayer: Lord, Your love embodies the earth. Open our hearts to receive You for who You are. You are the living God. Your grace is bestowed upon us new each day. Lord, help us to delight ourselves in Your holy presence. Don't allow us to push our relationship with You to the side, but to give You priority in everything that we do. We will spend the rest of our lives expressing Your goodness, so with everything we will sing of your praises. Your righteousness covers us day-by-day. Our tongues will declare You are Lord. We are forever grateful. In Jesus' name we pray, Amen.

# March 10

*Then shall ye call upon me, and ye shall go and pray unto me, and I will hearken unto you.* (Jeremiah 29:12)

When we realize life is bigger than us, we will see the true heart of God. Our purpose in life is to be a part of His family. Each of us are individual body parts, which fit together as a whole body in Christ for God's good cause. Surrendering our desires for God's will keeps us in alignment with Him. We will no longer indulge in self-pity parties, always asking, "what about me." Instead our delight will be found in God. God knows the specific thoughts and plans He has for us. Plans to use us to bring glory to His name while edifying us in the process. Everything God does is for His good pleasure, and it develops our relationship with Him. God is such a giving Father, not only has He orchestrated our lives to fit into His plan but gives us complete satisfaction during the process. Accepting that God has great plans for us allows us to pray with a heart of contentment. Our prayers will be in accordance with what God wants to do in the earth, and God will perform the very things we ask of Him.

Prayer: Lord, You do all things well. Renew our minds to know the truth of who You are. Your plans for us far exceed anything we could ever think of. Your wisdom is unexplainable. All of Your ways are perfect. Help us to deny ourselves to be captivated by Your love. Your love, which calls us into perfect fellowship with You, to be used by You for Your glory. We will be Your willing vessels- work through us. God have Your way now and forever. In Jesus' name we pray, Amen.

# March 11

*Then God saw everything that He had made, and indeed it was very good. So the evening and the morning were the sixth day.* (Genesis 1:31)

There is good in you. Regardless of our stature or what accomplishments we have achieved, at some point we have all felt as though we weren't good enough. These feelings of self-defeat developed either though other's opinions or our own negative opinion of ourselves. Luckily for us, we no longer have to succumb to anyone's view of us when we have God's perception- and He says we are VERY GOOD. *Everything He created He already blessed and placed His divine purpose inside of.* Negative thoughts about our self-worth do not come from the throne of heaven. Yes, we may engage in activities that are not conducive or have characteristics contrary to God's will. He makes these areas in our lives known to us and guides us towards getting on the right track. God's intent for all things created is for His good pleasure. There is greatness inside of each of us, and God is trying to pull it out and show us how to walk in our maximum potential. By staying close to God, He reveals how much He loves everything about us. The more time we spend with Him, the more knowledge we obtain in regard to how pleased He is with us- the precious gift He created. His works are perfect and pleasing, goodness resides in you.

Prayer: God of all things created, You called life into being for Your perfect plan. Give us wisdom to comprehend how much You love us. You are concerned with every aspect of our lives. You give wisdom to sustain us on a daily basis. We draw close to You Lord. Reveal Your marvelous works to us. Thank You for esteeming us. We know we are the children of the Most High. You love us with an everlasting love. Heal the lost and touch the broken-hearted. We receive Your love today. In all things we give thanks. In Jesus' name we pray, Amen.

# March 12

*If any man serve me, let him follow me; and where I am, there shall also my servant be: if any man serve me, him will my Father honour.* (John 12:26)

In our serving we are to always be where God is, not trying to get God to conform to where we are. In our seeking after Him we take our position as subordinate and yield to the respect due our Master. Our act of service requires we relinquish ourselves to the full use of God as our guide through life. We know as we follow Jesus we are being led to a place where He has traveled before. On our journey, our safety and satisfaction is guaranteed. God is where we are going and He travels alongside of us. Not only do we find delight in being wherever Christ is. we also obtain honor from the throne of grace. God looks upon us with great pleasure at seeing His children enjoying acts of obedience. Our concept of servitude has been distorted by the world's standards of thinking servants are run-of –the-mill; when in actuality being a servant is the most distinguished honor in the kingdom of heaven. Jesus came to the earth to serve, and because of His service we are able to spend eternity with God. Just imagine what our act of service would do for those around us as we impact the world with God's glorious light.

Prayer: Lord, we exalt Your name on high. We are here to be used by You. Teach us how to serve You with our entire being. Where You lead we will follow. Wherever You are that is where we long to be. You are our Shepherd. We are pleased to listen to Your commands. In Your presence is the fullness of joy. Thank You for walking beside us and being our light in this dark and evil world. We deny ourselves, kill everything in us that is not like You. All glory and praise belongs to You. In Jesus' name we pray, Amen.

# March 13

*God is spirit, and those who worship him must worship in spirit and truth.* (John 4:24)

God, being a Spirit, puts a whole new emphasis on how we should worship. He is not confined by time or limitations. He is free to do whatsoever He desires for His creation. Heaven and earth belong to Him. At the command of His voice all things surrender before Him. Many refuse to realize how awesome and powerful God is. It is by His grace that we are not consumed. His loving nature invites us in to worship Him for who He is. O' how great it is when we grab hold of who God is and begin to worship. Then we experience the Shekinah glory- the manifestation of His presence. We fail to recognize His presence that is always in the earth because we have so many other distractions fighting for our attention. Make a declaration today that no matter what we face, we will make it a priority to worship God in spirit and in truth. God is a holy being. Nothing can encompass His greatness. In our human intellect we are not able to comprehend the extent of His greatness. The encounter we experience with God, although great, is only the tip of the iceberg. Everything about Him exudes glory and deserves our honor and praise. When we allow ourselves to think about God in all of His glory, the Master of the universe, we will discover He is- Magnificent and Holy, and our worship will instantly change. Worship is surrendering every ounce of us in adoration toward God. Love responding to love. We have to get excited about the God we serve. No longer will we allow our circumstances to determine our level of worship, instead our love for God will stimulate our adoration for Him. Think about His goodness and let our love for God be louder than our worries about life. God is among us give Him honor!!

**"I tell you," he replied, "if they keep quiet, the stones will cry out." (Luke 19:40)**

Prayer: Lord, we give You honor, glory and praise. You are more than enough. Search us inwardly to examine our hearts. Lord, remove all forms of distractions right now. We will make a choice to press in Your presence and give You the honor You deserve. You grant us life everlasting and we say thank You. Give us an authentic praise. Lord, let us experience You like never before. In Your presence Lord, You take us higher and higher in You. Lord, we sing a new song of adoration. You are so righteous. Pour out Your Spirit and let us be aware of You. Speak into the atmosphere and we will obey Your voice. God, we bow in reverence. In Jesus' name we pray, Amen.

## March 14

*And I heard a loud voice saying in heaven, Now is come salvation, and strength, and the kingdom of our God, and the power of his Christ: for the accuser of our brethren is cast down, which accused them before our God day and night.* (Revelation 12:10)

Don't you dare beat yourself up for another moment. God loves us and knows the times here on earth will be difficult. Satan stands before God on a daily basis, trying to remind God of our wrongdoing. Just as the devil is in heaven accusing us, he uses different tactics here on earth to discourage us. You could be in the middle of prayer and the enemy will constantly remind you of things you have done in the past. If we give way to the devil's tricks it will cause us to get off track. Our only focus should be on God and God alone. The devil knows his time is almost up. He is trying everything within his limited power to lead God's creation astray. The devil will not be able to have his way with us because we know who we are in Christ Jesus. We know Jesus is our salvation and our strength. God sees us through the blood of Christ- restored and redeemed. Nothing can separate us from His love. Deception is a method satan tries to use to blind us from the truth of God's word. God teaches us satan's devices; we have to counteract satan's stumbling blocks by reminding ourselves whom we belong too. God has given us POWER to trample over satan and his forces (Luke 10:19). Don't waste your energy another day worrying about what oppositions are coming your way. Stand flatfooted in the Word of God and speak to mountains until they move. We have the very power of God Himself living on the inside of us. The deceptive nature of the enemy is to make us overwhelmed so that our primary focus is on what is going wrong. Kingdom principle is to ONLY trust God. He is our strength, power and refuge. Give everything to Him. Submit to God, Resist the devil and he will flee (James 4:7).

**And they overcame him by the blood of the Lamb, and by the word of their testimony; and they loved not their lives unto the death. (Revelation 12:11)**

Prayer: Lord, You are Good. You are righteous, Holy and All Powerful. Touch the hearts and minds of Your people. Remove all forms of discouragement. Lord, when the enemy comes in with lies and temptation, bring all of Your words back to our remembrance. We know we are the sons and daughters of the Most High. Power is in us. You fight every battle and know everything that will take place before it happens. Be our strength. We will not complain when the evil one tries to tempt us. We will rejoice in You. You rule heaven and earth. Continue to teach us who we are in Christ. Shift our focus off of the negative and only on Your kingdom and Your righteousness. All is well. We honor You now and forever, in Jesus' name we pray, Amen.

# March 15

*Since we have these promises, beloved, let us cleanse ourselves from every defilement of body and spirit, bringing holiness to completion in the fear of God.* (2 Corinthians 7:1)

God declares that we are the temple where He dwells. Since we have accepted God's invitation to live in us, we must make room for the King of Glory to reside. Often, we find ourselves in a battle between trying to get to God when God is trying to get to us. He said He would make His dwelling among us and walk among us (2 Corinthians 6:16). Here Paul is teaching us how to recognize the full Presence of God by cleansing ourselves and remaining pure. Our bodies and spirit have the potential to be filled with God's glory or the lust of the flesh. It is our job to separate from the things that wage war against the Spirit of God inside of us. Preserving the purity of our body and spirit requires us to respect the notion that God is here. When we consider the shows we watch, the music we listen to, the conversations we entertain, and what we do with our spare time, we must realize God is in the midst. Putting God before us when we make choices will safeguard us against feeding our lustful desires. His love will captive us; inviting us to share in the mysteries of His heart, that special place where God makes all things new.

Prayer: God, we honor You as Holy. This life is a gift. Use us for Your purpose. Thank You for dwelling among us. Thank You for holding our hand and wiping our tears. Wherever You are that is where we want to be. Lead us on the narrow path of righteousness. Loose the cord of bondage and let Your people receive the fullness of who You are. There is no better place in all the earth than in Your Presence. Lord, You created all things and we submit ourselves to be used by You. Work in us as Your holy vessels. We submit our bodies and spirit to You. Hallelujah! In Jesus' name we pray, Amen.

# March 16

*Now therefore come, let me give you advice, that you may save your own life and the life of your son Solomon.* (1 King 1:12)

When you have godly mentors and people of character in your life, their advice is priceless. Many times we are faced with situations or have made decisions out of a lack of wisdom. Having someone to pour into your life in a godly way will help you see things in a different light. God will speak through people and others who may have experienced the very thing you are going through. "A man hath joy by the answer of his mouth: and a word *spoken* in due season, how good *is it*!" (Proverbs 15:23). Words of wisdom and encouragement at the right time can change our entire attitude. God loves when His children are able to lean on each other. Everyone at some point in time will need someone to comfort them and will need to be a comforter for others. Wisdom and good advice go a long way. In some instances it can save a life. There is no greater feeling than to know someone cares about you. We know Jesus cares about us and has given us the Holy Spirit as our guide. Following His example of receiving godly advice and giving godly advice will enhance the kingdom of God in the earth.

Prayer: Lord, You are good and Your mercy endureth forever. Lord, I pray for all of Your children to engage in positive relationships. Send mentors, people of God to pour into our lives. Raise us up to be that godly influence in the lives of others. As we continue to allow iron to sharpen iron we will seek Your face for wisdom, knowledge, and understanding. "Blessed is the man who walks not in the counsel of the wicked, nor stands in the way of sinners, nor sits in the seat of scoffers; but his delight is in the law of the Lord, and on his law he meditates day and night" (Psalm 1:1-2). Fill the earth with Your Presence. In Jesus' name we pray, Amen.

# March 17

*For no prophecy was ever produced by the will of man, but men spoke from God as they were carried along by the Holy Spirit.* (2 Peter 1:21)

When we read the Bible, it's kind of hard to argue with what is written therein. Many of us want to interpret God's words to try to make it fit around our lifestyle and personal desires. God's Word is not up for debate. Everything He has spoken is for a reason. His divine purpose has inspired men to write what they received from heaven. Prophecy is God's voice directly from heaven. It is not filtered with human will; everything God wants us to know He reveals it to us. No one knows the heart of God except His Spirit. He has freely given us His Spirit to bring all things back to our remembrance and to keep us filled with everything we need to function in the earth. God's Word is filled with power and glory sent to purify our hearts. As lovers of the gospel, it should be our daily task to soak in God's Word to see what plans He has for our daily journey. Every word from heaven showers us with life. It brings us closer to our Father. The Holy One who has a perfect plan for us to enjoy the life He has prepared for us. When we receive His word, it is not time for argument but a time of agreement. We have entered into a covenant with God, filled with thousand of promises. God is trying to get us to see life beyond ourselves. Many may shy away from surrendering their will for God's will because it requires commitment and sacrifice. Not knowing what God has planned for us far exceeds anything we could ever purpose for ourselves.

Prayer: Lord God Almighty, You are awesome. Open our eyes to see You as You are. We are Your sons and daughters made in Your image; birthed into the earth to subdue it and to have dominion. We take possession over all You have spoken in Your word. Your Word is true. It is life unto our very bodies. Nothing is impossible with You. Fill us with Your Holy Spirit. Your Spirit searches Your heart and reveals to us what You require of us. We say "here I am, ready to be used by You." Remove anything that will try to keep us from following You. We will be doers of Your word. Each of Your children are made in greatness. Our lives are filled with Your holy Presence. Continue to shine Your light through us. In Jesus' name we pray, Amen.

# March 18

*And when he looked on him, he was afraid, and said, What is it, Lord? And he said unto him, Thy prayers and thine alms are come up for a memorial before God.* (Acts 10:4)

Our prayers are worship before God. Jesus teaches us to pray in this manner: ***Our Father which art in heaven, Hallowed be thy name. Thy kingdom come, Thy will be done in earth, as it is in heaven…*** (Matthew 6:9-13). The framework of this prayer is a petition for God to allow us to join in with what He is doing in heaven. Our worship acknowledges God as Sovereign and we submit ourselves to Him in joy, knowing that His will is the best life can offer. Our prayers are guaranteed to reach heaven. ***"And the smoke of the incense, which came with the prayers of the saints, ascended up before God out of the angel's hand"*** (Revelation 8:4). Not only do our prayers reach heaven, you know what else reaches heaven? Our complaints, doubts, fears and unbelief. We should not want God to have to filter between our faith and our unbelief. When we pray we are coming into agreement with what God has already said. If we are unsure about what God says about a situation, we have tools to research His Word. We have the Bible along with technology where we can search for scriptures based on topics and others who are spiritually mature. It brings God great pleasure to answer our prayers. Our prayers, aligned with God's Word are sure to be heard and answered. Prayer is a time of worship and celebration, an opportunity to enjoy the presence of God.

**You will show me the path of life; in Your presence is fullness of joy, at Your right hand there are pleasures forevermore. (Psalm 16:11)**

Prayer: Heavenly Father, we are thrilled and delighted to soak in Your Presence. There is no greater place in all the earth. God, we invite You to dwell in us. Open our heart to desire more of You. Your words are life to us. You speak truth in every situation. Renew our minds to come into prayer with a godly focus. Permeate our heart with Your concerns. We know that You will add all things to us. Lord, there is nothing undone in Your kingdom. Visit the earth to saturate us with Your Spirit. Lord, we need You! We give You the highest praise, Hallelujah. In Jesus' name we pray, Amen.

# March 19

*Blessed (happy, blithesome, joyous, spiritually prosperous—with life-joy and satisfaction in God's favor and salvation, regardless of their outward conditions) are the meek (the mild, patient, long-suffering), for they shall inherit the earth!* (Matthew 5:5)

There God goes again, trying to bless us. He is showing us the many things we receive as a result of being called into His kingdom. Having a meek spirit is something we have to work on in order to develop this attribute fully. Jesus said, "*learn of me; for I am meek*" (Matthew 11:29). This lets us know we have only obtained a meek spirit through Christ. As we surrender our old nature and walk in our new nature of God, we begin to develop His characteristics. There are many benefits associated with inheriting the attributes of God. He is teachings us on a daily basis how to employ His mannerisms. A meek spirit is one who is humble, teachable, patient, a person who decides to see the positive in every situation. Taking on this attribute allows us to inherit the earth. We are able to enjoy life because our focus is found in God. We are not easily moved when situations arise. Hearing God's voice is a priority in our daily activities. Seeking after God is our desire, and we find ways to learn about what He is doing in the earth. One who pursues God is sure to find the right path leading to blissfulness.

Prayer: Lord, we love You. You are the greatest gift we could ever ask for. Thank You for saving us. In love You have captured our hearts. You went a step further to show us the way of life. Lord, continue to teach us Your ways. We surrender before You. Teach, lead, guide and destroy everything that is not like You. You know the reason You created us. Let Your fire burn in us to walk in right standing with You. We make a choice today to be filled with Your Spirit. All glory belongs to You. In Jesus' name we pray, Amen.

## March 20

*As far as the east is from the west, so far hath he removed our transgressions from us.* (Psalm 103:12)

The biggest misconception people have regarding God is that He sits in heaven looking for ways to punish us. This mindset tends to focus more on what we do wrong than on what we do right. The intent of God creating us was to have perfect fellowship with us. God longs to interact with us and share His great nature with us. When sin entered the world it caused a separation. Thankfully, we have been redeemed by Jesus and can enter His presence once again. Now is the time to renew our minds by transferring our negative thoughts and any feelings that imply we aren't good enough for God's love. God built our frame, He knows the very ins and outs of our being. He knows our thought process and every decision we will make before we even contemplate making it. Yet, He still loves us. We have a found the way back to our perfect fellowship with God through Jesus. Looking at life from God's loving perspective is the only way we should live. If we find ourselves living contrary to the will of God, His Spirit will convict our hearts. If we ask for forgiveness, God is sure to do just that. He is not like man to bring it up later. He removes it from His thought process. As humans we have a hard time accepting the fact that God forgives us, because we are always looking for the "why" factor. The fact of the matter is, God loves us and His purpose for creation is to commune with us, not to condemn us.

Prayer: Lord, You are awesome. Lift every broken heart; enter every home where Your people are fighting battles within themselves. You cast all of our transgression into the sea of forgetfulness. Break the chains of bondage. Allow Your people to walk in the Spirit. We are free in Christ Jesus. Nothing is too hard for You. Minister to our point of need. Shift our focus to be set on Your love. Your everlasting love that keeps us in the palm of Your hand. Glory to Your name, In Jesus' name we pray, Amen.

# March 21

And they took knowledge of them, that they had been with Jesus. (Acts 4:13b)

Inviting Jesus into our lives on a daily basis is sure to produce tangible evidence of our intimate connection. Coming before the throne of grace guarantees we leave different from whence we came. Everything can be laid before the Father; even the hidden parts of our heart where we refuse to let anyone else enter can be restored through Christ. God wants to be involved in every part of our being. Not until we surrender ourselves over to Him will He be able to function through us to His fullest capacity. We have to take the limits off of God. He is willing –and longing to do supernatural things in our lives. The word supernatural is not a cliché to be used by the church to make mention of the power of God. It is the very evidence of God performing in such a way that is impossible otherwise. God has so much He wants to do in the earth and is searching for a willing vessel to perform His marvelous works. The problem we face as children of God is our inability to be STILL and allow God to work. Not only do we have to spend time with Jesus, we have to change the structure of our time with Him. No longer should we come before God with our hand out, instead come seeking God for His divine will for our lives. In seeking God and His kingdom agenda, all of our needs will be met far above any request list we could have ever presented. Being in His presence produces unexplainable power and joy. His glory will go before us, astonishing those we come into contact with, having our very lives point them to Christ.

Prayer: Lord, fill us up until we overflow. You are the true and living Word. We exalt Your name on high. Enter into our hearts, homes, jobs, relationships, communities, and nations –everywhere. Lord, there is no place on this earth that is hidden from You. Your people need You. Thank You that you hear our prayers and are quick to answer. Work on us, help us to be still and know that You are God. You know the end from the beginning. Let us shift our energy from always asking how you are going to do things to offering praise and thanksgiving. We come before Your throne for Your divine order and plans for our lives. As we enter Your gates with praise on our lips let our time with You reflect in our daily living. So that men will know You are holy and inquire of You. We desire nothing above You. You are our joy. In Jesus' name we pray, Amen.

# March 22

*Beloved, do not be surprised at the fiery trial when it comes upon you to test you, as though something strange were happening to you.* (1 Peter 4:12)

Surprise means to be caught off guard. God prepares us for the many things we will endure in life and tells us to be prepared when we are tested by trials. It is important to know first that God loves us, and second NOTHING can happen to us unless God allows it. Living in the earth has tainted our mind to look at hardships in a negative way. We feel anxiety and emotional distress when problems arise due to being uncomfortable. For some reason our normal routine has been interrupted and we are not content with things being out of control. God is so strategic with mankind. He instructs us to rejoice instead of getting upset. One may ask, "how do you expect me to stay calm when destruction is at my doorstep." God's answers prove satisfying as we are grounded in a living hope – God. He is our All in ALL. His command for us to rejoice is teaching us what trials really mean. Trials are not permitted to destroy us or cause us to lose hope. We are tested in order for God's glory to be revealed. Through our test we grow in wisdom and knowledge and are strengthened by God's power. Our relationship develops more as we are placed in situations where only the hand of God can bring us out. Deciding to rejoice instead of wallowing in self-pity or unbelief is a choice. Whatever type of energy we place on a situation will determine the outcome. When trouble arises we can obey God and rejoice and see the manifestation of His glory. Or we can complain and stay in the testing phase longer than God has intended

Prayer: God, You sit on high. Open our eyes to live this life in the Spirit under Your guidance for our lives. There is so much You are trying to teach us -only if we would listen. Open our ears today to hear what You are speaking. Speak to our heart, build our strength in You. Everything about You is pleasing and perfect. ***My brethren, count it all joy when ye fall into divers temptations; Knowing this, that the trying of your faith worketh***

***patience. But let patience have her perfect work, that ye may be perfect and entire, wanting nothing***. (James 1:2-4). Lord ,we love You. In Jesus' name we pray, Amen.

# March 23

*This news about Jesus spread throughout Judea and the surrounding country.* (Luke 7:17)

During the time Jesus walked the earth, the people were under Roman leadership. Those of Jewish descent were the children of promise, yet they were in captivity to the Roman laws of the land. They were waiting for a Savior to deliver them from the bondage they were in. When Jesus arrived on the scene many believed in Him but many did not. For those who accepted Jesus in their heart and believed in the many miracles He performed, every prophecy spoken about Jesus was fulfilled right before their very eyes. What did they do with this incredible experience? They ran to tell any and everyone about their encounter with Jesus. Jesus' mere presence changes the atmosphere. We heard about Jesus and made a choice to make Him our Lord and Savior. Every person walking this earth has an innate need for a Savior. Since we have found the way, the truth and the life, we too must carry the gospel to our brothers and sisters worldwide. We live in a society fixated on obtaining the latest information. What a time in God it would be if our obsession for kingdom business outweighed the latest fashion or reality television show. As saints, we have the responsibility to let God live through us. Thinking back over how far we have come in Christ should ignite a fire within us to run and tell others how great our God is.

Prayer: Lord, You are the true and living God. You created the heavens and the earth. All things exist because of You. We acknowledge You today. Build our strength. Give us a spirit of boldness to speak Your Word in truth, spreading the good news everywhere we go. Give us opportunity to speak about Your goodness. One encounter with You will change the course of this generation. Lord, visit us. Send down Your power and shift the atmosphere. Humble our hearts. We submit to You this day. Have Your way. You get all the glory. In Jesus' name we pray, Amen.

# March 24

*He seeing this before spake of the resurrection of Christ, that his soul was not left in hell, neither his flesh did see corruption.* (Acts 2:31)

There is no reason to doubt God. The only time we doubt God is when we choose to do so. We have to make a conscious effect whether to believe God at His word or not. David, a pioneer of faith is mentioned here during Peter's sermon to the crowd at Pentecost. He gives an account of Jesus' resurrection being prophesied through David. God promised David that the Son of God would come through his bloodline. God spoke beforehand about Jesus, promising He would raise Him up to sit on the right side of His throne. This declaration was given to David through a word. David believed God so much that He saw the vision take place before it occurred. Fast forward approximately 1,000 years and Peter and the disciples were able to witness what David stood in faith and proclaimed. After the resurrection of Christ, Peter gave account of these things, assuring the people that God's word is true and there is no reason for doubt. "***Therefore let all the house of Israel know assuredly, that God hath made the same Jesus, whom ye have crucified, both Lord and Christ***" (Acts 2:36). No longer can we look at the words in the bible or what God speaks to us in our private time as a possibility. It has to become our reality, seeing God's words as flesh. Something tangible that we have already received. When we are able to see what God says for our life it will change our entire outlook. It will cause us to operate in accordance with what God has promised. Our hearts will be filled with joy and our days with hope, weakening the ability of anxiety to rest in our souls. Knowing for sure what God says is the only conclusion for our lives.

Prayer: Lord, You have created all things for Your glory. Open our eyes to see what You have already predestined. Align our thoughts with Yours. Reduce the possibility of doubt. Let our natural response be to trust You and to walk upright with You. We tend to stray away due to uncertainty. We make a choice today to believe only the report we hear from You. This goes for every aspect of our lives. You have made every possible provision for everything we will ever need. So we come to the source for all things. Fill us with Your Spirit now and forever. We love You. In Jesus' name we pray, Amen.

# March 25

*But the word of God continued to spread and flourish.* (Acts12: 24)

Everything in life will at some point perish. Only God's word will stand and live on forever. It will be with us in eternity. Our house, car, bank account, or most prized possession, will one day succumb to the sands of time. As we understand the value of God's Word and the power embedded within it we develop a better outlook on life. God called all things into existence by His words. He only speaks words of perfection and restoration to build us up. His words show us our unique self, reflecting how we are created in His image. The Apostles were able to see God's word in the flesh through Jesus, and after His resurrection they had the task of spreading the word to all ends of the earth. They were persecuted on every side, even to the point of martyrdom. How could something that resembles such power cause such division? It was not God's word, it was those who decided not to believe. Followers of Christ made a choice to continue to spread God's word in spite of all of the hardships they faced in life. We have not yet suffered to the point of bloodshed following after Christ (Hebrews 12:4). Our mission is to proclaim Christ as the one and only Savior must continue to be accomplished. After all, the word of God has power. As we speak it into the atmosphere we must not concern ourselves with whether or not people will adhere to God's word. As vessels, our job is to plant and water the seed- only God can give the increase (1 Corinthians 3:6).

**For the word of God is living and active, sharper than any two-edged sword, piercing to the division of soul and of spirit, of joints and of marrow, and discerning the thoughts and intentions of the heart. (Hebrews 4:12)**

Prayer: Lord, like Moses on the holy mountain we come before Your presence and say, "here I am." Use us for your most holy work. Lord, we will speak of Your excellent grace and mercy. The love that you show everyday will be on our tongues. You are good.

Cleanse us from the inside out, that we have room for You to dwell within. Fill us until we overflow. Let our worship be authentic and our praise exude Your name until we worry no more. You are greater than any desire. Hallelujah! We bless You God. In Jesus' name we pray, Amen.

# March 26

Abraham was now very old, and the Lord had blessed him in every way. (Genesis 24:1)

A life in God is a life fulfilled in every way, to include every internal and external need. God desires to bless us (Luke 12:32). Abraham is no different than you and me. He too was a child of God, called to obedience and to stand on God's word through faith. Abraham paved the way for us, being an inheritor of the blessings of God. He was used as God's vessel to show how much God loves His creation. Abraham made a choice to surrender his will by submitting to the will of God. He believed everything God spoke concerning His life. As a result of being created by God, we have received blessings in our lives. According to our ability to develop the measure of faith that God has already instilled in us, determines the degree to which we receive all that God has for us. The Lord blessed Abraham to see old age, and looking over His life, the bible says He was blessed in ***every way***. We have been designed to be fulfilled (blessed) in all aspects of our life and have the opportunity to achieve it. Submitting ourselves to God through prayer, reading His word and obedience opens the door for God to trust us and pour out His blessing upon us. The truth is, every person walking this earth is blessed. The first thing which lets us know we are blessed is the mere fact that we have breath, and then second, because God created us. I don't want to deny God the opportunity of giving me the supernatural blessings just because I am so caught up in myself that I miss out on what He wants to do in my life. We must long for, seek after, and accept the goodness of God. Through faith, stand on God's word and allow Him to bless You in EVERY WAY.

Prayer: Lord God Almighty, You are excellent. Lord, You seek out ways to bless Your people. You have countless plans for Your people o prosper as we draw closer to You. Lord, it's not about material gain but a relationship with You. Our lives are enriched by Your holy presence. Every ounce of Your being adds value to our lives. Forgive us for allowing anything to stand in the way of

You blessing us. Command Your angels to be on post, working in our lives. Pour out Your power from heaven to bless us in every way. Let faith become our lifestyle and obedience be in our first choice. God, You are good and Your mercy endures FOREVER. In Jesus' name we pray, Amen.

# March 27

*You have made them to be a kingdom and priests to our God; and they will reign upon the earth.* (Revelation 5:10)

Because of the works of Christ on the cross, we have been redeemed as God's children. The blood of Jesus granted us access back into God's presence. We have now become a kingdom and priest to God. A kingdom is the place where God lives. God now lives in us. A priest is a servant; we are now servants of God. Since God lives in us and we serve Him, it is only proper for us to reign in the earth. As a chosen people we have victory over every aspect of our lives. We reign in our attitudes, emotions, relationships, families, finances, ministry, careers, etc. God has called us to victory. As God operates through us, we will only involve ourselves in things that yield God's divine purpose for our lives. If we find an area in our lives where we do not have dominion, it's time to self-reflect. Come back to the drawing board. Repent if need be; seek His plan and adhere to His instructions to take our proper position as a priest of God. God has already blessed us to be rulers in the earth (Genesis 1:28). Living beneath our potential is, in actuality, not obeying God and mishandling our time on earth. Align with the commands of heaven and be victorious, for what God has said is so in heaven and in earth.

**To the one who is victorious, I will give the right to sit with me on my throne, just as I was victorious and sat down with my Father on his throne. (Revelation 3:21*)***

Prayer: Father, You are the beginning and the end. You are worthy of all praise. Honor is what we render to You this day. Forgive us for not walking in victory at all times. You said the righteous are bold as lions. Develop Your character in us. As we commune with You, show us Your glorious splendor. Open our eyes that we may see. Open our ears that we may hear what is taking place in heaven and rule in the earth. We have power over every authority in this earth. We are whole, righteous, free and redeemed by the blood of Jesus. We are forever grateful and we bless Your name, praise shall continually be on our lips. In Jesus' name we pray, Amen.

# March 28

*That at the name of Jesus every knee should bow, of things in heaven, and things in earth, and things under the earth;* (Philippians 2:10)

Jesus is exalted as high in heaven and in earth. At the name of Jesus every knee will bow and every tongue will confess Him as Lord. When we stand before the Lord and receive our judgment, the magnitude of His holy presence will bring us to our knees. Our free will to choose whether or not to worship Him will be negated. In His presence, our spirits will be consumed by His glorious splendor. Beyond our control, our spirit will yield to God's command and our lips will offer praise and honor to His name. God's glorious presence will cause ALL things created to bow and worship. It will not be beneficial to wait until the Day of Judgment to render praise to Him. We can exalt Him now in the earth and experience His presence daily. God is a consuming fire, destroying everything in us that would hinder us from total worship in His presence. It shouldn't be our desire to be forced into giving God praise when He deserves our highest act of gratitude. We can obey God now. Allowing God to exercise His ownership of us while we are on earth is preparing us for a life with Him in eternity. When we see Jesus and give account for our life, the relationship we have with Him now shouldn't change. We should continue right on loving Him and worshiping in His presence. It shouldn't be that when Jesus cracks the sky that we try to change our behaviors. God is teaching us to love, honor, and spend intimate time with Him now as preparation for what it will be like in eternity. We will continue worshiping God and reverencing His name as we were doing in the earth. God is alive and living. Our lives should be a reflection of heaven. In heaven we'll worship God daily. On earth we can worship God daily. In Heaven we'll obey all of God's commands. On earth we can obey all of God's commands. God is omnipresent, invite Him in and enjoy heaven on earth.

Prayer: Jesus is the name above every name. You are exalted above everything in earth and in heaven. We make a choice today to honor You every day of our lives. Your awesome power is welcomed in our heart. Fill us with Your spirit. The fruit of our lips will bless Your holy name. Lead us on the narrow path of righteousness for Your name's sake. We will bless You now and forever. You are the great and living God. In Jesus' name we pray, Amen.

# March 29

*For unto us a child is born, unto us a son is given: and the government shall be upon his shoulder: and his name shall be called Wonderful, Counsellor, The mighty God, The everlasting Father, The Prince of Peace.* (Isaiah 9:6)

Imagine a world without Jesus. Close your eyes and walk around in darkness without help or guidance and you will quickly see the destruction you'll encounter. The world without Jesus is just like that, filled with darkness. We were once a part of the dark world, living our lives day-by-day, not knowing the doom that awaited us. But God said "It is not so," and sent His only begotten Son to bring us into His kingdom. God didn't send temporary comfort, He sent a piece of Himself in the earth to become EVERYTHING we will ever need. He is **Wonderful** – great beyond measure, satisfying every desire. **Counsellor**- yielding perfect judgment. **The Mighty God**- there is no one greater; Alpha and Omega, who is, who was, and who is to come. **The Everlasting Father**- lover of our souls, mercies are new every morning. **The Prince of Peace**-made us whole and complete in Him, nothing by any means can harm us. Jesus is a gift given to us to enjoy and find pleasure in being called into His presence. There is no worry in God because He has become all we will ever need. There is no limit to His matchless grace. Our hope is set in Him; everything has been given to us through Christ Jesus.

Prayer: The earth is the Lord's, and the fullness thereof; the world, and they that dwell therein (Psalm 24:1). God, everything belongs to You. Thank You for thinking of us every day as You bestow Your grace and mercy on us. You are Wonderful, Counsellor, The mighty God, The everlasting Father, The Prince of Peace. We recognize You as Lord of our lives. We invite You in to have Your proper place in our heart, mind, body and soul. Permeate our spirits with Your holy presence. Have Your way in us. Nothing that concerns us is too hard for you. We find rest in Your arms. Bless You God for being everything to us. In Jesus' name we pray, Amen.

# March 30

*but you shall love your neighbor as yourself: I am the Lord.* (Leviticus 19:18)

Most often, as a society, the concept we have of love is backwards. We love those who love us and treat others with kindness when their behavior warrants favorable actions. We're always looking for justification to love one another. She was nice to me so I'll be nice to her. He was rude to me, now I'll be rude to him so he understands how I feel is the attitude we often take. God has commanded us to love our neighbors as ourselves for a reason. God teaches us to be holy, because He is holy. Our conduct must be a reflection of who God is. Loving our neighbors as ourselves is displaying the love of God in the earth. ***"No one has ever seen God; but if we love one another, God lives in us and his love is made complete in us"*** **(1 John 4:12).** We're not even complete when we fail to love others. If we considered others above ourselves the world would be a better place. Instantly there would be drastic change. All form of evil stem from corrupt intentions and a lack of love. Going out of our way to consider the needs of others will help us to have compassion for others. Instead of thinking of ways to pay people back for the wrong they have done to us, we can use difficult situations to exhibits God's love. Just think for a moment how effective we could be if we chose to show love to others even after they behave in a nasty or disrespectful manner. When people display impolite behavior they are waiting on a reaction, it's like they feed off of negative energy. Deciding to obey God by displaying love shifts the atmosphere and has the power to change your heart and the heart of the person being discourteous. God's love does that. He is Lord of our lives and wants full control of our actions. How we respond or fail to respond to others displays who lives on the inside of us. As God's children, we aim to please our Father, having a heart of love draws us closer to God allowing us to shine His light on others.

Prayer: God, we love You. Thank You for first loving us. Lord, some of us are struggling in the area of love. We have been dealing with bitterness, unforgiveness and strife in our heart. Help us to know the depth and length of the love of Christ, which surpasses knowledge. Your love seeks us out daily. We receive it today. Transform us by renewing our minds to push past offence and make a choice to love our neighbors as ourselves. Not based upon circumstance or action, but simply because Your love works. It has power to destroy the yoke of bondage. Freedom belongs to Your people. Heal every heart, restore every relationship, and build our strength, as we stand strong in You. All glory belongs to You. In Jesus' name we pray, Amen.

# March 31

*And Elijah said to Ahab, "Get up, eat and drink, for there is a sound of the rushing of rain."* (1 Kings 18:41)

Everything that happens in the earth first takes place in heaven. How did Elijah hear the sound of rushing rain when there was no physical indication of a rainstorm about to take place? After all, there had been a drought for over three and a half years. Elijah stood on the word of God. God already informed Elijah that there would be a drought and rain would only return at His word. ***"As the Lord, the God of Israel, lives, before whom I stand, there shall be neither dew nor rain these years, except by my word"*** **(1 Kings 17:1).** Elijah's intimate relationship with God kept him in tune with what God was doing in heaven. God reveals to us everything He wants to do in our lives. He has given us His word to help us know what will take place. Praying on a daily basis builds our personal relationship with God and allows us to grow in His wisdom. God is not a secretive God, He wants us to enjoy the fruits of His glorious splendor. Heaven is always producing a sound; we have to open our ears to hear what is taking place in the spirit to prepare for the move of God. Elijah simply reacted off of God's word and got into position to witness what God had promised would take place. Elijah didn't live by "what if;" He took God at His word. Believing if God said it, it is surely going to happen. As we intertwine our hearts with God, He will reveal things to us and we too will hear the sound of heaven way before we see the manifestation in earth. This will motivate us to stand firm in our faith, being confident of the plans of God.

Prayer: Lord God Almighty, we bow before Your holy presence to worship at Your feet. Your plans are perfect. What takes place in heaven is far beyond anything we could ever imagine. We are delighted that You consider us as Your children and have invited us on the journey to experience Your greatness. Cleanse us of doubt and fear, which get in the way of us believing Your faithful word. We want to hear the sound of heaven today. Your people need You. Have Your way in this earth FOREVER. In Jesus' name we pray. Amen.

# April 1

*But this command I gave them: "Obey my voice, and I will be your God, and you shall be my people. And walk in all the way that I command you, that it may be well with you."* (Jeremiah 7:23)

Obedience is always better than sacrifice. Obeying the commands from God displays our love for Him. We have come to the conclusion that God's plans are far better than ours. He designed the blueprint for our life. Following His instructions is beneficial to us. Failure to do so causes us to go backward instead of forward. ***"But they did not obey or incline their ear, but walked in their own counsels and the stubbornness of their evil hearts, and went backward and not forward"* (Jeremiah 7:24)**. When we choose to adhere to the plans God has for us, we embark upon a great path. God only instructs us in things to bring glory to His name and to satisfy our soul. In obeying the voice of God we give God full control over our lives. It is impossible for God to steer us in the wrong direction or have us to engage in useless activity. Everything He requires of us is used as an ingredient to build our character to become more and more like Jesus Christ. God takes His covenant serious. When we decided to come into His presence by accepting Jesus as our Lord, He regarded the invitation as a sacred act. God keeps us accountable and entrusts us with His plans. Obeying God is a privilege; we have been given the opportunity to showcase the love of God by allowing Him to fulfill His purpose in and through us. Whatever God has called us to do works together for His perfect plan and for our good, satisfying the deepest part of our soul. Walking with God is a pleasure; we have obtained freedom to enjoy the best parts of life that only He can provide.

Prayer: Lord, You have the key to all things possible. We are not concerned with material gain, but desire to grow and develop in the way You have ordained for our life. Lord, we need You to move in our hearts and minds. Give us a heart to obey Your voice. Your plans far exceed anything we can imagine for ourselves. We'll walk with You and see what You are doing in heaven and reflect it in the earth. We want to have an encounter with You like never before. Your plans are what we desire. Search us inwardly and remove anything that keeps us at a distance from You. Ignite a fire within us to seek after You. You are perfect, and Your plans are pleasing. Give us patience to wait on You. Glory and honor belong to You. In Jesus' name we pray, Amen.

# April 2

*Bless the Lord, O my soul: and all that is within me, bless his holy name.* (Psalm 103:1)

It is our innate will to bless God. We were created to worship our Lord and Savior. Everything we are is because of Him. When we tap into what God has for us, we find delight in blessing Him at all times. Not for what He can do, but for who He is. A relationship with God fills every void in our life, supplies all of our needs, and secures our place in eternity. Blessing God with all that is within us requires us to honor God as Sovereign. We make up in our mind God is Lord over every aspect of our lives and we choose to bless Him. It is our choice to bless Him. Every choice we make will produce a subsequent result. The product of blessing God only produces a life full of His loving grace. God is good all the time. Our offering of praise to Him displays our appreciation for Him choosing us to be a part of such a great fellowship. Also, it displays our awareness of who He is, what He has done in our lives and what He continues to do. There is no greater love than to be in the will of God, aligning with the angels saying, "holy holy holy is the LORD Almighty; the whole earth is full of his glory."

Prayer: Lord, there is none greater than You. You are King of kings. You called earth into existence. There is nothing too hard for You. God, we are delighted to bless Your holy name. You are faithful, loving and kind. Continue to shine Your glory upon us. With all that is within us we will sing praises to Your name. In Jesus' name we pray, Amen.

# April 3

*And let the peace of God rule in your hearts, to which also ye are called in one body, and be ye thankful.* (Colossians 3:15)

We are one with God. He resides on the inside of us. Whether or not we yield to His presence is up to us. What an awesome experience it is for us when we make the choice to allow God to govern our heart. He only supplies us with tools that are beneficial to us, for the purpose of fulfilling our greatest potential in Christ Jesus. Walking with God is an enjoyable time of fellowship where He is sure to minister to our souls. Everything we have need of is found in God. He is our Creator and has given us a manifold amount of gifts. One being peace, God has called us to peace. God's peace allows us to maintain joy regardless of any circumstances we encounter in life. It's our natural position as kingdom citizens. If we allow the peace (Present nature) of God to exercise ultimate power and authority over our hearts and our lives, we will never be the same. God's ability to rule in our hearts is a part of God's original intent for mankind. When we surrender ourselves to the governing of His power in us we will never be disappointed. God will continue to build us up in His holy attributes, giving us balance in life and a peace to cover us in all things. Nothing is greater than being under God's control. His peace is a gift to us, a safe haven where we grow and develop, resting in His arms.

Prayer: Peace I leave with you, my peace I give unto you: not as the world giveth, give I unto you. Let not your heart be troubled, neither let it be afraid (John 14:27). Jehovah Shalom, we bow in Your presence. You are a Great and Mighty God. You bestow so many gifts on us on a daily basis there is no way we could ever repay You for Your kindness. All the days of our lives praise and thanksgiving will be in our mouths. God, go to every home and pour out Your peace. Rule and abide in the hearts of Your people. Destroy the yoke that comes to interrupt the peace You have given. We are Yours. We belong to the kingdom of heaven. No weapon that is formed against us shall prosper. In Jesus' name we pray,

Amen.

# April 4

*But blessed are your eyes, for they see: and your ears, for they hear.* (Matthew 13:16)

God is always trying to teach us so many marvelous things. Our heart must be turned to Him and be transformed to His way of operating. God is always speaking because He loves fellowship and desires to reveal His plans to us. Failure to adhere to God causes us to put little emphasis on the tools we been given access to. God has given us keys to the kingdom. This is an awesome privilege where we are able to come to the throne of grace and hear directly from God. It is a blessing to have eyes that see the way God sees things. He teaches us about our current situations, giving us warning and guiding us on a daily basis. Our ears are open to hear His voice from heaven directing our footsteps in His perfect plan. Apart from God's will, everything we do will be done in vain. Submitting ourselves to the Spirit of God is of great benefit to us. God is delighted to reveal His deepest thoughts and aspiration to His beloved. Hearing from heaven lengthens our days and adds joy to our lives. God has already completed His master plan for our lives. He sits in heaven, rejoicing as we come into alignment with what He has already done. He is the only one who can open our eyes to see the beautiful plan He orchestrated long ago. Today we choose to devote our heart, soul, and mind to God to see the manifestation of His glory.

Prayer: Lord, You are perfect. Our hearts rejoice because of who You are. You are El Shaddai-God Almighty. You command every aspect of life. God there is no one greater than You. We exalt Your name today. Lord we surrender our entire being before You. Renew our minds today. Forgive us of all unrighteousness. Cause us to seek after You and only You. You know the end from the beginning. You called us into Your kingdom. Your love keeps us day-by-day. Jesus we bless You. God, have Your way in us. Open our eyes and ears to see and hear from heaven. We choose Your plans above our own. Your name will forever be praised. In Jesus' name we pray Amen.

# April 5

*And Jesus, looking at him loved him, and said to him, You lack one thing: go, sell all that you have and give to the poor, and you will have treasure in heaven; and come follow me."* (Mark 10:21)

It's very important to love those who lack. As Christians we must have compassion for those in the body of Christ. When we see others who are struggling in their faith, our natural response should be to love them. Jesus began cultivating us from the first day of our acceptance of salvation to where we are now. God has always loved us. He is leading and teaching us in kindness. This love is the foundation of our relationship. We are to show the same sympathy towards others. People learn best by love. Our nose should never be turned up toward another person who has a need, especially among the body of believers. Many of us lack in some area, God is the only one who can judge us. In His judgment He offers perfect ruling to show us the correct way to walk with Him in righteousness. No one has reached the place of perfection, we all have room to grow in our relationship with Christ. Staying close to Him and walking in the Spirit, we are able to learn the attributes of God and be transformed on a daily basis. Our eyes must stay on God to help us stand firm in our faith. Our relationship with God is continuous; He is constantly revealing new things in us, helping us to grow and develop in Him.

Praying: Our Father which art in heaven, Hallowed by thy name. Thy kingdom come. Thy will be done in earth, as it is in heaven. Lord, You sit high and look low. You see the hearts and minds of all Your people and You love us with an everlasting love. Continue to teach us how to love others and to offer comfort and compassion. Give us a heart of empathy. Let love be the universal language for all mankind. Open the gates of heaven and pour out Your blessings. Your love calls us close to You. We will store our riches in Heaven. You get all the glory and praise. In Jesus' name we pray, Amen.

# April 6

*The wicked flee when no man pursueth: but the righteous are bold as a lion.* (Proverbs 28:1)

One of the characteristics God has instilled in us is boldness. God created us not to fear anything we face. So much so, that God tells us multiple times in the Bible to fear NOT. Our countenance is built on God's ability to fight for us. The things we face in life are no match for what God is doing in us. He fights our battles and gives us confidence to perform. Fear is a tactic the enemy uses to try to keep us from accomplishing things in life. Fear tells us we aren't capable of completing certain tasks by magnifying the potential of failure. When we take the stance God has given us to go after life bold as a lion, we can stare fear and the devil in the face and say, "If God be for us who can be against us." We know the enemy seeks to devour us, but God's power shelters us. He has given us the ability to trample every attack the enemy could possible think of. "***And ye shall chase your enemies***, and they shall fall before you by the sword. And five of you shall chase an hundred, and an hundred of you shall put ten thousand to flight: and your enemies shall fall before you by the sword" (Leviticus 26:7-8). God has so much confidence in us He instructs us to chase off our enemy. Nothing should cause us to draw back into a shell and relinquish our purpose due to being afraid. No longer will we allow fear to linger over our heads, echoing lies in our thought process. From this day forth we will walk bold as lions, receiving the blessings of God.

Prayer: Heavenly Father, we bow in worship before You. Thank You for teaching us how to take our proper position in the kingdom. We are joint-heirs, You have instilled Your Spirit in us. All things are possible with You on our side. The enemy has no authority over us. We will no longer listen to his lies. We are blessed, righteous, and full of hope. We pull down every stronghold that tries to stand in our way. We will only believe what You declare from heaven. You have commanded that we fear not. There are more with us than who fight against us. Victory belongs to the LORD. May Your blessing rest on Your people. Selah (Psalm 3:8). All glory belongs to You. In Jesus' name we pray, Amen.

# April 7

*And the LORD turned the captivity of Job, when he prayed for his friends: also the LORD gave Job twice as much as he had before.* (Job 42:10)

The thing I love about the story of Job is there is no indication of how long Job had to endure hardship. This is an encouragement to us as believers who know in this life we will have tribulation. In our waiting on God, we can find rest in His promises of hope. Time is not a limitation for God. When He says enough is enough then that's the end. When God decides to turn our situation around it is for certain that everything we had to endure will be well worth it. Every tear will be dried, every broken heart will be healed. God is a restorer and only operates on purpose. What we go through in the natural has no power to destroy us in our spirit. God dwells in us and has established us in Christ Jesus. Our job is to be patient during tribulation and to be constant in prayer; asking God for strength and wisdom to live through everything we will experience. Trusting that if God allowed it to make it to our doorstep there will be glory in the lesson we learn. God is sure to turn our situation around at His appointed time. He is a restorer; He can do anything. In the midst of trials we must remove ourselves and let God in to have His way. The end result is already guaranteed, and when God shows up He always exceeds our expectation. Our praise in the hard times shouldn't dwindle but grow greater, knowing God is working on our behalf.

Prayer: God, You are the LORD of increase. Increase our ability to stand strong in Your might. Jesus did everything for us. This life we live is only for Your glory. You know every situation that will ever take place. You promised if we trust in You we will never fail or be forsaken. We find hope in You being our strong tower. Thank You for every lesson we will have to learn. Develop us spiritually so we will be equipped for the work You have for us to do in the lives of others. As Your servants, we are here to perform Your duties. Give us the strength to press our way through difficult times. We give our burdens to You. You control all things. We exalt Your name on high. In Jesus' name we pray, Amen.

# April 8

*Humble yourselves in the sight of the LORD, and he shall lift you up.* (James 4:10)

Nothing is higher than God, and He is trying to teach us the principles of heaven. We draw close to God by esteeming and exalting Him. We must crucify our flesh, coming empty before His throne in order to be filled by His Spirit. Since God dwells in us, our act of humbling ourselves shows reverence to His presence. It is important to relinquish our self-imposed desires and allow God to impart His purpose in us. After all, the requests that we long for are of no comparison to what God has predestined for our lives. Being humble requires us to put aside what we want and honor God's heart above our own. This does not imply we aren't to dream or to have aspirations and set goals for ourselves. God is showing us how important it is draw close to Him so He can show us the great things He has prepared for us; things that will satisfy us beyond our wildest imagination. Having a humble attitude prepares us to experience God. Our mindset no longer insists on getting our own way, but on trusting God to order our steps. God searches for people He can work through. When God shows up, there is no limit to the power He'll perform in us and through us. No façade, no masks, no boasting, no esteeming ourselves- just us yielding to His presence.

Prayer: Lord God, You are King of all things created. What an honor it is to fellowship with You on a continuous basis. Thank You Jesus for giving us access to the Father's throne of grace. Lord, we humble ourselves coming before You. We exalt Your name on high. Lord, perform Your work in us. As You speak, help us to listen and obey every one of Your commands. Whatever You have planned for us we submit our ways to You. We acknowledge You in all our ways. Transform us by renewing our minds to know the hope to which you have called us. Perform Your powerful works through us that all the earth will see Your glory. You are marvelous! In Jesus' name we pray, Amen.

## April 9

*Now faith is the substance of things hoped for, the evidence of things not seen.* (Hebrews 11:1)

To understand faith, we have to understand how the kingdom of God operates. God's word never returns to Him void. Every promise in Him is "yea" and "amen." By us believing, we come into agreement with God's original plan. What God has ordained will not be revoked. When we have doubt we are not on the same course with God, hence we may not see the manifestation of our prayers. Faith is the only thing that pleases God. It says, "God, I know You love me, You created me to be a part of Your perfect plan. I come into agreement with the plans of Your heart and am willing to be used by You." Then we can ask anything in Jesus' name and know God will do it for us. We have to get away from the self-centered mindset of only having faith for things that are beneficial for us. Our substance of things hoped for and evidence of things not seen are for the body of Christ as a whole. For instance, if we are believing God for a job, our prayer should be asking God to place us in a establishment where our witness is needed and His name can be glorified. Then God can add all things needed on a personal level because we sought first the kingdom of God. Whatever we believe God for in faith according to His will is beneficial to the kingdom. As we deny ourselves by seeking what God desires first, He is willing to do exceedingly and abundantly above all that we can ever ask or think. He does this because He knows we belong to Him and we have discovered His plan is better than the plans we have for ourselves.

Prayer: Lord, You reign forever. We join in with the angels and sing holy, holy, holy is the Lord God Almighty. Develop our faith within us. Keep us on the right path with You. In our personal time with You show us the things that are pleasing in Your sight. What are the plans You have for us to accomplish in the earth. Use us as Your ambassadors to show how mighty You are. We will be the example to show to the world that You are alive. Let Your love flow through us. Help us not to waiver from whatever we believe

You for. What You say will come to pass. "Blessed is the man that trusteth in the LORD, and whose hope the LORD is" (Jeremiah 17:7). We will bless You forever. In Jesus' name we pray, Amen.

# April 10

*He who calls you is faithful; he will surely do it.* (1 Thessalonians 5:24)

Before anything came to be in the earth, God first called it into existence. He called our destiny before our parents even met. Everything needed for us to fulfill our purpose is already inside of us. Walking in the Spirit will keep us on the path God has already planned, and everything God instilled on the inside of us will manifest. The deepest desires we formulate in our mind have been God-inspired according to His master plan. It is God's good pleasure to give us all things (Luke 12:32). Being under the construct of God's master plan, He puts His calling in us, gives us an appetite for it and then allows us to trust Him to see it through to fruition. Everything you have every dreamed about will come true when You trust God. He is faithful to accomplish mighty things in us if we allow Him too. It is our heritage to walk in close proximity with God, reflecting the plans of heaven here on earth. God needs humans to operate through to display His glory. The goal you have festering around inside your spirit is sure to occur. Though it tarry, wait for it; because it will surely come, it will not tarry (Habakkuk 2:3).

Prayer: God, You are the bright and morning star. You are magnificent and holy. Lord, Your plans for creation far exceed anything we could ever imagine for ourselves. Thank You for the plans You have for us, which are to prosper us. Reveal Your glory through us in the earth. Let those with doubt have faith to wait upon Your hand. Your timing is perfect; Your ways are without error. Fill the earth with Your power. Ignite a fire within us to go after our dreams and aspirations. Being confident of this very thing, that he which hath begun a good work in you will perform it until the day of Jesus Christ (Philippians 1:6). We worship You. In Jesus' name we pray, Amen.

# April 11

*But even the very hairs of your head are all numbered. Fear not therefore: ye are of more value than many sparrows.* (Luke 12:7)

Your perception of yourself should only come from your value in God's eyes. Humans are quick to disqualify you, always looking for a reason to prove you are not worthy of things in life. This is not the value of creation given from heaven. God has carefully crafted each of us together in His divine perfection, and if we are willing to seek His face we will understand the extent of our importance. On a daily basis, we judge ourselves against our neighbors by placing value on their opinions of us. We allow others who have no authority to validate our worth. Instead of putting emphasis on what the world thinks, we ought to take the time to see ourselves from God's view. He has a count of every hair on our head. Every minute detail about our being is magnified as extraordinary in His sight. It is impossible to even measure our self-worth using human standards. Now is the time to look in the mirror and tell yourself, "I am loved, I have life, and I am valued by God." Don't waste another second in self-denial by comparing our lives to that of others. King Jehovah has already stamped and approved us as "worthy."

Prayer: Lord, You reign as All Mighty in all the earth. Your glory fills the atmosphere. We sit in awe of You. Lord, thank You for first loving us. Take the scales off of our eyes to see our worth according to the way You see us. We bind up depression and low self-esteem. Bless the heart and mind that feels they are not worthy of this life You have given. In all aspects of our life, expand our thinking to know we belong to You and all things are possible to them that believe in Your Son Jesus Christ. You went to great lengths to show us Your love. Lord, we will not deny it by thinking badly about ourselves. Your value is on our heads, we are a royal priesthood, dearly beloved. We are forever grateful. In Jesus' name we pray, Amen.

# April 12

*For thus saith the high and lofty One that inhabiteth eternity, whose name is Holy; I dwell in the high and holy place, with him also that is of a contrite and humble spirit, to revive the spirit of the humble, and to revive the heart of the contrite ones.* (Isaiah 57:15)

What an honor it is to have God, who is holy and sits on high, abiding in us. His divine nature separates Him as Sovereign in all things, yet He considers the ones He created and dwells with us. His love is everlasting, always looking for ways to restore life to our soul. He searches the earth, looking for a place to inhabit. He shows us how to embrace this love by having a contrite and humble spirit. This is a spirit of repentance and modesty, exalting God's way above our own. As we reflect these characteristics, we open ourselves up to God's holy presence. There He comes in to inhabit our very being. God restores life to us by pouring His strength and energy into our hearts, teaching us how to operate in the world. His love is showcased as He is the Ruler of this earth and still considers us to share in His glory. With this great expression of love, our love for Him grows as we experience how much He cares. Our hearts are filled with joy, knowing God- who can do all things and who is all things, finds great pleasure through living in us.

Prayer: God, You are amazing. You rule the earth and all things that exist. Yet You desire to lodge with us Your people. Thank You! Your love restores, heals, sets free and gives us hope on a daily basis. Find our hearts open to Your holy presence today. Remove anything that stands in the way of You residing in us. Transform our mind. We ask for forgiveness for anytime we fail to obey Your commands. We long for You to dwell in us. We are made whole only because of You. Make Your home in us. All glory belongs to You. In Jesus' name we pray, Amen.

# April 13

*And when the tempter came to him, he said, If thou be the Son of God, command that these stones be made bread.* (Matthew 4:3)

One thing we know for sure, there is a real adversary in the earth that desires to destroy us. Jesus, being the Son of God was not exempt from being tempted by the devil. The tempter comes only to KILL, STEAL, and DESTROY. In the wilderness the devil tried to persuade Jesus away from the assignment God sent Him to earth to fulfill. The devil is the master of trying to blind people from seeing their true identity in God. Like Jesus, we have to be far ahead of the tempter by knowing for certain who Jesus is to us, and what we are in Him. The devil asked Jesus a rhetorical question (IF thou be the Son of God) trying to insinuate that Jesus didn't know His true identity. You see, no one can make you believe a lie when you already know the truth. This is the tactic satan uses against us on a daily basis. He tries to tell us lies about who we are and about situations in our lives, trying to keep our minds off of the truth of what God has already promised us. Being assured of who we are in Christ by having continuous communication with Him through reading His word, prayer and other avenues, we come into true knowledge. Now, when the devil tries to trick us, because he comes again and again, we have our shield of faith, which is able to quench all the fiery darts of the wicked (Ephesians 6:16).

Prayer: Lord, You are holy and righteous all glory and power are found in You. Thank You for being our shield and protection. Your Spirit leads us in all things and there is no weapon that is formed against us that shall prosper. We know who we are in Christ Jesus. We are the head and not the tail, we are holy, elect, beloved, a peculiar people, a holy nation called into covenant with YOU. Nothing shall by any means harm us. We bind every attack the enemy has planned for us, and those we love. We put on the full armor of God and stand firm in our faith. We will no longer believe the lies of the enemy but every word that comes from heaven. We are blessed and are seated in high places in Christ

Jesus. We bless Your name forever. In Jesus' name we pray, Amen.

# April 14

*And I will make of thee a great nation, and I will bless thee, and make thy name great; and thou shalt be a blessing:* (Genesis 12:2)

God has called us into His presence as His own. Since the beginning of creation, God has looked on us with the intent to bless us and cause us to be a blessing to this world. The first thing God promises Abram is that a great nation shall come from his lineage. Holy nations, which like Abram, have faith in God and stand in agreement with God's covenant. Then God goes on to say as a holy (great) nation, there are benefits associated with being the seed of the Most High God. His blessings flow to us and through us, giving us the ability to bless others. The blessings of God sanctify us, covering us with His standard of holiness and calling us close to Him to see all that He has for us. Standing under God's covenant we have access to the multitude of great things He has prepared for us, and the pipeline then flows freely from us to others. As we receive the gifts of life being sanctified by God, we use our lives to bless others and the ripple effect continues on. This establishes us as a great nation; one who loves God, and adheres to His voice. In return, we walk in the promises of Abraham and are a blessing to the earth. As a result of God's love, we have access to unthinkable treasures and the ability to showcase God's promises to all mankind.

Prayer: Lord, You are so thoughtful. You consider all things created. There are unlimited amount of treasures stored up for those who love You. As You continue to bless us we will bless others. Prepare us to always be ready to bless someone we come into contact with. As we seek Your face and Your kingdom, we will continue to grow in Your love. Help us to stand in obedience to Your Word. Not always coming with our hand out but with praise on our lips, exalting You for who You are. You are holy, righteous, loving, kind, forgiving, compassionate, and understanding. We will forever praise You. In Jesus' name we pray, Amen.

# April 15

*In every thing give thanks: for this is the will of God in Christ Jesus concerning you.* (1 Thessalonians 5:18)

Giving thanks is a command from God. It brings Him great pleasure to see us offering up praise and adoration. God says it is His will that we give thanks in everything. Putting so much emphasis on having a grateful attitude illustrates how important it is. To give thanks simply means to show appreciation and honor for something or towards someone. We understand when we allow thanksgiving to flow from our hearts it keeps us in the right frame of mind. As we have given our life to Christ, we understand we are now under His authority and have yielded ourselves to Him. Our lives are in His hand and God covers us, leading us on a path of love. Regardless of the state we find ourselves I,n God's love is always nearby. This gives us a reason to be thankful. It is not by our own strength that we are functioning in the earth. The very course of our life is in the palm of God's hand. Realizing this gives us the ability to trust in the LORD with all our heart and lean not on our own understanding (Proverbs 3:5). We know God has every aspect of our lives under control. Giving thanks in EVERYTHING then becomes a natural response, as we trust in God's unfailing love and His faithful nature.

Prayer: Lord, we thank You for this day that You have given to us. Thank You for all that You do, all that You have done and all that You have planned for us. You created us with a purpose that is pleasing to You. We yield ourselves to You today and make a vow to stop worrying about things that are out of our control. You have commanded us to give thanks and that is what we shall do. We thank You for everything. All of Your ways are perfect and pleasing. Thank You for nurturing us and keeping us close to You. We will forever sing of Your praise and glory. In Jesus' name we pray, Amen.

# April 16

*Then came she and worshipped him, saying, Lord, help me.* (Matthew 15:25)

Far too often, instead of worshiping God for who He is and asking Him for help, we try to negotiate with God. Our conversations tell Him how angry we are about our situation and how unfair we feel we have been treated. It's not usually until we realize God is not moved by our unstable emotions that we take into consideration His commands for us in our times of desperation. It's easy to say I trust in the Lord at all times, but when situations arise, actually going through them requires strength far beyond our own. Thank heaven for our Father who calls us to cast our cares on Him. It is true He can carry the weight of the world. The only way to get through difficult times is to lose ourselves in Him. In our human nature alone we can't fathom the hurt and pain associated with hardships. God, knowing this, has given us clear instructions and demonstrations through people in the bible on how to get through these difficult times. During our time of despair and times of joy, we are charged to praise God. When unfavorable situations arise, IT's OK to ask God for help! God delights in being the pillar holding His people up. This allows our faith in His unfailing love to carry us through our circumstances. Instead of replaying the misery over and over in our head, we must exude praise from our lips. Worshipping the God who is in control of all things. Faith is the only thing that moves God. Praise coupled with faith not only keeps us sane, it also gives us a constant reminder of the All-Mighty God we serve.

Prayer: Lord, there is no other in the entire universe greater than You. Your love keeps us close to You. Thank You for being our place of refuge. We can't do anything without You. We put all of our trust in You. Help us in every situation we find ourselves in. Lord, even in that dark place where we don't understand what is taking place around us, we know You are sovereign. You are on the throne. You are concerned and have compassion for Your people. Send Your host of heaven to protect us and open our minds to Your principles; our mouths will be filled with Your praise and with Your glory all day long. All honors belong to You. In Jesus' name we pray, Amen.

# April 17

*And Balaam answered and said unto the servants of Balak, if Balak would give me his house full of silver and gold, I cannot go beyond the word of the LORD my God, to do less or more.* (Numbers 22:18)

Nothing, including riches, fame, lust or desires, should be able to entice us to go against the command of God. His commands come from His holy nature and are assigned to fit into His perfect plan. We have gained access into His secret place and decided to give God authority over every aspect of our lives, where we make sure we hear and obey the commands of God. We should not add anything to it nor take away from anything He says. This goes for us personally or when God speaks to us on behalf of others. What God says is sovereign, and there is no error found in His guidance. It is our desire to get to a place of intimacy with God where we hear His voice and only speak what we hear from His throne. When this scripture says, "I cannot go beyond the word of the LORD my God, to do less or more," it is stating the end of the matter. When God speaks things happen. As He sends forth His command, everything yields to His voice. There is nothing in this earth that can distort the Word of God. Instilling this principle in our spirit will open our eyes to the secure dwelling we have in Christ Jesus, enabling us to experience the freedom we have in our Father. His word is PERFECT, everything He does has purpose and as we follow Him we embrace the life of perfection He created us to have. "The law of the LORD is perfect, converting the soul: the testimony of the LORD is sure, making wise the simple" (Psalm 19:7).

Prayer: LORD, Your faithfulness is everlasting. You have given us life and all things to sustain us through the days. All day long we seek after Your voice. Open our hearts, ears, and minds to hear from heaven. Let every aspect of the day enlighten us to Your loving presence. As we look around and see the beauty of Your holiness we will rejoice. Lord, no matter what comes our way we will stand on Your principles. Adhering to the commands You have set in place for a specific purpose. Not one word from Your throne will return to You void. It is our desire to only speak what we hear from YOU. In all things we give thanks. In Jesus' name we pray, Amen.

# April 18

*My mouth is filled with your praise, and with your glory all the day.* (Psalm 71:8)

Every day when we rise, we have a choice on what we allow to flow from our mouth. God has given us commands on how to live an abundant life and it starts from the inside of our being. What flows from our mouth is what resides in our heart. If it is hard for us to sing praise unto our God; we must ask God to perform heart surgery on us this day. God created us to worship Him in Spirit and in truth. As we come into the knowledge of who God is, worship will be able to flow from our heart and out of our mouth. The very act of worship is honoring God for who He is. It is us, exalting Him for being in our lives and responding to His awesome love. Often, we have so many other things built up in our heart that there is little room to think about the goodness of God. Every day we should be able to speak words of adoration to the true and living God, giving Him glory and honor at all times. The scripture reveals "our mouth is filled with God's praise and with His glory." In order to have our mouth filled with God's praise, we have to consciously feed ourselves God's Word. We have to know God for ourselves on an intimate level, and when situations arise, God's praise will flow from our lips. As children of God, our hearts are filled with God's praise because we know God for who He is and He has shown us our true identity in Him. Being in Christ, we have the mind of Christ, and His mind says we are in right position with God. Knowing who we are in Christ and who He is in us fills our mouth with praise where it will be hard for us to keep quiet.

Prayer: Lord God, thank You for filling us with praise. You are our shelter, refuge and place of safety. We bless You for who You are. You have given us the fruit of life. All that we have need of is found in You. We seek first Your kingdom and Your righteousness, and all things will be added to us. Be a lamp unto our feet and a light unto our path. All things are found in You. Search our hearts and fill us with Your splendor that Your praise will flow from our lips all the daylong. We will praise and give

You honor on purpose. "Casting down imaginations, and every high thing that exalteth itself against the knowledge of God, and bringing into captivity every thought to the obedience of Christ" (2 Corinthians 10:5). In Jesus' name we pray, Amen.

# April 19

*He that dwelleth in the secret place of the most High shall abide under the shadow of the Almighty.* (Psalm 91:1)

There is a secret place where God lives, a place of divine comfort where all the cares of the world are cast at His feet, and in return we experience His loving nature. God is always in the midst of her and makes countless attempts for His creation to come into this place of sacredness. Those who love God run to this place and allow His Spirit to inhabitant every aspect of their lives. It is not only sought after in times of need, but we make our abode there. Our lives are centered on remaining in God's presence. It is our position in the kingdom of heaven to experience pure bliss. As we make it our lifestyle to find rest in the secret place we find exuberant satisfaction in having all of our needs met, living under the shadow of the Most High. Though trouble may arise on every side, our position in His presence will not change. He has made provision for us and commands His angels to keep watch over us. Making every way possible for us to know we are not journeying the course of life alone. Remaining in the secret place of the Most High fills us with confidence, shinning light on the path ahead where we find rest under the shadow of the Almighty.

Prayer: Lord, You alone are Holy. Righteousness resides with You. Thank You for inviting us into Your secret place. A place where you cover us with songs of deliverance. Prepare us to go higher. Lord, there is no greater experience in all the earth than to see You for who You really are. Holy, righteous, loving, kind, peaceful, merciful, El Shaddai, Jehovah-jireh, Emmanuel. Lord, we can go on and on. Most dear to our heart we call You Abba Father. Everything that concerns us concerns You. Lord, do a new thing in the earth. Show Your face; let Your name be glorified throughout this entire earth. All things are possible to him that believes. We say glory to Your name. In Jesus' name we pray, Amen.

# April 20

*Now go ahead and send a message to the Jews in the king's name, telling them whatever you want, and seal it with the king's signet ring. But remember that whatever has already been written in the king's name and sealed with his signet ring can never be revoked.* (Esther 8:8 NLT)

There was a decree sent out to destroy all of the Jews (God's chosen people) during the reign of Queen Esther. Esther was of Jewish decent and pleaded with the King to have mercy towards her people. God's favor was upon Queen Esther and the King heard her appeal for the Jews. However the King had already sealed a decree to destroy the Jews with his signet ring, indicating it could not be broken. To counteract this ruling the King gave Esther and her uncle Mordecai free will to write another decree in his name to protect the Jews. God always has an alternative plan to supersede the enemy's plan to destroy us. We are His chosen people, His elect and beloved generation. It wouldn't be in God's character to sit back and watch us be destroyed. We, like Esther and Mordecai, must use God's wisdom against the strategies of the enemy. God's favor is covering us, shielding us from the evil plots arranged for us. God will use us to stand for the welfare of our family, community and our nation as His royal priesthood. He has placed in our hands the power to bind and loose on earth according to His power. We have obtained access and been given the keys to the kingdom of God to have dominion in the earth. God is All-powerful and works through us and has given us authority over the enemy, so nothing can harm us (Luke 10:19).

Prayer: Lord, You are good and Your mercy endures forever. Lord, we put on Your full armor today. You have given us every tool necessary to have victory in the earth. We have power through You; every spirit is subject to us. Give us wisdom and boldness to stand on Your word. Whatever is taking place in the earth will not destroy us. We are more than conquerors. No matter what it looks like, send Your ministering angels to cover and protect us. Help us to counteract spiritual warfare by studying

Your word and knowing who we are in Christ. We have a spirit of power, love and a sound mind. Fear and defeat are not from You. So today we choose to walk only in the gifts of the spirit. Everything is under Your control and You fight for us. We have the victory in You. Hallelujah! Glory to Your name. In Jesus' name we pray, Amen.

# April 21

*And I say also unto thee, That thou art Peter, and upon this rock I will build my church; and the gates of hell shall not prevail against it.* (Matthew 16:18)

Insert your name right where Jesus mentions Peter in this scripture. “And I say also unto thee, That thou art Nicole...” Jesus has welcomed each of us into His kingdom to share and experience His glory. At the onset of accepting Christ we were made aware of our true identity. In Christ alone is where we find our true selves. God has enabled us to be a part of His plans and the expansion of the body of believers in the earth. We, as His disciples, have been charged with the task to live as His children, showcasing His glory to the world. Jesus is our foundation. He is our cornerstone that holds all things together. Daily we are able to grow in the knowledge He bestows upon us, which helps us to develop and become more and more like Him. Jesus is our High Priest and has given us a solid foundation, where He is able to work through us. We have become the dwelling place of the Most High and must yield ourselves and acknowledge what this really means. God makes our spirit the place He inhabits. Through His Spirit, He permeates our entirc being, growing us as His holy temple. Within us is the place where God lives (the kingdom of Heaven). What a joy to know God loves us so much He has given us access into His Kingdom.

Prayer: Lord God Almighty! We sing glory to Your name. You are the King of Kings and Lord of lords. All power and majesty is in Your hands. We say, “yes” to You building Your church within us. Develop us, mold us, and transform us to be more and more like You. Remove all manner of sin from us. Forgive us of our sins. Show us the truth of Your word. Open our eyes to our true identity. Grant us a spirit of discernment to only allow things that will mature us and draw us close to You to take residence in our spirit. We receive Your love today. Thank You for establishing us with Jesus as our foundation. We trust and believe that the gates of hell shall not prevail against Your church. The place You have created, Your dwelling place. Lord, we give You honor. In Jesus' name we pray, Amen.

# April 22

*My sheep hear my voice, and I know them, and they follow me:* (John 10:27)

God will never hide anything from us concerning our purpose. God uniquely created each of us as His ambassadors to fulfill our part in His perfect plan. Everything we need to successfully complete our task on earth has been given to us. Jesus is our Shepherd, and as His flock we follow the path He has already travelled. Daily, we open our ears to hear the plans of heaven and come into agreement with everything He is speaking to us. Being the followers of Christ we know Him as our Lord. We understand everything He does is to bring glory to the Father. God's plans are satisfying and pleasing. It is a great honor to be called into the kingdom of Jesus and to be trusted with such a great task. It is our responsibility to ensure our ears are attentive and we dedicate intimate time with God to hear what He is speaking to us. Once we hear, we are to listen and follow the directions, which only leads to valuable outcomes. Reading God's Word and inviting God into every aspect of our lives helps us to know Jesus more and more. The more time we spend with God, the more deeply we come to know and trust Him. Our joy is anchored in knowing we are following Jesus, who is leading us to eternal life where we will dwell in the house of the Lord FOREVER!!!

**~If You lead me I will follow~**

Prayer: Lord, You are King of all things created. We honor You! Help us to have an attentive ear, to know Your voice and the voice of another we will not follow. Shield us, lead us and guide us on the narrow path of righteousness for Your name's sake. You are not a man that You should lie. Everything You say is true. Lord, thank You for thinking so highly of us that You have given us step-by-step instructions on how to be more than conquerors. Your lovingkindness grants us new mercies day-by-day, and we say, Thank You. Father glorify Your name in us. In Jesus' name we pray, Amen.

# April 23

*Now when Ezra had prayed, and when he had confessed, weeping and casting himself down before the house of God, there assembled unto him out of Israel a very great congregation of men and women and children: for the people wept very sore.* (Ezra 10:1)

It was common for the leaders in Israel to cry before God on behalf of the people. Ezra's heart broke upon learning of the children of Israel's sin. As the high priest, he immediately went to the source, repenting and pleading for their disobedience. As the people saw Ezra before the Lord, their hearts too became heavy with conviction and they joined Ezra's plea and repented before the Lord. This is a valuable lesson we can practice today; when we fall into temptation and commit sin, we should band together and lift each other up. Instead of pointing fingers and casting judgment-leaving people to endure the snares of life alone, we can stand side-by-side before the Lord. Encouraging each other can help lift the burden of feeling guilty and aid in the process of remaining obedient to God. Unity in the body of believers is beneficial to all. We all belong to Christ and function as many parts of the body. When one part isn't functioning it affects the entire body. Being supportive in the process of repenting is very important. We can offer comforting words, assuring each other of God's love in hopes of turning from sin and walking according to the Spirit. Two are always better than one. In times of transgression, the last thing we need is to be alone. So the next time you hear of someone who has made a decision contrary to the Word/will of God, offer prayer and God's love.

Prayer: Behold, how good and pleasant it is when brothers dwell in unity! (Psalm 133:1). Father, we magnify Your name. Thank You for being a living example of love and unity. You never leave us alone. While we were yet in sin You sent Your Son to die for us. As we walk this earth, help us not to cast judgment but to band together, being in one accord, lifting each other up in prayer. When we see others struggling we will offer support and speak in love, displaying Your affection in the earth. We all belong to the body of Christ and will continue to teach and correct each other in love. Remove pride and judgment from our spirit. Open our hearts to have compassion and mercy. As You love, we will love as well. Your ways are pleasing and add value to our lives. Whatever you do in word or deed, do all in the name of the Lord Jesus, giving thanks through Him to God the Father (Colossians 3:17). In Jesus' name we pray, Amen.

# April 24

*Ye have heard how I said unto you, I go away, and come again unto you. If ye loved me, ye would rejoice, because I said, I go unto the Father: for my Father is greater than I.* (John 14:28)

We have confidence in the promise of eternal life in Christ. He came that we may have life and that we may have it more abundantly. His promise is for us to have a secure dwelling place where we have open fellowship with Him. Nothing can deter His plan of eternity for those who believe and accept Jesus. His work was fulfilled as He walked the earth, submitting Himself to every command of God in order to show us how to function in our true identity. Now He sits at the right hand of God interceding on our behalf. He is in heaven, preparing a place for us to reside with Him forever. Jesus being with the Father gives us reason to rejoice. He is no longer bound to human limitations, as when He walked with the disciples. Now He sits in the presence of the Almighty, speaking on our behalf. God, being ruler of the universe, listens to the voice of His Son and is more than willing to receive us as we have received Jesus. After all, this is the plan of God to showcase His love to all of mankind.

Prayer: Greater love has no one than this: to lay down one's life for one's friends. Father, You sent Your only begotten Son to die for our sins in order for us to be reconciled back to You. Your love moves mountains and is chasing after us. We accept the works of Christ and hold dear to our hearts the newfound hope that we have in Him. We rejoice, knowing all things are under His feet and wait in expectation for His return. That when He returns He may see us being diligent in the task You have assigned to us. Help us to walk always in the Spirit, adhering to all of Your commands. Thank You for securing our future by giving us eternal life with You. You are the greatest gift of life. Glorify Your name in us. In Jesus' name we pray, Amen.

# April 25

*Let the word of Christ dwell in you richly in all wisdom; teaching and admonishing one another in psalms and hymns and spiritual songs, singing with grace in your hearts to the Lord.* (Colossians 3:16)

We are unable to learn in life apart from reading and being taught. Bishop T.D. Jakes once said that reading is imperative to everything God has available for us to receive. He made the analogy of those who attend school. A person enters school as a student and yet can come out as a doctor. The DNA of the person didn't change, only their intellectual ability was stimulated and fed knowledge. The same is true for the Saints of God. God has transformed us; we are new creatures in Christ Jesus. We have received from God every blessing we will ever need to fulfill His purpose on earth. Spending time in His word on a daily basis will allow us to be transformed (renewed mind) into the very image of Christ. Failing to allow the word of Christ to dwell in us richly (abundantly), we are unable to know what God desires of us. His word is set in place to help us grow and develop Godly character. We are God's reflection in the earth. Our knowledge of how to operate only comes from above. When Christ returns, He is coming to find us operating as a reflection of Him. ***"Beloved, now are we the sons of God, and it doth not yet appear what we shall be: but we know that, when he shall appear, we shall be like him; for we shall see him as he is"*** **(1 John 3:2).** The word shows us right from wrong, teaches us how to love and how to express God to others. We are on assignment, and only through the teachings of God can we display His image in our lives.

Prayer: Heavenly Father, we adore You. Establish Your word within us. Give us a heart to seek after You. Your word is power and gives life. It changes all those who believe and receive what You have to offer. Lord, we are forever thankful for Your kindness in giving us instructions in life. You never leave us without hope. Everything we need in life is found in You. So let the word of Christ dwell richly in us in all wisdom, teaching and admonishing one another in psalms and hymns and spiritual songs, singing with grace in our hearts to You Lord. You are so amazing. Glory to Your name. In Jesus' name we pray, Amen.

# April 26

*But he that is spiritual judgeth all things, yet he himself is judged of no man.* (1 Corinthians 2:15)

We have been given wisdom from God. Wisdom, which stands in connection with what is on the very heart of God. Living by the Spirit, we have obtained the mind of Christ. We have come into agreement with God's plans and are able to comprehend the meaning of His word. God is so gracious; He wants us to grow in knowledge. He created us to live as the very image of His Son Jesus Christ. Being a reflection of Christ, God instills us with insight to make sound judgment. We are able to implement God's precepts into our daily living and live our lives according to God's greatest potential. Every situation we encounter in life can be filtered through God's wisdom and He is sure to give us spiritual understanding in how to conduct ourselves. Having the mind of Christ, we have gained a sensory to evaluate all things and make decisions, which are pleasing to God (In essence will be pleasing to us). Being led by God's Spirit, we will only engage in things that are in right standing with God. Whatever God has planned concerning us, He will also reveal to us. As we walk in alignment with God, allowing His Spirit to influence our mind, every choice we make will yield favorable results. When God is in the midst of what we are doing, there is nothing that can stand against us. God wants us to open our minds to His Spirit, releasing the pressure of trying to do things on our own. Helping us to experience the benefit of being His beloved children.

**You are not alone- Don't do life all by yourself.**

Prayer: There is none like You in all the earth. God, You are more than words can explain. Your splendor and glory fill the earth. Thank You for calling us as Your own. Your plans for us only lead to beneficial outcomes. Everything about You produces love. Keep our minds stayed on You. Show us the truth of Your word. Let faith cause us to believe in everything Your Spirit is trying to show us on a daily basis. We will make a conscious effort to sit in Your presence to grow and develop into the very image of Christ. Destroy every ounce of our flesh. Develop our ability to discern between good and evil and to always choose righteousness. In all things we give thanks. In Jesus' name we pray, Amen.

# April 27

*But God, who is rich in mercy, for his great love wherewith he loved us,* (Ephesians 2:4)

To obtain some insight on how much God loves us, we have to take a look at how it all started. You see, God created all things. Today, many people disregard the fact of being created by God. We live under the notion that somehow we just appeared here on earth and life just happens because the stars in the universe lined up. This is not the case. God is on the throne, carefully orchestrating His plans for creation. He sits in expectation and is excited when His beloved acknowledges the truth of His love. Embracing God's love allows us to be made whole. We obtain spiritual insight and function with the confidence of God being our devoted Father. It's important to understand God chose us first. It is because of His great plan we are uniquely created to enjoy and explore the earth. Born with a sinful nature, we were living under the power of darkness. God, looking at His great creation, would not dare allow us to be separated from His original intent of being joined together with Him. His love makes it possible for us to take our predestined position in the kingdom as His heirs. He pours out His compassion on us because we belong to Him. We are the apples of His eye. His love for us makes it impossible for us to miss out on our God-given purpose. Literally being delivered from the snares of death, God opened the gate into His kingdom. Through the nature of His love, He couldn't bear to see us die to the lies, deceit and tricks of the enemy. His love is readily available and an innate part of who He is, and what He is trying to give to us on a daily basis.

**Love is here, will you accept it?**

Prayer: Father, You are so gracious and kind. Without You, our lives have no meaning. Thank You for loving us. Your love has carried Your people throughout time. Everything You do is based on Your loving nature. Open our hearts to receive Your love, to operate in it and to express it to others. You abound in great mercy and loving-kindness. You are the light of this world. Continue to shine through us. Use us for the uplifting of Your kingdom. Ignite Your fire within us to walk boldly, proclaiming how great You are. Thank You for being our Father. We will bless Your name forever. In Jesus' name we pray, Amen.

# April 28

*And from Jesus Christ the faithful witness, the firstborn of the dead, and the ruler of kings on earth. To him who loves us and has freed us from our sins by his blood.* (Revelation 1:5)

Living our lives conscious of the precious works of Christ will open our eyes and allow us to experience a great time on earth. Just think about it, Christ came to the earth to show us how God operates. We are able to see the love He has for us as an example. This example shows us how to operate in our true identity, the very image of God, Jesus and the Holy Spirit. Jesus' life and ministry revealed the very heart of God. He revealed who we are in Him and uncovers the greatness that He has instilled in us. Every word of God proves true. Not only has the Bible been tested and proven by people in times past, Jesus also came as the living example to show us the true quality a relationship with God entails. Jesus is a faithful witness. He sits in the face of God and reflects everything He sees the father doing then turns around and discloses it to us in order for us to join in on God's master plan. As our living example, Jesus embedded our hearts with the fruit of God's nature. Our eyes are open to the freedom we have obtained by the works of Christ. The works of Jesus were established so we could come into the knowledge of who God is, what God wants to do in our lives, and how we can effectively witness to others. As we come boldly to the throne of grace, we know we serve a God whose love captivates our soul to make us better. His love draws us close to Him, only to disclose the awesome plans He has prepared for us to partake in.

Prayer: Thank You Father for inviting us in to reside with You. You are the true and living God. Your love has captured our hearts. It is by Your plans that we walk the earth. Everything You do is in hopes of us recognizing Your greatness in order for us to experience true life with You. You sent Jesus in hopes of us seeing our true self in Him. Open the eyes of our heart to see the plans You have for us. Your desire is for all creation to join in fellowship with You. All that You have prepared for us is for our benefit.

Send Your revelation to this earth. Help us to be in alignment with what is taking place in heaven. All of Your plans bring us hope and lead us closer to You. In all that we do we give You praise. In Jesus' name we pray, Amen.

# April 29

*I tell you, he will give justice to them speedily. Nevertheless, when the Son of Man comes, will he find faith on earth?* (Luke 18:8)

God is always watching and looking for ways to get us to experience His great nature. As humans, sometimes we only depend on God or cultivate our relationship with Him when things are going our way. God is not pleased with this one-sided behavior because it breaks His heart. He wants us to acknowledge Him as Lord through every circumstance. In the good times and bad times, God has given us principles to stand on. We understand He has already established our future in Him. Our hope is anchored in His unwavering love. Our faith tells us on the challenging days, "if God be for us who can be against us." No matter what situation we find ourselves in, our love and attitude toward God should never change. Our promise of eternal life and the seal we have in the Holy Spirit stand as our ammunition for our faith. We are confident that as we endure, it only pushes us closer to God. We know everything that He does is for our benefit. Regardless of what we face in life, we can always depend on God and rely on our trust in Him to carry us through. We are living this life with the promise of spending forever in His presence. What we face today will not hinder what He has already purposed for us. It is essential that we renew our mind each day to ensure that when Jesus does return, He finds us standing firm in our faith, NOTHING WAVERING. "Now the just shall live by faith: but if any man draw back, my soul shall have no pleasure in him" (Hebrews 10:38).

**Just live by faith**

Prayer: Lord, you are good and your mercy endures forever. There is no greater love than what you pour out on us every day. Continue to build our confidence in you. Help us to be bold as lions, spreading your gospel throughout the earth. We want to come into alignment with what you have planned for us in heaven. As Your willing vessels, prepare our heart for worship and to be obedient to You at all times. This life we give to You to fill the earth with Your glory. All praise belongs to You. In Jesus' name we pray, Amen.

# April 30

*When life is heavy and hard to take, go off by yourself. Enter the silence. Bow in prayer. Don't ask questions: Wait for hope to appear. Don't run from trouble. Take it full-face. The "worst" is never the worst.* (Lamentations 3:28-30 MSG)

God is merciful and full of compassion. As we journey through life, we will encounter times where we wish God could allow us to surpass the turbulence. No one enjoys difficult situations. We will experience some dire situations that may even seem unbearable. In these moments we have to grab hold of God's hand and remind ourselves of His faithfulness. God is still on the throne, and as we go through different circumstances we have to place our hope in Him alone. He sees all that we go through and help is always available. In the midst of our situation we have to command our mind to focus on God's compassion which will NEVER fail us. We have to do whatever it takes to stand still and know that God is in control. If we have to read every scripture about our situation, lay on the altar or seek counsel to keep our mind on Jesus, so be it. One thing we know for sure is His word is true and He is pleased to deliver us. What we endure someone else is enduring as well and others have already overcome that same situation. Our courage comes from knowing God is never unaware of what is taking place in the lives of His children. He has given us the ability to bear every season of our life. As we activate our faith, we can praise God in the middle of unfavorable circumstances and know God fights every battle for us.

Prayer: Lord God Almighty! We worship You. You are marvelous. Lord, we are nothing without You. God, You have truly prepared us for all things on earth. You told us that, in this life we will have trouble. You warned us about our adversary, and have given us every tool to be conquers in this earth. We have power and dominion to trample over every serpent and snake, nothing shall harm us (Luke 10:19). We put on Your full armor today and go out, prepared for what we will encounter. Your strength is our protection. We bow before Your throne, have Your way in us. Thank You for never leaving us or forsaking us. Our hope is in You. Blessed is the man who trusts in the Lord, and whose trust is the Lord (Jeremiah 17:7). God, we love You. In Jesus' name we pray, Amen.

## May 1

*And the Lord blessed the latter days of Job more than his beginning. And he had 14,000 sheep, 6,000 camels, 1,000 yoke of oxen, and 1,000 female donkeys.* (Job 42:12 ESV)

Everything about God leads to increase. As we are being led by the Spirit of God, our lives will only go in an upward direction. We may face many obstacles, and even make some bad decisions that seem to get us off course. In these instances, we are never too far out of God's reach and His ability to reel us back in. His plans for us can never be destroyed; so long as we are obedient and trust in His word we are able to enjoy His promises. Job had not done anything wrong in God's sight, yet his life was completely rocked upside down and hit from every angle. He had to endure tremendous challenges, including the death of his children, loss of property and his ailing health. Even in our winter storms we find ourselves developing in the characteristics of God to our benefit. Trusting in God will ensure we are always in a state of maturing. God's desire for mankind is to excel and to prosper in the purpose He has planned for us. Whenever we find ourselves in a season where we don't understand all that is taking place around, us we can rest assured God is still in the midst. Seasons may change but God will not. God is always making sure all things work together for our good, where His name will be glorified. To include the things that may cause us discomfort. One thing for sure is we can always depend on God. As we trust in Him we will grow in His wisdom and knowledge. As we expand spiritually, God is always extending His hand toward us, pouring out His blessings to get us to know Him more and more. It is God's will that we increase in learning and obtain our benefits from heaven. When we wait on God to see how His plans unfold we are never disappointed. It is His great pleasure to bless us and to safeguard our life in His unfailing arms.

**God is working!**

Prayer: Almighty Father, we bless Your name. If we are

completely honest with ourselves we will face difficult times in our life where our faith may waiver-causing unbelief to set in. Thank You for never letting go of our hand. You always encourage us and stay true to Your Word. In Your Word we find many promises of hope. Your word is faithful to accomplish what You have already ordained for it to perform. Teach us how to trust and wait on You to operate in our lives. During seasons of unfamiliar territory we will grab hold of Your hand a little tighter and stand firm in our faith. You are faithful. All things are possible to him that believes. We will bless You forever. In Jesus' name we pray, Amen.

# May 2

*Know therefore that the Lord your God is God, the faithful God who keeps covenant and steadfast love with those who love him and keep his commandments, to a thousand generations.* (Deuteronomy 7:9)

We are the only ones who change in our relationship with God. We can either grow closer to God, or by our own willpower drift away. We experience the beauty of His loving nature when we decide to draw close to Him. God is the same yesterday, today and forevermore. When we came to know Him we were introduced to all of His glorious attributes. None of His characteristics fade over time. He is God of all things created, lover of creation and faithful to those who believe. God is more than amazing. He spends all of His time trying to get us to recognize the gem that we have in Him and the jewel that He sees us as. Not only does God walk with us hand in hand each day, promising and fulfilling the abundant life as we follow Christ, but His grace extends to a thousand generations to come. What God did for the people in the Bible He'll do for us. What God does for us, He'll do for the generations who come after us. His hand is not waxed short, He never runs out of love, power or the ability to provide for His creation. Therefore we are confident that the love of God will never fail. It's always available to us if we are willing to receive it.

Prayer: Hallelujah! Glory to Your name. It is such an honor to be called Your children. We exalt Your name in all the earth. There is no greater love than what You show toward us everyday. Your promises are Yes and Amen. You search for opportunities to bless us. We are forever grateful. Thank You for establishing a covenant with us. Your promises are sealed and can never be broken. Open our hearts so we can comprehend the love that You have for us. Your love heals, forgives, and makes us whole. All that we need is found in You. We will bless You and teach the next generation about Your splendor. Lord, You are marvelous, magnificent and holy. We give You all the praise. In Jesus' name we pray, Amen.

# May 3

*When a man's ways please the Lord, he maketh even his enemies to be at peace with him.* (Proverbs 16:7)

"If it is possible, as far as it depends on you, live at peace with everyone" (Romans 12:18). In this life we will encounter difficult people. At times we will be on the other side of the prayer where someone is praying for the way we treated them. As we live in the Spirit we will be convicted whenever we conduct ourselves in a manner that is unbecoming as Saints of God. Laying pride aside, we are to go to our brother and sister and express our mistake in hopes of rectifying the issue. If they choose to still walk in anger it is no longer on our plate. We have asked God for forgiveness and did our best to resolve the matter. Also we will encounter those who are jealous of us or for whatever reasons don't like us. They make it a point to cause us pain and to be hostile toward us. In whatever instance we find ourselves face to face with an enemy, we know God is in control. Our enemies have no power over us except for what we relinquish to them. God instructs us to bless those who curse us and to pray for those who mistreat us (Luke 6:28). We are to overcome evil with good. Our primary focus is not on who likes us as it is on being in right standing with God. Walking in the Spirit we will at all times seek to treat others with care and courtesy. Finding pleasure in the sight of God, He will make even our enemies to be at peace with us. As we seek God He works on them and ensures peace surrounds us covering all of our days.

Prayer: Lord, we bless Your name. Lord, we will stand on only what You say in Your word. You have called us to peace. Harmony lives with us. We will not allow pride or strife to rule in our house. We will walk in the fear of the Lord, which causes men to depart from evil. Goodness and mercy shall follow us all the days of our life. Help us to be slow to anger and to rule over our spirit of flesh. Nothing shall harm us or cause us to react in evil. Bless those that curse us and heal those who mistreat us. Help our enemies to know You as Lord and Savior. Let peace be the universal language coupled with love. All things are possible in You. Restore broken relationships, heal wounds, and break down walls of pride, strife, jealousy, and envy. Restore Your people to walk in the fruit of the Spirit expressing love, joy, peace, longsuffering, gentleness, goodness, faith, meekness, and temperance. All glory belongs to You. In Jesus' name we pray, Amen.

# May 4

*And the publican, standing afar off, would not lift up so much as his eyes unto heaven, but smote upon his breast, saying, God be merciful to me a sinner.* (Luke 18:13)

God, through the works of Christ, is the only one who offered us salvation. It was not of our own doing that took the place of our judgment beside the works of Christ; a decision God made before any of us came to be. He knew the condition humans would fall into and made atonement to ensure the path was always available for us to reach Him. His love saves us from our flesh that is present within us. God is holy and cannot deal in the presence of sin. His presence consumes sin. The wages of sin is death. Every one of us has participated in sin. Thankfully, we have been forgiven. God's grace washed us clean. We must never forget how kind God is in allowing Jesus to come to the earth to be the ultimate sacrifice. We should never think of ourselves to be so righteous that we forget all that God has forgiven us for. By remaining humble we are able to spread God's grace throughout the world. When we see others still living in sin, we can relate. We should never look down on them or get to a point were we are not able to fall on our knees and ask God for forgiveness even for others. According to God's nature, every day we fall short, His love keeps us close to Him by looking at us through the blood of Jesus. Be humble. Say, Lord I'm not worthy but I thank You for Your grace. My deeds say death, but Your love says life.

**Go Jesus!**

Prayer: Hallelujah! For our Lord God Almighty reigns. Lord, You are excellent! My God, My God, Your grace is everything. Because of You we have eternal life. Lord, You saw us in our sin and said it is not so with my people. You make it impossible for us to go through life without knowing You exist. We can look all around and know that You are alive and active in the earth. With humble hearts, we fall on our knees to exalt Your name. We give

You total praise, reverence and honor. God, You saved us from the pit of hell. Lord, when we didn't know right from wrong, You called us into Your kingdom. Lord, we are forever grateful. We are lost without You. Save Your people who may not know You or fail to submit to Your way of life. Let our life be a living testimony. Help us to be authentic in sharing how Your love saved us. Meet us at our very point of need. In all things we give thanks. In Jesus' name we pray, Amen.

# May 5

*I will make thy name to be remembered in all generations: therefore shall the people praise thee for ever and ever.* (Psalm 45:17)

We too first came to know God by the kindness of someone telling us about a great God. At some point we were introduced to a God who cares and loves us. Someone took the time to share his or her liberty with us, in hopes of us coming into the knowledge of Christ for ourselves. Praise God for those who are not selfish in spreading the Good News. It is because of the Saints around the globe that we know God as our personal friend and Savior. Now the torch is in our hand to continue the legacy of our Father. In our daily activities and the way we conduct ourselves, we shall express the greatness of God. Many people watch our lives, and by seeing the goodness of God may come to know Him for his or herself. God has also given us the task to boldly proclaim His goodness. As humans, we like to share everything else, so why not share the greatest gift of all? Some are waiting on our testimony, and if we keep quiet it may prolong them knowing God. Living in the Spirit, we have embarked upon a great lineage that has open door access to all who believe. There is more than enough grace and mercy to go around for everyone walking this earth and then some. With every ounce of our being, we should be screaming from the mountaintop how great our God is.

Prayer: Heavenly Father, we exalt Your name. We will speak about Your goodness all day long. We will make it our business to tell the world how great You are. It's because of You that we are free to live this life in abundance. You have opened our eyes to receive the love and care that You so eloquently pour out each day. Lord, we pray for the Words to speak concerning Your goodness. Let our lives speak of Your glory. You are the King of all things created. We will share all that You have done for us with the world. Letting them know You are not partial. The same love You have for us You have for them. Hallelujah! You are excellent. In Jesus' name we pray, Amen.

# May 6

*The sacrifices of God are a broken spirit: a broken and a contrite heart, O God, thou wilt not despise.* (Psalm 51:17)

*Going through the motions doesn't please you, a flawless performance is nothing to you. I learned God-worship when my pride was shattered. Heart-shattered lives ready for love don't for a moment escape God's notice.* (Psalm 51:16-17 MSG)

The Hebrew word for sacrifice is Karbanot – to draw close to God. The ultimate purpose for everything we do is to be in close proximity with God. We offer God our sacrifice because we love Him. We must be careful not to go along with rituals, in doing so we deny God's power the ability to work through us. God searches our hearts. He travels the earth to find His children who have a desire for Him. Looking into our hearts He understands the motive behind everything that we offer Him. Our heart is where we treasure the Spirit of God. God is purging us on a daily basis, clearing all of the clutter from around our heart in order to fill us with His virtue. It is our choice whether or not we surrender ourselves to Him and ask for more awareness of His Spirit. God wants us just the way we are, so we can glorify His name as He transforms us. As we draw close to God, our hearts have to be in tune with what God is trying to do in us. God cannot work in the midst of pride and arrogance. A broken spirit is one that is ready to be cultivated by God; it's when we relinquish our own ability and allow God to build us in His image. Having a broken and contrite heart is when we are in touch with God's love and determine we are nothing without Him. Failure to adhere to His commands should immediately bring us to repentance where we desire to seek after and rely on His unfailing love. These attributes draw us close to God, and in the brokenness of our spirit before God we are able to obtain all that He is offering for us to be His holy vessels in the earth.

Prayer: Heavenly Father, You are so great. Lord, search us inwardly and judge our heart. Have mercy upon us, open our eyes to see the error in our ways and forgive us. Lord, thank You for never being far away from us. We will be the nation that adheres to Your commands. When You look into our hearts, You will see the love we have for You. Let Your virtue be present in everything we do. Where we try to push You out of our lives, reveal it to us so we can make the necessary adjustments. Lord, we give You all of us. There is no plan better than what You have already established. As Your royal priesthood, it is our pleasure to serve You. Let our worship be authentic as we think about Your goodness and praise You according to Your excellent greatness. We will keep our minds stayed on You. In all things we give You glory. In Jesus' name we pray, Amen.

# May 7

*So will I sing praise unto thy name for ever, that I may daily perform my vows.* (Psalm 61:8)

There are many things we make sure to accomplish on a daily basis, and praise should be at the top of the list. We are not rendering honor to a figment of our imagination. Our praise comes before the King of all things created, a faithful and just Father. Our God, who watches over us all the days of our life to ensure we enjoy our time on earth as we magnify His name. Uttering sweet words from our lips is a bonus that we are thrilled to do on a daily basis. To think about the goodness of God changes our entire countenance. When we find ourselves in a bad mood, we can open our mouths to praise God, and I guarantee our attitudes will instantly change. We won't easily fall into temptation or engage in pity parties because our mind, heart, and mouth will be focused on the goodness of God. Speaking about God brings back to our remembrance the many times He has helped us before. His goodness and love will be at the forefront of our mind, and we confess all that we are grateful for. Studies have shown that individuals who state three things they are grateful for in the morning and repeat it at night are healthier and happier. Being grateful in the form of giving God praise puts things in the right perspective. There are a lot of things to worry about. The bible tells us that in worrying we aren't able to add anything to our life (Matthew 6:27). Giving praise, honor and glory through thinking about the goodness of God will make our hearts merry, reminding us of the great love of our Daddy in heaven. We will find joy in esteeming God and making sure our praise and our actions are pleasing in His sight at all times.

Prayer: Lord, You are our praise. As we think about Your goodness and all that You are, all that is left to do is to say "Thank You." You are the God of all things. Your mercy and grace keep us every day. Forgive us for any times we fail to praise You. We make a vow to praise Your name at all times, no matter what we face in life. We know You are on the throne. Nothing is too hard for You. You will never forsake us or leave us without help. Praise will continually be on our lips. You deserve all the honor and glory. In Jesus' name we pray, Amen.

# May 8

*And Jesus said, Who touched me?* (Luke 8:45)

Jesus was in the midst of a large crowd of people and asked who touched Him. There were many people encircled around Him, I'm guessing being in close proximity everyone was touching each other. Even His disciples marveled at His question, knowing they were in a crowded space. Jesus felt virtue leave His body and inquired who had received the power of God. There was one whose faith drew her to Jesus. She came believing Jesus could heal her of her ailment. All she needed to do was to press into His presence and just touch His clothes, and immediately she was healed. This teaches us so many valuable lessons, one being that faith activates the power of God in our lives. God sees us in our situations, and has given us every tool necessary to receive what we need from Him. We will not receive from God if we fail to believe what His word says is true. We have to determine in our heart that our Father will not withhold any good thing from us. Our faith is the only thing that moves God. Without faith, it is impossible to please Him. He sits in heaven, encouraging us to use our God given power to stand on His word by exercising our faith. Not believing whole-heartedly deters what God is trying to do for us. We see in the bible many times how excited Jesus was about people who exercised their faith. We have to trust the God we serve is able to do the IMPOSSIBLE. When we fail to believe, we shut ourselves off to the marvelous things God wants to perform in through us.

Prayer: Thank You Father for allowing us to see another day. Your grace and mercy meet us every morning. Thank You for giving us an example in the works of Your Son, Jesus. As we grow in our faith we come believing Your word is true. Your ways have been tried and proven. There is no fault in You. You are not a man that should lie, or the son of man that You should repent. What You say will manifest. We will only speak what You speak and believe what You believe. Continue to pour out Your wisdom. As we walk this earth we will do everything in faith. Transform us to know who we are in Christ. Get the glory out of us. We love You so much. In Jesus' name we pray, Amen.

# May 9

*Again the word of the Lord came unto me, saying,* (Jeremiah 24:4)

Today is a new day. Praise God we made it. With joy on our lips we turn to God to see what is on His heart each new day. Communing with God is first priority, a necessity that we cannot live without. Failure to inquire of the Lord only leads to self-hurt. God speaks to us on a daily basis. His word is full of instructions, wisdom, comfort and revelation for each day's journey. Our daily bread is readily available, all we have to do is reach out to receive it. Again, the word of the Lord comes to us, speaking directly to our point of need. Wherever God is taking us, He is sure to prepare us. God will instruct us in whatever He requires us to do. Never will we find ourselves lost without a cause. His loving nature ensures we are fully equipped for each day, along with power to endure the experience we'll face that day. "For in Christ all the fullness of the Deity lives in bodily form, and in Christ you have been brought to fullness. He is the head over every power and authority" (Colossians 2:9-10 NIV). Christ made it easy for us to have assurance in the truth of God's word. Everything He speaks manifests, and there is a specific word for each of us to enjoy on a daily basis. All we have to do is apply ourselves by opening the Bible, which nourishes our spirit. Building us up in our most holy faith, pushing us in the direction of the narrow path of righteousness.

Prayer: Lord, You are alive and living. Though the LORD be high, yet hath he respect unto the lowly (Psalm 138:6). You care for Your people and we are forever grateful. The sole purpose of creation was to showcase Your love. We exalt Your name. Thank You for loving us. Your word is powerful, and full of life. It has the ability to transform situations. Enlighten the eyes of our heart in order for us to know the hope in which You have called us. Lord, we will read Your word everyday and adhere to Your commands. We will delight ourselves in Your ways. You alone are worthy and we give You all honor and praise FOREVER! In Jesus' name we pray, Amen.

# May 10

*And it shall come to pass, that before they call, I will answer; and while they are yet speaking, I will hear.* (Isaiah 65:24)

God's says "Tell the righteous it will go well for them" (Isaiah 3:10). It is never the question whether or not God hears our voice in prayer. God hears everything, but based upon the position of our heart and God's timing we are guaranteed to receive His promises. God commands us to love Him with our heart, soul, strength, and mind. Doing this makes all things well with us. God is the creator of everything and has so graciously invited us close to Him to enjoy the fruits of His kingdom. When we determine in our hearts to love God by being obedient to His word, we tap into the many blessings He has stored up for us in heaven. Do we live our life with our hand out, only seeking God for His great benefits? No, we merely are reaping the benefits of being Kingdom heirs. It's God' decision to bless us. Based upon His loving nature, He has given us the tools to ensure we receive every spiritual blessing in heavenly places. God is just that good! He has crafted a system of principles, calling us into fellowship with Him so we experience true life with Him. In coming into His presence and basking in His glory, the very needs of our heart are met. As we delight ourselves in God, He is in turn granting the desires of our heart. Oftentimes we make it so hard when God is trying to get us to relax. He is simply saying, come to me; I promise you'll enjoy our time together. When we humble ourselves, giving God the very best of our entire being, He handles every aspect of our lives. Before we can even form our lips to pray, the answers come forth.

**God is waiting to hear from you.**

Prayer: Lord, You are Mighty. Jesus, give us a heart of obedience. "But seek ye first the kingdom of God, and his righteousness; and all these things shall be added unto you" (Matthew 6:33). Lord, You created all things that exist. You know every one of our needs, wants, and desires. All You are asking of us is to seek You. Lord, open our heart to Your wisdom so we can deny ourselves and come before Your throne of grace. All power and majesty belong to You. Lord, help Your people to know and understand Your love and grace, Your kindness that calls us each day. Lord, all You want is a generation who will listen to Your voice. Lord, here we are. Speak to us that we may hear You clearly. It is a delight to sit in Your presence and experience Your great nature. At all times we will bless You. In Jesus' name we pray. Amen

# May 11

*But first he must suffer many things, and be rejected of this generation.* (Luke 17:25)

The grace of God entails God pouring out His love to all mankind. Many people chose to reject God and the works of Jesus, not realizing that even breathing in and out is an act of the grace of God. They decide for whatever reason to live life according to their own standards, failing to grab hold of real life, which can only be found in Christ. Jesus came to earth for the sole purpose to show the love of God. His love stretches so far it cannot be contained. Jesus suffered many things on earth, including being rejected by His own people. The very people He helped to create. It is devastating for God to look down from heaven and see a generation of people who are choosing to reject Him. In hope of us repenting and turning our heart towards Him, He has given us chance after chance. Jesus suffered so we could have the opportunity to come to God and say, "please forgive me." God's loving nature is slow to anger because He waits for the day when we will surrender our life to Him. *"Don't you see how wonderfully kind, tolerant, and patient God is with you? Does this mean nothing to you? Can't you see that his kindness is intended to turn you from your sin?"* (Romans 2:4). The unbeliever is not the only one who suffers God. We cause God grief as well when we fail to love our neighbor or adhere to the voice of the Holy Spirit. There is nothing we can do to cause God to retract His love. What we have control over is how we embrace His love and how we show our appreciation to Him and those around us. Our daily duty is to walk in righteousness and respond to God's love with love.

**Don't let it be too late!**

Prayer: Lord, You are Marvelous. You are our praise. Everything about You is perfect. Search our hearts and show us the error of our ways. As the kingdom of God resides in us, teach us how to function as kingdom citizens. As Lord in our lives, instruct us in our daily task that Your name may be glorified throughout the entire earth. We embrace the love that You give us each day. You are always trying to show us how much You care about us. Thank You for calling us into Your kingdom. Thank You for another chance. Thank You for never leaving us. Thank You for always being our protection and wisdom. All that we are is because of You. In thought and deed, we will bless Your holy name. In Jesus' name we pray. Amen.

# May 12

*Wherefore, my beloved, as ye have always obeyed, not as in my presence only, but now much more in my absence, work out your own salvation with fear and trembling.* (Philippians 2:12)

Obedience to God tells Him we are trustworthy with the assigned task He has predestined for our lives. As His sons and daughters, we were all born with a specific assignment (purpose) that fits into the overall plan for creation (We all matter). In order for God to get glory out of His creation, we have to come into agreement with Him and adhere to the commands of His Spirit. God is constantly revealing Himself to us, in that He has also given us a free will to either obey or do things our own way. In doing things our own way, we are essentially showing God we are not responsible for the task He has assigned us to. As believers, our desire is to reverence God and show the world the goodness of being called into His kingdom. Our lives should display the work of Christ to the world; we shine as bright lights, drawing others to inquire about the goodness of our Father. As living testimonies, it is our pleasure to be likeminded with Christ, following the example He set forth through being obedient. It is an honor to acknowledge God as the head of our life. We are to arrange our life around God to ensure His plans can be manifested through us. Since we have been given the choice on how to conduct ourselves in life, we must make a conscious effort to always honor God in everything we do. Knowing that we will ALL give an account to Him on how we utilized the time He gave us. His grace and mercy can stand as a memorial, continually reminding us how fortunate we truly are.

Prayer: Lord, we love You. You are the most precious gift in all the earth. Lord, we are forever blessed to have You as our Father. Your love is on display every day. Thank You for always watching over us and leading us according to Your plan. Touch our hearts and open our minds to follow the example of Jesus at all times. Crucify our flesh, as we adhere to every one of Your commands. You show us the pathway of life. In Your presence is joy. Nothing can compare to Your greatness. By Your love we are able to know the purpose of our life. You created us to worship You and to enjoy open fellowship with You. We invite You in our hearts to reign supreme. Obedience will be our way of life. God, we honor, reverence, and fear Your holy name. In Jesus' name we pray, Amen.

# May 13

*That the God of our Lord Jesus Christ, the Father of glory, may give unto you the spirit of wisdom and revelation in the knowledge of him:* (Ephesians 1:17)

In God's exceeding kindness, He has given us access into His marvelous power. He wants the eyes of our heart to be open to the great riches we have obtained by believing in Him by way of accepting Jesus Christ. As children of God, we have inherited the glorious riches of Christ. We have obtained EVERY spiritual blessing in heavenly places. It is God's great pleasure for us to know and understand His immeasurable power. The same power that raised Jesus from the dead is available and working through us. It is God's desire that we no longer conform our mind to think according to limited constraints. With the Holy Spirit as our seal, we have access into the mysteries of God. God wants us to see beyond our physical limitations and grasp the depth of His wisdom. As we grow in Christ, our knowledge from day to day is expanded. We should not be the same as we were last week. As we spend time with God, we are constantly being exposed to His knowledge, teaching us how to operate and function according to His standards; which can only be known through learning how to trust in Christ and being led by His Spirit. The Spirit will expose us to God's predestined plans for us. Through God's loving nature, He is excited to reveal Himself to us. He doesn't want us to walk around in darkness, but in the light of His freedom. We are kingdom citizens; it must now become our nature to understand and operate in God's unlimited power.

Prayer: Lord, we give You glory. Exude Your loving grace upon this earth. We thank You for being so kind. You have given us the gift of life. We are now made alive by Your awesome power. Grant us spiritual wisdom to understand and walk in Your great power. We are kingdom citizens who have keys to Your kingdom. We will not accept the lies of the enemy which come to blind us to the access we have in Christ Jesus. Take the scales off of our eyes. Give us witty ideas and ways to prosper in this earth.

In all that we do, let Your name will be magnified. As the body of Christ, help us to walk in our divine purpose. As Your ambassadors, let our work be pleasing in Your sight. Bless You God for being holy. In Jesus' name we pray, Amen.

# May 14

*For this is the love of God, that we keep his commandments: and his commandments are not grievous.* (1 John 5:3)

God's ordinances are set in place to help us maximize our time on earth. God instructs us in our daily pursuits in order to show us how to live in accordance with His plans for our life. He sees the path ahead, and time with Him prepares us for everything we will encounter. His laws build our character to know how to deal with others. His wisdom shows us how to deal with our daily affairs. God has arranged creation to be able to rely on Him for all of our needs. In our own intellect we are not capable of journeying through life alone. Yes, there are many successful people according to the world's standards who are not a part of the body of Christ. Their level of success is measured by human standards. God measures success by whether or not we accept His Son in our life and follow His commands. We received the jewel of eternal life, which is far greater than anything we can achieve in this life. Following God's commands expresses our love for Him. We find delight in pleasing God, the lover of our soul. We have come to an understanding of God's love for us. Knowing His love called us into fellowship with Him, saving us from a world of darkness. Our eyes have been open to see His marvelous works and His wisdom is made readily available to us. Everything God does is for our benefit. His commands teach us we are victorious and have power to overcome every obstacle in life.

Prayer: Lord, You are marvelous. In this life we will never be able to express how great You are. With every ounce of our being we will exalt Your name. Thank You for saving our souls. Your love called us out of darkness into the kingdom of Your Son Jesus. We are grateful. We honor You for giving us commands on how to experience the best life You have prepared for us. We will be alert and have a sober mind and yield to the guidance from Your Spirit. Instruct us in Your plans. Open our heart to obey everything that You require of us. It is our desire to please You. Wisdom and knowledge are found in You. Pour it out to us in abundance. We will forever bless Your name. In Jesus' name we pray, Amen.

# May 15

*They kept also the feast of tabernacles, as it is written, and offered the daily burnt offerings by number, according to the custom, as the duty of every day required;* (Ezra 3:4)

In the Old Testament, the people of God had to abide by daily rituals of offerings for every occasion before God. Their offerings came before God as a sacrifice, and worship in time of fellowship with the Father. God instructed them in specific time-consuming sacraments in order to prepare their hearts for worship. God looked upon the people's offering and accepted it according to the condition of their heart. We learn in Genesis 4:4 how God respects offerings which come from the depth of our heart. The instructions on how to present daily offerings before God required special attention to the tedious task. In preparing the exact gift, before God allowed time for the people to prepare their hearts for worship. In preparation they were able to think about God's goodness and bring the best they had to offer. This requires continuous steadfast love. By the grace of God, we are now able to come before the throne of grace by way of Jesus Christ, who became our sacrificial offering once and for all. We stand before God, honoring Him with our whole heart and obedience to the guidance of the Holy Spirit. Although we don't have to physically prepare animals and other sacraments, we must ensure our heart is ready for worship. This means taking time to sit in God's presence, reading His word and really thinking about His goodness, repenting of every sin and giving God the best of us. It is not our daily task to come before the throne with our hand out, screaming "gimmie gimmie." We should enter in God's presence with a heart of gratitude, thanking God for being ruler in our lives. Our daily sacrifice to God is embracing who He is and loving Him for being so great!

**God is here!**

Prayer: Lord, You are the Captain of this world. You are in control. NO matter what may seem like is going on, You know the days ahead. We honor You for being God. We love You for saving us from this evil world. Lord, continue to keep us in Your loving presence. Open our heart to honor You for who You are and not for what You can do for us. Help us to enjoy the life You have given to us. We will always put You before us and look to You for guidance. We pray for Your wisdom to fill our hearts. In all that we do we will acknowledge You. You receive the glory, honor, and praise, forever. In Jesus' name we pray, Amen.

# May 16

*Now My soul is troubled and distressed, and what shall I say? Father, save Me from this hour [of trial and agony]? But it was for this very purpose that I have come to this hour [that I might undergo it].* (John 12:27)

Everyone is created with purpose. Jesus' purpose was to save the world. In His human form, He experienced pain and the agony of being rejected and having to be brutally hurt by the people He came to assist. In His despair, He made the choice to grab hold of God's unfailing hand and allow God's name to be glorified. He pressed His way through, knowing the end result would demonstrate the power/love of God. In the midst of trials, we too should ask ourselves whether or not we'll choose to complain or will we say, "Father glorify Your name"? We are a chosen race, a royal priesthood, sent to the earth as vessels of God. Some of the things we have to endure in life may not be pleasing, but will always have purpose. What God has designed inside of us is for us to exude His glory throughout the entire world. Anything that we suffer through in accordance with God's plan is a blessing. God uses us as living examples to prove to the world His excellent greatness. We have been given the awesome opportunity to make our Father proud. As we look adversity in the face and refuse to whine, but rather say "Lord have Your way," the good news is God predestined us for our purpose. He goes before us and prepares the way, and looks back to guide us through. He gets the glory out of everything we go through for the kingdom. We obtain satisfaction in fulfilling our purpose and God is pleased with our obedience.

Prayer: Father of all things, you are so worthy to be praised. Your name is exalted high above the earth. We bow down in total reverence. Lord, do in us the very thing You have intended even before the foundation of the earth. As we look to Jesus who came to the earth and did only what You instructed Him to do, we will follow His example of obedience and perseverance. Get the glory out of everything we do. Whatever Your plan is for us we say, "yes," with a willing heart. God, You know the end from the beginning. Open our hearts to follow Your lead. Pour out Your Spirit to continue to lead us on the path of righteousness. God, You are faithful, loving and kind. We magnify Your name. Father, we love You. In Jesus' name we pray, Amen.

# May 17

*And ye shall know the truth, and the truth shall make you free.* (John 8:32)

Jesus is the truth. Every word from Heaven bears witness of the goodness of God. Jesus came to the earth so we might be able to look into the mystery and destiny that God created us to operate under. As our living example, He took on human form to show us the power and authority we possess as kingdom citizens. Jesus is the Word of God, which became flesh. All of His attributes teach us how we are to function as Children of God. If we continue seeking God and adhering to His word, we will enjoy the freedom that has been given to us. Anything done contrary to God's divine purpose holds us in bondage. We are under the authority of the Most High. Like Jesus, whatever God speaks should be the echo we send forth in the earth. Our freedom in Christ allows us to dream beyond our wildest imagination. It opens the door to opportunities where we are able to exude the beauty of God's holiness. It abolishes fear and doubt, and we are able to function in our fullest capacity. The truth of God is all around us, but we must know it for ourselves. God's word must be embedded in our heart. We must yearn for it and seek after it as constant food that nourishes our spirit. Acknowledging the truth of God establishes a certainty of who God is, and acceptance of His Word as the truth which has set us free.

Prayer: Lord, we honor you. Thank You for setting us free. Some of us are unaware of the bondage we are in when as we fail to adhere to Your voice. Help us to hear only what You say in heaven. We will stand on Your truth. We know for sure that You are the living God. Your ways are perfect. Open the eyes of our heart. We invite You in to rule in us. We will abide with You forever. We find our perfect rest in Your arms. Shine Your light on this world; pour out Your wisdom in abundance. All glory belongs to You. In Jesus' name we pray. Amen.

# May 18

*This day the Lord will deliver you into my hand, and I will smite you and cut off your head. And I will give the corpses of the army of the Philistines this day to the birds of the air and the wild beasts of the earth, that all the earth may know that there is a God in Israel.* (1 Samuel 17:46)

God has given us power and authority to trample over everything in the earth. There is nothing stronger than the strength God has placed within us. David had a personal relationship with God. He believed God was all-powerful. His mind was set on who God said He was, and what God said we, as His children, possess in this earth. Our mindset has to be in alignment with what God says about us. God says we are the head and not the tail, and that NO HARM shall overtake us. When we come into battle with things in our life, we have to call it according to our position as kingdom heirs. This strong, overpowering Philistine Goliath was intimidating. He chastised the people in Israel for over 40 days, spouting insults, telling them their worth and what they could and could not do. David refuted the tactics of fear Goliath tried to control the Israelites with by standing on the truth of God. David disregarded the fact that he was literally fighting against a giant who had the ability to destroy him. Instead, he utilized His faith and stood on who he was in Christ and surrendered the battle into the Lord's hands. God only needs willing vessels to believe He is the Lord of hosts and He will fight every battle for us. This day the Lord says He will deliver us from ALL snares of the enemy so His name will be glorified.

Prayer: God, You are All-Powerful. You are the great "I Am." Thank You for the power You have given us to trample over every serpent. Nothing can come against us. You are our shield and buckler. We find rest in Your arms. Lord, build us up in our most holy faith to stand strong on Your word. On a daily basis, we are attacked by various distractions that try to plague our mind. Shield us from the plans of the enemy. Give us a heart to discern between good and evil. Shut the door of destruction. Pull on our heart to walk after You. You lead us only into great and marvelous things. Transform us by the renewing of our minds. We cast down every imagination that tries to exalt itself against You. We will stand on Your word and only believe what You say as truth. Lord, we love You with everything that is within us. In Jesus' name we pray, Amen.

# May 19

*The Lord taketh pleasure in them that fear him, in those that hope in his mercy.* (Psalm 147:11)

God is pleased when we are able to trust Him as our first resort. It delights our Father when He is able to see us standing upon His Word and executing His statutes in our daily living. God has given us the blueprint of life. Laying the foundation of our hope in Him, as we allow the Holy Spirit to guide us we will encounter unknown territory. With God on our side we are able to stand on His word and press forward, allowing our faith in Him to be our strength. On a daily basis, God is trying to develop our trust in Him. He will allow us to go through certain situations to see if we will lean on Him or try to take matters into our own hands. Yielding to God produces pleasure in His sight. He is able to entrust us with the plans of the earth. Our life goes beyond our personal needs as we are ambassadors for Christ. Our lives are a daily display of the glory of God. Living in fear of the Lord teaches us to only seek after the things that are on the heart of God. Our determination to rely on God's word, His power, and His timing showcase our faith in Him. We are depending upon a God who is compassionate and gracious. Our hope is securely anchored in His unfailing love. All of this sounds nice, but if we don't believe it in our hearts and actually live it out, it is pointless. God takes pleasure in us putting our faith into action, as we are sheltered in His mercy.

**God is all.**

Prayer: God, with our hearts lifted up to You we sing praises to Your throne. You alone are God. You are worthy. You created the heavens and the earth. All things belong to You. Your name is to be exalted in all the earth. As Your willing vessels we will magnify Your name. Take pleasure in us, as we fear You. Your law will be found in our hearts and displayed in our actions. Search each of us individually and cast out all manner of sin. Anything that isn't like You we ask for forgiveness in Jesus' name. We will hope in Your mercy and lovingkindness, which You so graciously give us.

Goodness and mercy shall follow us all the days of our life. Thank You for always thinking about us Your love has no bounds. Your mercies are new every morning. Hallelujah! In Jesus' name we pray, Amen.

# May 20

*My soul is also sore vexed: but thou, O Lord, how long?* (Psalm 6:3)

God hears every cry from our heart. In Christ, we are taught to call upon the name of the Lord at all times. Bringing our supplications before the throne of grace is usually the easy part. It is while waiting on God's response where we find that our hearts become heavy and weary. We don't enjoy waiting too long for anything in life. When we feel God is not moving at the speed of lightning we become discouraged, not knowing that everything God is going to do is already done. Everything we have need of is already in position, just waiting to catch up. It brings comfort to our soul to know for a fact that God hears every prayer. He sees all that we go through and has compassion on our situations. In the midst of waiting on time to catch up with the promises of God, we shall fill our time with praise; praising God according to His excellent goodness. Praise takes our mind off of our needs in order to glorify God, who is always working on our behalf. Our exaltation develops our patience and teaches us to be content in every situation. Thinking about God's grace and mercy will encourage us and help us endure during times of difficulty. God's hand is not overwhelmed where He isn't able to perform the very deeds we request. So, in our time of waiting we will bless the name of God. He hears and will deliver in His perfect timing. So, instead of asking God How long, we shall declare how long will we praise You Lord? The answer is forever, no matter what life brings our way.

**God always answers every prayer!**

Prayer: Father, You are so great. Lord, there is nothing we shall desire in this earth that You have not already prepared for Your people. Open our hearts to receive from heaven today. In our time of waiting let our hearts be filled with Your stature. Fill us until we overflow with Your glory. You are the very thing we need. God, with one word, "Jesus," all things change. God, we thank You that every one of Your promises are "Yea and Amen." It is well with the kingdom of God. You are greatly to be praised. In Jesus' name we pray, Amen.

# May 21

*Giving no offence in any thing, that the ministry be not blamed: 4 But in all things approving ourselves as the ministers of God, in much patience, in afflictions, in necessities, in distresses,* (2 Corinthians 6:3-4)

All of our actions should be carefully thought out and pleasing in God's sight. Does this mean we'll be perfect? The answer is absolutely not. It is our conscious desire to follow after Christ, who will shine His perfection through us. As humans, we will often make mistakes and find ourselves at the feet of Jesus. This is no excuse to come down hard on ourselves, it only showcases that without God's Holy Spirit guiding us, we will fall short every time. God has trusted us with the ability to make a conscious effort to seek Him in all things. Since we have a free will, as believers it is God's hope that we live our lives as obedient servants. Outsiders are constantly looking at how we function. They look for reasons to validate claims of Christians being hypocrites. Or they look for a reason to join the faith. Whichever the case, we have been given the opportunity to use our lives as ministers, "servants" unto God. As His servants, we should utilize every opportunity to allow Christ to shine through our actions. All that we do should bring glory to His name. One practice I have implemented in my life is to consider Jesus as physically being the room with me at all times. Would He be pleased with my behavior is the question I pose to myself. During those times when we don't get it right, we must immediately repent and allow God to help us change our behavior. Our greatest mission in life is to spread the gospel. Our testimony must be authentic and not cause people to turn away.

Prayer: Lord, we love everything about You. Your grace meets us new each morning. As Your servants, we will not let Your seed fall on unfertile ground. We will go and make disciples. Correct every area of our lives where we are not pleasing You. Continue to teach us all of Your principles. Build us up in our most holy faith. Lead us by Your Holy Spirit so we know which way to go. As we devote time with You, pour out Your wisdom. Help us to be slow to speak, quick to listen, and slow to anger. Let us do all things in love, loving our neighbors as ourselves. Shine Your light through us. Use us to manifest Your plans in the earth. You alone are holy. In Jesus' name we pray, Amen.

## May 22

*For he performeth the thing that is appointed for me: and many such things are with him.* (Job 23:14)

Everything in life will not make sense. God's infinite wisdom far exceeds our intellectual capacity. We are not in a position to question God's judgment. His ways are higher than our ways; everything He does has divine order. As humans, this is a hard reality to digest. Embracing God's love helps us during times when we don't understand all that is taking place around us. God has promised us many things, most importantly that our home is in heaven. As His ambassadors in the earth, we have to accept the times of great joy along with times of sorrow; knowing that everything works out for our good. Today's trials can very well be the power we need for tomorrow. God's plans are perfect and pleasing. When we find ourselves in unfavorable situations we have to stand firm in our faith, trusting God knows what He is doing. By nature, when things feel uncomfortable we tend to react according to our emotions. As God's royal priesthood, we have surrendered our will for His, and whatever plans He has for us we must yield to. God has called us for a specific purpose; we can trust that what He is doing has been carefully arranged and predestined. We can go into every situation, allowing our faith to be our comfort. We will not look at the problems but look to God, who has appointed each of us for such a time as this.

Prayer: God, You are the great "I Am." All things are under Your control. Open our hearts to hide Your Word within us. You know every plan You have for us. We surrender our will for Yours. Help us to live by faith and not by sight. Expand our knowledge; bestow Your wisdom on us like never before. Thank You for opening the gate into Your holy kingdom. In Your presence we find fullness of joy, and at your right hand are pleasures forevermore. All praise belongs to You. In Jesus' name we pray, Amen.

# May 23

*Now the just shall live by faith: but if any man draw back, my soul shall have no pleasure in him.* (Hebrews 10:38)

God is moved by one thing, and that's faith. Faith to believe God will do according to His will, whatever we ask for in Jesus' name. When we walk in the Spirit, we will only be led to desire the things God has already purposed for us to have. If you are trusting God for something, be encouraged you WILL receive it at the appointed time. It gives God great pleasure to give His children great things (Luke 12:32). Every aspect of our life has already been calculated and accounted for. There will never be a time where God is caught by surprise. Where we often waiver in our faith is in the area of consistency and persistency. Persistence is the ability to accomplish a task regardless of any opposition that gets in the way. In this life, we will have to preserve our way through adverse circumstances. We have to determine in our heart and mind that no matter what it looks like, we will get to the finish line. Consistency requires that with each new dynamic of life we utilize our faith. Faith is not something we take on and off, or put on the shelf until the next time we need it. Our faith must be in action at all times. As we grow in Christ, our faith will develop and evolve. Faith is the driving force for everything we set out to accomplish. **"And everything that does not come from faith is sin" (Romans 14:23).** When we overcome one challenge, we usually get comfortable and take our garment off, failing to realize we need it at all times. Faith has to always be at work if we want to achieve the greater works Jesus has ordained for us to do in this earth.

**Verily, verily, I say unto you, He that believeth on me, the works that I do shall he do also; and greater works than these shall he do; because I go unto my Father. (John 14:12)**

Prayer: God, You are so merciful. Your glory fills our hearts as we honor You. NOW faith is the substance of things hoped for and the evidence of things not seen. Hallelujah!!!! God, we will live by faith and not by sight. We will run this race with endurance. Help us to see what You see in heaven. The plans You have ordained before the beginning of time, You orchestrated everyday before any of them came into play. Lord, take our hand and lead us. You are a lamp unto our feet and a light unto our path. Remove the scales from our eyes. Soften our hearts. Let us only speak what we hear from heaven. Command Your blessings to overtake us. We remain confident that we will see Your goodness in the land of the living. We give You glory. In Jesus' name we pray, Amen.

# May 24

*But thou, when thou fastest, anoint thine head, and wash thy face;* (Matthew 6:17)

Fasting is a time of denying our flesh in order to seek God. This time of seclusion is an opportunity for God to unveil His power through us. Yes, we can receive God's power by being in right standing with Him, but there is something unique about making a special sacrifice to seek God's face. As we deny our own pleasures, we give God the opportunity to fill us with His power. It is a statement to God that we are willing to forgo things we enjoy to hear from heaven. Fasting should be incorporated in our continuous relationship with God. Jesus teaches us certain things will not take place in life without prayer and fasting (Matthew 17:21). God is trying to get us to expand our spiritual capacity. Whatever we decide to give up for a set period of time to devote ourselves to God in prayer and studying His Word equips us for our kingdom purpose. During this time, we are able to hear God more clearly. Our spiritual ears are more in tune, and God's Word can reside in the open space we now have as a result of this solitude. Our purpose for fasting is to hear directly from God concerning His will for our life. God is trying to get us to go beyond fasting only when we need something from Him in our personal lives, because He promises to supply all of our needs. We must incorporate a balance throughout our time of fasting. This can be done by going into our time of isolation, motivated to be led by the Spirit and allowing God's power to work through us. The goal of fasting is to expose God's glory!!!!!!

Prayer: God, we give You glory and praise. Teach us the true meaning of fasting and prayer. Let our time of devotion be meaningful. Search our hearts and prepare us for worship. Let our praise meet You at all times. Thanksgiving will be our universal language. Silence any influence that will hinder us from our time with You. Let Your Spirit guide us and speak to us when we need to begin a fast. Give us strength to endure as we receive Your glory from heaven. Time alone with You is unexplainable. It is an absolute joy to indulge in Your holy presence. Thank You for inviting us in to experience You. You are our expectation and we are fully satisfied. In Jesus' name we pray, Amen.

# May 25

*The Lord would speak to Moses face to face, as one speaks to a friend. Then Moses would return to the camp, but his young aide Joshua son of Nun did not leave the tent.* (Exodus 33:11)

Shame on us, if we only seek God when we need Him. Not only does it defeat the purpose God designed us to experience, but we miss out on precious time with Him. Time with God is impossible to fabricate. Our attitudes must be right when we come before Him. God knows the difference and searches each of us inwardly and deals with us accordingly. His desire for us is to get to a place where our greatest delight is the time we spend with Him. As we enjoy the presence of our friends, times of laughter and memories fill us with joy. These feelings fail to compare to time spent with God. Our greatest feelings of excitement will never compensate for time with God. He is our JOY; time with Him is a pleasant delight. It stimulates our spirit, uncovering the purpose He created each of us for. Wisdom and all power are found in Him. The very plan for our life, answers to questions, peace, comfort, joy and just plain ole love are found in Him. The love of God is pure and satisfies all of our needs. We should be persistent in ensuring we spend time with God. Time has no limit in God's presence. As we relinquish our heart, allowing Him to orchestrate the course of our meeting time, we leave empty of ourselves and full of His splendor. Some days we'll have to act like Joshua and stand in His presence uninterrupted by time and immerse ourselves in His glory. What a time it will be to forget about all the matters of the world to marinate in God's presence!

**There is Great Joy in the Face of God!**

Prayer: Father, thank You for being Holy, righteous, and altogether worthy. You alone deserve all honors. We exalt Your name on high. There is no one like You. You do exceeding abundantly above all that we can ask or think. You are the great "I AM". In Your presence is where we long to be. If You fail to lead us, we will be led astray. Send Your angels before us and guide us on the path of righteousness. As we set aside time daily to commune with You, help us to take our mind off of outside influences. Allow our worship time with You to be authentic. Blow our mind like never before. Do a new thing in us. We come with a great expectation. Let Your plans be established in us. We long to please You. Lord, have Your way in this earth. We give you glory now and forever. In Jesus' name we pray, Amen!

# May 26

*Great peace have they which love thy law; and nothing shall offend them.* (Psalm 119:165)

God's law gives great understanding. Jam-packed with wisdom to order each of our steps in life. When we allow God's Word to saturate our heart, His peace embodies our entire spirit. We find joy through daily devotion, where we grow and expound upon His precepts. This not only satisfies our inner man but also helps us make decisions, ultimately enriching our overall well-being. Every ounce of our existence is sheltered by God's unfailing love. We become anchored in His statutes and are not moved by opposition. Loving everything about God and His word keeps us longing for more of Him. God is constantly pouring His wisdom into the lives of those who love Him. We find refuge in His presence and become regenerated through His power allowing His attributes to be displayed. Everything pertaining to God's statutes instills His wisdom within us. Abiding in the peace of God prepares us for the day of adversity. When the challenger comes we will be girded in God's peace, allowing nothing to cause us to stumble or get off track.

Prayer: God, we give You glory. All of Your precepts were established to give us life. We exalt Your name on High. We long for Your presence. Teach us good judgment and knowledge: for we have believed your commandments (Psalm 119:66). We will hide Your Word in our heart so we will not sin against You. Your word is established and will live on forever. Our hope is set in You. We will only seek after the things that You love. Wherever Your glory is, that is where we long to be. Saturate our hearts with Your presence. Order our steps in Your word: and let not iniquity have dominion over us (Psalm 119:133). You are Alpha and Omega, it all belongs to You. In Jesus' name we pray, Amen.

# May 27

*Because of Christ and our faith in him, we can now come boldly and confidently into God's presence.* (Ephesians 3:12)

Jesus came proclaiming good news. His message came forth to ignite the fire inside of us to come with confidence to receive the promises of God. God has prepared so many great things for us since the beginning of time. Through Christ Jesus, we now have access to come boldly before the throne of grace to receive the unsearchable riches of God. These riches go far beyond material possessions. These riches encompass God's power being poured into us to transform the earth to walk in accordance to the purpose God has ordained. As we come before the throne of grace, we are confident to receive the plans God has for each of His children. In God's presence, we experience open fellowship with our Creator to know and understand God's intention for all mankind. The very things we believe God for come to fruition as His Spirit leads us. This open gate into God's holy presence is showcased to the world. As God's elite nation, we have power and authority to reveal God's strength through our lives. God is calling us to turn toward Him and see the promise He has specifically prepared for us to accomplish as individuals and execute them with boldness. We have obtained access into the mystery of heaven, into the very thoughts and desires of God; where He willingly pours out His plan into the lives of those who diligently seek Him. We were not created to live in fear, but to come with boldness and confidence, grabbing hold of everything God has stored up for us in heaven.

**Heaven is Real!**

Prayer: Lord, You are good and Your mercy endures forever. There is no one like You. Lord, We thank You for always thinking about us. You have carefully orchestrated everything strategically for us to come into Your presence and receive the very gift of life. We have open access to Your awesome splendor. Nothing can compare to You. LORD, continue to lead us and guide us on the narrow path of righteousness. We shall be planted like a tree by the rivers of water, that bringeth forth our fruit in our season. Our leaves will not wither; and whatsoever we do SHALL prosper (Psalm 1:3). We exalt Your holy name. We love you Daddy. In Jesus' name we pray, Amen.

# May 28

*Neither shall they say, Lo here! or, lo there! for, behold, the kingdom of God is within you.* (Luke 17:21)

God has invited us into His kingdom as His children to reign and rule by His authority. It is an invisible society of God's elect who have accepted His Lordship by allowing His attributes to flow through them. God's kingdom resides on the inside of us. It is not a place that we can go to visit. It's a covenant relationship with God where we have obtained access to every spiritual blessing in heavenly places. We exercise our kingship when we allow the Holy Spirit to guide us, keeping us in right relationship with God. "For the kingdom of God is not meat and drink; but righteousness, and peace, and joy in the Holy Ghost" (Romans 14:17). The kingdom of God is us tapping into the spirit God has placed within us to obey His commands and fulfill His will in the earth. As we walk in God we are exercising our kingdom authority in the earth. Being led and empowered by God exercises our kingdom ability. The kingdom of God is hidden from the ungodly. We have obtained access through Jesus Christ. God has given us keys to perform His divine miracles in the earth. The kingdom of God is within us to accomplish EVERY plan God has put into place. We are citizens of the most holy place. We are to reign, rule and produce only what is being fed to us from God above.

Prayer: Lord, You are good and your mercy endures forever. Lord, You are the King of our hearts. Thank You for inviting us into Your kingdom. You have all power. Open our eyes to the tools we have in order to reign as kingdom citizens in this earth. You have given us power and authority to accomplish Your plans. As Jesus was obedient, help us to follow in His footsteps as He said, we would do greater works. Lord, only by Your strength. Help us not to be afraid, but to be bold for the kingdom of God. To walk in the divine authority You have given us. We pray the kingdom of God over our families, churches, schools, children, friends, against violence and all manner of evil. Lord, send Your power to this earth and establish Your kingdom in Your willing/obedient vessels. When we hear Your voice we will say, "Here, I am, send me." All power belongs to You. In Jesus' name we pray, Amen.

# May 29

*Let your gentleness be evident to all. The Lord is near.* (Philippians 4:5)

God has instructed us to rejoice always in Him. He is never far from us. When we search for Him He will be found. Most of our anxiety comes from the unknown. We are uncertain how different situations will turn out and result to becoming over-anxious. Or we allow anger and frustration to build up within us, causing our countenance to change. Resting ourselves in the Lord calms our spirit as we follow His instructions, NOT to be ANXIOUS or to WORRY about anything. But in ALL things, bring them before God in prayer and supplication with THANKSGIVING. In return for us laying the cares of our heart at the feet of our Father, He gives us peace. If we come, believing God is able to handle all the cares of our heart, we will experience the peace that surpasses all understanding. This type of calmness can only be found in God. Experiencing hardships in life are inevitable. When we take on the burden of trying to calm the storms of life, it takes a toll on our inner man. Our heart becomes weighed down and pressure begins to build up. If we allow God's power and strength to work in our lives it will relieve all of the pressure. Failing to release the negative energy festering within us will result in the overspill of ungodly character. When we are at peace we are able to share the peace of God with others through our gentle spirit. Letting the world know Christ is near; He is always working in the lives of those who diligently seek Him.

Prayer: God, You are KING of kings. Your power is glorious! ***You formed the entire universe with Your Words***. All things belong to You. Lord, You see each of us individually and know the desires of our heart. Thank You for considering us today. You have all power and majesty in Your hand. We believe You will do a mighty work in the lives of Your people. You reign in all the earth. Everything is under Your command. Command Your angels to stand post in our lives working on our behalf. Thank You for opening the windows of heaven to always produce harvest in our life. Our life is lived only for You. Have Your way. We will forever exalt You. In Jesus' name we pray, Amen.

# May 30

*Being then made free from sin, ye became the servants of righteousness.* (Romans 6:18)

The Word of God teaches us that we are slaves to whatever we obey. When we were living in the world we obeyed and executed the commands given by our flesh. Now, as saints of God we are free from sin. Christ has given us the grace to denounce the power of sin in our lives and to adhere to the influence of the Holy Spirit. Since we are now in Christ, we are instructed to use every ounce of our being in following the commands of God. When we were living in sin, we were bearing fruit to death. Now our works lead us to God and eternal life. God shined light on sin so we could see the separation it causes between Him and us. His love is so astounding that He couldn't fathom us being out of fellowship with Him. Our commitment to obeying His commands opens the door to great opportunities. Whatever we give our heart to is the very thing we will reap. As kingdom citizens, we are assured that our stance in God will only yield works that glorify His name and produce righteousness within us. The same energy we used to obey the lust of our flesh is the same level of extreme we must exercise in obeying the voice of God. While we were in the world we were bold in our mess. Now we are instructed to use all of our energy to command our bodily members to obey the voice of God.

**Watch God blow your mind!**

Prayer: Lord, we bless Your holy name. You are great and do all things well. Lord, in our sin You were thinking about us and saw us in our fullest potential. Thank You for Your wisdom. You understand every aspect of our life and desire for us to come into the knowledge of Your Son, Jesus Christ. Shine Your light on our lives. Show us whatever isn't pleasing in Your sight. Help us to have understanding of Your Word to know how to function in life. Teach us Your ways. We submit to You. We commitment ourselves as Your holy servants. To hear and obey Your voice. God, we are forever grateful. In Jesus' name we pray, Amen.

# May 31

*But the land that you are going over to possess is a land of hills and valleys, which drinks water by the rain from heaven, a land that the Lord your God cares for. The eyes of the Lord your God are always upon it, from the beginning of the year to the end of the year.* (Deuteronomy 11:11-12)

God has given each of us authority in the earth. We have the ability to govern the natural resources we need to be a well-established body of believers in the earth. Through the power of God we are able to possess great things. Christ must be the cornerstone and foundation of our homes, careers, and ministry. Yielding all things to God establishes the many plans He has for us. God will only guide us on the narrow path of righteousness. His hand of protection will cover us in all of our endeavors and cause the work of our hands to flourish. The desires of our heart will manifest, as they are inspired from Heaven. God's favor will shine down upon His land and His people producing everything that we need. God will ensure our every need is supplied because our trust is in Him. We have denied ourselves and made a choice to follow after the Almighty God. From His throne flows the river of life. In the midst of the stream we receive our nutrients and ability to continually reproduce. From the beginning of the year until the end of the year God is watching over the land of His people. He takes delight in pouring out His blessings. All who come to Him and drink from the river of heaven are fully satisfied.

Prayer: God, You are a marvelous wonder. The true and living God. What an honor it is to know how much You care about us. You know us down to every single detail. Your grace secures our life. We are made whole in You. Your eyes watch over us and You are in the midst of all that concerns us. Thank You for always covering us and supplying all of our needs. We will continue to walk in Your statutes and serve You with our entire being. You are Holy and we bless Your name, in Jesus' name we pray, Amen.

## June1

*And he believed in the Lord; and he counted it to him for righteousness.* (Genesis 15:6)

God speaks to each of us individually. Our purpose in life is derived from God's perfect perspective. As God's creation, we all have a place in God's plan. Abraham heard the voice of the Lord and believed everything God promised. Abraham's faith aligned with God's covenant. Although Abraham didn't see the full extent of the promise in the natural, he based His faith on God's Word. He believed if God spoke it, it would manifest at the appointed time. God's Word is the fuel that ignites our faith. Faith always comes before the manifestation. We have to believe what God is saying to us directly. Daily communication with God prepares us to receive our directives for our life. God gives strategic plans concerning our individual desires, the needs of our family, our community, and how we are to impact this world. We are each a piece of the magnificent puzzle God has uniquely put together. We each add value to the earth. God is trying to get us to hear His voice so we can go out and be fruitful. As God speaks to us, we are able to obey in confidence and see God's plans come to fruition. God has specific goals set for each of us. Adhering to God's voice develops our relationship with Him, it also rewards us as we contributes great value to our society. God is speaking, what will your response be?

Prayer: Father God, You are holy. There is none like You in all the earth. Thank You for creating us in Your image to reign and have authority in the earth. Our ears are open to Your voice. Speak to us and we will respond in faith. We know Your Word is true and will not return to You void. It is our desire to be in right standing with You. Help us to remove all distractions. We will take time out to fast and pray to hear what You are saying in heaven. We come seeking You. You know the thoughts and plans You have for us. Unite our hearts with Yours. Give us a willing heart to trust and rely on You alone. In all things we give thanks. In Jesus' name we pray, Amen.

# June 2

*And when the queen of Sheba heard of the fame of Solomon concerning the name of the Lord, she came to prove him with hard questions.* (1 Kings 10:1)

The Queen of Sheba heard about Solomon's fame concerning THE NAME OF THE LORD, and it enticed a curiosity within her. She set out to see for herself the virtue everyone claimed Solomon possessed. This effect of God's anointing in the earth should still ring out in the ears of people all around us. When people consider you and me, are they able to see God doing mighty things in our lives? Fame and recognition is not the position God will call all of us to. Wherever God has placed us is our platform to glorify His name. His power working through us should spark curiosity in others to inquire about God. People should be able to glorify God as a result of our life. The Queen of Sheba came because she heard about a God who, through the life of King Solomon, was doing great and mighty things. This report resonated so deeply within her spirit that she gathered a group of her assistants, prepared gifts and went to see what the Lord was doing. When people see us do they see God? Or are we so conformed that people are unable to set us apart as saints of God. These are real questions we must ask ourselves. Our lives must be lived in such a way that it inspires others to want to know about the God we serve. We are walking epistles, always on display in order to expand the Kingdom of God.

Prayer: Our Father which are in heaven, Hallowed be thy name. Lord, You are magnificent and holy. Let Your work be done through us. Let everything we do bring glory to Your name. We die to ourselves. Nothing apart from You will ever last. Pour out Your wisdom upon us. Transform our thinking, by renewing our mind. Help us to be willing to live a spirit filled life. Let our life draw all men unto You. Our actions and entire lifestyle will be a testimony of Your greatness. Correct us in every area where we have failed to submit to Your commands. We will honor and praise You forever. In Jesus' name we pray, Amen.

# June 3

*He also that is slothful in his work is brother to him that is a great waster.* (Proverbs 18:9)

God has ordained every day for us to accomplish His will in the allotted time He has given. Many things get in the way of us utilizing our time wisely. Often, we are torn between our personal desires and God's plan for our lives. We set out to be useful with our time, only to end the day feeling overwhelmed by not accomplishing every task on our list. When we place God before us, He will instruct us on how to utilize our time. We will hear the still small voice calling us back into focus when our mind and actions drift. His plans inspire the desires of our heart; the will of God will become the very thing we long to accomplish. Our own stagnant behavior throws us off course sometimes. Too many distractions can cause us to become lazy. In God, we must esteem to do only the things God has called us to. Being lazy has no place in the kingdom of heaven. Working according to God's plan will stimulate our inner man to desire to be useful with our time. God created us and knows the gifts placed inside of us. Staying close to Him will open our eyes and help us to work diligently. Setting our eyes on Jesus will guide and instruct us in our daily pursuits. God teaches us not to succumb to idle habits. He declares a lazy (slothful) person is like brother to a waster. A lazy person is one who wastes the precious time God has given us in order to fulfill our own desires or when we make the choice to do nothing by ignoring our obligations. Forgetting to seek God's hand at all times will lead to the road of unfulfilled purpose. God is knocking on the door of our heart in order to show us the right path for our life. His guidance places us in a position to accomplish great things. As we submit our ways to the Lord, He will establish the work of our hands. Everything done in God is twofold; He is glorified and we grow closer to Him, expanding our joy in Him. Staying close to God opens our heart to wisdom and gives us the power to utilize our time wisely each day. Our obedience also blesses those around us. Imagine if someone's victory was determined upon us walking in our purpose. Could we really live with the fact that we failed someone else because we refused to use our time wisely.

**Earth Needs You!**

Prayer: Lord, You are the Great "I AM." You are the very air we breathe. Nothing is impossible with You. Thank You for considering us as Your own. We will forever praise You. God open our eyes to come before You, seeking You first, Your kingdom and Your righteousness. We will have no thought for our lives. We know You are in control. You set all things in motion. God, Your wisdom fills the earth. Help us in our daily pursuits to have a kingdom focus. We come to receive our daily bread. Open doors for us to glorify Your name. Laziness does not reside in us. Help us to be useful of our time and energy and to work towards all things that produce good fruit in our lives. Your name will forever be praised. In Jesus' name we pray. Amen.

# June 4

*Glory in his holy name; let the hearts of those who seek the LORD rejoice!* (Psalm 105:3)

God alone is marvelous. When we think about His nature our hearts can't help but to rejoice. His wonders are innumerable; His hand is always among His people. His words go forth to perform miracles in our life and to build us up as His loving disciples. Everything about Him is centered on His loving nature. Our hearts are esteemed to magnify His holy name. At the remembrance of His holy works our spirits shall rejoice. We are reminiscent of how God saved us. We are forever blessed by His constant presence in our life. His name is to always be exalted. Our hearts remain attentive to His presence by speaking of His glory. His deeds should always be found leaving our lips. We can shout to the world how great our God is. Our song of praise shall join in with the angels each day as we give thanks to our Father. We are glad to serve God and worship Him in Spirit and truth. His love has never failed us. His guidance always leads us, and our confidence in Him benefits all who accept Him. Our hearts rejoice in knowing God is "All Sufficient." He has thought about everything and orchestrated all things to fit into His perfect plan. Blessed are those who hunger and thirst for righteousness, for they will be filled (Matthew 5:6 NIV).

Prayer: Jehovah, Great God, Ruler of all things, we exalt Your name this day and forevermore. There are no words to express Your excellence. With every ounce of our being we will give You glory. Our life will be living examples of the great impact You have made in our lives. As our Father we are thrilled to serve at Your feet. Our hearts rejoice as we seek You continuously. You are always before us. We devote our lives to loving You. God, you are the greatest gift. We honor, praise, and exalt Your holy name. Thank You for being our King. In Jesus' name we pray, Amen.

# June 5

*But without faith it is impossible to please him: for he that cometh to God must believe that he is, and that he is a rewarder of them that diligently seek him.* (Hebrews 11:6)

Faith, the assurance of things you believe God for, although You cannot see them. It's our ability to trust in the power of God to do all things. By faith we understand NOTHING is impossible for God. In our own strength we cannot accomplish the promises of God. Exercising our faith is the only thing that moves God to work in our life. We must first believe that God is. We believe that God is everything. God is whatever we need Him to be in our life in every moment. He has placed before us the keys to the kingdom of heaven; we have open access to every spiritual blessing based on our confidence in Him. Our ability to trust God keeps our mind at ease. We are certain of the things He has promised us and are able to structure our lives in accordance to His word. As we accept God's word as truth in our life, we are able to obtain everything God has prepared for us. If God were to show us all of His plans for us we would be blown away. Our faith keeps us at thc feet of Jesus, yearning for more of Him. We desire the very things He desires for our life. Manifestation of God's promises inspires us to seek Him and develops our faith. God works in our life based upon our confidence in Him. If we fail to believe in His promises we will not receive the blessings from heaven. Not only does our faith draw us near to God, it releases rewards in our life. God will not force His blessings on us, we have to believe and receive what is already available for us.

**Will you believe God today?**

Prayer: Father, we adore You. In faith we rise every day to bless Your holy name. You are the bright and morning star. Your love embodies the earth. It is full of Your goodness. God, without faith we fail to please You. Thank You for teaching us the way to Your heart. We believe, and have confidence in everything that pertains to You. Help us to exercise our faith in all that we do. Now faith is assurance of things hoped for, and the evidence of things not seen. Lord, give us Your eyes to see Your splendor always before us. Unlock the door to our heart so we can walk in alignment with Your unfailing Word. As our Shepherd, we will follow You. We believe only what You say. With all praise we say, thank You. In Jesus' name we pray, Amen.

# June 6

*And he cried and said, Father Abraham, have mercy on me, and send Lazarus, that he may dip the tip of his finger in water, and cool my tongue; for I am tormented in this flame.* (Luke 16:24)

The rich man cried out after waking up in hell. He raised his eyes to see Lazarus, who was humble in life and had a relationship with Christ, in the presence of Abraham. During the rich man's life he put more emphasis in temporary things than on His relationship with Christ. The Bible does not go in depth to explain what his exact thoughts were concerning Christ. It only shows us that during the rich man's life, he wasted his time being focused on material things. "There once was a rich man, expensively dressed in the latest fashions, wasting his days in conspicuous consumption" (Luke 16:19). The poor man lived a humble, meek life, content with what God allowed Him to have and was rewarded greatly. You see, everyone is promised two things, to be born and to die. Where we spend eternal life is left up to us. The rich man chose to experience the good life while on earth, and in return forfeited eternity with God. The poor man chose to live with Christ on earth and now spends eternity in glory. Ask yourself the following questions, "Am I living for today's glory or for God's glory to be evident in my life?" This scripture shines light on the reality of heaven and hell. While it was too late for the rich man to change the course of his life, he pleaded for Abraham to have mercy on him and to send Lazarus back to warn his family members. God's mercy is available to us on a daily basis, it's so important to grab hold of His grace. Our prayer for our family members and ourselves is to realize the truth of who God is before it's too late. God's door is open for us to seek Him while He may be found.

Prayer: Jehovah, You are the ruler of this universe. All things exist because of You. Thank You for showing us the reality of life in Christ. We pray for those who fail to honor and devote their life to You. Dispatch Your ministering angels to touch our hearts that we may trust and believe in You. Help us to walk in obedience and to reverence You in all that we do. We pray for every unbelieving heart to be softened and open to Your love. We invite You in our homes, neighborhoods, schools, jobs, and all public establishments. Help people to come into the kingdom before it's too late. God, with You all things are possible. Thank You for pouring Your love out on us every day. We magnify Your holy name. In Jesus' name we pray, Amen.

# June 7

*Do all things without murmurings and disputings;* (Philippians 2:14)

As a child of God, it is important that we appreciate everything God does on our behalf. As we know, God is always watching over us. His protection meets us every day. It is His grace and mercy that leads us throughout our life. In response to God being so faithful, it is important for us to have a heart of gratitude. God asks that we obey all of His commands in order for us to shine as lights in this dark and evil world. We have been trained by the response of the world to naturally complain and argue when unfavorable situations arise in our life. This is not the response of the kingdom of heaven. When we are being led in the Spirit we have the mind of Christ. God is guiding us only through the path that He has prepared for us. His perfect hand orchestrates everything He does in our life. We have no need to complain or argue when God is in control. His ways are faultless and only lead to righteousness. God created us to have dominion and authority in the earth. Everything we do and say has power to either add to our life or take away from it. Words of murmuring and disputing go into the atmosphere as particles of destruction. It adds no value to our life. With our eyes set on Jesus, we will not have the energy to complain, our hearts will be filled with joy as we trust in His guidance. This is not natural, as some many of the things we see around us teach us to complain. With discipline and literally making a conscious effort to be different, we have to decide to be thankful instead of rehearsing words of murmurs and complaints.

Prayer: Father God, You are the light of our life. We are honored to be called into Your presence. Lord, teach us the ways of heaven. Let our hearts be filled with praise and worship. As we are led by You, help us to understand that although times may get rough and we feel the need to complain, we will allow Your Spirit to take control. We know it will not always be like this. We have victory in Christ Jesus. We are overcomers. Help us not to argue with the intent to hurt others, but to disagree in love. Let love be the universal language that falls off of our lips and is being rooted in our hearts. Teach us to always keep Your statutes at the forefront of our mind. Hide Your word deep within our heart that we sin not against You. Let us shine brightly in this dark world. Drawing all men unto You. Let our life be a living testimony. Giving You honor, glory, and praise forever. In Jesus' name we pray, Amen.

## June 8

*Because you are precious in my eyes, and honored, and I love you, I give men in return for you, peoples in exchange for your life.* (Isaiah 43:4)

God's love is pure. He loves us because He is pleased with His creation. We were created to share in His love in open fellowship. He gave His Son just so we could see the magnitude of His love. The Bible is a personal love letter to each of us. Each passage points to the love of God. He has carefully created all things and has promised to be all things to us because of His great love. God doesn't see us the way we see ourselves. He looks past mistakes, scars, and feelings of defeat. He sees us in our purest form. We are precious in His sight, honored and loved. It gives God joy to see us enjoying the life that He has given us. It puts a smile on His face when we recognize who we are in Him and yield our life to being led by Him. We are the apple of His eye. Everything about creation is based upon building a loving relationship with our Father. God goes above and beyond to showcase His love on a daily basis. We have the gifts of His Son, His Spirit, and His Word to confirm His love is real. Knowing God as a personal friend helps us realize His love is true. As our relationship develops and we trust in His unfailing Word, our life will manifest every promise He has made. All of His promises were formed in love. If you ever feel like you are lost or unloved, stand on the truth of His Word and know God not only loves you, but will give nations in exchange for you. Now that's true love.

Prayer: Lord, You are Great. You are God. You are everything. Our words could never express the gratitude we have for You. You created us to experience Your love. You have prepared so many great things for Your people because of love. You watch over us and protect us because of love. You are honored to be our Father, despite our shortcomings. You love us beyond our mistakes. Your love washes us clean. Your love teaches us right from wrong. Your love gives and gives and gives. We are forever thankful that we cannot be separated from Your love. Lord, You are awesome. We will forever give You glory. In Jesus' name we pray, Amen.

# June 9

*Now when Daniel learned that the decree had been published, he went home to his upstairs room where the windows opened toward Jerusalem. Three times a day he got down on his knees and prayed,* ***giving thanks to his God, just as he had done before.*** (Daniel 6:10)

Can you give thanks to God in every season? Daniel's faith was tested immensely. With the thought of death at his doorstep, he made the wise choice to give thanks. He didn't allow his situation to alter his reverence toward God. Thanksgiving must be rendered to God according to His excellent greatness, not according to our emotions or current circumstances. To be honest, this is easier said than done. Praising God through the rough times is imperative to our growth and development as believers. We were never promised a peachy clean life. Obstacles are inevitable; God is looking at how we respond in every situation. Will you trust me, He ponders? We should know we have an advocate, Jesus, who is always interceding on our behalf. He has experienced everything that we will ever encounter and has gone through the storm with grace and dignity. One of the hardest things for us to do during a storm is to wait on the Lord to intervene in the midst of our difficulty. It sounds easy to quote scriptures such as, "But they that wait upon the Lord shall renew their strength," but when adversity shows up it requires unwavering faith- real action. Daniel was faced with the decree that if he prayed, he should be put to death. Just think about that, he had to choose between his faith or obeying the laws of the land. In our daily life, we will face obstacles that seem unbearable. In these moments, our faith has to be developed, deciding that our only option is to stand on the Word of God. This life changes like the wind; we must be anchored in the Lord so we are not blown away at every sight of trouble. We have to mediate day and night on the scripture to constantly remind ourselves of the God we serve. When the storms of life come, we will be able to respond with giving thanks, because we know nothing is a surprise to God. He knows everything that will happen and has guaranteed we will overcome.

Prayer: God, You are excellent. Your love is overwhelming. Thank You for always thinking about us. We know every good and perfect gift comes from above. You are always looking for ways to show us Your glory. Open our eyes to see You in every situation. We will always place Jesus before us and stand firm on Your Word. You have promised to never leave or forsake us. If God be for us who can be against us is our daily prayer. Nothing in this life has the power to destroy us. You have given us the strength to be built up in Your mighty power. Continue to watch over us as we continue to exalt Your name and to give thanks at all times. You are the great “I AM.” Your grace is more than sufficient and we say, Thank You. In Jesus’ name we pray, Amen.

# June 10

*[That you may really come] to know [practically, through experience for yourselves] the love of Christ, which far surpasses mere knowledge [without experience]; that you may be filled [through all your being] unto all the fullness of God [may have the richest measure of the divine Presence, and become a body wholly filled and flooded with God Himself]* (Ephesians 3:18 AMP)

God's love is not something one can fathom through mere words; it can only be experienced. When I came into the faith, I was a lost soul longing for a foundation, a connection to fill an empty void that was in my heart. As soon as I allowed God to take permanent residence within my inner being, I was instantly satisfied. Everything I longed for internally was given to me as a gift. God knows each of our spiritual and natural needs, and we are only made whole through Him. Paul is trying to get the church of Ephesus to fully grasp the love of Christ. The love of Christ produces evidence through us as we allow Him to permeate our heart. The love of God is not conditional or based upon our good merit. It exists solely because of who God is. This love comforts the broken heart, gives food to the poor, restores relationships and forgives and abolished sin. There is no depth to God's love, it can NEVER run out. Our knowledge (involvement) of God's love is based upon our FAITH. We experience God's love according to our individual level of belief. Truth be told, God's love is all around us, it's based upon our sensibility to God's Spirit whether or not we are aware of it. As we allow Christ to abide in our inner being, we can appreciate our time with God and recognize His love all around us.

Prayer: Lord, Thank You. Open the hearts of Your people today to enlighten us to the full awareness of Your great love. Overwhelm our hearts with Your presence. Open our eyes, get into our hearts and pour Your Spirit on us. You are a faithful God. You think of ways to display Your love towards us. We will not deny Your fellowship. We run to You with open arms and accept Your grace and mercy which is new everyday. In Your presence in the fullness of joy and at your right hand are pleasures forevermore. God, we love You, In Jesus' name, Amen.

# June 11

*Then Jesus said to his disciples, "Whoever wants to be my disciple must deny themselves and take up their cross and follow me."* (Matthew 16:24)

As we read this scripture, one may ask why would Jesus require us to deny the very thing He created? The answer is found in the works of Adam. Ever since sin entered the world, we were all born with a sinful nature. Sin resides within us because of the evil that fills this earth. Sin is very present in this world, and it is a requirement for each person to make an individual choice to accept the works of Christ to receive deliverance from our sinful nature. Christ is inviting us to come into the light. As we deny ourselves, we are denouncing every ounce of our sinful nature to be led and inspired by Christ Himself. God is trying to release us from sin's influence that is present all around us. As we accept salvation (deliverance) in Christ and follow after His principles, we are able to live the life God created us for. God created us with the intent to dwell with us in unhindered fellowship. With sin present He is not able to interact with us. Christ is our gateway back into God's covenant for His people. This is a scripture of freedom in Christ, where we are able to receive the gift of true life. Christ only leads us to places He has already prepared, where God receives all the glory and we receive fulfillment as we accomplish God's original intent for life.

Prayer: Lord, You are amazing. God, our hearts are lifted up before You. You are the joy and strength of this earth. Thank You for giving us hope in Your Son Jesus. We have a new life, a life of freedom. Open our eyes to the things You are doing in us. Help us to know Your voice, and the voice of another we shall not follow. Help us to deny ourselves on a daily basis. We know You will never lead us astray. Everything You establish brings glory to Your name and is beneficial for all creation. Pour Your Spirit upon us as we go out with a Spirit of boldness to declare Your love to this entire earth. It is our desire that everyone experience Your love. Help us to be sensitive to Your Spirit to hear and obey. God,

You are the ruler of our lives. We praise Your holy name. In Jesus' name we pray, Amen.

# June 12

*You built a reservoir between the two walls for the water of the Old Pool, but you did not look to the One who made it, or have regard for the One who planned it long ago.* (Isaiah 22:11)

There will never be a time in our life when we will not need God. God has created us to be reliant upon Him. Society has made it appealing to be self-sufficient and promotes self-reliance along with the strength that stems from being independent. Being self-sufficient is glorified and relying on others is frowned upon. This is not the way God desires for us to operate. As we live life, we will quickly realize it is IMPOSSIBLE to live totally independent. Since birth, we have relied on the help of others. God is the ultimate help and should be our first choice in all matters. We need God to help us in everything. It may seem like life is manageable without the guidance of others, yet in reality this is far from the truth. What if there was so much more God wanted to show us or to do through us? What if God wanted to give us a strategic plan where we could maximize our time and accomplish so much more in less time? In God's kingdom, His wisdom far exceeds ours. His hand is readily available to guide us into the predestined plan for each of our lives. God's hand in our lives is most effective. He is the creator of all things and understands how all things operate. It benefits us to seek His support in everything we do. It's imperative that we stop trying so hard to be self-sufficient and fall into the arms of our loving Father. We have obtained access into an inheritance that shall never perish. We have resources, and God's hand covers us and will sustain us throughout life. Most importantly, we have a Savior who is: Wonderful, Counselor, The Mighty God, The everlasting Father, The Prince of Peace (Isaiah 9:6).

Prayer: Mighty God, we come to You with a heart of repentance. Purge us that we may be pleasing in Your sight. Forgive all manner of sin found in us. Get to the root of all contention and flesh that tries to stand against Your Spirit within us. We accept Your garment of praise. We exalt Your name throughout all the earth. Pour out Your wisdom upon us. Give us spiritual insight to always seek You first. Your way is the only path we desire to follow. In everything we will seek You. Help us to find joy in obeying Your commands. Knowledge from the world is meaningless unless it comes from You. We will filter everything through Your Word and adhere to Your Spirit within us. In all things we give thanks. In Jesus' name we pray, Amen.

# June 13

*However, do not rejoice that the spirits submit to you, but rejoice that your names are written in heaven.* (Luke 10: 20)

In Christ we have everything. One must be careful never to boast about the freedom found in Christ. Jesus teaches us a valuable lesson through telling His disciples the greatest victory is not in having power over satan, but in knowing our name is written in heaven. This principle shows how to keep our mind in a right perspective. Our time on earth is temporary. The hardships we endure are only a test. As children of God, we have power and authority over satan and his demonic forces that try to invade our lives. Our primary focus shouldn't be on satan and his tactics, but to be thankful that God has saved us by His grace. We spend too much time giving energy to trials and tribulations instead of thanking God for the end result that is already promised to us. Instead of directing our energy towards constant battles in our mind over issues, we can make a conscious effort to rejoice. Rejoicing is an expression of joy and celebration. We are able to have joy because we know it's God's strength that helps us through our difficulties. He finds pleasure in working things out on our behalf. God has done more than enough to deserve our exaltation. With a new outlook on life we can wake up each morning, thanking God for knocking on the door of our heart and welcoming us into the kingdom of His Son Jesus.

Prayer: Lord, You are strong and mighty. You have won every battle that will ever be fought. God, we give You praise for always knowing the purpose for Your creation. We celebrate the life You have carefully orchestrated for us. You have opened our hearts to eternal life with You. We magnify Your name for saving our souls from the evil that plagues this earth. Keep our minds stayed on You. We will consider it pure joy whenever we face trials of many kinds (James 1:2). We know You fight on our behalf. We have overcome the evil intentions of this world by the blood of Jesus and the word of our testimony. Your praise will continuously fall from our lips. There is no one greater than You. We devote ourselves to You whole-heartedly. In Jesus' name we pray, Amen.

# June 14

*And the apostles said unto the Lord, Increase our faith.* (Luke 17:5)

We fail to utilize our faith whenever we allow unbelief to set in. We are able to exercise our faith by trusting in the promises of God. We have to make a conscious decision to stand on the Word of God while waiting patiently for the manifestation of what we are hoping for. God has already instilled faith within us. Our job is to put our faith to work. Whether what we believe God for is big or small, faith is always required. Doubt/fear are presented as tools to prohibit us from standing firm in our reliance on God's Word. They are nothing but mere distractions. We must realize faith is our servant. It works for us. This principle has to be embedded in our mind to influence us to always have confidence in what we believe God for. If we fail to employ our faith, we will get nothing in return. As we exercise our faith according to God's plan for our lives we are able to come into alignment with God's power. There is no limit to the things God is trying to open our eyes to see. He is always attempting to get us to live our best life. Our faith prepares us for the future, while placing us in position to always be able to exalt God. Our faith is already increased, it's time to use it.

Prayer: Lord, King of all creation, we bow in total reverence to Your name. All glory belongs to You. Lord, You see every person and You know our issues. You know the areas where we struggle and You love us the same. Today we make a pledge to trust in Your Word as truth. We will believe every Word that flows from heaven. We will search the scriptures concerning our lives and the plans You have for us. We will only speak what we hear You speak. Renew our minds to trust in the unseen. We have confidence in the things we hope for. You are a good Father and will never withhold any good thing from us. There are some who have believed You for some time now and feel like giving up. We place all of our concerns before You. Give us the patience to endure knowing we will see the promise at the appointed time. We will not become frustrated while waiting in You. We will exalt

Your name and rejoice. You are Alpha and Omega. Your name be praised forever. In Jesus' name we pray, Amen

# June 15

*And he said unto me, My grace is sufficient for thee: for my strength is made perfect in weakness. Most gladly therefore will I rather glory in my infirmities, that the power of Christ may rest upon me.* (2 Corinthians 12:9)

God will go to the very extreme to get us to realize how much He loves us. As we have come into fellowship with Him, He guards our covenant with a divine protection. He orchestrates our life to where we have no other choice but to trust Him. He will allow obstacles and the course of life to present itself and watch in expectation for us to grab hold of His hand. Hardships are inevitable, every person walking this earth will experience them at one time or another. In that instance, God is cheering us on from Heaven saying, "Cast your cares on Me." Relying on God's power teaches us how to remain in His peace at all times. Many of the things we face are only presented to see whether or not we will allow God's strength to be exhibited in our lives. God's ability and His strategic plan supersede any wisdom we could ever formulate in our own ability. So whether it's a bill, relationship problem, health, emotional or spiritual imbalance, God's grace is more than enough to cover us as we get through any season of difficulty.

**Your Grace is Enough for Me!**

Prayer: God, Your love is magnificent. It covers us from day-to-day; we are in awe of Your greatness that searches for opportunities to be present in our lives. We say thank You for orchestrating the end from the beginning. You have planned our expected end and it only points to victory. We grab hold of Your hand and submit into Your care every issue that enters our mind. Nothing is too hard for You. Clear our minds; relieve anxiety, pressure, depression, oppression, doubt, and fear from Your people. We will only stand on the promises You gave us. You created us with the spirit of love, power, and a sound mind. Shield us in the power of Your might as we put on Your full armor to stand against the schemes of the devil. All power and praise we give to You. In Jesus' name we pray, Amen.

## June 16

*And ye shall be my people, and I will be your God.* (Jeremiah 30:22)

God is forever Sovereign over all things. If we determine to make God ruler in our lives He will show us the pathway of life. There is no doubt about God being in control, yet He has given us free will to decide if we want to surrender ourselves to Him. God uses the conjunction "And" in scripture, "and ye shall be my people" to teach us that in order for us to be God's people we must accept His grace and live in His Word. God will always be God. It's our choice if we want to join Him in allowing Him to govern every aspect of our lives. God has created us to be dependent upon Him because He wants to ensure we receive all that this life has to offer. When we are connected to God, He will only deposit things in us that are beneficial for our growth. He will strengthen us with His power and enable us to prosper in everything we do. As His chosen people we have to yield every thought and decision to Him and walk in His Spirit. God takes His role in our lives seriously. He has already completed every work that will take place in the earth. As we align ourselves with Him, we will uncover the hidden treasures of His heart and walk under His divine protection. When we allow God to maximize His sovereignty in our lives we are shielded, protected, comforted, healed, restored, rejuvenated and made whole. God has so much He is trying to get us to receive; all we have to do is accept His grace. We must devote ourselves to Him as His chosen people, and allow Him to be God in every area of our lives.

Prayer: King of Kings, You are the Lord over all things created. Thank You for choosing us to be Your people. We surrender our lives before You today. Lord, You have the blueprint of life. We will sit before Your throne and receive our daily bread. Let Your word pierce our heart that we are always found abiding in You. We invite You into our hearts to be God. Be God in our finances, relationships, careers, ministries, and in everything that concerns us. You know the plans that You have for us and we submit ourselves to You. Thank You for always thinking about us and trying to get us to open our eyes to Your goodness. Shield us in Your protection. Only goodness and mercy shall follow us all the days of our life. We give Your name praise. In Jesus' name we pray, Amen.

# June 17

*If ye then be risen with Christ, seek those things which are above, where Christ sitteth on the right hand of God.* (Colossians 3:1)

We must allow God to renew our minds on a daily basis. As we focus our energy on His purpose, we are able to experience the abundant life. God, being the source, needs us to trust and rely on Him. We are to pursue His plans on a consistent basis in every area of our lives. It's a daily task for us to come to God through prayer and reading His Word. During this time of devotion we receive His knowledge that is available for us to grow and develop in Christ. All of our needs are available and within arms reach when we see and pursue after the Creator. Having our mind renewed teaches us the importance of following Christ. We understand we are not wasting our time on vain things that will perish in the end. Everything we are doing is being stored up in heaven where we have an eternal reward. God gives us the following principles to help us put on our new man: we are to walk in mercy, kindness, humbleness of mind, meekness, longsuffering, forbearing one another, forgiving one another, love, and peace (Colossians 3:12-15). Since we are hid in Christ, our spirit will desire the things of God. Christ becomes the most important aspect of our existence and we gain pleasure in pursuing the commands of His heart and to be walking in right standing with God.

**And whatever you do, whether in word or deed, do it all in the name of the Lord Jesus, giving thanks to God the Father through him. (Colossians 3:17)**

Prayer: Thank You Lord for this day. This is the day that You have made, we will rejoice and be glad in it. We have made a promise to seek after You all the days of our life. Those things, which are in heaven come to develop us and to teach us how to exalt Your name in the earth. Continue to bestow Your wisdom and knowledge upon us. Let us walk in the new man that You have created in us. We deny the lust of the flesh, the lust of the eyes, and the pride of life. It is our delight to pursue right standing with You and to walk in obedience at all times. Open the ears of our heart to hear Your voice clearly and adhere to Your commands. Let our natural response be yes. All glory belongs to You. In Jesus' name we pray, Amen

# June 18

*But Peter said, Ananias, why hath Satan filled thine heart to lie to the Holy Ghost, and to keep back part of the price of the land?* (Acts 5:3)

During this time, the apostles and the people following Christ were suffering great persecution from the religious leaders who did not believe Jesus was the true Messiah. Nevertheless, the followers of Christ prayed for boldness and were determined to be of one accord. They decided collectively to sell all of their possessions and bring the profit to the apostles in order to distribute between everyone according to their needs. The bible tells us they had great grace upon them and every need was met (Acts 4:31-37). Now we meet Ananias and his wife, who sold a possession and instead of bringing all of their profit to the apostles, they kept a portion for themselves. The intent of their heart was to offer a sacrifice to God, but their motives were not right. They knowingly tried to trick the people of God into receiving their tainted offering. This lesson teaches us many things, first we see there is nothing hidden in the sight of God. God will reveal the motives of our heart when they are not pure before Him. We also learn God is not interested in sacrificial offerings when we fail to provide Him with the proper respect. God would rather we not give or refrain from actions than to accomplish them through deception. Everything done in the dark will come to the light. God's presence exposes darkness. His attributes of purity are not imposed to cause us harm, but to teach us how to operate in uncontaminated devotion towards Him. Self-control must be exercised whenever we are presented with temptations. Satan can only suggest things; we are the ones in control of our actions. We have to guard our heart so we refuse to give room towards anything contrary to God's commands or allow them to take root within us. Ananias and his wife lied about money and were fatally punished. We must examine the motives of our heart and pray to God, asking for forgiveness in any areas of wrongdoing. This will allow us to come before God with a clean heart ready for devotion.

Hear the supplication of your servant and of your people Israel when they pray toward this place. Hear from heaven, your dwelling place, and when you hear, forgive. (1 Kings 8:30)

Prayer: God, we thank You for being God. Thank You for always hearing our prayers. Your arm is not waxed short, there is nothing impossible for You. Lord, search us inwardly. Wherever you find polluted motives within us, remove them so we can honor You with a pure heart. Show us the error in our ways. Forgive us for not giving You the proper respect in all aspects of our lives. Continue to allow Your Spirit to teach us right from wrong. Develop our spirit of discernment. Let us spend quiet time with You to grow in Your doctrine. Let everything we do and say bring honor to Your throne of grace. You are the light of this world and the light of our life. In Jesus' name we pray, Amen.

# June 19

*Then he showed me Joshua the high priest standing before the angel of the Lord, and Satan standing at his right side to accuse him.* (Zechariah 3:1)

Satan is always before God, trying to accuse us of our many sins. You should be happy about this. Why, because he is before OUR Father trying to convince Him of our wrongdoing. Just like any parent, we know we will not easily allow anyone to degrade, manipulate or harm our children. Not only does he go to God to make accusations, he also tries to enter our minds by reminding us of our past mistakes. God, being a loving Father, stops satan in his tracks and reminds him of his place in the pit of fire. God sees us the way He created us, in our purest form. He has cleansed us from the filthiness of sin and clothed us in fine garments. Since God sees us for who we really are, we too need to see ourselves in the same manner. Instead of allowing the lies of the enemy to replay over and over in our head, we must stand on the truth of who God says we are. God says we are clothed in His righteousness. "I delight greatly in the LORD; my soul rejoices in my God. For he has clothed me with garments of salvation and arrayed me in a robe of his righteousness, as a bridegroom adorns his head like a priest, and as a bride adorns herself with her jewels" (Isaiah 61:10). As we walk in obedience to Christ, we are able to obtain wisdom to resist the tricks of the enemy and only stand on the promises of God. Whenever we are presented with negative thoughts or temptations, we are to remind ourselves of who we are in Christ. God has chosen us as His royal priesthood, a holy nation, His special possession; nothing can distort the way God sees us. It's our choice whether or not we hold fast to our righteous form or fall victim to the accusations of satan.

**My God today!**

Prayer: Yahweh, thank You for standing firm against satan's tactics to destroy us. You have loved us beyond our weakest moments. Your grace has allowed us to come before Your throne.

Thank You for cleansing us with Your garment of holiness. Impart Your truth in us. Teach us how to accept only what You say as truth. Open our eyes to see ourselves the way You see us. Help us to look at each other through the eyes of grace. Dispatch Your angels on our behalf. Give them the power to fight on our behalf. Thank You for not leaving us in this world alone. We have hope in You. We are forever grateful. With every breath within us we worship You in spirit and truth. In Jesus' name we pray, Amen. To God be the glory!!!

# June 20

*And if ye call on the Father, who without respect of persons judgeth according to every man's work, pass the time of your sojourning here in fear:* (1 Peter 1:17 KJV)

Our time on earth is very precious. God has given us the gift of life to enjoy creation and open fellowship with Him. With God's grace at the forefront of our mind, we are able to orchestrate our day in accordance to His order. In every decision, we are to consider the sacrifice Christ made for us and conduct ourselves in honor of what He did for us on Calvary. Jesus removed us from darkness associated with sin, and we are now living lives devoted to God. We are forever conscious of God's grace watching over us. As God's elect, we sanctify ourselves daily by being obedient to God's Word. We do not conduct ourselves as those who do not know Christ. Our conduct is measured against God's principles. As foreigners in this earth we look to heaven for guidance, making it our goal to hear from God and act in accordance to His commands. We understand we will give an account of everything we do and use this knowledge as a driving force to always show admiration towards God. What we do and what we don't do all matter to God. We are here for a specific purpose. Every day is filled with extreme assignments, and as we are in divine connection with God, our source, we have grace to fulfill all of them. What would happen if every person walking the earth devoted himself or herself to God and really walked in purpose? "Jesus," this earth would be a better place. Although we cannot control the decisions of others, we can make a conscious choice with everything within us to live life sold out for the kingdom of God. The secret to life is realizing our actions not only affect us but everyone around us. The gift God placed inside of us fits together in a perfect puzzle for mankind. Do not be the missing piece.

**You matter to God!**

Prayer: Lord, You are the light of this world. Thank You for shining light on us and showing us the true meaning of life. In all that we do we will give reverence to You. Transform our thought process. Help us to consciously obey each of Your commands. Develop Your heart within us. Teach us how to love, honor and cherish one another. We will live as Your servants. It is our desire to please You. Guide us on the narrow path of righteousness for Your name's sake. Let our conduct and conversation bring honor to Your holy name. We bless You now and forever. In Jesus' name we pray, Amen.

# June 21

*If ye oppress not the stranger, the fatherless, and the widow, and shed not innocent blood in this place, neither walk after other God's to your hurt:* (Jeremiah 7:6)

Here we find God teaching His people how to refrain from indulging in false worship. They thought that they gained power by merely coming into the temple. God corrected them and revealed to them that He is not concerned with the act of worship but with our heart of worship. God looks at our motives and our attitude. He watches us on a daily basis to see how we interact with others and how we follow His commands. To engage in true worship, God must be at the forefront of our mind. When we spend time with God developing His characteristics, our demeanor will exude the traits of His Spirit. The more we learn about God the more equipped we are to function in life. When we come before Him to worship we are able to come with a clear heart because we have prepared ourselves by walking with Him continuously. Does this mean we will be perfect and get it right every time? No, but we will be striving to hear from God and make a conscious effort to govern ourselves accordingly. As we focus on God we can be corrected as we make mistakes. When we mistreat others, or put other god's before Him we are practicing false worship. Worship by definition means to love, adore, devote, and to respect a person or thing. So whatever we put our energy towards is receiving our worship. God is a jealous God, and rightfully so. We were created to worship HIM alone. In doing so, we find the beauty of life; the choice is ours. As for me and my house we will serve the Lord.

**Worship is free but it cost Jesus everything!**

Prayer: Elohim, we bow down in reverence before Your throne of grace. There is no other god we will serve but You. Your name is great in all the earth. We choose this day to honor, respect, love, and to adore You alone. We will set You before us at all times. Open our hearts to hear and obey Your commands. Let love be our natural response. Teach us how to operate in unity with all of mankind. Forgive us if we have ever placed any natural thing before You. Whether it be work, family, friends, recreation, or material possessions, nothing is more important than giving Your name praise. God, in You we find all things; we come to You first giving You our best praise. All things belong to You. We surrender our will, asking that Yours be done in us. In Jesus' name we pray, Amen.

# June 22

*Into thine hand I commit my spirit: thou hast redeemed me, O Lord God of truth.* (Psalm 31:5)

God has given us the opportunity to make conscious decisions on how we will nurture and cherish the life He has given us. We are faced with the choice on how to act in all circumstances. For those who love the Lord, we find it right to commit our spirit into the hands of our beloved Father. God knowing all things and having prepared all things for us is the best choice. It takes a lot of self-control to follow the commands of God. We have to deny ourselves on a daily basis to be led by the Spirit of God. We have to command our thoughts and bring them into alignment with God and His principles which teach us how to operate and function in this earth. As we develop these characteristics, we will have to exercise these attributes by utilizing our faith. As we commit our spirit to God we are showing God that we trust His plan for our lives more than we desire to fulfill the lust of our heart. We have obtained knowledge of the truth of His Word and believe everything He has promised. Our faith is secure in knowing God will guide, protect and establish His will through us.

Prayer: Lord, You are the light of this world. All things exist because of You. We are forever thankful. Into Your hands we commit our spirit that You may teach us how to operate. Open our eyes to see You for who You are. Help us to take time out of our day to soak in Your presence to grow and to develop in Your word. You created all plans, and we come to receive our daily bread. Nourish us with Your greatness. You are the source of life. With all praise we say glory to Your name. In Jesus' name we pray, Amen.

# June 23

*But even the very hairs of your head are all numbered. Fear not therefore: ye are of more value than many sparrows.* (Luke 12:7)

God cares so much for us. Every little thing that concerns us concerns Him. He desires we grow and develop by utilizing the fundamentals of His Word. In our daily situations, He understands the pressure we face as we experience the issues of life. Anything we face in life can be found in the book of life (the Bible). God knows we need comfort and assurance to get through many obstacles, and He is constantly encouraging us. While in the middle of heartache, setbacks, and devastations, we may feel as if we are all alone. God's Word shines light on the fact that we can fall into His arms and allow Him to work on our behalf. So often we hear we are to lay our burdens down, but in the midst of turmoil we find it hard to let go. It is a command to cast our cares upon God, so our energy can be focused on kingdom assignments. It's time out for carrying our own burdens for longer than the desired time. We have an advocate, Father and friend who anticipates us giving Him our despair. God is so in love with us that He counts the very hairs on our head. He knows everything and can handle all things. It's time to rest in Him.

**"LORD I give it to You."**

Prayer: Alpha and Omega, You are the great "I Am." You are marvelous in all Your works. We submit our life to You today. Let Your kingdom come. God, there are some who are dealing with great turmoil today, we pray that You step down into our situations and show us the light. Let us find hope in trusting You. Help us to take that leap of faith by giving all of our concerns to You. We release the heavy burden into Your hands. We refuse to walk around with the weight of the world on our shoulders. You are more than able to deliver us out of any circumstance. Pour out Your wisdom. Let Your word be found in our heart and flowing from our lips. In all that we do we will give honor to Your name. You are forever blessed. In Jesus' name we pray, Amen.

**Come unto me, all ye that labour and are heavy laden, and I will give you rest. (Matthew 11:28)**

# June 24

*Then will I sprinkle clean water upon you, and ye shall be clean: from all your filthiness, and from all your idols, will I cleanse you.* (Ezekiel 36:25)

We need to be cleansed on a daily basis. What we endured yesterday positions us for the growth we will develop today. We come asking God to cleanse us by renewing a right spirit within us. We understand the war taking place between our flesh (carnal nature) and the Spirit. We refuse to yield to the temptations of our flesh by holding onto the Word of God that we have hidden in our heart. The Word of God purifies us by showing us our own error and bringing to our remembrance the works of Christ. It is with our new heart that we will worship God, humbling ourselves in His presence, being totally reliant upon Him. We will worship Him in spirit and truth, casting all our cares at His feet and not giving way to the obstacles that come to distract us. "Therefore, if any man be in Christ, he is a new creature: old things are passed away; behold, ALL things are become new" (2 Corinthians 5:17). As we hide ourselves in Christ we will allow His spirit to orchestrate the course of our day. Operating in our new creation, we will showcase to the world the splendor of our Holy God, who has transformed us into His very image.

**He makes all things new!**

Prayer: Jehovah Shalom, God who gives peace, we adore You. Your very presence is where we long to be. Thank You for the open invitation. Cleanse us from all outside influence that doesn't come from You. Allow the commands from heaven to control all our actions. Purify our hearts to be in alignment with Your covenant. Remove our heart of stone and replace it with Your heart of flesh. Out of our heart flow the issues of life. We need You to operate on us this very second. Open our eyes to see the beauty of our new creation in Christ. Help us to allow Your presence to dwell freely within us. In all that we do we honor You. In Jesus' name we pray, Amen.

# June 25

*Jesus stopped and ordered them to bring the man to him. When the man came near, Jesus asked him, "What do you want me to do for you?" The blind man said, "Lord, I want to see again."* (Luke 18: 40-41)

Every day Jesus meets us, asking this very question, "What do you want me to do for you." We are alive because of who God is. His abundance of grace meets us new each day. Our faith is dependent upon what we are willing to receive from God. Jesus already knows what we desire and has already prepared for us beyond our wildest imagination. He is sitting back, waiting on us to come to Him and receive the abundance He has stored up for us. When we make a declaration, we are putting our faith in the things God has already arranged for us to have. God is everything, has everything, and will give us all things. As His heirs, we have rights to the things of the kingdom. As we walk in righteousness with God, we are able to come to our Father and receive what we ask for. This pertains to a clear mind, stable emotions, right perspective, a heart of love, finances, employment, restoration, healing- whatever it is, God WILL provide. Are we willing to ask? We miss out on a lot of opportunities and blessings from God because we simply fail to ask or we ask amiss. God has commanded us to seek Him first, His Kingdom and His righteousness and He will add all things unto us (Matthew 6:33). It gives God great pleasure to give us His innumerable blessings. God is an awesome provider. This day He is waiting to pour out the blessings of heaven. What do you need Him to do today? Our request is only a prayer away. Let God in Your heart and request your desire, believing you have already received it in Jesus' name.

Prayer: Lord, You are the great "I Am," ruler of the universe. Our love is forever kindled for You. Thank You Father. We shout in victory, thanking You for Your grace and mercy that follow us all the days of our life. We pray for the desires of our heart to be fulfilled in You. We believe Your Word as truth, and we have what You have promised us. All glory belongs to You. Develop our faith to study the scriptures and to speak only the things that You speak in Heaven. Pour out Your wisdom in this earth. We honor You. In Jesus' name we pray, Amen.

# June 26

*Even so faith, if it hath not works, is dead, being alone.* (James 2:17 KJV)

*So you see, faith by itself isn't enough. Unless it produces good deeds, it is dead and useless.* (James 2:17 NLT)

Now faith is the substance of things hoped for, the evidence of things not seen. Faith is us believing the Word of God, although we can't see what we hope for. We know that as we exercise the principles of God those things we once were unable to see begin to manifest themselves. We believe by operating in God we will see the evidence of the things we hope for. Our faith inspires us to act in accordance with what God has purposed us to do in order to see the fruits He has promised. When we fail to act upon what God has called us to believe, our faith is dead. It becomes stagnant. Our belief in God should produce good deeds. By faith we receive everything we hope for in accordance with God's will. We obtain strength and courage to come before God to receive His plans and then execute them. When God calls us to accomplish things in the earth they entail tasks we are incapable of accomplishing on our own. It is through our dependence upon God we are able to exercise our faith. He becomes our ability to do the impossible. In order to obey the voice of God, we first have to believe what God says is true. If we can't dream big on God's level, our faith will continue to lie stagnant. God wants to develop our faith. As we walk with Him, He will continue to give us witty ideas to expand our faith in Him. By listening to the voice of God and walking in our purpose, we receive the promises of God and our faith will always remain active. What we hope for will manifest out of what we once couldn't see, but always believed God would perform.

**God is Faith!**

Prayer: Lord, You are Mighty in Battle, You are our strength. You are all we need in this life. Lord, we love You for allowing us to have hope. We trust in Your promises. We solely depend on

Your Word. Your Word breathes life, heals, restores, and keeps us safe. Without You we are nothing. Create in us a clean heart. Let our joy be found in You. We desire to seek You in all things. Develop our faith; help us to trust in Your unfailing love. We press toward the mark for the prize of the high calling of God in Christ Jesus. All that we do we will do in faith. All glory belongs to You. In Jesus' name we pray, Amen.

# June 27

*Sing unto God a new song; play skillfully with a loud noise.* (Psalm 33:3)

Every morning we should have a fresh praise from our heart for God. As God traveled with the children of Israel through the wilderness, He provided new manna (food, substance) every day. It fell fresh with the dew each morning and God commanded them to only eat what was provided for that specific day. If they attempted to save manna for the following day, it would be rotten by morning. This showcases the great love of God and how He provided their essential needs each day. There was no lack within the entire camp. As we come before God, the utterance of our lips should be sparked by us reminiscing on the goodness of God. God does more for us in a day than we could ever do in a lifetime. God deserves our best praise. Our song of gratitude should be full of exaltation, expressing how great He is. There will never be a time where we will run out of reasons to bless God for His goodness. Our thanksgiving should be so continuous that time runs out before we think to stop lifting up His name. As we meditate upon God's goodness, it stirs up excitement within us to where our praise is uncontained. As we think about the goodness of God we will offer up a new song, thanking God for the new things He does each day. No two days are ever the same. We are wiser and stronger than we were yesterday; this day we will shout with joy, expressing our love for our Father.

**I was glad when they said unto me, Let us go into the house of the Lord. (Psalm 122:1)**

Prayer: Lord, You are marvelous!!! There is none like You. We sing unto You a new song, a song of gratitude. We are forever thankful for all You have done for us. With every ounce of our being we will magnify Your holy name. We will think about Your excellent greatness and praise You for who You are. You created the entire earth, everything belongs to You and yet You love us with an everlasting love. A love which has no limits, a love that will never be retracted. We sit in honor of You. Our hearts are lifted toward heaven singing, "How great thou art." We join the angels in continuous worship. You are the Lord who is holy. We praise You now and forever. In Jesus' name we pray, Amen.

## June 28

*Then the people rejoiced, for that they offered willingly, because with perfect heart they offered willingly to the Lord: and David the king also rejoiced with great joy.* (1 Chronicles 29:9)

As we give to the kingdom of God, we experience joy and understand the true meaning of "it's better to give than to receive." There are many ways to offer our worship to the Lord. Whenever we offer worship to God, it must be done from a pure heart. David was living by example before the children of Israel. He set aside an abundant offering to give to the temple of God. His generous gifts encouraged others to give willingly as well. David recognized how important it was to financially support the place of worship. The temple was built solely on generous gifts from people who gave from their heart. They rejoiced in knowing God's palace was well taken care of. God is not concerned with how much we have; He looks at the motives behind what we do with what we have. We give to the kingdom with an understanding that everything belongs to God. It is a gift placed under our care, and with great joy are we able to give a portion towards the upbuilding of God's physical church. Purposing in our heart to give to God allows Him to replenish us and secure all of our needs (2 Corinthians 9:7-11). Our offering comes before God as a thankful praise. We are honored to bless others and use our resources to include our money and talents as instructed by God. We accomplish this cheerfully understanding God is our source and provider. Everything we have comes from God, with great pleasure we present our gifts before Him.

Prayer: Lord, You are marvelous. The work of Your hands cannot be numbered. It will take eternity to express our thankfulness towards You. You are forever holy. Lord, give us a perfect heart to keep Your commandments. Develop within us a cheerful heart to give unto the kingdom. All we purpose in our heart according to Your will, we will offer willingly. We rejoice before Your throne. We give You every ounce of our being. Keep our mind on You and not on material things of this world. Open our eyes to see that all good things come from heaven. We adore you and bless Your name forever. In Jesus' name we pray, Amen.

# June 29

*With him will I speak mouth to mouth, even apparently, and not in dark speeches; and the similitude of the Lord shall he behold: wherefore then were ye not afraid to speak against my servant Moses?* (Numbers 12:8)

We'll only receive from God what we seek after. If we desire more of God, we have to be willing to spend more time with Him. We must set aside time for prayer, fasting, and time of seclusion from the outside world to hear from God. During these times we develop our relationship with our Father. God is not a respecter of persons. He loves each of us the same, and is willing to reveal Himself to anyone willing to accept Him. Spiritual growth is contingent upon what we value as important. If we desire more of God we will receive it. God's position is always secure; He is always available for fellowship. Moses was called a friend of God because he was faithful, humble and trustworthy (Numbers 12:3, 8). He spent time with God, listening to everything God was teaching Him and then implementing it in His life. Moses spent so much time with God that his characteristics resembled the form of God. He sought God's face and didn't leave His presence until He received his daily bread. This testament should encourage us to take time to sit in God's presences on a daily basis, listening to His voice soaking in His glory. Allow God to grow through us by engaging in daily intimate communion with our friend, and see what great plans the Father has for us on this specific day.

**No two days are the same!**

Prayer: Lord, You are faithful. You are magnificent and holy. There is none like You. God, we die to ourselves today. We too like Moses want to be able to speak to You openly without any limitations. Help us to be humble, faithful and trustworthy. Let our natural response to Your commands be yes. Everything You command is for our benefit. Open our eyes to see the joy we obtain by being in relationship with You. Remove all forms of distractions that try to take the place of us seeking You. Lord, you said if we seek we will find. We are searching for You. We will be diligent, consistent, and committed to our time with You. We give You proper place as head of our lives. There is nothing more important than You. With our entire strength we bless Your holy name, Hallelujah. In Jesus' name we pray, Amen.

## June 30

*Be strong and of a good courage, fear not, nor be afraid of them: for the Lord thy God, he it is that doth go with thee; he will not fail thee, nor forsake thee.* (Deuteronomy 31:6)

God is all about acceleration. All our time on earth should be times of progression, not digression. God has not called us to be stagnant in our life. With His attributes flowing within us we have the ability to prosper. God designed us to grow in every area (spiritually, financially, relationship, career, and ministry). Everything we put our hands to should increase, as these are the fundamental characteristics of God. He is perfect, whatever He establishes grows and multiplies. When we find ourselves at a crossroad between fear and faith, we have to consider the allegiance of our trust. We have to examine ourselves by renewing our thought process. God being in the midst of everything we set out to do has to be embedded in our mind. God said, "**for the LORD thy god, he it is that doth go with thee**." Fear should not take precedence over the fact that God is walking with us. Whatever it is that we face, be it a career choice, ministry idea, relationship challenge, we have to trust God is working for it out for our good. Focusing our energy towards operating in faith allows God to pull His purpose out of us and enables us to complete His plans in the earth. We are citizens of the kingdom of the Most High. We belong to an eternal kingdom under the rule of a Mighty God who owns all things. This alone should ignite fire within us to face fear, worry, disappointment, and encourage us to take God's hand to proceed in excellence.

Prayer: El Shaddai, God Almighty, we take Your hand today to walk with You into our destiny. Lord, You know the end from the beginning. You have set all things in order. You have established the course of our life. We accept Your plan with an open heart. We place all of our trust in You. We cast all of our cares upon You, You are our refuge and very present help in trouble. Fear does not belong to Your children, so we exchange it today for faith. Faith to trust every Word that proceeds from heaven. You have ordained us for such a time as this. Help us to expose our gifts by operating in Your love. We thank You for Your continuous compassion. Ignite fire within us to be strong and courageous. We will accomplish every assigned work for the kingdom. All glory and praise belong to You. In Jesus' name we pray, Amen.

# July 1

*And seek the peace of the city whither I have caused you to be carried away captives, and pray unto the Lord for it: for in the peace thereof shall ye have peace.* (Jeremiah 29:7)

Kingdom principles teach us to consider others above ourselves. God makes it possible for us to consider the welfare of others because in Him we know we have everything we need. God always instructs us to pray for others, even if their current behavior does not warrant our desire to pray for them. This kind of consideration for our society helps establish peace in the earth. Our prayers for our nation and those in authority make life a better place for all. Although we are not under the eternal control of those in our government or lawmakers in our towns, we are subject to their rule. We have to operate under their sanctions. It is imperative that we summon the hand of God concerning the earth we live in. This allows the right people to be placed in office, and the rules and regulations for our society to be God inspired. Prayer for our nation's protection is for our well-being and prepares for future generations to come. As we request God to govern the hearts of the land, we are included in the peace God bestows upon our country. Our prayers should be for our school system, law enforcement, local and national government. As we look around we see the turmoil taking place in our society. God has giving us the antidote in 2 Chronicles 7:14. "If my people, which are called by my name, shall humble themselves, and pray, and seek my face, and turn from their wicked ways; then will I hear from heaven, and will forgive their sin, and will heal their land." God has carefully given us instructions on how He intervenes in the cares of the earth. Our position is to pray and heed God's instructions.

**What would happen if we all prayed?**

Prayer: Lord, You are so amazing. We come before Your presence on behalf of our nation, our leaders; local, state, and national government. We pray for all those in authority. Grant peace in the earth. Watch over the nation and keep Your people safe. Order our steps to stay in line with Your will. Give those in leadership wisdom to govern by Your standards. Show us how to operate with the welfare of all people in mind. Watch over the affairs of the land. We praise Your holy name. In Jesus' name we pray, Amen.

# July 2

*The Lord delights in those who fear him, who put their hope in his unfailing love.* (Psalm 147:11)

Do you want to please God? We must first understand what God takes pleasure in and what He despises in order to learn how to develop and operate in godly character. Wisdom teaches us how to fear God. “The fear of the Lord *is* to hate evil;Pride and arrogance and the evil way, And the perverse mouth I hate” (Proverbs 8:13). When we hate those things the Lord hates, we are showing reverence toward Him. To fear God is to worship God. We are making a conscious effort to refuse to partake in any behavior contrary to the commands of God. God is concerned with the condition of our heart; out of our heart flows our behaviors and principles which fuel our actions. God hates all manner of sin because it separates us from Him. He takes no pleasure in casting judgment upon His creation. He desires for all of us to find joy in despising the evil intentions of this world. God finds pleasure when we deny the flesh and develop spiritual characteristics; grabbing hold of His hand of mercy and living in hope.

Prayer: Heavenly Father, we surrender all before You. In Your presence we render glory. Search the depths of our heart. Transform our very nature; impute Your characteristics within us. Develop each of Your attributes within us. Open our eyes to the splendor of Your beauty. Remove from us the heart of stone; place in us Your heart of flesh. We long to operate in ways that please You. We will worship You according to Your great pleasure. We hate anything that is not like You; give us the strength to overcome by Your power. We sit in awe of Your greatness. In Jesus’ name we pray, Amen.

# July 3

*Wherefore he is able also to save them to the uttermost that come unto God by him, seeing he ever liveth to make intercession for them.* (Hebrews 7:25)

Jesus holds the office of High Priest. As High Priest, he has made atonement for us once and for all. He also speaks to God on a continuous basis concerning each of us. Jesus came to earth in the form of man by stepping down from heaven to relate to us on our human level. He teaches us through His experience in life that,, although trials arise, if we keep our eyes on God we will overcome. He accomplished all of this in order to continually go before the Father on our behalf. In communion with God, I can see Jesus saying, "Father the temptations they are facing are difficult, don't hold it against them. Look at them through me, the Holy One. I take on their pain and strife." Christ is combating it for us. It's like an assembly line, the enemy distracts us with obstacles, we give them to Jesus, and Jesus takes them to the Father. Our job is to trust in the one who is constantly in the face of God working on our behalf. We surrender opposition into the hands of Jesus and are able to focus our energy on our kingdom assignments. Jesus is more than able. He has already carried our burdens on the cross. He is trying to get us to put down the very things He has already died for. We were called to enjoy the promises and intimacy with the Father.

**Give it to God!**

Prayer: King of glory, Ruler of the universe, all praise belongs to You. Thank You for being our High Priest. Thank You for pleading our cause even now. Lord, You see our life and You have made plans for each moment we walk this earth. We stand in awe of Your splendor. The wisdom You display in crafting such a unique creation to carry out Your plans. Into Your hands we commit our will that You may work through us. We glorify Your name, In Jesus' name we pray, Amen.

**Come unto me, all ye that labour and are heavy laden, and I will give you rest. Take my yoke upon you, and learn of me; for I am meek and lowly in heart: and ye shall find rest unto your souls. For my yoke is easy, and my burden is light. (Matthew 11:28-30)**

# July 4

*These things I remember as I pour out my soul: how I used to go to the house of God under the protection of the Mighty One with shouts of joy and praise among the festive throng.* (Psalm 42:4)

Why should we pour out our heart to God when God knows everything already? Great question, when we pour out the concerns of our heart it builds trust in God. We are saying, “Lord, I give You everything because I know You are the only one able to guide me in life.” As we release the issues of our heart to God, it takes the load off of us and helps to fight off depression. Talking to God, we will uncover the strategic plans He has for our lives, helping us deal with things that challenge us. In His presence, we are able to see the error in our own ways and exchange our way of thinking for His perfect plan. Nothing done in the earth is a secret to God; only when we bring it to Him is He able to intervene. In our time of confessing the cares of our heart, the Spirit brings back to our remembrance the times in the past where God has shown Himself to be faithful on our behalf. No issue or concern is outside of God’s reach. He is able to answer every prayer and calm every nerve within our spirit. Another word for pour is transfer. God wants us to transfer the cares of our heart onto Him so He can satisfy every request. His love longs for us to come before Him on a daily basis with our arms out ready to receive His blessings. “Do not be afraid, little flock, for your Father has been pleased to give you the kingdom” (Luke 12:32).

Prayer: Take this time to pour out your heart to God.

# July 5

*And David sent messengers unto the men of Jabeshgilead, and said unto them, Blessed be ye of the Lord, that ye have shewed this kindness unto your lord, even unto Saul, and have buried him.* (2 Samuel 2:5)

Kindness is one of the many attributes of God. It is bestowed upon us every day. In kindness, God is patient toward us. He shows us love in every form possible to get us to receive it with open arms. The kindness shown to us is reciprocated and is to be shown to others around us. Living in the world today, it is often taught that we should be concerned with our own lives before focusing on the welfare of others. What about those who are in despair, who are incapable of helping themselves? Our acts of kindness can change the course of someone's life. When we choose to display love towards others they are able to see the beauty of God. At some point in our lives we will all need someone to lean on. When we are able to be the helping hand it puts a smile on God's face. Instead of always looking for self-motivated ways to get ahead in life, we should consider how we could be a blessing to someone else. As we pour out, God is pouring into us. We will never run out of ways to bless people. God is always evolving His characteristics within us. We may have the very thing someone needs to keep them from going over the edge. Let's take time out and see how we may help one another.

**I need you, you need me, we're all a part of God's body!**

Prayer: Hallelujah Lord, You are so worthy of praise. We welcome You into our hearts; transform us from the inside out. Help us to stop thinking only about ourselves and think about the needs of Your people. Put words of kindness on our lips. Help us to consider the feelings of others. Give us a spirit of compassion and kindness. Show us what is on Your heart that we may be in line with Your grace this day. We pray for every person who is going through a difficult time. Send Your ministering angels to help encourage us. Turn our sorrow into joy. Let this time of growth be a blessing. God, in all that we do we give thanks. In Jesus' name we pray, Amen.

# July 6

*I know thy works: behold, I have set before thee an open door, and no man can shut it: for thou hast a little strength, and hast kept my word, and hast not denied my name.* (Revelation 3:8)

God has a purpose for everyone and everything He created. As we make a commitment to Him, He is thrilled to show us the pathway of life. Being led by the Holy Spirit places us in our predestined position for doors to be opened. God has already written the book of life; fulfilling our potential is based on our ability to yield to the Spirit of God. As we commit to God, we obtain His strength to complete every task in life. God knows the obstacles we will face as we journey through life. As they arise, God is in heaven cheering us on, encouraging us and giving us insight and strength for today's journey. In our own human ability we will experience burnout trying to achieve the highest level of potential that God has prepared for us. Laying our cares at His feet enables us to follow His steps into the doors of our destiny. Our destiny lies in God's hands. There is nothing that can hinder us from getting to our purpose except if we get in our own way. God is our shield and protector, always looking for ways to get our attention to be committed to Him. As we commit ourselves to Him, we find everything in the will of God will be fulfilled through us no matter what opposition we encounter.

Prayer: God, You are holy, righteous and full of glory. Thank You for always having a plan for our lives. Lord wherever You want us to go we will follow You. Wherever Your glory is we long to be. We submit our plans into Your hands. Ignite Your fire within us to fulfill the destiny You have placed inside of us. Open our hearts to receive the plan You have for our lives. We commit our lives into Your hands, lead the way. We worship You in spirit and truth. In Jesus' name we pray, Amen.

# July 7

*But Peter put them all forth, and kneeled down, and prayed; and turning him to the body said, Tabitha, arise. And she opened her eyes: and when she saw Peter, she sat up.* (Acts 9:40)

Everything God is trying to get done on behalf of mankind requires a willing vessel. God uses us as His body parts to perform His work in the earth. He has all power and is waiting to exhibit it through His children. After the death of the disciple Tabitha, her friends, knowing the connection Peter had with Jesus, sought him out for help. They believed He could turn this devastating situation around. When Peter arrived, mourners reflecting on how good of a person Tabitha was welcomed him. Peter could not be deterred by overwhelming emotions; he cleared the room to seek the one with power. Peter knew apart from Jesus he could do no good thing. He kneeled down and prayed to God, yielding to the Holy Spirit, allowing God to work through Him to perform the miracle of resurrection. It wasn't in Peter's power that Tabitha was raised from her death bed, it was God working through Peter. God is alive and wants to be active in each of our lives. Executing miracles showcases God's power and causes others to believe in Him. We are the body parts of Christ; whenever impossible circumstances arise we are to seek God and allow Him to work through us. Bystanders will see the power of God and give testimony, causing others to believe in the true and living God.

Prayer: Lord, Your love saturates us. We welcome You in our hearts with open arms. Take full control of our lives. Exercise Your authority in us at all times. We yield our desires to Yours. Make us over, renewing our minds. Transform us from the inside out. Use us as Your willing vessels. Help us to hear that still small voice. Command us this day in our assignment. In everything that we do we will do it to bring Your name glory. All praise belongs to You. In Jesus' name we pray, Amen.

# July 8

*And, behold, the veil of the temple was rent in twain from the top to the bottom; and the earth did quake, and the rocks rent;* (Matthew 27:51)

Christ paid it all for you and me to enter into the presence of God. Without Christ we would have been eternally separated from God. In love, Christ bore our sins on the cross, scorning its shame, and granting us access to God. God cannot dwell in the presence of sin. In the temple there was a veil which separated the holy place from the Most Holy place. "And thou shalt hang up the vail under the taches, that thou mayest bring in thither within the vail the ark of the testimony: and the vail shall divide unto you between the holy place and the most holy" (Exodus 26:33). There, only the High priest could enter to give a sacrifice on the behalf of others. Jesus' blood on the cross became the ultimate sacrifice for us. Now, when we come before God the works of Christ have cleansed us. There is no longer a veil or a need for someone to go in on our behalf. Christ's sacrifice granted us the opportunity to experience an intimate relationship with God without hindrance. Now, as soon as we sin we must come ourselves asking for forgiveness and turn away from contrary behavior. Thanks to Christ, we are dead to sin. His blood freed us from the bondage associated with sin. We are now free to live in the Spirit and follow God without condemnation. This day we remember the death of Christ and the power of God that raised Him from the dead. Thanking God for loving us so much to send His Son to bring us back home. What an example we have in Christ, who took His assignment with dignity only to experience human torture on our behalf.

Prayer: Lord, You did it all for us. Our life is praise before You. You are the reason we live each day. Thank You for the work on the cross. Now we can come boldly before the throne of grace to worship at Your feet. Your love encompasses the earth. It is filled with Your glory. You are so wonderful. We will spend the rest of our lives thanking You for calling us back to You. We die to our flesh that You may live in us. We love You forever. In Jesus' name we pray, Amen.

# July 9

*And* he that searcheth the hearts knoweth what is the mind of the Spirit, because he maketh intercession for the saints according to the will of God. (Romans 8:27)

There is never a time when we are left alone on earth. God is always with us; we also have our friends Jesus and the Holy Spirit interceding on our behalf. Even in our deepest despair, the Spirit is reporting to God the deepest issues of our heart and God responds. What an awesome team of advocates we have as saints of God. We are strengthened on every side. There are more who work for us than there could ever be against us. When we take the time to reflect on the goodness of God, we can see Him at work in our lives. Not to mention every day was written for us before any of them came to be. "You saw me before I was born. Every day of my life was recorded in your book. Every moment was laid out before a single day had passed (Psalm 139:16). As we walk in the Spirit, yielding to the commands of God, we are able to enjoy the fruits of righteousness. Setting our eyes on Jesus, we experience the greatness of being led into the destiny God has prepared for us. We don't have to question whether or not our life is being lived on purpose. We are assured by allowing the Spirit to guide our every step. The Spirit only leads us in the things God has instructed of Him. Securing our life in His hands, encouraging us each day; teaching us to operate in our position as heirs to the kingdom.

**Be Kingdom Minded!**

Prayer: Lord, Thank You, Thank You, Thank You. Not only did You call us by name, but You have given us help in all things. Without Your guidance we are blind. Everything You instruct us to do brings glory to Your name. Crucify our flesh today to be led by Your Spirit. God, this is a constant struggle as we live in the world. Let Your Word pierce our heart to understand the truth within. Help us to be doers and not only hearers of Your Word. Develop our faith as we hope in Your promises. We surrender all to You. Your name will forever be praised, In Jesus' name we pray, Amen.

# July 10

*Keep thy foot when thou goest to the house of God, and be more ready to hear, than to give the sacrifice of fools: for they consider not that they do evil.* (Ecclesiastes 5:1)

In this fast-paced world we live in today, it's hard to find quiet time to just sit and listen. Although we may feel our lives are filled to capacity, in our time with God we must be able to push everything aside in order to hear the sound of heaven. God is always in position, He teaches us how we ought to come before Him, ready to hear all the plans He has prepared for us. So often we find it easy to check the block during prayer by submitting our supplications like reading a grocery list and saying Amen without taking the time to ask God what His plans are concerning our life. When we change the order of our prayer we are able to pray the way Jesus teaches us in Matthew 6:10 when he says, "Thy kingdom come, Thy will be done in earth, as it is in heaven." After giving reverence to God, our ears should be open to hear what God is saying. God wants us to respect our time with Him. We obtain more as we come to God with an open and pure heart, ready to receive everything He has to offer. He knows all of our needs. He wants us to surrender by turning to Him in acknowledgment. When we come to God in prayer, allowing the Holy Spirit to take over, we can receive everything our hearts desire to ask of Him.

**God what is on Your mind? Reveal it today!**

Prayer: God, You are the King of glory, The LORD strong and mighty, The LORD mighty in battle (Psalm 24:8). We give You reverence today. We come with an ear to hear what is taking place in heaven. Speak into the lives of Your people, let us hear Your voice. Remove all distractions. We will make it our priority to sit in silence and hear what You are speaking. We give You all the praise. In Jesus' name we pray, Amen.

# July 11

*And let the beauty of the Lord our God be upon us: and establish thou the work of our hands upon us; yea, the work of our hands establish thou it.* (Psalm 90:17)

There is nothing worse than starting a project and not completing it (Ecclesiastes 7:8 Finishing is better than starting). We begin each task with good intentions and hopes of seeing it through to fruition, only to find out sometimes we allow life to get in the way, and for one reason or another we may fail to complete our mission. Either through our own negligence or other obstacles, which arise. God wants us to be mindful of our time and energy while on earth. Our time here is short in comparison to the time we'll spend in eternity. We have to focus our energy on the things of God. This may sound boring to most, but if you really think about it, God places our gifts and aspirations within us. Everything good comes from Him. As we align with His Will, the desires of our heart are what He has predestined. We find joy in yielding our plans before the Father, knowing it is in Him that our dreams will be established. Everything God begins He finishes. As we submit our plans to God, we are confident that they will be established. "Commit thy works unto the LORD, and thy thoughts shall be established" (Proverbs 16:3). Lay every dream you have within your heart before God. Seeking His direction and walk in His promises and see the manifestation.

**Dream Big and watch our Big God fulfill them!**

Prayer: Lord, You are strong and mighty. You are everything. Thank You for sharing Your love with us. We are forever grateful. We submit our plans to You. We give You the desires of our heart that You establish the work of our hands. Give us the confidence to achieve our goals and aspirations. Let our gifts manifest in the earth. Ignite Your fire within us to finish every task You set before us. We understand that whatever we put Your hand to will be established. Thank You for choosing us to be Your beloved children. We give You the glory in Jesus' name we pray, Amen.

# July 12

*And he taught, saying unto them, Is it not written, My house shall be called of all nations the house of prayer? but ye have made it a den of thieves.* (Mark 11:17)

Prayer is an essential part of our relationship with God. It is the very gateway to us learning the attributes of God, hearing from Him and enjoying fellowship with Him. Jesus was disappointed about the condition of the temple. People were selling and buying merchandise instead of using the temple as a sacred place of worship. Jesus taught how important it is for His house to be a house of prayer. Prayer goes directly to the Father. We are able to cast our cares at His feet, relinquishing everything to receive strength and encouragement in return. Showing reference in God's house and in our lives allows God to speak directly to us concerning everything that is going on. We can turn on the news and see the devastation-taking place throughout the world. There is always a need for prayer. We also have so much to be thankful for. There is a lot God protects us from on a daily basis. God is holy and desires to teach us how to operate and function as Heirs to the kingdom. Making prayer a priority ensures we are always in alignment with everything God is trying to pour into our lives and the lives of those around us.

**Don't miss it, by missing God!**

Prayer: Lord, You are the King of kings, Lord of all the earth. Everything is because of you. We acknowledge Your goodness in the earth and are pleased with Your works. We surrender ourselves to be taught how to incorporate prayer in our daily lives. Let our words come before You as a sweet aroma. Teach us how to pray; show us how to wait diligently to hear from You. We don't want to be anywhere unless You are in the midst. Guide our tongue, instruct our hands, and establish everything in our lives. With gratitude we are honored that You never sleep nor slumber. You are always available to commune with us and we say thank You. We give You all honor and glory. In Jesus' name we pray, Amen.

# July 13

*And the word of God increased; and the number of the disciples multiplied in Jerusalem greatly; and a great company of the priests were obedient to the faith.* (Acts 6:7)

The Word of God increased, spreading across many regions saturating the minds of thousands of people. By hearing the Word of God they were compelled to join fellowship with God, adding to the church of Christ daily. God's love speaks directly to the heart of those who will listen. When God pierces our heart with the truth of His Word, our entire nature begins to change. His grace is captivating, drawing us in and prompting us to yearn for more of Him. The Word must first be in our hearts in order for it to grow in the earth. Failing to read God's Word will keep us in darkness, shielding us from the things God is trying to awaken within us. As we develop and grow, our experience is available to be shared with those around us. Our excitement about the truth of God's Word can ignite an interest in others. Applying God's Word to every aspect in life develops our faith and keeps us in alignment with heaven. The power embedded within God's Word draws people in, causing us to desire to be obedient to His every command.

**Whom have I in heaven but You? And besides You, I desire nothing on earth.**
**(Psalm 73:25)**
**God is All!**

Prayer: Lord, You are the very air we breathe. By Your grace we are able to enjoy life. Lord, we place our lives in Your hand. We invite You into our hearts. Have Your proper position as head over our lives. Teach us how to evangelize. Minister to our souls, so we can be effective in the community. As we seek Your face daily, send us revelation and understanding. We will stand on the truth of Your Word, speaking it in love. Let the words of our mouth and the meditation of our heart be acceptable in Your sight (Psalm 19:14). Your Word is power, strength and truth. It has changed us and is causing us to become more and more like You.

Thank You for speaking to us and never leaving us alone. We bow down in honor before You. In Jesus' name we pray, Amen.

# July 14

*Now when Daniel knew that the writing was signed, he went into his house; and his windows being open in his chamber toward Jerusalem, he kneeled upon his knees three times a day, and prayed, and gave thanks before his God, as he did aforetime.* (Daniel 6:10)

When do we thank God? The correct answer is at all times. Thanking God should not be limited to our emotional state. When things are going well with us we honor God, and then as soon as challenges arise, we succumb to the pressures of life. When trials arise or unfavorable circumstances cause our emotions to get out of whack our lips shall mutter, "Lord I thank You." We are able to thank God because He has already orchestrated our entire life. Our expected end is guaranteed to be victorious as we rest in God. Daniel knew there had been a decree put into the law stating if any person were to pray to any god beside King Darius, they were to be killed. There is no greater torment on earth than to knowingly face death. The possibility of dying did not deter Daniel from his normal fellowship with God. He continued in his daily communion with God and refused to allow outside influences to cause his faith to waiver. Daniel offered thanksgiving as he normally did. This is a great principle to follow as we are in covenant with God. Our eyes must always remain set on God. When obstacles arise we can thank God as we normally do; understanding that our gratitude is not based upon what we see, it's based upon knowing the God we serve.

**Nothing Shall Deter Us from God!**

Prayer: God, You are Alpha and Omega, You are the Lord of the earth. All power belongs to You. You have granted us peace in abundance. Lord, we thank You that we are whole today. Thank You for always being in control of every aspect of our lives. Although at times it may seem rough, we know You are alert and in touch with our reality. You are not surprised by anything we experience. No matter what we have to endure in life, our eyes will be set on You. We will always place Jesus before us as the Author and Finisher of our faith. We trust You. Thank You for an expected end. Your plans for us are good and promote our well-being. We will forever give You thanks. In Jesus' name we pray, Amen.

# July 15

*"On that day," declares the Lord Almighty, "I will take you, my servant Zerubbabel son of Shealtiel," declares the Lord, "and I will make you like my signet ring,* ***for I have chosen you****," declares the Lord Almighty.* (Haggai 2:23)

There should never be a question whether we have purpose in life. God's sole reason in allowing us to grace the earth is a part of His divine plan. Each of us are individually unique in His eyes. He has predestined us to fulfill great things on earth. We are able to see the goodness of God as we look around at the wonderful things in the earth. The sun is in position and accomplishes the set task God created it for. Just like nature, we have an internal connection with God, which maintains our life line. We are connected to greatness, and as a result should be producing such in the earth. If we are unaware of the plans God has instilled in us, all we have to do is ask. God will be more than willing to grant us insight into the gifts He has placed on the inside of us. Once we come into agreement with God's plans we must execute our assignments. We will not obtain a greater satisfaction throughout our lifetime that can be compared with the joy of walking in God. His plans not only bring about His divine purpose but it pleases us all at the same time. In God, we don't have to worry about "what if;" our constant meditation is from heaven as we hear the voice of God saying "***for I have chosen you.***"

**Before I formed you in your mother's womb I knew you! (Jeremiah 1:5)**

Prayer: God, You are the source of our life. We breathe because You allow it. We rejoice this day, thanking You for Your loving kindness. Open our hearts to seek Your face to know the plans that You have so eloquently established for us. Give us godly visions to see what You have prepared for us in heaven to come in alignment with the grace you have bestowed upon us. Build our confidence to operate in faith, believing in Your Word concerning our lives. Stir up the gifts You have placed inside of us. Let us walk in purpose all the days of our lives. Lord, You have been so gracious to us, we worship in Your presence now and forevermore. In Jesus' name we pray, Amen.

# July 16

*If we live in the Spirit, let us also walk in the Spirit.* (Galatians 5:25)

If we are to be led by the Spirit we are going to have to deny ourselves every day. It requires that we make a conscious effort to adhere to the promptings of the Holy Spirit by submitting ourselves to the commands of God. Our flesh and God's Spirit within us are in a constant battle. However, we are assured God is the victor. As we become doers of the Word we are feeding our Spirit with the nourishment that will enable us to resist temptation from our flesh. God has given us every tool to live a successful life. Yielding to God's Spirit is beneficial in helping us to develop godly character. Temptation is sure to knock on each of our doors because we are human. Our faith steps in during these tests, allowing us to draw on the strength of God's power by standing on His Word. The devil is not bothered when we attend church, or that our prayer life is intact; what shakes the enemy is our ability to stand on the promises of God and remain steadfast during times of distress. Staying before God prepares us to exercise His principles at all times; equipping us to be the light of the world. There is no fault in being led by the Spirit, it breathes life, directs our path and builds us up with wisdom. Every step we take should be governed by God. His Spirit within us helps us to do all things well.

**But the fruit of the Spirit is love, joy, peace, longsuffering, gentleness, goodness, faith, Meekness, temperance: against such there is no law. (Galatians 5:22-23)**

Prayer: Lord, You are Mighty, Awesome, Powerful and full of goodness. Your name will forever be praised. Lord, we yield to You this day. Sanctify us in Your holy presence. God, we bow down in exaltation, asking for forgiveness of all manner of sin. Wash us, search us inwardly. Transform us to be made into Your holy image. Lord, help us to die to our flesh. Don't allow us to be comfortable having a form of godliness, but denying the power thereof (2 Timothy 3:5). Help us to turn from the lust of the flesh and follow after You. Your plans far exceed anything we could think of for ourselves. Your love compels us to obey You. Keep us close. All power and majesty belong to You. In Jesus' name we pray, Amen.

# July 17

*To Him be glory in the church and in Christ Jesus throughout all generations forever and ever. Amen (so be it).* (Ephesians 3:21)

What God did for David, Daniel, Noah, Joshua, Mary, Abraham, Isaac, Esther, and Ruth, He can and will do for us. His power far exceeds anything we can begin to imagine for ourselves. It actually pleases God when we dream big. He is our biggest encourager and I believe He often wants us to dream outside of the box. His love supersedes any mistakes we have made or will make. God deserves glory (honor, revere) for who He is. God has prepared our lives distinctively to ensure we are able to function at our fullest potential. He delights when we are able to enjoy our experience with Him on a continuous basis. God finds delight when we come into the knowledge of who He truly is. As we know Him, we are able to fully become aware of who we are. Our identity is hidden in Christ. The more time we spend with Him, learning and developing in His nature the more we are equipped for this life. God wants to show us the mysteries of His heart. It is in His presence where we find the fullness of joy and at his right hand treasures for evermore (Psalm 16:11). We have been granted full, not partial access through Jesus to come boldly before the throne of grace to bear every part of our being before God. As we yield, He pours more of Himself into our hearts, filling us with His splendor. There is not a day that goes by where God isn't showering us with His love. To Him be glory!

**God, use me for Your Glory!**

Prayer: Lord, Your love surpasses understanding. How awesome it is to know You care for us. Thank You for looking past our shortcomings and seeing the greatness You placed inside of us. Help us to see ourselves in the same manner. We glorify You for being who You are. You are a perfect Father. You have redeemed us, and we say thank You. Fill us with Your wisdom that we may function as heirs to the Most High. Lord, we bless Your name forever, in Jesus' name we pray, Amen.

# July 18

*And if these [neighbor nations] will diligently learn the ways of My people, to swear by My name, saying, As the Lord lives—even as they taught My people to swear by Baal—then will they be built up in the midst of My people.* (Jeremiah 12:16)

God's promises reign forever; His covenant cannot be broken. He promises to be in the midst of those who trust Him. As His beloved children, we are living in a world among some who choose not to believe God exists or who fail to follow His commands. This should not discourage us in our efforts of exercising kingdom principles. Our lifestyles in Christ should be affecting the world with God's way of doing things. Pollution of the world should not be the strongest force of influence in our life. Our lives are a living testimony of our acceptance of Jesus Christ and how He has given us a new identity. In our new identity, we are able to share with the world how awesome God is. We understand if anyone is a friend of the world they are an enemy with God (James 4:4). Our greatest concern shouldn't be what we can obtain in life; it should be our ministry to the world trying to influence and be an impact to them, shining a light on Christ, showcasing who He truly is. The welfare of our neighbors should be upon our heart as we see many dying from a lack of knowledge. Our lifestyle should draw people in to inquire about God's greatness. God's love is to be radiant in the lives of His people, shining light on the evil of this world causing unbelievers to turn from sin.

**Let your light shine!**

Prayer: Lord, we honor You. We come for our assignment today. Touch our hearts with Your ministry. Train us in the way we should go. Influence our lives in such a way that it shines through our pores. You are the light of this world. Use us as Your vessels to complete Your plans in the earth. Oh, how great it is to be loved by You. Your love is everlasting and incomparable. Nothing can take Your place in us. Help us not to be selfish, and encourage us to spread the gospel among the world. Build our strength to speak about Your goodness and encourage us to lift up our neighbors. All praise belongs to You, in Jesus' name we pray. Amen.

# July 19

*It is in vain that you rise up early and go late to rest, eating the bread of anxious toil; for he gives to his beloved sleep.* (Psalm 127:2)

Worry can add no value to our life. It is natural for us as humans to experience restless emotions when uncomfortable circumstances arise in our life. God has given us precise directions to guide us through. First, He tells us if He is not involved in every aspect of our lives we are operating in vain, working, but adding no value to the course of our life. Secondly, if we incorporate God in every aspect of our lives we have established a solid and secure foundation. Although it may look challenging, God is in control. We don't have to worry ourselves by losing sleep, constantly rerunning the events over in our head or beating ourselves up about a mistake. Without God, we establish plans aimlessly. Our trust must be anchored in our God, who never sleeps nor slumbers. Who knows the end of a matter before the beginning and has orchestrated every detail of our existence before the foundation of the earth. You will eventually burn out, we continue functioning without God. God has everything we will ever need in the palm of His hands. It's a daily requirement to surrender before His presence. Allowing God to establish the course of our path, knowing it will produce only righteousness and total fulfillment. Well then, you may ask what about those people who are successful and deny Christ. The answer is by what standards is their success measured? As believers we are living to live again. We have hope and believe we will spend eternity in heaven with God. I often wonder how God and I will laugh when I get to heaven and He shows me all the things I worried about, all of my fears and the many things I missed out on due to not trusting Him. God has so much more for us, we have to allow Him to be Lord over every aspect of our being.

**God Knows!**

Prayer: God, You are Supreme in our lives. We submit ourselves before Your presence this day. Establish the work of our hands. Pour out Your splendor upon the earth and into the lives of Your beloved children. Your love covers us. Your love compels us to obey Your voice. The voice of another we will not follow. Pull us back in if we shall ever stray. Forgive us of all manner of sin. Cleanse us of disobedience, unbelief, doubt, fear, anxiousness, worry and all malicious intent. Search us inwardly, washing us in Your mighty power. Allow Your Word to reside deep within our hearts, causing our spirits to align with You. We call heaven to the earth in the lives of Your people; abundant living in every aspect. We bless You God. In Jesus' name we pray, Amen.

# July 20

*Blessed be the Lord, who daily loadeth us with benefits, even the God of our salvation. Selah.* (Psalm 68:19)

Many ask the question, how can I not worry when faced with adversity in life? God gives the answer in His Word over and over. We are covered by God's protection. As soon as our feet hit the ground in the morning, God has already prepared us for the day. He has imputed in us every necessity we need to sustain us through the day. God never sleeps or takes a day off from sending His angels to be on post around us. He is trying to get us to open our heart to the principles of heaven and walk according to our position as kingdom citizens. God is our salvation, He bears the burden of every trick the enemy tries to throw our way. We were not called to the earth to live in a state of despair. God has a solution to every challenge. "Even to your old age and gray hairs I am he, I am he who will sustain you. I have made you and I will carry you; I will sustain you and I will rescue you" (Isaiah 46:4). The bible says, **God loadeth us with benefits on a DAILY basis.** We are without excuse when it comes to blessing God for being everything to us at all times. There is not a day that goes by where God forgets to supply every one of our needs. Our nourishment is always found in Him. He relinquishes our daily bread and equips us every day of our lives. From the time we were born until the day we return to Him we are covered by His grace. It brings God great pleasure to see us rejoicing in the blessings of life.

**But let the righteous be glad; let them rejoice before God: yea, let them exceedingly rejoice. (Psalm 68:3)**

Prayer: Hallelujah! Lord, we bless Your name. We rejoice in Your presence. You have searched the earth to find Your people praising You. There is no greater way we can express our gratitude for Your loving-kindness. We will exalt You at all times; praise will continuously be on our lips. Our hearts are full of joy, thanking You for supplying our every need. We will lift our eyes to You daily and wait for Your instruction. This is Your life, have

Your way. Lead us on the narrow path of righteousness for Your name's sake. In all that we do we give You glory, in Jesus' name we pray, Amen.

# July 21

*Better is one day in your courts than a thousand elsewhere; I would rather be a doorkeeper in the house of my God than dwell in the tents of the wicked.* (Psalm 84:10)

As long as we live on earth we will not be able to find any place in all existence that can compare to being in the midst of our holy God. Being in God's presence consists of us giving Him proper position in our lives, which is first place. A lot of times we are so eager to get the day started, as we live in a fast paced world. From personal experience, when I give God the first part of my day through total devotion, God holds the time for me. What I mean is, everything else falls into place; as if I have more time to accomplish my goals for the day. We can seek His face on a daily basis by setting aside time to hear from Him, He will surely guide our every step. As we draw close to Him, He releases everything we need to sustain us. "For the Lord God is a sun and shield; the Lord bestows favor and honor; no good thing does he withhold from those whose walk is blameless" (Psalm 84:11). He is always available; He is constantly waiting in expectation for us to acknowledge His splendor. Oh, but when we do we experience gratification like never before. His love compels us to return day after day. Giving God full reign of our being satisfies our soul. A day apart from Him should cause us to miss being in His presence. Luckily for us, grace meets us each day; we have ample opportunities to come and soak in His presence. There is nothing more important than quality time with God. As we take time to soak in His presence, His glory fills us and we are able to radiate His goodness in the earth. In His midst we receive everything we have need of. Even the things we weren't aware of. As we sit before Him in total surrender, we are able to gain an unexplainable awesome worship experience. We enjoy our time with God by being led by His Spirit. No two days are the same. He'll tell us how long, turn music on or off, bring a note pad, sit in silence or whatever the case may be. What we receive for sure is an opportunity to grow in deeper connection with the Creator of all things, our Father, Abba!!

**Rejoice, today God is here!**

Prayer: God, we could search the entire universe and nothing would compare to You. Your love compels us to draw close to You. Everything about You produces goodness. Open our hearts to receive You at all times. Don't let us allow anything to distract us from sitting in Your presence. God, lead us on the path You have made straight for us. Everything we need is in Your hands. We submit ourselves before You. Thank You for allowing us to see a new day. God, You are marvelous. With all praise we say glory to Your name. In Jesus' name we pray, Amen.

# July 22

*Is not this the word that we did tell thee in Egypt, saying, Let us alone, that we may serve the Egyptians? For it had been better for us to serve the Egyptians, than that we should die in the wilderness.* (Exodus 14:12)

Whenever we allow negative thinking to overwhelm us, it will cause us to become stagnant. It can paralyze us, causing us to deny the power God is trying to exhibit through our situation. At the onset of opposition the children of Israel succumbed to the lies of the enemy. Seeing their foes caving in on them, they turned to Moses and wished they were back under the Egyptians' abusive hand. They considered their desolate state as slaves to be better than death. Their negative thinking had them believe they were not worthy of the freedom God created them to abide in. They refused to even try to put up a fight; their first instinct made them believe they would be defeated. Not understanding they were under God's authority and He was their weapon. The devil attacks us in our mind to make us believe we are not equipped to overcome challenges and we are not worthy of the things God has prepared us for. He feeds us lies which strip down our confidence to make us believe God is not present. Not only is God present, He has already prepared the end result before any situation ever occurs. Moses responded to their negative thinking by placing the attention on God and His principles. **"And Moses said unto the people, Fear ye not, stand still, and see the salvation of the LORD, which he will shew to you to day" (Exodus 14:3).** The only thing standing between us and overcoming opposition is our faith and time. God has already secured our future. When unfavorable situations arise, our first instinct should be to stand on the Word of God. Standing on God's Word destroys fear and helps us remain steadfast as we wait on the LORD to show us the strength of His hand.

**Be still and Know that I Am God!**

Prayer: LORD, You are so amazing. The earth bows in

reverence to Your name. Lord, You understand how overwhelming life can be. We have been conditioned by our society to think negative about what life presents to us. Turn our negative thinking into trust. We no longer want to be reliant on what we see. We will stand on Your Word and exercise our faith. Knowing the truth is, You fight for us and victory is ours. You rule the earth; everything is Yours. Therefore we will not fear, instead we will praise Your holy name. Help us as we wrestle with negative thinking by renewing our minds on a consistent basis. As soon as thoughts rise up that are contrary to Your will we will cast them down. We love you, in Jesus' name we pray, Amen.

**Finally, brethren, whatsoever things are true, whatsoever things are honest, whatsoever things are just, whatsoever things are pure, whatsoever things are lovely, whatsoever things are of good report; if there be any virtue, and if there be any praise, think on these things. (Philippians 4:8)**

# July 23

*And they straightway left their nets, and followed him.* (Matthew 4:20)

What does it mean to follow Jesus? As Simon and Andrew dropped everything in an instant to follow Christ, we too must do the same. Every day when we get up we ought to lift our eyes to God and say, "Lead me." Laying aside everything to follow Christ brings us to a place of great refuge. We must understand the significance of our steps being ordered by God. He created everything. Nothing will come as a surprise to God. Every single day of our lives are already established in the book of life. Why wouldn't we seek the Author and Finisher of our faith? Most times we find it easier to make decisions for ourselves until we receive the revelation that God has our best interest at hand. It is beneficial for us to submit our plans to God, as a result they guarantee manifestation. God has many great plans for us. My Pastor says it all the time, "there are a millions ways to do things and God wants to give us the most strategic plan possible." When this happens we eliminate wandering down the wrong path and wasting the time God allotted us on earth. We all know time is one thing we will never be able to get back. We find pleasure in allowing God to orchestrate the plans for our lives. His purpose is the only true fulfillment we will ever obtain in life. Not only do we experience fulfillment, but abundant living in all aspects. As we lay aside every weight and sin that easily entangles us (Hebrews 12:1), we are able to appreciate our freedom by evaluating all things in accordance with God's Word. Jesus will only lead us to places He has already prepared for us. As we carry out our assignments we are assured the outcome will bring glory to God and develop us. Guidance from God is sheltered by security, and produces courage for us to endure the course set before us with inner peace. Knowing every decision composed by God has been thought out, tried, proven, and yields perfect results.

**Trust Jesus – it's the Only WAY!**

Prayer: God, You are holy. You thought to give us life and to sustain each of our days. As we walk this journey, You are right beside us, encouraging us every step of the way. Thank You for guiding us. Even in the midst of stubbornness, procrastination and disobedience, You never took Your eyes off of us. Forgive us for every time when chose not to consult Your throne. Open the eyes of our heart to follow after Christ. We surrender all. Nothing is more important than You. We put You first in all things. The earth is Yours and the fullness thereof. There is nothing we can do apart from You. We appreciate the life You have given us and will spend it in communion with You. Glory and praise we offer to You, now and forever. In Jesus' name we pray, Amen.

# July 24

*A man who lived there answered, "And who is their father?" So it became a saying: "Is Saul also among the prophets?" After Saul stopped prophesying, he went to the high place*. (1 Samuel 10:12 NIV)

When God transforms us, our entire demeanor will change as God is reconstructing the nature of our heart, burning off every attribute contrary to the characteristics He has instilled in us for the edifying of His kingdom. Saul was the first king appointed by God to the children of Israel. God instructed the prophet Samuel to give Saul specific guidance on how God would pour out His Spirit upon him. Everything the LORD spoke came to fruition. As soon as Saul turned to leave Samuel's presence, God changed His heart. God transformed Saul in such a way that when He returned to his hometown, people didn't recognize him. He was among the prophets prophesying; this prompted the people to inquire with such statements as "What has happened to the son of Kish?" (1 Samuel 10:11). They knew his lineage and did not associate Saul as being a chosen vessel of God. HA!!!! God's plans supersede popular opinion or any confinement man tries to place over our head. God predestined us to accomplish specific things in the earth. "The Spirit of the Lord will come powerfully upon you, and you will prophesy with them; and you will be changed into a different person" (1 Samuel 10:12 NIV). When God changes us, our old self must die. We are now hidden in Christ to perform the works of the kingdom. People should associate our works with our Father. Looking at our lives, it should be a reflection of heaven's fragrance exuding from our being.

**Be like Your Daddy, God and big brother Jesus!**

Prayer: Lord, You are so amazing. Words can't express Your greatness. You have filled our lives with such joy; we stand in awe of You. LORD, we ask that You touch our hearts today to accept the freedom that You have given to us. Release pressure from our lives from trying to be perfect. Let us find rest in Your bosom.

Help us to enjoy the life You have given us. As You walk hand in hand with us, let us get lost in the splendor of Your marvelous glory. We relinquish all forms of anxiety, doubt, fear and unbelief. As You have poured Your Spirit out among us let us walk in liberty, trusting You at all times. Let our life resemble Your greatness that when people see us they see You. Lord, we don't want to be phony, so as we come into Your presence on a consistent basis, burn every ounce of our sinful nature off of us. Thank You for Your power. In Jesus' name we pray, Amen.

# July 25

*But the Master said, "You don't need more faith. There is no 'more' or 'less' in faith. If you have a bare kernel of faith, say the size of a poppy seed, you could say to this sycamore tree, 'Go jump in the lake,' and it would do it."* (Luke 17:6 MSG)

Faith is not distributed in quantities pertaining to each person's condition. Jesus tells the disciples faith is embedded in their Spirit as a gift from God. Our faith to believe God can raise someone from the dead is no different from having faith to believe we will get a specific job. The difference is our level of development. My pastor uses the analogy all the time that two people have the same amount of muscles in their body. One person who develops and exercises their muscles will reflect it in their physique. While the other person may not display the muscular body type of a body builder, they still have the same amount of muscles, they are simply under developed. Faith is exercised by believing God will perform according to His Word, even though we can't see it at the present moment. Humans have put conditions on faith, structuralizing it to fit into boxes. When Jesus said faith is a part of our DNA, it's a command to exercise it. The power instilled in our faith gives us the courage to trust God no matter what life looks like. God is trying to take the scales off of our eyes, to help us realize our identity. Faith gives us hope to stand strong in the truth of God's Word. We know everything He says is true. Why then do we waiver at different times in our life? I believe it is because we have been trained to react to the conditions of life instead of operating in our position as kingdom citizens. We have to get to a place where we operate according to God's principles and what He has taught us. *He said fear not, He said do not be anxious, He said I will never forsake you, He said you are more than conquerors; He said I will fight for you, He said I will heal you.* He has covered every possible scenario that will ever present itself in our lives. Our commitment to obedience requires us to trust God by applying our faith at all times.

**Faith that works!**

Prayer: Emmanuel, we bless You! Be with Your people today. God give us faith to believe, faith to obey, faith to operate as Your children. We want all of You. We surrender every negative object that stands in the way of us trusting You wholeheartedly. We will praise You according to Your excellent greatness. Your Word has been tried and proven, it will NEVER return to You void. God help our unbelief. Jesus is a fence around us. We relinquish control of every aspect of our life. Search us inwardly; purge us to see the truth of Your Word. Remove the scales from our eyes. We want to experience life with You like never before. God, we will wait in Your presence until we hear from You. We are open to Your voice. Hallelujah, glory to Your name. In Jesus' name we pray Amen.

# July 26

*The sacrifices of God are a broken spirit: a broken and a contrite heart, O God, thou wilt not despise.* (Psalm 51:17)

The opposite of have a broken spirit is having a hard spirit. One that is shielded from allowing God in to transform aspects that are not of Him. A wall has been put up where the Holy Spirit is shut out, and is unable to deposit the greatness of God. God requires that we let down our guard, allowing ourselves to be broken before Him. In this manner He is able to cultivate our being by imputing in us the fruits of righteousness. A broken spirit is adherent to the commands of God's Spirit and functions according to kingdom principles. God is near a broken spirit; He is able to dwell in the midst without restriction. A broken and contrite heart is inviting to God, it tells Him we revere Him and without Him we are nothing. Honoring God with a heart of repentance displays respect for God's Word. As we dwell with God, allowing Him to be embedded within us, it will break our heart to break God's heart. The only opposition hindering us from having the courage to repent is pride. Pride puts up a barricade between God and us. God is trying to get directly to us. Having an open Spirit allows us to hear from God when we err, and forces us to respond accordingly. If our heart and actions don't align with God's commands, our prayers and acts of reverence become hindered. God doesn't require that we are perfect, but He wants us to be open to Him working through us. As we allow God to dwell within us, we adhere to correction and turn from contrary behavior. Having a broken spirit; a broken and contrite heart says to God that we make mistakes and are not too proud for correction and guidance. It's a humbling act, respecting His Supreme authority as LORD of our lives.

**For thus saith the high and lofty One that inhabiteth eternity, whose name is Holy; I dwell in the high and holy place, with him also that is of a contrite and humble spirit, to revive the spirit of the humble, and to revive the heart of the contrite ones. (Isaiah 57:15)**

Prayer: Lord, we render praise, honor, and glory before Your throne. You are worthy of all the praise. We invite You in to dwell in our midst. Search us inwardly, remove all iniquity, and wash us clean. Do a thorough inspection of our heart, mind and spirit that we may be found holy. Work out every aspect that is contrary to Your commands. Reveal to us the things that are hindering us from going deeper in You. We come to develop an authentic uninhibited relationship with You, where we dwell in open fellowship. Cause us not to boast in our works, but to acknowledge You in all things. Let us find no greater joy than to soak in Your presence. Thank You for ALL that you do on a consistent basis. We love You. In Jesus' name we pray, Amen.

# July 27

*And whiles I was speaking, and praying, and confessing my sin and the sin of my people Israel, and presenting my supplication before the Lord my God for the holy mountain of my God;* (Daniel 9:20)

Daniel's intimate time with God taps into the different dynamics of their relationship. He spoke to God as a friend, prayed to Him as a Savior, confessed before Him as Sovereign, and presented his supplications as a Provider. God is so awesome to be one Spirit, but everything we need all at the same time. It's important that we understand the holistic capabilities associated with our God. He is EVERYTHING we will ever need. Developing a relationship with God is no different from the relationships we have with other humans in the sense of open communication. We are able to speak freely with God, enjoying His presence (Just a little side note: God knows everything about us). There's nothing we can hide from Him. Yet, He still wants us relinquish our fears and trust Him. In our relationship with God we will never get to a place where we are above reproach. We all need to be replenished and washed in the Holy Spirit on a continuous basis. Humbling ourselves to always come confessing our mistakes, seeking for better ways to be more like Christ. God doesn't require us to be perfect; He wants us to be honest. Honest in our submission before Him; understanding our wisdom comes from Him. When we take this approach by surrendering our hearts before Him in free fellowship, we can begin to enjoy a loving relationship with our Father. Any matters on our heart can be shared in God's presence. There we find no room for judgment or embarrassment, only times of intimacy and true revelation. We come to the knowledge of who we are and how God wants to operate in our lives. Oftentimes people ask the question, well how do I pray? What do I say to God? The answer is talk to him like you talk to your friends. Be open with Him. Tell God about Your day, ask God how He is and allow the Spirit to take over. Its promised to be a rewarding time in His presence.

**I was glad when they said unto me, let us go into the house of the Lord!**

Prayer: Lord, we enter Your throne with a broken and contrite spirit. Forgive us of all of our sins. Wash us clean as snow, cast our iniquities into the sea of forgetfulness. Lord, thank You for forgiving us. You know every mistake and we are not too proud to say we are sorry. Watch over us, protect us and push us in the right direction. As we dwell in fellowship with You, help us to take the walls down. No longer will we place limits on you. You are free to invade our hearts, minds, and souls and become a permanent resident within us. All glory and praise belong to You. In Jesus' name we pray, Amen.

# July 28

*At midnight I will rise to give thanks unto thee because of thy righteous judgments.* (Psalm 119:62)

Sacrifice is required to obtain quality time with the LORD. Sometimes you'll have to give up your favorite television show or inform friends you aren't available in order to spend time with God. Alone time with the Master cultivates such unique characteristics within us that the more time we spend with Him, the more we long for His presence. There is never a time where we will not have a reason to be thankful. God does not force Himself upon us, yet He desires we receive His love. When we turn in reverence, our souls are satisfied. Rising at midnight exhibits a desperate yearning for God. God is not technical about a specific time, the psalmist uses midnight to illustrate a time of sacrifice. However we choose to plan alone time with God is beneficial. Planning exclusive time with God indicates NOTHING is more important than our relationship with Him. To surrender time which is borrowed anyway should be a joy and delight. Deciding to offer up our personal time to soak in His presence produces spiritual maturity. We prepare for many things, but nothing will ever be as important as our personal time with Jesus.

**You have said, "Seek my face." My heart says to you, "Your face, LORD, do I seek. (Psalm 27:8)**

Prayer: As the days continue, we will surrender our time before Your throne. We dare not forget about Your loving-kindness that keeps us day-by-day. Your grace surrounds us. Command our soul to bless You. We will delight ourselves in Your laws at all times. Let Your plans become our plans. We will place nothing before You. Help us to be committed to the call of being Your children. There is no greater love than what You give freely every day. Help us never to become too busy to bless Your name. We love You, in Jesus' name we pray, Amen.

# July 29

*For neither did his brethren believe in him.* (John 7:5)

People may not believe in you or the God you serve. Jesus' own brothers were embarrassed by Him and tried to taunt Him. Jesus, being cognizant of this, operated with discernment in all matters. He didn't allow the lack of encouragement from those closes to Him to defer His purpose. Instead, He allowed God's power working within Him to speak for itself. We must not ever deny our destiny on account of someone else's opinion of us. We can't please people, neither should they be our focus. Our concentration is primarily set on God. Self-pity should never be our place of refuge. When we find ourselves focused on the opinion of others we become distracted from glorifying God (Trick of the enemy). Jesus warned us that the world would hate us, and encouraged us to count it all joy. Our faith has the power to overcome our fear. "He that speaketh of himself seeketh his own glory: but he that seeketh his glory that sent him, the same is true, and no unrighteousness is in him" (John 7:18). Keeping our mind on Christ allows the Holy Spirit to govern our actions. We remain in the right mindset by not allowing outside circumstances to paralyze us. People who ridicule you are condemning themselves by breaking God's commandments. We don't have to worry about others judgment of us; our chief focus is on kingdom business. After all, God said you are "perfect." He loves us with an everlasting love. The acceptances of men is not our guiding force in life. We have to settle in our heart that we are the children of God. His loves is more than enough.

**God is all!**

Prayer: Lord, You are amazing. Your grace meets us every day. God, watch over us; give us wisdom and discernment concerning all matters. Help us not to be thrown off track due to life circumstances. We will place our trust in You. Help us to have a kingdom focus to always be about our Father's business. We bind the hand of the oppressor, gossiper, and backbiter. No weapon that is formed against us shall prosper and every tongue that rises against us shall be condemned, for this is our heritage (Isaiah 54:17). With praise we magnify Your name. In Jesus' name we pray, Amen.

# July 30

*For what is our hope, or joy, or crown of rejoicing? Are not even ye in the presence of our Lord Jesus Christ at his coming? For ye are our glory and joy.* (1 Thessalonians 2:19-20)

Paul was overjoyed at the calling God placed on His life. Since his transformation, he yielded his life to spreading the gospel. Even through persecution he made sure people were able to hear the gospel of Christ. God entrusted him with the Word of truth. The Word of God which holds great power and has the ability to transform lives. Paul, being filled with God's spirit, longed for the churches he was commissioned to teach. He understood there was nothing more important in life than for us to dwell with Christ in eternity. As he spoke to the church of Thessalonica he made sure they knew his actions and words were sincere. Their salvation was so important to Him that He affectionately longed for them (1 Thessalonians 2:8). Not only did Paul and those who came with him preach the gospel, they also gave everything within their souls to help the people believe through faith in Jesus. They yielded to the Holy Spirit and were able to touch the hearts of the listeners. As they believed, their faith was exhibited through their actions. After Paul left the city he sent His disciples to establish the church of Thessalonica and to encourage them in their faith. Upon the disciples' arrival they found the church to be functioning in faith and charity. Based upon Paul's authentic teaching, the church was able to grow in faith. They grabbed hold of God's Word and allowed it to transform them wholly. Even though Paul was no longer in their presence, the most important thing (Christ) resided within them. Our job as Christians is to spread the gospel. We may only have a little time with some people. Our message must be sincere and governed by God Himself. When we allow God to use us, His power is forever embedded in His people and they become lovers of the gospel.

**And the Lord make you to increase and abound in love one toward another, and toward all men, even as we do toward you: 13 To the end he may establish your hearts unblameable in**

**holiness before God, even our Father, at the coming of our Lord Jesus Christ with all his saints. (1 Thessalonians 3:12-13)**

Prayer: God, You are the joy of our hearts. Nothing is greater than You. Your grace meets us every morning. We say thank You for Your loving kindness. Lord, there is no greater desire for You than for all mankind to believe in Your Son, Jesus Christ. Commission us with Your power to spread the gospel. Use us as Your body parts in the earth to magnify Your name. Let love be our universal language to spread toward others. Help us to love with agape love. Teach us to love without condition or to long for something in return. Place Your desires upon our heart. We pray for every heart around this globe to yield to Your love and accept You as Lord. We will forever bless Your name. In Jesus' name we pray, Amen.

# July 31

*If you are willing and obedient, you will eat the good things of the land; 20 but if you resist and rebel, you will be devoured by the sword." For the mouth of the Lord has spoken.* (Isaiah 1:19-20)

There is never any deficiency on God's part concerning His promises. He only has to say something once. Before the foundation of the world He made provision for each of us concerning our purpose. We have free will whether or not we choose to follow His plans. When we yield our life to God as obedient and willing vessels, we unlock the treasures He has stored up for us. Our treasures pertain to every aspect of our life. Relationships, prayers for family, peace, jobs, and finances can be hindered if we fail to adhere to every one of God's commands. God gives us instructions on a daily basis to keep us in line with what is taking place in Heaven. It's important to know everything He asks of us is for our benefit. Our task matures us and strengthens us as a body of believers. I remember when God told me to write my first book. He instructed me to take a semester off of school to accomplish His plan. Instead of listening, I tricked myself into believing I could go to school and write a book at the same time. It all blew up in my face. Faced with life's obstacles, I was forced to drop all my classes in the middle of the semester without even starting the book; all because of disobedience. I had no book and no credits that semester. God is serious about His Word; there is no compromising. He will not suffer us to accomplish a worthless task. Everything from God has great benefits, it behooves us to listen the first time and receive the good of the land. He loves us so much that He'll interrupt our life to cause us to get back on track to obedience.

**God Speaks clearly, now listen!**

Prayer: Father, we adore You. Your plans have been thought out, tried and proven to be perfect. On our best day we cannot compare to Your marvelous knowledge. Remove our pride today. Help us to yield to Your every command. When You speak, let

"Yes" be our natural response. When we don't understand, give us strength to trust You. Help us not to lean on our own understanding. You have an expected end for us. Help us to die to our flesh that we are not so consumed that we miss the mark. Open our eyes to see Your goodness. We would have lost hope if we didn't believe we would see the goodness of the LORD in the land of the living. (Psalm 27:13). Bless You God, now and forevermore. In Jesus' name we pray, Amen.

# August 1

*Beyond all these things put on love, which is the perfect bond of unity.* (Colossians 3:14 NASB)

There is no question whether or not God loves us. The doubt lies in whether we love God. Love is a simple thing that we as humans transform into something difficult. We put conditions on our love for God and for others. We consider our present circumstances to somewhat hold the key to the magnitude of how God will love us. If our lives are not together we feel as though God's love is somehow diminished. Or if we fail to accomplish something we try to associate it with His love slipping away. God is not like us. His love is entangled in His nature. It can never be separate from who He is and what He is trying to be in the lives of those He created. Love is a gift given to nourish our soul; it draws us to God and keeps us in His presence. We can't work for His love, it's something that has to be received and reciprocated to others. No longer do we have to put a charge over people's head, causing them to work for our love. God doesn't act in this manner and neither should we. We should wake up with love on our mind, searching for opportunities to show grace and mercy towards our neighbors. C.S. Lewis states, "Many things- such as loving, going to sleep, or behaving unaffectedly- are done worst when we try hardest to do them." He is teaching us to let our love flow naturally. There is no other way to learn how to love than from the Creator of love. As we bask in God's love, He will develop His attributes and love will become our natural response to life.

Prayer: Lord, we bless You! We sing praises to Your holy name. Because of You we are. There is no greater love in all existence. We stand in awe of You. Help us to receive Your love today. God, take the scales off of our eyes to see things the way You see them. This life is a gift. You have stored up riches and treasures for us. We can't even begin to imagine the greatness You have planned for us. You do this all because of love. Your love keeps us in perfect peace. Thank You for always encouraging us to be more like Jesus. We place our lives in Your hands to mold us and shape us into Your image and likeness. With our hearts lifted to You we give You glory and praise. In Jesus' name we pray, Amen.

## August 2

*"I am the Lord's servant," Mary answered. "May your word to me be fulfilled." Then the angel left her.* (Luke 1:38)

What an honor it is to serve at our Master's feet? Service in the kingdom requires total surrender to the Will of the Father. Every selfish ambition has to be checked at the door. We have invited Jesus in to reign as Lord over us. Our submission to God's commands breathes life into our bodies. It is the very source of our nourishment. As Jesus laid down His life for us, we ought to be willing to accomplish the will of the Father. Hearing God's voice will sometimes require us to deny pleasures in our life. As God's servants we should come before His throne, asking what we can do for the kingdom before we ask what He can do for us. He has already promised all of our needs would be met, and we are not to be anxious about anything. Knowing this better equips us for selfless service. When God speaks we respond with a "Yes". It may be a struggle, because there is a constant battle between our flesh and His Spirit. Our hope comes from knowing only the work we do for God will last. There will be no greater joy in life than pleasing God. Our life is to be spent preparing for Jesus' return. Everything associated with God embodies goodness; serving God satisfies our deepest need while expanding the Kingdom.

Prayer: Lord, there is no greater love than from above. Nothing we do in life will compare to what You have done for us. We will spend our life rendering honor and praise before Your throne. We are Your servants; tell us what You would have us to do. Remove anything that enslaves us and causes us to push You aside. Let us find no greater joy than to hear from You and to commit to obedience. Let obedience be our natural response to Your voice. Be our strength as we exercise our faith. All glory belongs to You. In Jesus' name we pray, Amen.

# August 3

*For I know the thoughts that I think toward you, says the LORD, thoughts of peace and not of evil, to give you a future and a hope.* (Jeremiah 29:11)

If God has our best intentions in His heart, who are we to contend with His Word? Our only response should be to get into position. We should position ourselves to hear from heaven on a daily basis to receive our instructions. We are traveling through unknown territory. We are unable to discern what tomorrow will bring, only God knows. Thankfully His thoughts toward us are to give us a future and a hope. A future guarantees we always have something to look forward to. Our hope strengthens us and enables us to enjoy the journey of life. God didn't say, I promise you a life without hardships. He said His intention is to give us a future and a hope. That's something tangible we can hold on to. We always come out on top in Jesus. Following God puts us into position to fulfill His destiny. Everything associated with God produces greatness. Instead of worrying, we need to focus on our connection with the Father. Having God plan our lives gives us hope, He is our joy. We have assurance that as we are following the commands of God everything works out for our good (Romans 8:28). Everything about Him is great and He has decided to share it with us. We can rejoice in God's thoughts towards us. His unwavering plans develop our character and teach us how to operate as kingdom citizens.

**What God has for me it is for me!**

Prayer: God, this life we live belongs to You. We count it as an honor for You to think about us the way You do. You love us beyond our deepest scar. You see us pure and unblemished. You are concerned with our circumstances and every aspect of our life and we thank You for being our Daddy! There is no greater love in all the earth. Instruct us in Your plans today. Let us grab hold of the hope that You have implanted in us. We rejoice, knowing You have ordered each one of our steps. Keep us in tune with Your plans. Let Thy kingdom come. Thy will be done in earth, as *it is* in heaven. We love you. In Jesus' name we pray, Amen.

# August 4

*I was glad when they said unto me, Let us go into the house of the Lord.* (Psalm 122:1)

I remember the first time I experienced an encounter with Jesus, feelings of completeness overwhelmed my body. From that day forward I longed for every piece of Him. He sparked a fire within my heart that no one could put out. The love and security I had been searching for my entire life was filled in an instant. God's love is that compelling. It saturates our hearts, filling it to capacity until it overflows. Every attribute of God draws us closer to Him. His love purifies who we are and we trade in our brokenness for His marvelous peace. Spending time with God changes everything. There's nothing too hard for Him; and there is nothing He is not aware of. He's able to deal with everything we release to Him. Coming to God literally shifts the course of our day to join in alignment with His plans. God never intended for us to experience anything in life alone. His presence is where the fullness of joy is and at His right hand are pleasures forevermore (Psalm 16:11). Not only do we have the grace to come boldly before His throne, we ought to count it as a privilege. There are many places across the world where the mention of the name of Jesus warrants death. Here we have freedom to come into His house to worship and give Him glory in open fellowship. It's beyond gratifying to enter into His presence to bless His name.

**Will you come?**

Prayer: God, You deserve all the glory and we render it to You. No greater love will we ever know than what You supply. Every one of our needs are met according to Your glory and riches in Christ Jesus. You have considered our days. You walk with us on a consistent basis. Nothing is hidden from Your sight and yet You still love us. God You are worthy. Fill our hearts with gladness. We delight ourselves in Your presence. It is with great honor that we reverence You. In Jesus' name we pray, Amen.

# August 5

*Do not err, my beloved brethren. Every good gift and every perfect gift is from above, and cometh down from the Father of lights, with whom is no variableness, neither shadow of turning.* (James 1:16-17)

God is the Father of love. Everything He does is for our benefit. His position in our lives is to cultivate us into the original image of greatness He conceived at the onset of creation. It is imperative we understand the issues of life and know what is and isn't from God. Many times God is trying to get us to open our eyes to the problems around us. Not to be mistaken with God trying to tempt us into any bad situation. Nothing bad comes from God, only what is good and perfect comes from heaven. Being the loving God that He is, He teaches us how stand firm when tempted by evil. He says don't allow it to throw you off course. Our ultimate goal in life is to serve God. We have an adversary whose only job is to steal, kill and destroy. When our faith is being tested, we are certain God is not the mastermind behind deception. God is our refuge and strong tower; we can run to Him for protection. We are able to obtain wisdom and instructions on how to endure each obstacle. When our faith is tested, we are able to exercise our total dependence on God. His loving nature only produces goodness, righteousness, and gifts to blossom us. He is not fickle in His actions toward us. His purpose for creation is for us to dwell in fellowship with Him. He doesn't waste our time by trying to trip us up with difficulties, but when they arise He is right there beside us, encouraging us in His Mighty power. The closer we are to God, through reading His Word and becoming doers; the less affected we are when satan comes to tempt us.

**Be Free!**

Prayer: God, we thank You. We know we have freedom in You. We are free to enjoy life. We know nothing harmful comes from above. Lord, search our hearts thoroughly to remove all manner of sin. Transplant Your Word deep within our heart, let it blossom during times of despair. When faced with obstacles let us run to You asking for wisdom and discernment. You have all the answers; nothing comes as a surprise to You. You know each day, before any of them come to be. Let Your love fill our hearts. Build our confidence in You not to worry about ANYTHING. We lay every concern at Your feet and run this race with endurance. All glory belongs to You. In Jesus' name we pray, Amen.

# August 6

*The lot causeth contentions to cease, and parteth between the mighty* (Proverbs 18: 18 KJV)

*You may have to draw straws when faced with a tough decision.* (Proverbs 18: 18 MSG)

Casting lots was a practice where people would throw rocks, and depending upon where they landed it revealed God's Will. It also serves as an encouraging practice promoting humility. In this scripture, the wisdom being taught is encouraging us to have humility as we trust God. Many times in life we will be faced with difficult decisions where many choices could produce favorable outcomes. Using the metaphor of drawing straws or casting lots encourages us to make a decision based on God's principles. When we gave our life to God, He took our covenant agreement seriously. He has aligned our life with what is written in the lamb's book of life. He often allows us to experience times where we aren't immediately able to come to a decision. In these instances we are able to depend upon His Holy Spirit to guide us in the right choice. We can lay out all possible decisions before God and listen for guidance. Sometimes God will speak clear as day and show us exactly what to do. God is not reluctant in sharing his heart with us as His children. It may warrant us to set aside additional time for prayer and fasting. Wherever we are led, we are assured God is right there beside us. One common practice we can always apply towards our decision is to search God's Word. As we grow in God, He prepares us for our future. Our steps are ultimately being ordered by Him. If we yield to God we will come into alignment with everything He is orchestrating behind the scenes. "A man's heart deviseth his way: but the LORD directeth his steps" (Proverbs 16:9). As long as we continuously turn our hearts toward God, He will continue to fill our hearts with His desires, establishing our steps directly along His path.

**Follow Jesus straight to destiny!**

Prayer: God, all we can say is THANK YOU! Thank You for ordering our steps. We may feel like the decisions we make are based on our own power, but we know You are the driving force. You open doors that no man can shut and close doors that are not conducive to Your perfect will. We surrender our plans to develop a heart for You. Work in us to be obedient to Your voice. When faced with a tough decision, we will meditate on Your Word and walk in Your path. We know You have already established this life for us. We will keep our eyes on You. Lead us on the narrow path of righteousness for Your names sake. Help us to find delight in Your Word and allow it to transform us into the image of Your Son Jesus. Every day is ordained by You. Help us to get out of the way, so Your name may be glorified. With all our might we praise You. In Jesus' name we pray, Amen.

# August 7

*Therefore said he unto them, The harvest truly is great, but the labourers are few: pray ye therefore the Lord of the harvest, that he would send forth labourers into his harvest.* (Luke 10:2)

There is never anything wrong with kingdom principles. The default is always found in us. Failing to see things the way God sees them blocks our production for kingdom work. Jesus lets us know the kingdom of God is always yielding fruit. The issue lies among the workers not being able to plow the field. He encourages us to pray to God, the Lord of Harvest, to send forth His workers. Our prayer is for the saints of God to come together in unity, seeking God for kingdom assignments. Are we so concerned with getting ahead in life that we forget God? I hope not. Because God has specific instructions for each of us. In today's society, it is easy to get caught up in working diligently towards the next promotion, degree, or trying to make ends meet that we push the purpose of God to the back burner. The reality is, when we place God first and His kingdom THEN all things will work together for our good (Matthew 6:33) I have never met anyone who wholeheartedly followed the plans of God and failed. Nope! It's impossible; He is the Lord of harvest. His plans only yield bountiful fruit. It is our duty as disciples to always be found doing the work of the kingdom. God is so amazing that when He thought to create us He instilled our personal desires. Now, as we walk in our purpose we find satisfaction as well as obedience to the will of God. Our purpose is tied up in the Kingdom of heaven. The gifts God has instilled in us are the necessary tools we need to be effective workers for Christ. Everything we do for God will produce good fruit and draw people to Christ. Consistency, commitment and faith are important work ethics. Jesus tells His disciples to pray for workers right before He sends them out to evangelize. This shows us the magnitude of the work that needs to be done to fill the earth with the knowledge of God. You and I can't do it alone, we need help. God is waiting to pour His Spirit upon willing vessels to ignite the fire within us to receive the harvest.

**A life with God is worth living!**

Prayer: God of mercy, grace, and loving-kindness, we come before Your throne of grace, giving You total reverence. Establish the work of our hands. Ignite fire within us to always be found doing the work of the kingdom. We bind up laziness and procrastination. Whatever plans You have for us, we yield to Your command today. Show us the work of the kingdom and let us be diligent in completing every task You give us. We pray for workers to come into agreement with heaven today. Remove idols from our life which take the place of our work for You. Let our time be utilized wisely. All glory belongs to You. In Jesus' name we pray, Amen.

# August 8

*Behold, the former things are come to pass, and new things do I declare: before they spring forth I tell you of them.* (Isaiah 42:9 KJV)

*Indeed, the former things have come to pass, Now I declare new things; Before they spring forth I proclaim them to you.* (Isaiah 42:9 MSG)

God has called us in righteousness (right standing with Him) for us to be His body in the earth. Everything we do should bring Him glory. He illustrates the power of His glory as He gives the prophet Isaiah the characteristics of the coming Savior. His glory is so powerful that if we allow it to flow through us, people would be drawn to Him by the multitudes. "He shall not cry, nor lift up, nor cause his voice to be heard in the street" (Isaiah 42:2). Jesus didn't have to go out screaming He was the Son of God or profess He had power. God placed His spirit upon Him, allowing His splendor to draw the people in. People heard of the miracles that were taking place in His life and came to see what was going on. God needs willing vessels to pour His Spirit upon to fill the earth with His glory. As we come before Him, He is able to reveal things to us and we are assured they will take place in the earth. He wants us to get to a place where we come without restraints, just a pure heart ready to hear from God. He will never force Himself upon us or allow us to tarnish His name. When we surrender ourselves before Him, He is able to fill our hearts with His virtue. We are able to allow the Spirit to lead us in everyone of our decisions and our assignments in the earth. People will be compelled by His glory and come seeking His face.

**God speaks and it happens!**

Prayer: God, You are ruler of the universe. Power and glory belong to You. You are the great and living King. There is none above You. Lord, we surrender our heart before You. We bow down in total reverence to Your name. We ask for Your Will today, we say "yes" to the assignment . Use us for Your glory. Let Your light shine brightly within us. In all things we give You thanks. In Jesus' name we pray, Amen.

# August 9

*And he said unto him, Arise, go thy way: thy faith hath made thee whole.* (Luke 17:19)

Ten lepers met Jesus as He entered a village in Jerusalem, crying out to the Master for healing. After being cleansed, nine continued on their way without rendering thanks unto Jesus for their miracle. One turned, being humble, falling at His feet to give thanks. In response, Jesus says, " Arise, go thy way: thy faith hath made thee whole." Faith is a continuous belief process that must be exercised every day. The nine other lepers were healed in their body from the disease of leprosy, but it would only be a matter of time before they would cry out for mercy again. When we fail to acknowledge God as supreme by giving thanks, we condition our relationship. Constant communion with God is required to keep us in a perfect state. Not perfect by the world's standards with no fault, but being complete and maturing in God. Wholeness is only found in Jesus, He equips us with every necessary element to sustain us throughout life. Only coming to Him for our needs to be met puts stipulations on our relationship and stunts our growth. God wants to heal every aspect of our lives, not certain areas. When we come to Him on a daily basis, layers of our sinful habits are being stripped away. Thankfulness reminds us we did not save ourselves. We have an advocate who speaks on our behalf and invited us into His presence to sit with Him in heavenly places. "And God raised us up with Christ and seated us with him in the heavenly realms in Christ Jesus" (Ephesians 2:6).

**A thankful heart goes a long way!**

Prayer: God, You are the great "I Am." We render honor and thanksgiving before Your throne of grace. Thank You for the continuous opportunity to come before You. With boldness we come professing our love for You and this life You have given unto us. Jesus, we are totally satisfied in You. Wherever we find ourselves today You are right there in the midst. Help us to be a great host. Be pleased with our life and our actions. Where we need help, convict us. Strengthen us in areas where we need growth. Thank You for never giving up on us. Have mercy on us. Forever we are grateful. We bless Your holy name. In Jesus' name we pray, Amen.

# August 10

*For the earth shall be filled with the knowledge of the glory of the Lord, as the waters cover the sea.* (Habakkuk 2:14)

Many people in the world tend to focus on negative aspects of life instead of shining light on the positive. Not to deny the terrible things taking place around us, but there are just as many great things taking place as well. There are clouds of witnesses who sacrifice their time on a daily basis through selfless service. There are people interceding on our behalf continuously. Our energy must be focused on the truth of God's Word. When we allow His Spirit to teach us we are able to fill the earth with His knowledge. God has given us every tool necessary to function effectively; it's our choice whether or not we practice what we have learned. God's greatness is all around us. As we aim our attention on reading His Word and allowing it to transform us, we become better equipped for the challenges of this present day. Our daily focus will be based upon us growing spiritually and displaying His splendor throughout all the earth. Accepting God's principles and applying them in our daily living will display His greatness in the earth, drawing people in to experience His glory. Having the mind of Christ, which means the attitude of Christ, our focus will be on the kingdom. As we face challenges we will stand on God's word and respond accordingly. We will not succumb to the pressures of life. This is a distraction from the enemy to get us so overwhelmed that we detour from God's purpose. Issues of life are great opportunities for us to stand firm and see the salvation of the Lord. In this manner, others will see the strength and power of God and seek to know the God we serve.

**Use every opportunity to bless God!**

Prayer: Lord, Your glory fills this earth. Open our eyes to see Your goodness. You will remain at the forefront of our mind in all things. When our mind drifts, bring it back into alignment with Your Will. Everything about You is perfect. We surrender our heart, mind and soul to You. Fill us with Your wisdom and knowledge. Teach us how to make godly decisions. Help us to always be conscious of our behavior, in everything that we do in order to allow Your glory to shine through us. Forgive us of all iniquity. Our life will be a living sacrifice unto You. You deserve all the glory. In Jesus' name we pray, Amen.

# August 11

***And it came to pass*** *on the seventh day, that they rose early about the dawning of the day, and compassed the city after the same manner seven times: only on that day they compassed the city seven times.* (Joshua 6:15).

Every word that proceeds out of the mouth of God shall come to pass. God gave Joshua and the children of Israel specific instructions on how to conquer the land of Jericho. God's directions guided Joshua with the following statement "**and it shall come to pass.**" God wants us to open our eyes to see the power embedded in His Word. When the time came for Joshua and the camp to conquer Jericho scriptures states, "**And it came to pass**." This confirms how God governs His Word. God's plans are sure to take place if we stay in alignment with His Will and are obedient. As faithful stewards constantly before God, the only thing that stands between us and seeing the manifestation of God's promises in the natural realm is time. God already wrote the book of life, our story is already finished. Our daily communion with God prepares us to better experience the chapters within God's predestined agenda. He waits in expectation to show us how to overcome the obstacles of life, and to teach us how to endure in peace. God's presence supplies us with wisdom to maximize our time on earth, fulfilling His purpose. Knowing the power entrenched in God's Word gives us confidence to watch and wait for the manifestation.

**Though it tarry, wait for it!**

**God hath spoken once; twice have I heard this; that power *belongeth* unto God. (Psalm 62:11)**

Prayer: Jehovah, You are He who is able to do exceedingly and abundantly above all we can ask or think. Nothing can hinder Your love in the earth. Teach us how to hear from heaven. Show us how to be watchmen looking for the manifestation of Your Word. We know once You speak it, it shall come to pass. Prepare our hearts and minds to be in position to walk in our purpose at all times. You are the Holy One whom we adore. In Jesus' name we pray, Amen.

## August 12

*Come and see the works of God, He is awesome in His deeds toward the children of men.* (Psalm 66:5 MSG)

God does all things well. Our appeal to the world is our testimony. The great works of our Father are on display as we exalt Him for His greatness in our lives. The many miraculous things He does on our behalf will never go unnoticed. We were walking the earth as blind men until God opened our eyes to the light of His glory. Now we are able to see God's goodness all around us. The great and mighty works of His hands are constantly before us. His eyes watch over us day-by-day, and it brings Him great pleasure to work on our behalf. "For the eyes of the LORD run to and fro throughout the whole earth, to shew himself strong in the behalf of *them* whose heart *is* perfect toward him" (2 Chronicles 16:9). When others see our life in Christ, there should be a clear distinction of God's principles producing newness in our life. Not only do we receive a new identity, our character changes to God's original intent for mankind. We are able to experience the many blessings of living a life of freedom in Christ Jesus. God's supreme love is uncontainable. It must be shared with the world, inviting them to partake in God's loving grace.

**I have seen you in the sanctuary and beheld your power and your glory. (Psalm 63:2)**

Prayer: Lord, You are remarkable. Everything You do is for the greater benefit of Your beloved. We are humbled to be considered as Your children. There is no greater honor than to serve at Your feet. We sit at the feet of Your altar and exalt Your name. We praise You according to Your excellent greatness. There is no greater love than what You have instilled in us. Life is nothing apart from You, and with You we are made whole. Thank You for looking over us on a continuous basis. Everyday in Your arms is sweeter than the day before. We will shout with joy, expressing to the entire world how great Your love is toward all. Every ounce of our being praises You. In Jesus' name we pray, Amen.

# August 13

*So when they continued asking him, he lifted up himself, and said unto them, He that is without sin among you, let him first cast a stone at her.* (John 8:7)

A very important principle in the kingdom of God is: Do not judge (Matthew 7). When we take it upon ourselves to condemn others for their behavior, we are saying God is not worthy enough to do His job. Our main focus in helping those around us is to correct them in love. If we see our neighbor performing ungodly behavior, we have the right to inform them of their wrong by speaking the truth in love. We are to show mercy and kindness, helping them to realize their behavior in hopes of them coming to repentance. Prayer is essential as well; it opens the door for God to intervene. God is the only one who understands the outlining circumstances. He sees the motives and what causes people to engage in such behaviors. It's important for us to remember we are not above reproach. We must consider our life before Christ and how merciful He is towards us. Ridiculing someone for their behavior is the last thing they need. Oftentimes we allow our emotions to steer our actions, when Jesus teaches us otherwise. By following the principles of Jesus we are to restore those who find themselves outside of God's will. "Brothers, if anyone is caught in any transgression, you who are spiritual **should restore** him in a spirit of gentleness. **Keep watch on yourself**, lest you too be tempted" (Galatians 6:1). This is how Christ called us out of the world of darkness. He brought us back into the right position through love and mercy. He was not constantly before us, reminding us for our wrong behavior. Encouragement is the most effective way to help someone modify his or her behavior. Our purpose in life is to bring souls into the kingdom; we can help others by showing agape love.

**Don't you realize how patient he is being with you? Or don't you care? Can't you see that he has been waiting all this time without punishing you, to give you time to turn from your sin? His kindness is meant to lead you to repentance. (Romans 2:4)**

Prayer: Lord, You are amazing. You are more than worthy of all the praise. Your loving-kindness called us into Your holy kingdom. Thank You for always looking at us with grace. We are in no position to judge or condemn our brothers and sisters. Teach us how to restore them back to You. Teach us how to show compassion and mercy. Let us not esteem ourselves to be better than anyone. Give us a humble spirit. God, help Your people who are in need. We fall before the altar of grace today with a humble heart. Have Your way in restoring our souls. Remove the desire of sin from our heart. Lead us on the narrow path of righteousness for Your name's sake. In all that we do, we give You glory. In Jesus' name we pray, Amen.

# August 14

*If you believe, you will receive whatever you ask for in prayer.* (Matthew 21:22)

Our entire relationship with God is based on faith. Our ability to trust and believe God's Word is the key to everything in life. God has created us to prosper in all areas. Every tool needed to sustain us is already within us. Keeping our mind on Christ and standing firm on His promises helps us to receive the things of God. Every prayer of the righteous is heard. It goes before God and He tends to each one accordingly. "The smoke of the incense, mixed with the prayers of God's holy people, ascended up to God from the altar where the angel had poured them out" (Revelation 8:4). Nothing said in faith will go unnoticed. God is careful to consider each one of our concerns. As we trust in Jesus we are able to ask God for anything in faith and see it manifest in our lives. God is pleased to give us our heart's desires. What we think we have planned for ourselves God is already willing to give us. His plans include hopeful futures where we are able to function in our fullest potential. Never allow fear, doubt or unbelief to keep you from bringing your request to your Father. All requests made in accordance with His will are predestined and will be granted.

**We believe, help our unbelief!**

Prayer: Lord, You are mighty and wonderful. Thank You for hearing our prayers. The things we have on our heart are already in Your plans to give to us. You have created us to dwell in Your presence and to receive Your goodness. Everything in the earth belongs to You, we come asking in faith for You to grant our heart's desire. Prepare us for the things You have stored up for us. Help us to be in position to receive all that You have to offer. Develop our character to be able to live in accordance with Your will. Shape us into Your vessels. Help us to use our lives as Your servants. Give us a kingdom mindset. We accept the authority You have given us and will do all things to bring You glory. In Jesus' name we pray, Amen.

# August 15

*Look, I am coming soon! My reward is with me, and I will give to each person according to what they have done. I am the Alpha and the Omega, the First and the Last, the Beginning and the End.* (Revelation 22:12-13)

Our life is forever on display before our Father. Everything we do in the name of Jesus is set before Him as a sweet aroma. He also considers the things that we do which are contrary to His will. He has spent countless time preparing us to operate through His Spirit. Through His Spirit we are able to know what God has ordained for us to do. Walking in the Spirit keeps us away from fulfilling the lust of the flesh. We can walk away from things that we know are not of any benefit. We must realize everything we do is being sown either in righteousness or towards wickedness. When we obey God and sow in righteousness, we are assured of our reward. It pleases God when we accept the revelation of being a new creation in Christ and adjusting our entire life to function with Christ inside of us. Then God is able to get the glory out of everything we do. Our life in the earth becomes useful and goes before God as a memorial; displaying ourselves as His children, walking in alignment with His will. When Jesus returns our life should be able to continue in the same manner. Our today should be a reflect of our behavior in heaven. We should not be in shock or in a state of trying to get things in order. It will be too late. God teaches us every day how to allow the His Spirit to keep us in right standing with Him. Our works shall be contingent upon what we hear from the Father on a daily basis. On the day we meet God face to face, we will hear the satisfying words, "Well done, my good and faithful servant."

**God, You are welcome here!**

Prayer: God, You are everything. All power belongs to You. You created earth and all mankind for Your glory. It's a pure honor to sit at Your feet and to soak in Your presence. God, You control the universe. At Your voice everything stands still. Control every aspect of our life so we can do the work of the kingdom. Blessed are they that do his commandments, that they may have right to the tree of life and may enter in through the gates into the city (Rev 22:14). Everything You do is based upon our relationship. Thank You for always calling us by name to commune together. Lord, help us to enjoy this relationship we have with You. Let us delight ourselves in Your commands. Fill us with the fruits of Your Spirit, that we may experience all of You. Bless You for being who You are. In Jesus' name we pray, Amen.

# August 16

*But they that wait upon the Lord shall renew their strength; they shall mount up with wings as eagles; they shall run, and not be weary; and they shall walk, and not faint.* (Isaiah 40:31)

When we remain in close proximity with God we are able to obtain strength to endure each day of our life. God never runs out of energy or becomes tired from working on our behalf. All power belongs to Him; He is the source of our ability to function in the earth. In everything we must consult God, who is willing to lead us on the right path. Daily communication with Him develops balance in our lives and keeps us from being bogged down with the cares of life. Situations will not overwhelm us; we will be able to take on each task as it arrives with the strength of the Lord. We're graced to have the ability to come to our Father and express the issues/concerns of our heart knowing He understands. As we release them to God, He in turn reinforces His power within us. Walking with God helps to eliminate seasons of being burnt out. When our mind and body need rest, God's wisdom will instruct us on exactly what to do. God has given us this life to enjoy. His plans have been carefully thought out. His Word gives us guidance each day on how to maximize our energy and enjoy every day here on earth.

**For the joy of the Lord is your strength. (Nehemiah 8:10)**

Prayer: Lord, You are the great "I Am." There is none in all the earth like You. Thank You for equipping us with power and strength each day. Establish a firm foundation within us. Help us not to grow weary in well doing. Let us put all of our energy into serving You. In You we have strength to accomplish each day with joy. Heal the broken-hearted, restore the lost and teach us to trust You in all our ways. Help us to enjoy the life You have given us. Pour out Your peace that surpasses all understanding. Renew our minds, create in us a clean heart and renew a right spirit within us. All glory belongs to You. In Jesus' name we pray, Amen.

# August 17

*So I sent messengers to them, saying, "I am doing a great work, so that I cannot come down. Why should the work cease while I leave it and go down to you?"* (Nehemiah 6:3)

When Nehemiah's enemies heard he had rebuilt the cities walls they sought to destroy him. Our enemy conspires against us on a daily basis. We must remain focused by being spiritually intact and on guard, watching to uncover the plans of the adversary. Being in divine alignment helps us to notice the tricks of the enemy. When we are focused on God's business (Matthew 6:33), God reveals things to us and will prepare us before distractions arise. He gives us discernment before, during, and after things take place. Never take your focus off of doing the will of God. Distractions come to get us off course from God's will. We have the power to stop distractions right in their track. We are able to discern between what comes from God and what comes only to hinder our progression. The things of God come to uplift us in order to add value to our life. Distractions are not in line with God's will and may come out of left field to shift our focus. Staying in daily communion with God by mediating on His Word day and night enables us to recognize disruptions. God is strategic, orderly, and faithful to complete all tasks. He doesn't play games and is always willing to keep us striving toward spiritual growth. We must understand and recognize the difference between the two; choosing to remain focused at all times.

**Focus is our map guiding us into tomorrow!**

Prayer: Lord, You are Alpha and Omega. The thoughts and plans You have for us are thoughts of peace and not of evil, to give us a future and hope. We call upon Your name to keep our minds steadfast and on You. We will not be moved by distractions. We look to Jesus, the founder and perfecter of our faith. Help us to discern between good and evil. Let our focus be directed to You and the assignment that You have placed on the inside of us. With all of our strength we lift our hands in total worship before You.

Overpower us with Your glory to run this race with endurance. Help us to only use our energy on things that will cause us to grow closer to You. In all that we do, we give You glory. In Jesus' name we pray, Amen.

# August 18

*Love never ends.* (1 Corinthians 13:8)

As we celebrate love, we can't help but to think about the love of God. His love is enduring, perfect and endless; a gift given to each of us before we were even formed in the womb. We are able to experience His love daily as we breathe in and out and enjoy the wonders in the earth around us. A love not based upon our actions or our accolades, but upon His nature. God loves because it's a part of who He is. He so kindly pours His love upon us each day, showing us how to operate as His children. We show the world we love God by our obedience and the love we show each other. Love that is pure and full of hope is what we find when we think about our Father Jehovah. No matter what we do, there is nothing we can do to earn more of His love or for Him to retract it. It's embedded in His being and is seen in all the earth. A love that goes beyond time, teaching us the strength therein is certain to stand forever. A love able to fill every void; turning rainy days into rays' of sunshine. God's love is rewarding, as its very existence offers us benefits of experiencing true life in His presence. In His presence is fullness of joy; and at His right hand are pleasures evermore (Psalm 16:11).

**Love is a gift!**

Prayer: Lord, this day we take time to celebrate the very thing You created, love. There is no love apart from You. Today we celebrate You. The gift of love is what we are able to experience every day as we walk this earth. Everything You do is because of love. In love You keep us in perfect peace. You sent Your Son to redeem us based upon love. You restored us through love. All things point to You loving us with an everlasting love. A Love that goes beyond conditions and our circumstances. Even when we don't acknowledge You, You still bestow Your love upon us and we are forever grateful. This day and forever more we will celebrate You for first loving us. In Jesus' name we pray Amen.

# August 19

*And the apostles said unto the Lord, Increase our faith.* (Luke 17:5)

There are many areas in our life where, on a continuous basis, we must seek God to increase our faith. Our faith is continuously being exercised, and depending on the circumstances it may cause us to react to each of them differently. In one area we may find it easy to depend on God. Then when faced with something unfamiliar, feelings of doubt and unbelief may arise. Thankfully, we are able to lay our reservations before the Lord and allow Him to develop our faith. Focusing on God's Word will get us to a place where we believe Him without question. Experience with God shines light on the emphasis God puts on His Word. Many times we want to believe, but when time exceeds itself we grow weary. Our focus is on not seeing the manifestation immediately, instead of believing what God has promised. God needs us to get to a place where our only outlook is seeing what He has predestined. Failure must never be an option. We must continue to speak the Word of God over and over until it is embedded in our spirit. God can only work through our faith. Faith joins in agreement with what God has already spoken into existence. His Word is very precious to Him and can only be fulfilled when we come into agreement with Him. "Can two walk together, except they be agreed?" (Amos 3:3). God only requires us to utilize our faith toward things that He has already graced. Everything we do in Christ is based upon our faith in God. Our faith should never become stagnant, but always be evolving, and maturing; believing all things are possible to Him that believe.

**Your grace is enough!**

Prayer: Thank You Father for Your grace and mercy. Lord, we give You our unbelief today. In any area where we have doubt, we give it to You. Your Word is tried and proven to be true. Only distractions keep us from focusing on You. We vow to make a conscious effort to trust You by not leaning on our own understanding, but in all of our ways acknowledging You. You know the end from the beginning. Time is in Your hand, continue to watch over us. We will exercise our faith and practice Your principles in our daily living. You get all the praise. In Jesus' name we pray, Amen.

# August 20

*But the wisdom that is from above is first pure, then peaceable, gentle, and easy to be intreated, full of mercy and good fruits, without partiality, and without hypocrisy.* (James 3:17)

Foolishness is the opposite of wisdom. With are hearts turned toward God, it is not our desire to lively foolishly. We seek to reflect the very image of our Lord and Savior, possessing His attributes. Wisdom from above is clearly defined as being pure and peaceable. When we find ourselves exhibiting attributes contrary to what God produces in heaven, we are no longer exhibiting wisdom from above. When we feel we have a right to react with bitterness, anger, malice, envy or jealously, we have to examine our hearts to check our motives. Although life's issues may cause these feelings to arise, we must be careful not to allow them to dwell within our spirit. Doing so would not be wise. The wisdom from above is what we are seeking to present to the world. His wisdom is uncontaminated, full of purity and able to heal our brokenness. Our emotions must be under constant evaluation. Filtering our behavior through God's Word will show us what is from Him and what is not. This realization helps us to stay in line with what benefits our spiritual growth and proves we are not yielding to things contrary to the will of God.

**Wisdom is the principle thing!**

Prayer: Lord, we are honored to serve You. Teach us how to discern between good and evil. Help us not to be foolish in our ways but to allow wisdom from above to rule in our lives. We relinquish envy, strife, bitterness, hate, anger, unforgiveness, jealously, and any other characteristic that is not from You. Let wisdom teach us how to be patient and to have a gentle and quiet spirit. Let us be quick to listen, slow to speak, and slow to anger. All the glory belongs to You. In Jesus' name we pray, Amen.

# August 21

*And when he putteth forth his own sheep, he goeth before them, and the sheep follow him: for they know his voice.* (John 10:4)

Jesus is the Good Shepherd; he watches over His sheep, protecting and preparing us for His return. When we hear His voice we respond with, "Here I am," ready to receive our daily bread. We understand the significance in drinking from the fountain of life where we never will thirst again. Our spirits are filled to the brim and overflow with His virtue. Everything He sets out for us to accomplish is for His glory. We find great pleasure in being led by Him through the pathway of life. Each time He calls is as if it were the first time; the excitement never gets old. Great joy is found in being called by Jesus, our hearts fill with pleasure. We know His voice; it's sweet and tender, always creating new ways for us to enjoy His presence. We find delight in being the beloved of God. Without hesitation, we submit our lives to Him and follow the glory set before us. There is no confusion in Him. He is known by His splendor and tested by His works and proven to be faithful every time.

**Today when you hear His voice, harden not your heart!**

Prayer: Lord, we worship You. Forgive us all manner of sin. Transform us, renew our mind that we may be acceptable and pleasing in Your sight. You are our Good Shepherd. We flee from the voice of strangers and follow after righteousness. Remove anything that comes to hinder us from hearing Your voice today. With praise and gratitude we thank You. In Jesus' name we pray, Amen.

# August 22

*For such as be blessed of him shall inherit the earth; and they that be cursed of him shall be cut off.* (Psalm 37:22)

As we allow God to order our steps, we are assured of the righteous journey ahead. Everywhere our feet trod in Christ is sure to lead us into our destiny. We are the righteousness of God. As we yield our life to Him and allow His Spirit to work through us, we are able to receive the many blessings He has prepared for us. Since we have left the kingdom of darkness and are now in the kingdom of Jesus Christ, we understand there are certain promises that belong to us. We no longer have to wish or hope aimlessly, but are now confident in what God has promised us. In Him we have an inheritance. No one can steer us in the wrong direction or make us get off track unless we allow it. With our eyes set on God, He will order our steps by only leading us to places where His grace awaits. As we come into our rightful position, we find great pleasure in doing things God has already prearranged for us. Life becomes easier and obstacles are no longer seen as burdens, but as tools to strengthen our faith. God's ability to bless us is never a matter of our own power but is based on God's love. A love that God passionately pours out every day in hopes of us opening our hearts to receive it.

**We are already blessed!**

Prayer: God, You are our life. All power belongs to You. You are the very air we breathe. Life would be meaningless without You. Thank You for calling our name each day to come into Your presence to meet with You. We come with an open heart and mind to receive everything You have for us this day. Your blessings meet us each day, and we say thank You. Before the day begins, You know our every step. We take time out to acknowledge Your greatness and Your lovingkindness that keeps us in fellowship with You on a continuous basis. Lord, keep us close, You are our strength. We find great pleasure in You ordering our steps.

Everything You do is perfect and we are forever grateful. We love You, in Jesus' name we pray, Amen.

# August 23

*Many shall be purified, and made white, and tried; but the wicked shall do wickedly: and none of the wicked shall understand; but the wise shall understand.* (Daniel 12:10)

Don't ever become discouraged when you see others outside of the faith enjoying life. You see, the outward appearance of what seems fun, in reality only lasts for a season. We will all stand before God to give an account of what we have done with our life. Only things done through His Son will be counted as righteousness. He will not take into account how much fun we had, or how much money we made. Our very hearts will be on display before Him. Our attributes and characteristics will speak for themselves. We won't be able to persuade God with our self-indulged excuses. Only what is done for God will be written in the Book of life. Take joy in knowing your life is now hidden in Christ. Everything we do in righteousness will go before us as merits, stored up to showcase our obedience. Life outside of Christ may look enticing, but it stops there. It can add no value to the precious life God has given us. So don't grow weary in well-doing, our harvest is on the way. Our reaping will surpass any moment of excitement gained outside of God's Will. In Christ, we are able to enjoy life. After all, that is why He came to the earth. Christians should not give the impression that life is over or boring. God wants us to experience the pleasures here on earth through enjoying our time and spending it doing things we enjoy. This can all be done while serving Him and without compromising who we are in Christ.

**Enjoy life, it's a gift!**

Prayer: God, have Your way in our life. Fill us with Your attributes and let our life come before You as a sweet aroma. Renew our minds to stay focused on living according to Your righteousness. Help us to be thankful for the life You have given us. Let us find contentment in everything You have created for our enjoyment. Ease our mind from the pressures of the world to live according to popular opinion. Teach us how to be holy in everything we do. All praise belongs to You. In Jesus' name we pray, Amen.

# August 24

*And it came to pass after this, that David enquired of the Lord, saying, Shall I go up into any of the cities of Judah? And the Lord said unto him, Go up. And David said, Whither shall I go up? And he said, Unto Hebron.* (2 Samuel 2:1)

God is to be consulted before we set out to do anything. By His instructions we are able to travel the road He has already prepared for us. As we follow His Spirit, we understand what He is speaking in Romans 8:30, *"and these whom He predestined, He also called; and these whom He called, He also justified; and these whom He justified, He also glorified."* We don't want to be any place where God's glory isn't present. Seeking God before we make decisions allows us to maximize our time. We can ask God specific questions pertaining to our life and know He is going to give us clear directions. We are able to trample over fear as we travel through life being led by God's Spirit. Fear tries to cripple us by telling us we aren't good enough, or we will never accomplish our goals. With God as our leader, we know His plans never fail. Pursuing God in all things is the only sure way to live life and reach our fullest potential. God waits in heaven to hear from us daily in order to give us our daily bread. Just think about all of the wonderful plans God has for every person He created. What devastation we will experience if we wait to get to heaven to receive all that God has for us. We will not wait! We can ask God each day to enlarge our territory and to bless us indeed (1 Chronicles 4:10). Each day we should exhaust everything God has prepared for us in that day. We miss out when we allow the busyness of life to steal our time and forget to seek God.

**God first, everything else will follow!**

Prayer: God of all creation, we glorify Your name. With all thanks we praise You for being our true and living God. We come seeking You for Your plans and instructions on how to live our lives. Teach us everything we need to know. Bless us with Your wisdom and understanding. As we meditate on Your Word day and night, let it transform us by renewing our mind. Instruct us in all that we do. Give us clear direction; order our steps in Your Word. Help us to listen and obey Your voice above all other influence. We are forever grateful that Your plans are for our good. Everything You do is perfect, thought out, and benefits Your kingdom. In all things we give thanks. In Jesus' name we pray, Amen.

# August 25

*In thee, O LORD, do I put my trust: let me never be put to confusion.* (Psalm 71:1)

Whatever you need from God is only a prayer away. When you have a desire or need festering within your spirit, bring it before the LORD. He has created us to seek after His goodness so we will always be attached to the lifeline (Being in Christ). Seeking our own way to fulfill our desires and needs will always result in us not fully obtaining all that He has for us. Our way may work for a little while, but we will eventually end up asking God to intervene. God allows issues to arise in our life in order for us to lay them before His throne. In allowing God to work through us, His name is being glorified and we are not able to boast in ourselves. God wants the best for us and He is the only one who knows how to get it to us. Following after God will only lead us into places where God's grace is already waiting on our arrival. God is the only one who sees all, knows all and wants to prepare us for all things. Let's think about it, God wouldn't create us just to see us fail at this thing called life. Our trust in Him leads to the pathway of life where we are able to fulfill His purpose every time. Each day we are faced with the choice to walk in God's plan or to walk in our own plan. The best choice of course is to walk with God. He promised to lead us to a place of destiny where we are able to expand His kingdom. Where life can be a shining light on his glory. Where others can learn about the good news of Jesus Christ. It becomes a ripple effect, where our family, friends, associates, and community are all impacted by our life of obedience which shines light on God. What a blessing it is to show someone else the great things God has done for us. This opens the gateway for us to share that He will do it for them as well.

**My faith is not only for me but for my generation!**

Prayer: Lord, we lift Your name on high, complete your perfect work within us. Allow Your Spirit to operate within us. Open our hearts and pour Yourself deep within us. Remove everything that tries to take our attention off of You. In You do we put our trust. In You we live, and move and have our being. We submit our will to Yours. We come before Your throne of grace, seeking Your hand to work in our lives. Lead us not into temptation, but deliver us from evil. You order all the days of our life. All praise is Yours in abundance. In Jesus' name we pray, Amen.

# August 26

*But thou, O man of God, flee these things; and follow after righteousness, godliness, faith, love, patience, meekness.* (1 Timothy 6:11)

Our covenant relationship with God grants us access into the mysteries of His heart. There, we find out how to conduct ourselves and receive revelation from His Word. We obtain wisdom that surpasses understanding and equips us for our future. The world we live in is filled with things that are contrary to the Will of God and fight for our attention. Paul is very clear in his instructions to Timothy on how to conduct himself as a man of God. He explains the nature of evil and how it may seem enjoyable at the moment, but if God is not pleased with it, in the end we always end up harming ourselves. He warns us about unwholesome words, not teaching the words of Jesus Christ and not following God's doctrine. Apart from doing these things, we become vulnerable to the attributes of the enemy. It is very important for us to guard our heart and flee from such things. If we fail to allow God to produce the fruits of the Spirit within us, at some point evil will rear its ugly head in our speech, actions, and may become our lifestyle. We have to keep guard on everything that has the potential to influence us. This involves what we watch, what we listen to, our company, and what activities we engage in. Nothing should be able to compromise our faith. We give way to negative outside influences when we let our guard down. We say it's okay to watch derogatory and explicit things on television, I'll be ok. In actuality, we are becoming desensitized to things contrary to our beliefs and may end up accepting things that aren't favorable. One rule of thumb for me is to picture Christ physically being in the room. Would he be pleased with my behavior or what I'm engaging in? If the answer is "NO," then something must change. Our stance is to fight for the things God has instilled in us (righteousness, godliness, faith, love, patience, and meekness) which enable us to live with eternity in Christ at the forefront of our mind.

**God be pleased with my life!**

Prayer: Jesus, Your life is the reason we live. If it had not been for You we would be lost. Lord, help us to seek after You at all times. Let us run from all things that are contrary to Your purpose for our lives. Let us find joy in choosing to obey Your commands. Establish the work of our hands. We are dead to sin and alive in Christ. We will not yield to the tricks of the enemy. We will fight for our faith by trusting You with our whole heart. Reveal to us what it is You need us to do in the earth to bring glory to Your kingdom. All glory and praise belong to You forever. In Jesus' name we pray, Amen.

# August 27

*Instead of the thorn bush the cypress will come up, And instead of the nettle the myrtle will come up, And it will be a memorial to the Lord, For an everlasting sign which will not be cut off.* (Isaiah 55:13)

When we seek the LORD, we are able to align with our kingdom assignment by doing the very things God has called us to the earth to accomplish. In Genesis, we learn our purpose. “God blessed them; and God said to them, ‘Be fruitful and multiply, and fill the earth, and subdue it’” (Genesis 1:28). It is by these principles we see the way God operates in heaven. Everything He sets out to achieve is sure to happen. He gives us direct understanding of how we are able to function as we seek Him. Calling on God and adhering to His direction will allow us to only go to places and accomplish tasks that He has already set before us. No longer will we waste our time helplessly without a cause. God will lead us to the very place where He can use us to show forth His glory in the earth. When people see our works do they think of God? This should be a ringing question in our mind as we establish our goals and values in life. As we think of history, our names will one day be spoken of as vessels of God who did extraordinary actions for His kingdom. This can come in the form of the cure for cancer, reforming the judicial system, changing laws, establishing businesses, and so forth. We are all here to make a difference. Each day is an opportunity to shine bright in showing the world how much God cares! As we complete our assignments the world will see the splendor of our God and memorials will be in place. In the Bible, God led His people to very specific places and as a result they built memorials for Him and often named the place according to what the LORD had done. When God is the primary source in initiating our tasks there will be a sign of His presence to stand as a permanent monument.

**God I’ll do my part to expand Your kingdom!**

Abraham –And Abraham called the name of that place

Jehovahjireh: as it is said *to* this day, In the mount of the LORD it shall be seen. (Genesis 22:14)

Jacob- And Jacob called the name of the place where God spake with him, Bethel. (Genesis 35:15)

Prayer: God, You are the King of this universe. What a thrill and honor to be called Your children. We surrender all before Your throne of grace. Embed Your principles in us today that we may go out in joy and be led forth in peace. Whatever we put our hands to will prosper because You lead us on the pathway of life. All that You do through us is a reflection of Your power in the earth. Work in us that we may accomplish Your plans. Move us out of the way. We come before Your throne with a pure heart and clean hands, that we may be used for Your glory. Comfort us; help us not to grow weary in well doing. We will keep our eyes looking toward heaven for our strength. We rejoice with the angels today and forevermore. In Jesus' name we pray, Amen.

# August 28

*Henceforth I call you not servants; for the servant knoweth not what his lord doeth: but I have called you friends; for all things that I have heard of my Father I have made known unto you.* (John 15:16)

Everyone longs to fit in, to feel as though they are part of the in-crowd. Well, God's elite assembly is the best alliance to be a part of. After already granting us membership, He comes searching for us to cultivate our relationship through continuous fellowship. God's loving nature provides every member with his or her specific function, allowing us to share in His great joy. Jesus comes to us not only as a High Priest and perfect example, but also as a friend. Our Lord's characteristics encompass mannerisms to make us better individuals. His love for His friends draws us close to the Father, where we are able to receive the deepest desires of our heart. Walking in close relationship with our Friend establishes a covenant built to exceed time. There are no secrets that stand in the way of our growth in Christ. Daily, He pours out knowledge and wisdom to further our spiritual growth. His greatest joy is found in His friends abiding in Him. Receiving nourishment to produce abundant fruit that will remain, knowing without Him we can do nothing. As a friend, we are open to share our deepest concerns and aspirations. We include Him in the best parts of our life. No longer do we see Him as one whom we come to with our hand out. We are concerned about our relationship with our Friend and work towards cultivating it on a daily basis. For me, when I fail to spend time with Jesus, I miss Him and our time alone together. No two days are the same. Each day in His presence offers new glory and establishes a deeper connection. Like our earthly friendships, we must develop intimacy with Jesus. This is a great honor to be called His friend, He is thrilled to express His heart's desires and impart knowledge in us each day.

**What a friend we have in Jesus!**

Prayer: Lord, You are so amazing. You are the lifeline to our very existence. Thank You for cleansing us with Your Word, and allowing us to abide in You. As we are in You, and You are in us we, will bear much fruit. We are like a tree planted by the waters, and that spreadeth out her roots by the river, and shall not see when heat cometh, but her leaf shall be green; and shall not be careful in the year of drought, neither shall cease from yielding fruit. You see to it that everything we do prospers and all of our fruit shall remain (Jeremiah 17:8). God, in You we have everlasting life, hope, and confidence. We will bless Your name at all times and Your praise shall continually be in our mouth. In Jesus' name we pray, Amen.

# August 29

*Surely the LORD God will do nothing, but he revealeth his secret unto his servants the prophets.* (Amos 3:7)

Nothing of importance will ever be hidden from God's children. He takes all things into consideration and ensures we have every necessity in order to function in the world. Because He cares, He sets aside time to give warning before destruction and direction before the journey. When we carefully look at our lives, we can see the powerful hand of God cultivating us into our fullest potential. By God's loving nature, His plans for the world are revealed through His prophets (one who proclaims the will of God). God's declaration is not an assumption but a guarantee of what will take place. He is justified in everything He does. We will never receive punishment without a cause, nor will He withhold wisdom from us to obtain every good and perfect gift. He is an open book, anticipating and giving each of His children everything we need. Sometimes it's correction, comfort, redirection, encouragement and love. As we look around at society today, we need warning. We need someone to intervene on our behalf. We need to hear from God. What a world we would live in if everyone prayed and humbled themselves before God. I know wonderful things would take place. Unfortunately, not everyone will not humble themselves and pray. This is not a call to lose hope. God is still on the throne and cares for His people. We have to do our part and trust God and follow His commands. It is very important to heed His voice. Seeking His face every day could very well save our life. God can instruct us on what path to take that will benefit us and keep us out of harms way. It pleases God to give us His plans, the question is are we ALWAYS available to hear from heaven and obey?

**Speak Lord, Your servant is listening!**

Prayer: Hallelujah God, You are amazing. What an honor it is to bless Your holy name. God, You have created us to multiply in the earth. By Your plans all things were formed and continue to be.

Lord, we are in need of Your direction. Show us the pathway of life. Lead us in all of our ways. In everything we do we will acknowledge You as Lord. Reveal Your plans to us that we may take heed. Correct us in our wrongdoings. Don't let us get in our own way. Convict us when we fall short. Thank You for Your grace and mercy that meets us new each morning. We will continue to exalt Your name in all the earth. In Jesus' name we pray Amen.

## August 30

*For all the promises of God in him are yea, and in him Amen, unto the glory of God by us.* (2 Corinthians 1:20)

There are over 6,000 promises in the Bible. Assured vows God has prepared for His children that will manifest in our life as we believe and receive them. They cover every aspect of our lives from health, finances, peace, love, prosperity, our kindred and our mind, to name a few. Everything God promised will happen in our life. When He proclaims a thing it will come to fruition at God's appointed time. God's nature can only declare the truth. As His children who are led by His Spirit, we are a representation of Him in the earth. Since the Holy Spirit leads us in everything we do, our life should replicate His principles of reliability. Our words and actions should not waiver as the Holy Spirit is leading us. We are firmly grounded in the things God instructs us to accomplish, and are secure in knowing we receive every promise from heaven. We have a firm foundation in God, which means we can speak only the things He says in reference to every situation in our lives. I promise you that whatever issues or concerns we face in life, there is a Word from God in the bible concerning that matter. Praise God for the times we live in. Our generation is able to Google everything. If I need to know what God promises concerning my children, I can search the internet for "scriptures concerning children," or "what does the bible say about the promise for our children." Once the results come back, I can declare these scriptures over the lives of my children. This is true for everything we encounter. God has prepared us for this thing called life. Our hope rests in our Father establishing a well planned out life for His beloved children. Our position in this equation is to adhere and be aware of the promises through reading the Bible, spending time with God, and having the faith to receive. As the Holy Spirit leads us and we are compliant with God's instructions, we will reap a bountiful harvest. Being led by the Spirit will ensure our actions produce the intended goal of fulfilling our deepest desires and the predestined plans of God. It is God who anoints and calls us into obedience. God is trustworthy in fulfilling all of His promises; our position is to be faithful ambassadors of the kingdom. Doing such will bring joy to our lives, and in return, cause others to take notice and exalt and praise God by bringing glory to His name.

**Will you believe the promise of God?**

Prayer: Lord, Your grace is beyond sufficient. All that we are is because of You. Employ Your Holy Spirit to rule in our lives. Teach us to be dependable disciples, train us in following every one of Your commands. We long to please You. Thank You for always being dependable, and for working all things together for our good. There is nothing under the sun that You are not aware of. We receive every promise over our lives and declare and decree them right now in Jesus' name. In all things we give You thanks. With our hearts lifted towards You we bless Your name. In Jesus' name we pray, Amen.

## August 31

*Do they provoke me to anger? saith the LORD: do they not provoke themselves to the confusion of their own faces?* (Jeremiah 7:19)

God's gift of righteousness (right standing with God) is a free gift of liberty. It's not a notion to call us into submission to rule us with an iron-fist. God's call for obedience is strictly for our benefit. All of His commands are uniquely crafted for us to receive all of His promises. When we fail to obey His voice, we self-inflict pain. God knows the pathway of life and is trying to get us on board in order to see the manifestation of His predestined plans for us. Anything we do apart from God puts us in jeopardy of missing our assigned mission. It's imperative for us to always consult with God and follow His plans for our life. We understand God's plans are purposed specifically to produce greatness through us. Following God will enable us to walk through the doors of our destiny and maximize our time on earth. It is my deepest concern that we maximize the time we have in this life. One of the things that satan has mastered is causing us to fall prey to distractions. Every challenge, every upset, every obstacle is set in place to cause us to take our eyes off of God. Thanks to God, we are more intelligent than that. We have knowledge of the enemies plans and we are not ignorant of his devices (2 Corinthians 2:11). We MUST be spiritually inclined at all times. Knowing that whenever we turn from God and allow satan to trick us, we are essentially hurting ourselves.

**Victory is Ours TODAY!**

Prayer: Father, we adore You. You are the light of this world. All praise belongs to You. Teach us Your ways today. Help us to be clear about what it is You would have us to do with our time. Help us to make room for You at all times in order to hear Your voice. Be the strongest force of influence in our lives. Remove anything that stands in the way of our destiny or that comes to try to get us off track. Open our minds to receive from heaven today.

Renew our minds that we may be transformed. All glory belongs to You. In Jesus' name we pray, Amen.

## September 1

*The LORD hath appeared of old unto me, saying, Yea, I have loved thee with an everlasting love: therefore with lovingkindness have I drawn thee.*

God's call to fellowship is a rewarding adventure. It is designed for each of us to experience life on earth beyond the surface. His loving nature is always drawing us close to Him. Many of us have it backwards in thinking our relationship with God is some systematic form of strict rules and procedures, when instead, God is only trying to get us to receive His affection. His hand is always stretched towards us. He is never far away. Spending time with Him through reading His Word, and acknowledging Him throughout the day is an expression of gratitude. His love will always remain; it's our choice to receive it and enjoy it. "Behold, I stand at the door, and knock: if any man hear my voice, and open the door, I will come in to him, and will sup with him, and he with me" (Revelation 3:20). He is faithful to fulfill his lovingkindness towards us. His love never runs out or falls short of being able to satisfy our spiritual need for nourishment. As we think about the love of God, it captivates our being. God's love for us started way before we were even thought of by our parents. Once He thought of Creation, God's masterpiece of mankind that included you and me began. He hand-selected our parents, crafted our DNA, formed our tissue, designed our structure, cultivated our personality, and spoke us into existence before time began. He looked at all of His creation in awe! He loves all of us in our own unique manners and characteristics. Our stance is to be aware of this great love and bask in it. We do that by saying thank You God for loving me and accepting His embrace minute-by-minute everyday.

**God's love is enough!**

Prayer: God, You are the King of this universe. Your love is the greatest gift one could ever ask for. Saturate us with Your Spirit. We accept and acknowledge Your grace and mercy which You bestow upon us each day. Lord, by Your faithfulness You have called us into fellowship with Your Son Jesus Christ. Thank You for loving us at all times. We have confidence that nothing can separate us from Your love. Help us to establish love as our natural response to the world. Patience, longsuffering, kindness, faithfulness and joy will be the characteristics we will display in our actions. All praise belongs to You. In Jesus' name we pray. Amen.

## September 2

*Therefore he said unto Judah, Let us build these cities, and make about them walls, and towers, gates, and bars, **while the land is set before us**; because we have sought the LORD our God, we have sought him, and he hath given us rest on every side. So they built and prospered.* (2 Chronicles 14:7)

Asa, a ruler (King) of Judah dedicated his life to God. The bible states "Asa did that which was good and right in the eyes of the Lord His God" (2 Chronicles 14:2). As king, he commanded the people of Judah to seek the Lord and to follow the law and God's commandments. As a result, God gave him rest. During this time, previous kings and kings after him experienced battle. Although this was a period of rest for King Asa, he encouraged his people with the following statement, "while the land is set before us let us build." The word while indicates a set period of time. Asa understood the importance of utilizing his time wisely. He grabbed hold of the concept of being prepared before things arise instead of being caught off guard. He instructed the people to build walls, towers, gates, and bars for protection from intruders. In the event that another king and his army initiated an attack on Judah, they would be prepared. The scripture also reveals how, during this time, they sought the Lord. WOW! In pursuing God, they received a strategic plan to build a hedge of protection, and through their obedience they prospered. This is just like our great Father to give us warning and prepare us for the future. Even in periods of rest, we are instructed to seek the face of God. In God's face we receive plans and visions on how to stay abreast of what is taking place around us. This enables us to grow, mature, and to learn necessary skills to prepare for life's challenges. I promise this is true. In my own life, I have been in my daily devotion with God and He would instruct me to pray for peace and I would read scriptures on peace and receive insight regarding the topic. Later in the day, I would experience an event that would require me to stand firm in what I learned from God concerning peace. God wants us to be prepared and equipped in every manner. Seek His face and see what thus says the Lord.

**Seek ye first the kingdom of God!**

Prayer: Lord, You are so amazing. You are the bright and morning star. You are our righteousness. All things exist because of You. We come before Your holy presence, laying down every one of our cares. We exalt Your name. Reveal the very purpose for our existence. Order our steps in Your Word. Purify our hearts that we may have room for You to reside. As long as we are living, we will strive to follow all of Your commands. Let Your light shine through us. Bless the work of our hands. Enable us to subdue the earth and multiply in it. Help us to be pillars in our community and be the change needed to reflect Your greatness in the lives of Your people. As we delight in You, everything that we do will prosper. All glory and power belong to You. In Jesus' name we pray, Amen.

# September 3

*For what saith the scripture? Abraham believed God, and it was counted unto him for righteousness.* (Romans 4:3)

Faith is the only thing that enables us to believe the promises of God. We are able to place our hope in knowing that what God said will happen at the appointed time. Even though we cannot see it at the moment, we stand firm, knowing God will come through. Our relationship with God is based upon us believing what He said, and receiving daily revelation through our communication with Him. If, for a second, we lose hope, we waver in our faith and lose sight of God's direction. Faith is given as a free gift to encourage us in the things of God and in this life. It is guaranteed that if God said it, it will happen. Our faith helps us withstand the transportation process of God's promises from the spirit realm to the natural realm, where we are able to physically see the manifestation. It's easy to say we believe when we consider the bountiful list of promises set before us. God has equipped us to operate in faith when all odds are against us. It's not easy to endure when our faith is being tested, and we are waiting for long periods of time, but it's possible. When bills are due and there is no money, we have to see God as a supplier and refuse to lose hope. When our life is spiraling out of control, we have to trust God knows the thoughts and plans He has for us. God will allow us to encounter life and challenge us to utilize our faith. We have to be fully persuaded, strong in faith, and not consider any other outcome than what God has promised. The bible says Abraham, against hope believed in hope, that he might become the father of many nations (Romans 4:18). Abraham made a conscious decision to believe God's promise would overpower the desolate state he was currently in. By his faith, it was counted unto him as righteousness.

**Will you believe God!**

Prayer: Lord God Almighty, You are the very air we breathe. Nothing is more important than being in Your presence. Your will is the only perfect way known to man. We acknowledge You as El

Shaddai and thank You for Your grace and mercy. Watch over us this day. Direct our path and establish the work of our hands. Teach us Your ways. Show us the truth of Your Word. Help us to stay grounded in Your firm foundation. We believe what You have said concerning us and will follow You all the days of our life. Shine Your light upon us. All glory and praise is Yours in abundance. In Jesus' name we pray, Amen

# September 4

*And one cried unto another, and said, Holy, holy, holy, is the LORD of host: the whole earth is full of his glory. And the post of the door moved at the voice of him that cried, and the house was filled with smoke.* (Isaiah 6:3-4)

Your praise has power to change your surrounding circumstances. Often we allow our praise to be hindered by our current situation in which we find ourselves. If our mood is less than favorable, we give half praise. If the Lord opened some doors, then our praise is a little more elevated. God is searching for a people who will praise Him according to His excellence. "Praise him according to his excellent greatness" (Psalm 150:2). God instructs us to praise this way because He knows the end from the beginning (Isaiah 46:10). The other side of the mountain has already been established and revealed to us. We have to open our eyes and stand on the promises set before us. We know we have an expected end, and that ALL things work together for our good. We understand that we have an adversary who seeks to devour us. His only objective is to get our mind away from what God has already declared over our lives. When we follow kingdom principles we receive kingdom results. Numerous times in the Bible we are taught to render praise at all times, in good and bad seasons. God commands this type of response because His glory fills the earth, and when we release praise He is right there in the midst. His nature overpowers our circumstances and things begin to change at the sound of His voice. If we never initiate praise, which tells God He is everything to us, and that we trust Him; we are showing God that we have it all under control. There is power in praise; if we allow it to change the course of our lives we will save ourselves from a lot of agony.

**Will you praise God!**

Prayer: Lord of all creation, we worship You. All power belongs to You. You are holy, You inhabit the praises of Your people. Your glory fills this entire earth. We turn in recognition of

Your greatness and worship You in Spirit and in truth. At all times we will give thanks and praise to You according to Your excellent greatness. Everything You do is perfect and pleasing. With every breath we will give honor to Your name. As we look over our life we exalt You for always being there. Your plans for us far outweigh anything we could ever think of on our own. In all of our ways we will acknowledge You. You are the Holy Lamb of God and we are excited to be called into Your throne of grace. We consider it a privilege to sit at Your feet and receive Your commands. We surrender all to You. In Jesus' name we pray, Amen.

# September 5

*I have set the LORD always before me: because he is at my right hand, I shall not be moved.* (Psalm 16:8)

God should be our goal in life. He should be in the midst of everything we set out to do. God is the vision. He has set all things in motion. Whatever He puts His hand to will be accomplished. When we set Him before us, it releases Him into our lives to fulfill His perfect plan. He leads us to places where His provision waits on our arrival. His plans have already been accomplished, they await our predestined time of engagement. Our job as vessels is to keep our eyes on the Source. When God is before us He is a lamp unto our feet and a light unto our path. He clears the road of debris and we are able to continue on our merry way. A kingdom focus has to be embedded in our mind. This comes as we study His Word and apply it to our lives. When obstacles arise, we are able to be steadfast in hope. Rest assured, God knows every issue before it manifests itself in our lives and has already crafted a solution. Nothing can stand in the way of our God-given purpose unless we allow it. God is before us, leading, coaching, and encouraging us to take the next step. All we have to do is look up and see His glory. His glory energizes us to continue on the path of righteousness. Our vision must always consist of God being before us. Nothing should be magnified in our lives to consume the space of us seeing our Lord. His presence alone is powerful enough to dim every distraction and consume every obstacle. Self-awareness in your position in Christ will put things into prospective. Don't waste another day looking at life, wishing God would show up. Instead, look at God and He will show you life.

**Put it in perspective!**

Prayer: O' merciful Father in heaven above, we shout glory to Your name. Apart from You we can do no good thing. Remove the blinders from our eyes that we may always set You before us. Wherever You go, there we long to be. Be a lamp unto our feet and a light unto our path. Open doors for us that no man can shut. You will be magnified in our lives. Life will not consume us. We line up every aspect of our lives with Your Word. What You say is true, and we will trust You. Renew our hearts and minds, transform us to walk in obedience. Plant us by the rivers of water, and allow us to bring forth fruit in due season and allow everything we do to prosper. We love You. In Jesus' name we pray, Amen.

*God will be whatever you want Him to be in your lives. If you place Him as anything less than number one in your life, He will perform as such. You have to give God proper position in order for Him to render everything He has stored up for you.*

# September 6

*Jesus came and told his disciples, "I have been given all authority in heaven and on earth. 19 Therefore, go and make disciples of all the nations, baptizing them in the name of the Father and the Son and the Holy Spirit. 20 Teach these new disciples to obey all the commands I have given you. And be sure of this: I am with you always, even to the end of the age."* (Matthew 28:18-20)

Our lives are a living example of the goodness of heaven. As we obey our Father, we are able to show the world the proper way to function according to God's standards. When we live our lives pure before God, we are lights shining in the world. Others can see God through us. As His children, we are under His authority. We willingly release control of our own lives and follow His principles. As He teaches us, it will manifest in our behavior and we will teach others about God's goodness. We shouldn't keep the goodness of God to ourselves. Fear of being rejected or an outcast can be subsided when we allow the Holy Spirit to equip us. There are people in the world who are dying from a lack of knowledge; it could very well be our assignment to minister to them. Diligence, commitment, and constant communication with God prepares us for a time such as this. It's so important to discover God's will for our lives. Everyone has a place in God's kingdom; we are all many parts that form one body. "For as the body is one, and hath many members, and all the members of that one body, being many, are one body: so also is Christ" (1 Corinthians 12:12). Jesus instructed his disciples to go out to make disciples of all nations, and we have the same command today. A disciple is a follower of Christ. We know and experience great benefits in following Christ. Why would we want to keep it to ourselves? Our lives are filled with every blessing from Heaven. God is not a respecter of person and His grace extends to all mankind. He has enough power to supply every need of anyone who receives Jesus. Don't keep quiet another day.

**Let your light shine that someone may know Jesus.**

Prayer: Our Father which art in heaven, Hallowed be thy name. Thy kingdom come, Thy will be done in earth, as it is in heaven. Give us this day our daily bread. God we are under Your authority. All power and majesty is in Your hand. Teach us to follow the narrow path of righteousness all the days of our life. Help us to know Your voice, and never to follow the voice of another. Be the strongest force of influence in our life. Train us as Your disciples. Let our life be a living example of Your glory. When You prepare us to speak and minister to the lost, don't allow fear to keep us from trusting You. This is Your life, we say have Your way. In Jesus' name, we pray, Amen

# September 7

*But made himself of no reputation, and took upon him the form of a servant, and was made in the likeness of men:8 And being found in fashion as a man, he humbled himself, and became obedient unto death, even the death of the cross.* (Philippians 2:7-8)

Our greatest blessing in life is not in the things we can receive, but in the things we give. As Christ gave up His life as a servant of God, we are called to be likeminded. Our primary concern is not in what God can do for us, it is in what we can do for the kingdom. Our future is already secure and established; we know we will reside with God forever. As it pertains to this life our main focus has to be on God's purpose. God has called each of us to earth for a specific assignment. I heard a preacher say something so profound; he stated our testimonies shouldn't always be reactionary testimonies. That's when we get ourselves into a bind and God delivers us and we give a testimony. Don't get me wrong, God is our source and our supplier. What we seem to miss is this is not the only purpose for our life. Our life should consist of serving God with every piece of our soul. As his servants, the work we are doing for the kingdom should be our greatest testimony. Jesus did many miraculous things in the earth as a result of following the specific assignments His Father (God) gave Him. Then He said we are to do greater works! "Verily, verily, I say unto you, He that believeth on me, the works that I do shall he do also; **and greater** works than these shall he do; because I go unto my Father" (John 14:12).

**I was created for greater!**

Prayer: You are Alpha and Omega; the earth was formed for Your glory. God, you call all things into motion at the sound of Your voice all things respond to Your control. We sit at Your feet this day, asking for our assignment. Make us to be likeminded with Christ. Transform us by the renewing of our mind. Teach us to have the love of Christ, to be of one mind and not to consider ourselves, but to esteem others above ourselves. Let Your purpose be the greatest testimony in our lives. Let Your light shine through us, that darkness will be exposed by Your glory. God, we give You our lives that You may be glorified in all the earth. You are the reason we receive anything in this world by Your blessings. We surrender all before You. Not our will, but Your will be done, in earth as it is in heaven. In Jesus' name we pray, Amen.

# September 8

*Then Jesus beholding him loved him.* (Mark 10:21)

How hard is it for us to love people as they come to Christ; understanding they come with the world's percepts and a thought process that has not yet been transformed. It seems easy to poke up our nose at those who are still in the world and unaware of the grace given by Jesus. As we soon forget we were once that person on the outside looking into the kingdom of Jesus. We were converted as we accepted Christ, but we must not EVER forget where we have come from. Love is the only way to respond to people who are unaware of how to live for Christ. As time goes on, they will begin to develop a relationship with Him and their outward appearances and their inner man will align with the transformation that takes place in their heart as they accept Jesus. At all times, as children of God, we must express love in great measure. Love must be shown to unbelievers and to those within the body who make mistakes and need correction. This is the way God operates toward us. Grace alone has kept us from eternal judgment. Love corrects wrongs, builds confidence, and shows a reflection of who God is. No one on earth is without fault. We have ALL sinned. In the place of mistakes, we know firsthand it is not beneficial to outcast someone. That is the very opposite of what is needed. Instead, love is the answer. Having an understanding heart and taking the perfect mask off that we as Christians often wear and just be in the moment when someone is facing a challenge. Think about a time in your life when you made your biggest slip-up. God didn't correct us with an iron fist. He nurtured and corrected us in love.

**Love is enough.**

Prayer: God, You are Awesome, worthy to be praised. All honor belongs to You. With every breath within our body we praise You. Lord, thank You for always loving us. Even in our disobedience, love drew us close to You. God, teach us how to love others. Help us to consider ourselves in their situation and to never cast judgment. Love is patient and kind, not jealous or boastful, or proud or rude. It does not demand its own way, it is not irritable, and it keeps no record of being wronged. It does not rejoice about injustice but rejoices whenever the truth wins out. Love never gives up, never loses faith, is always hopeful, and endures through every circumstance (1 Corinthians 13:4-7). Let this love be found in us that You may get all the glory in the earth. In Jesus' name we pray, Amen.

# September 9

In all labour there is profit: but the talk of the lips tendeth only to penury. (Proverbs 14:23)

God makes principles for harvest very clear, WE MUST WORK. Before we see a return on our investment, we have to apply effort to achieve a set goal. Hopes and dreams will not be accomplished by mere aspiration. Aspiration must be fueled with diligence and consistent work, in order to see the end product. What God has placed inside of each of us is already guaranteed. The provision needed to accomplish God's work is readily available. "Then saith he unto his disciples, The harvest truly is plenteous, but the labourers are few" (Matthew 9:37). God is the Lord of harvest; it's His best interest that everything we put our minds to come to fruition. Jesus' heart was filled with compassion as He saw the people growing tired from working. God instructs us to not grow weary in well doing, because we will reap a bountiful harvest in due season (Galatians 6:9). Does this mean we are not supposed to get tired while working, NO. God is teaching us to follow His way of doing things, by operating in the strength of the Lord. His strength sustains and carries us through to see the end result (harvest, profit). There is a successful plan in each of us. God has never wasted any of His creation. That thing you dream about, the very thing you would work toward if money or condition weren't an issue, is the very thing God is saying if you trust Me I will do it for you. The sky truly is the limit.

**I Have Work to Do!**

**And he shall be like a tree planted by the rivers of water, that bringeth forth his fruit in his season; his leaf also shall not wither; and whatsoever he doeth shall prosper. (Psalm 1:3)**

Prayer: Lord of the Harvest, we pray for the laborers to come forth with a working heart. We will no longer allow fear to get in the way of our destiny. We believe what You have promised us. You said that once You have begun a good work, You are faithful to perform it. So we come seeking Your will, Your divine purpose. Everything we need is in Your hands. Teach us how to be diligent, consistent and faithful to the work of the kingdom. Push selfish desires out of our heart. Open our spirit to receive our assignment and work as Your servants in this earth. All glory and power belong to You. We love You and honor You. In Jesus' name we pray, Amen.

# September 10

*Thou hast given him his heart's desire, and hast not withholden the request of his lips. Selah.* (Psalm 21:2)

Trusting God enfolds multiple benefits, as we believe we receive. The original intent for mankind was for us to dwell in open fellowship with God. This meant we were to have every provision. There was no fear, no evil, no violence, heartache, pain, or anxiety. No cares of the world, only pure satisfaction in the midst of God continuously. We know sin entered the world through deception and caused a separation, and now through the works of Christ we have been graced to reenter God's presence. In His presence we have taken on a new character and embark upon our true identity in Christ Jesus. The original intent God has for each of us begins to manifest. God is now able to bring to our awareness His predestined desires which are embedded in our heart. As we pray and spend time with God, we discover our passions and deepest aspiration and make petitions before Him. It is through prayer that we get to God's heart. We have complete confidence in God's ability to answer every prayer. God is waiting for us to make our request before Him so He can give us what He already had planned before time began. He has promised not to withhold the request of our lips. Selah means stop and think. On a continual basis we are to reflect on God's answered prayers and thank Him at all times, causing us to take time to really contemplate on God's goodness. There will never be a time when God will not answer a prayer request that is asked according to His will. It is impossible for God to lie. If we delight ourselves in the Lord and commit our ways unto Him, we WILL receive the desires of our heart. Selah!

**When We Pray!**

Prayer: God, You are the bright and morning star. The light of this world. Alpha and Omega, everything we could ever need. Lord, thank You for considering our request. You are always available to answer and guide us in our path. We commit our ways to You. We are delighted to serve You. We come asking for the desires in of our heart, trusting and believing that all things are possible in You. Prepare our heart to receive the promises, which are Yea and Amen. If for any reason we are not in position for the things we request, develop us as we wait for the appointed time. We know You will not withhold any good thing from us. We are forever grateful for Your grace and mercy. We bless You. In Jesus' name we pray, Amen.

# September 11

*But even the very hairs of your head are all numbered. Fear not therefore: ye are of more value than many sparrows.* (Luke 12:7)

Even the little things concern God. He takes so much thought toward us that He knows how many hairs we have on our head. This example illustrates for us the significance of how much God loves each of us. At no point in our lives are we lost without a cause. If we turn toward heaven and seek our Father, we are sure to find comfort and strength for each of our concerns. God is very specific as He tells His people multiple times in the Bible not to fear or to be anxious about ANYTHING. We are to give thanks to God for being Mighty and powerful; more than able to carry our load. He releases the pressure of worry from our finite minds because we have too many other things we can be focused on. Worry causes us to place our attention and efforts on things instead of God. When God is the center of our concentration, we no longer find it difficult to trust Him when misfortune arises. "We have this hope as an anchor for the soul, firm and secure. It enters the inner sanctuary behind the curtain" (Hebrews 6:19). God has already made available everything we need. He teaches us how to conquer the thoughts of our mind that will cause us to believe otherwise. It is without doubt that God loves us. He loves us so much that He'll send His Son to the earth to die for us to realize He wants a relationship with us. The relationship He created us to have in the first place. If you ever for a second think you are not loved, remember the very hairs on your head are accounted for. God loves you and you should know it.

**Love is the universal language!**

Prayer: Thank You God for the truth of Your Word. It is impossible for You to lie or to break a promise. What You have predestined for us goes beyond our wildest imagination. You have not created us to worry or to live in despair. Comfort those who mourn this day. Revive those who are depressed, oppressed, or who have lost all hope. Let our faith be ignited today. Minister to our very point of need. All things are made new in Your presence. We acknowledge You. We invite You in to dwell among us. Lord, we worship You in Spirit and truth. In Jesus' name we pray, Amen.

# September 12

*And this shall be a sign unto you; Ye shall find the babe wrapped in swaddling clothes, lying in a manger.* (Luke 2:12)

God wants us to be so in sync with Him that we are unable to miss His signs. Before God does anything, He sends signs and wonders to confirm what our faith hopes for. Our life shouldn't be any different. Our intimate connection with God produces a level of communication where God has free access to reveal His plans to us. God longs to prepare us for every situation before we encounter them. As we draw near to Him, we develop a connection with Him. Our relationship with God teaches us His character, opening our mind to kingdom principles (God's order of operation). Daily communication allows God to shine light on His purpose for each of our lives. He is able to reveal our daily task helping us fulfill our destiny. As we spend more time being governed by the Spirit, we will receive visions from God. Confirmation follows to comfort our spirit and let us know God's Word is true. Prophecy is not to tell us what our future looks like as far as material gain is concerned, but to get us to see what is taking place in Heaven. God wants us to be aware of His divine plan for us. This is why the bible commands us to pray without ceasing and to seek God while He may be found. God is here! The question is, are we aware of His presence and willing to listen to His commandments no matter the cost.

**Everything that God says, comes true.**

Prayer: LORD, we bow humbled before Your throne, seeking a deeper relationship with You. What You are concerned with in Heaven, please place it upon our hearts so we can be in connection with You. You have called each day into existence before any of them came to be. Without Your guidance we walk around hopelessly. We are asking for Your wisdom, knowledge, and understanding. Let Your Spirit lead us on the narrow path of righteousness. In our time of consecration, teach us Your concepts and kingdom principles to govern our life. In all things we give thanks. We love You God. In Jesus' name we pray, Amen.

# September 13

*O house of Jacob, come ye and let us walk in the light of the LORD.* (Isaiah 2:5)

We all know there are two components of life's behaviors which include right and wrong. God makes it clear as he describes the evil as darkness and walking according to his standards of righteousness as light. In darkness, evil exists where we find all forms of hurtful behavior and actions. Light is where God resides and calls all of His children to dwell. It's where His attributes illuminate and cause a scent of his glory to fill the atmosphere. God, being so gracious, opens the door for us to stand before His presence of light as we walk with Him daily. Walking in the light produces in us the best life has to offer. We are able to see clearly and have a well-defined perspective. If we were to do a survey and ask humans what they wanted out of life, the majority, if not all, would venture to say fulfillment and satisfaction. We might mention personal goals and aspiration and good welfare for our loved ones. Well! Glory to God, this is what we receive as we walk in the light of the Lord. God has predestined each of our days to consist in total reliance on Him. When we choose not to obey His voice we slip into darkness and lose sight of the course we were once on. When He first thought to create us He designed a road map to get us to our final destination. He knows the course like the back of His hand. Every obstacle, intersection, and bump has already been set up for us to make it through the already traveled road. God joins us as we walk through our journey to ensure we receive everything He has prepared for us. As the light of the world, we can trust God by following His voice and walking in His path. A path is a way of travel which has been created for a particular purpose. Our purpose is to follow Christ and to display His glory in all the earth.

**Let your light forever shine!**

Prayer: God, You are the light of this world. Honor and glory are Yours in abundance. Open our hearts to receive all of You today. Remove everything that stands in our way or tries to hinder us from letting our light shine in all the earth. Your plans are perfect and pleasing, we will follow Your path of righteousness. We are Your sheep and hear Your voice above all other influence. Let Your Word be a lamp unto our feet and a light unto our path. All the days of our life we will walk with You. All the glory belongs to You. In Jesus' name we pray, Amen.

## September 14

*Will ye steal, murder, and commit adultery, and swear falsely, and burn incense unto Baal, and walk after other God's whom ye know not... But go ye now unto my place which was in Shiloh, where I set my name at the first, and see what I did to it for the wickedness of my people Israel.* (Jeremiah 7:9,12)

Blessed are the pure in heart: for they shall see God (Matthew 5:8). God is not so much concerned with our outward appearance of worship as He is committed to examining our heart. Many people play the role by attending church and proclaiming Christ, yet deny the very power that can save our lives. If our hearts are not committed and turned toward God, everything we do will be worthless. God inspects each of our hearts to see the true meaning of who we are. We can easily hide our thoughts from others, but not from God who sees our intent. He longs to purify our heart so we can be in right standing with Him. He has given us His Word, Jesus as an example and the Holy Spirit to help keep our heart in connection with Him. We are able to ask God to observe our inner being and help us develop a pure heart. Many think as long as we are not committing sins that are noticeable like adultery and murder, we are in the clear. God considers all acts of disobedience sin and judges each one accordingly. Doubt, fear, gossiping, lying, malice, anger, evil intentions are all things God hates. If we are quick to confess our sins and come to God on a daily basis to be continuously purified, we can live in right standing with Him. God is not pleased when we allow things to separate us from fellowship with Him. On the other hand, He will not dwell in the midst of sin. We have strength through His mighty power to resist all temptation of sin and enjoy open fellowship with our Father. Allow God to heal every broken area of your heart. The deep places of despair that we are afraid to talk about, God wants access to. The truth of the matter is, God already knows, so it's to our benefit to release it to Him and ask for help concerning the matter. Until we deal with everything that plagues us we will walk beneath the maximum potential God has created us for.

**Allow God to do heart surgery on you!**

Prayer: God, You are Alpha and Omega, nothing happens in this earth without You already knowing it. Search our hearts, examine us to the depths of our soul and forgive us of all manner of evil. Help us to understand that when we fail to operate under Your principles we are only deceiving ourselves. Wash us clean and purify our souls today. Get to the root of every issue that prompts us to act and react in any manner that is not pleasing in Your sight. Help us to resist temptation and to walk in righteousness at all times. Let the fruits of the Spirit, love, joy, peace, longsuffering, gentleness, faith, meekness, and temperance be found in us. All praise belongs to You. In Jesus' name we pray, Amen.

# September 15

*For it pleased the Father that in him should all fulness dwell;* (Colossians 1:19)

Jesus, the very image of the invisible God, is our perfect example of how to live a righteous life. He is God in the flesh, chosen to walk the earth and become a ransom for all of creation. His life illustrates the reason for creation to be in divine connection with God. God counted it as a privilege to fill Jesus' human body with His entire splendor. There was nothing hidden from Christ, all of God was within Him. He was completely human and completely divine all at the same time. Christ made room for God within His human frame. This relationship teaches us many ways to connect with God. Giving Christ the head position in our lives opens the gateway to the mysteries of God. We are able to obtain spiritual wisdom and understanding. God is trying to get us to become aware of our true identity, which can only be found in Christ. Christ has reconciled us back to God. There is no longer anything that hinders our relationship with God, except when we fail to operate in our freedom and deny the presence of God. God created us with every tool necessary for a purpose-filled life. Let God be pleased to dwell within us by releasing ownership of our mind, body and soul to the guiding of His Spirit.

**God, you are welcome here!**

Prayer: God, You are the Lord of this universe. For Your divine purpose, You created all things. We understand all of creation belongs to You. We deny ourselves before You today to take full ownership of every aspect of our being. Look over our lives. Search our hearts and call them into alignment with Your plans. We lay down our way of thinking and determine to seek Your wisdom and truth. We relinquish authority over our decisions, knowing that Your plans are perfect and pleasing. God, You know our days before they come, so we ask for Your guidance every day in every situation. Prepare us for the days ahead. Let us always be found seeking after Your kingdom and Your righteousness. In all things we give thanks. In Jesus' name we pray, Amen.

# September 16

*And the Lord visited Sarah as he had said, and the Lord did unto Sarah as he had spoken.* (Genesis 21:1)

God is a God of order. Everything He does has divine structure. His plans are uniquely crafted to always produce favorable outcomes. He orchestrates everything in His mind, speaks it into existence, and the plans manifest in the earth. In the beginning God created the Heavens and Earth. Nothing manifested until He spoke it into existence (Genesis 1). God opened His mouth and commanded every aspect of Heaven and Earth to form. God is big on communication. He has some specific things to say about each of our lives. We have confidence that when God speaks, His Word will never return unto Him void; everything will be established. just like He spoke to Sarah, He speaks to us today concerning promises He predestined before time began. As we read the history of the old testament, we discover countless accounts of God declaring what would soon happen. In every instance, we see the manifestation of what God proclaimed. Many times in the bible God prepared the people through disclosing His plans and preparing His children for what would surely come. God has never spoken a Word that has not taken place. He longs to speak with us as His children to reveal His divine order to us. We have to be willing and obedient to follow His instructions and to trust Him through believing every Word. Allow your ears to hear and your hearts to receive the spoken promises of God.

**God Said!**

Prayer: Glory to Your name O God. You are wonderful, marvelous, and worthy to be praised. God, all things are under Your command. We acknowledge Your glorious splendor. Open our ears so that we can hear from Heaven. We accept Your principles of declarations and speak Your promises over our lives today. We are kingdom citizens and share in the inheritance that You have given to us today. We are forever grateful for Your loving kindness. We love You. In Jesus' name we pray, Amen.

# September 17

*And the LORD answered me, and said, Write the vision, and make it plain upon tables, that he may run that readeth it.* (Habakkuk 2:2)

He has prepared every day of our lives to help us live up to our fullest potential.

God is looking for a servant who will hear the Word of God, write the vision, and take off to accomplish all that He is leading us to do. We are God's ambassadors in the earth. Everything God wants to accomplish in the earth requires a willing vessel. Daily communication with God prepares us for the journey ahead. God has already designed His plan for mankind. He is waiting on us to seek His vision for our lives. When we set aside time with God, we should have a notebook available to write down what God is saying. As we write the vision, God makes it plain to us how we are to prepare and accomplish it. He leads us to specific scriptures to help equip us for our assigned task. "Where there is no vision the people perish" (Proverbs 29:18). When we fail to ask God for direction, we waste our time/energy on things that are unable to benefit us. God doesn't want us to live in vain. He has designed us to function at a level of our fullest potential. If we are unaware of the purpose God has for us, we are to ask Him diligently and wait for a response. Once we receive the vision, we have to understand God has already made provision for the end result. He promises us the end, so we have something to work toward. He warns us not to worry about how long it might take to accomplish His goals, but to trust Him. When we make it through the process and reach God's purpose, our experiences confirm His Word. The very aspiration deep within us has been planted by God. As we desire to make our dreams come true, God is right there as our biggest cheerleader, cheering us on. The blessings of God are twofold; they build His kingdom and produce self-satisfaction at the same time. Go Jesus!

**Your life is already blessed~ Now walk in it!**

Prayer: Lord God of the earth, it's an honor to come into Your presence and reverence Your name. Take control of our lives today. Forgive us of our sins. Manifest Your glory in our lives. Lord, we come seeking Your divine will for our lives. Give us visions and help us to maintain momentum to see it through until completion. We will write it down and carefully yield to Your Holy Spirit to direct our path. Apart from You, we can do nothing. Prepare the way for us. Help us not to grow weary in well-doing. Command our focus to be on pleasing You. Give us a heart to be obedient to each of Your commands. Let "Yes" be our natural response to You. Lord, we love You. In Jesus' name we pray, Amen

# September 18

*Cast thy burden upon the LORD, and he shall sustain thee: he shall never suffer the righteous to be moved.* (Psalm 55:22)

Whatever pressures overwhelm our heart; God has already given us the grace to sustain us through it. Our present circumstances have no authority over us unless we give way to our hardships and allow them to defeat us. We are not children of fear who live without hope. We are assured that no matter what we endure, God is right there in the midst and has already established our expected end. Whether it is pressure from the outside world or internal issues that plague our mind, God has commanded us to leave our burdens at His feet. He is able to bear every obstacle and every form of opposition known to man. Nothing comes as a surprise to Him. He is probably more concerned when He sees His children walking around trying to carry the burden themselves. Instead of walking in our freedom, we act as if we enjoy hardships by ignoring the principle of casting our burdens upon the Lord. We understand every burden comes to test our faith, and when we give it to the Lord, we obtain a transformed mind, power and grace to wisely guide us through all matters of life. We are not to allow our emotions to get out of whack by complaining and living in fear, wondering when the Lord is going to show up. Casting our burdens upon the Lord gives rest to our soul. Whenever difficulties arise, our reaction should be, "Lord I am ready for the lesson." Victory is already promised; we might as well go through the test with joy and peace, and obtain wisdom as we expand our faith and dependence on God. Nothing can happen to us unless God allows it, knowing this develops our trust, because we know His desire is for us to prosper.

**God loves you!**

Prayer: O merciful Father, we exalt Your name on High. There is no greater name in all the earth. We cast every burden at Your feet that is on our hearts and minds. The issues that are constantly overwhelming our thought process we relinquish to You. This includes everything that tries to take our mind off of You. Anything we don't understand in our human minds we give to You for clarity and understanding. The issues that have been going on for years, and we feel as though they are too big to ever change, we give to You. You said cast our anxiety on You because You care. Thank Your for caring. Thank You for sustaining us and never allowing us to fail. God, Your power created the earth and has done miraculous things. We know You will not give up on us or leave us in despair. Renew hope today, set the oppressed free. Do a new thing; remove fear, doubt and unbelief. Lord, let us come into Your presence with praise and thanksgiving. We call You El Shaddai; You are everything we could ever need. All of our needs are met according to Your glory in Christ Jesus. Our hope is in You. We exalt You, In Jesus' name we pray, Amen.

# September 19

*My brethren, count it all joy when ye fall into divers temptations;* (James 1:2)

Whenever we are tempted by evil, we must understand it does not come from God. He never tempts us; neither can He be tempted by evil. "Let no man say when he is tempted, I am tempted of God: for God cannot be tempted with evil, **neither tempteth he any man**" (James 1:13). Our temptations come as a result of our lustful desires. The devil has been watching us since birth, in order to learn our mannerisms, the things we desire, and how we conduct ourselves in certain situations. This is the only leverage the enemy has to use against us. The enemy is not sovereign or all knowing. His only help comes from us falling into temptation. When we came into the kingdom of Jesus, the darkness of the enemy's plans were exposed. We obtained wisdom from God, showing us how to operate as heirs to our eternal inheritance- the Kingdom of God.

God teaches us to count the various forms of temptation as pure joy. From a human standpoint, we naturally want to respond with anger and sadness when unfavorable situations arise in our life. In Christ, we are able to have joy in our spirit because we understand what is taking place behind the scenes, and we must allow patience to have her perfect work, that we may be perfect and entire, wanting nothing (James 1:4). We aren't to get bent out of shape in difficulties, we have been commanded to have joy. It may not feel good, but God is more concerned with our obedience to His word then how temptations effect our emotions. Joy comes as we change our response to circumstances by not allowing our mood to be hindered; this way we are able to keep a right relationship with others. We are able to operate in joy, knowing that the tempting of our faith produces fruit in us. It makes us perfect and whole. It shows God's divine power at work. As we keep our eyes on God, He is able to manifest His purpose through us and everything works together for our good.

**It's not what it looks like!**

**Blessed is the man that endureth temptation: for when he is tried, he shall receive the crown of life, which the Lord hath promised to them that love him. (James 1:12)**

Prayer: Majesty, You are the light of this world. We exalt Your name on high. Everything You have thought concerning us is for our own good. Thank You for always being available. We ask for wisdom today concerning Your plans for our lives. We believe every Word in the bible is God-inspired to propel us into our destiny. We thank You that our destiny is not tied up in our failures, but in Your grace. Walk with us hand in hand, in order for us to stand strong on the day of temptation. We understand no one is exempt from being stalked by the enemy. We pray that by Your power his plans are destroyed right now. The evil he intended for Your people will not come to fruition. We will walk in righteousness, joy and love at all times. Let the fruits of the spirit be embedded in our heart and displayed in our mannerisms. We want all of You. Use us to bring glory to Your name. With all honor we praise You. In Jesus' name we pray, Amen.

# September 20

*And were continually in the temple, praising and blessing God. Amen.* (Luke 24:53)

Jesus had just risen from the dead and had come to dwell among the disciples and His followers. At first sight of Him, they were afraid, even after Jesus already informed them these events would take place. They knew the history, which was written in the Law of Moses and the words that were prophesied concerning Jesus. Yet still His followers were shocked and amazed, all at the same time. Jesus had to open their mind to comprehend everything that was taking place. Although He had already forewarned them, when He appeared after a brutal death, their minds were not immediately able to process the power of God raising Him from the dead. Here stood a man who had done many miraculous things in their sight. Everything Jesus spoke about was now coming to fruition right before their eyes. I can imagine the overwhelming rush of emotions they experienced as a result of Jesus' resurrection. At this point they were commissioned as witnesses to preach the gospel, which teaches us to repent and the power that released us from bondage (sin). Who wouldn't praise a High Priest such as this? Not only did they hear about the power of Christ, they experienced it firsthand. They kept their fire burning by staying connected to Him through praise and blessing God just for who He is.

**Take a moment to think about God and all that He is to you. Praise and bless His holy name. It will change the course of your day. Let your praise be authentic.**

**He is Worthy!**

Prayer: God of heaven and earth, all power belongs to You. How great is Your mercy and lovingkindness towards us. Without You we are nothing. Everything we are is a result of Your love. Lord, we open our mouths to bless You and praise You in the temple of holiness. God, You have done miraculous things in this earth, and in our individual lives. We are in constant remembrance of Your compassion and how You are everywhere at all times, and how You have delivered, protected, healed, and provided for our every need. We bow down in total reverence to Your name. When circumstances arise that seem unfavorable, replace our complaining with praise and thanksgiving. Open our minds to the understanding of the scriptures. We don't want to miss anything You are trying to teach us. With every breath, we worship You in spirit and in truth. In Jesus' name we pray, Amen.

# September 21

*Herein is love, not that we loved God, but that he loved us, and sent his Son to be the propitiation for our sins.* (1 John 4:10)

Propitiation means a turning away of wrath by an offering, that offering being the death of Christ. Instead of God giving us our just punishment, His anger was turned away when Christ became the sacrificial offering. Love is the only reason Jesus came to earth. His love overpowered the knowledge of His death on the cross. Knowing the pain and suffering He would have to endure, He said "yes" so that God could present Himself to us again. God goes through great measures to display His love to His creation. His love is a free gift that waits patiently for us to acknowledge and accept it. So often people feel as though they have to reach some level of perfection before they can come before God, when God is trying to present Himself to us in order for us experience His loving nature. Jesus did the work on the cross for each of us. Our job is to repent and accept Jesus, then rejoin fellowship with the Father. We were created to experience God's love; God holds our relationship in the highest regard. It grieves Him when we deny His fellowship. He went through great lengths to be reconciled to us by washing away our sins. Once we realize the love of God, we obtain a new outlook on life and are able to enjoy our experience with Him. This is the original intent for mankind. God being so loving He could not associate with sin, so He destroyed it in order for us to be able to come boldly before the throne of grace once again. Thank God for Jesus, we are kingdom citizens.

**He did it all for you!**

Prayer: God, You are the Prince of peace, Alpha and Omega, El Shaddai, Emmanuel, You are everything we need at all times. Lord, we can't even begin to imagine the depths of Your love. We honor You for creating us, for uniquely crafting us in our own individual uniqueness. Everything You do is perfect and a result of Your love. Open our hearts to receive Your love. Teach us how to display Your same love to others. Love is so powerful. Remove any hardness of our hearts so we are able to enjoy every second of our life. All praise belongs to You. In Jesus' name we pray, Amen.

# September 22

*I have been young, and now am old; yet have I not seen the righteous forsaken, nor his seed begging for bread.* (Psalm 37: 25)

Every good and every perfect gift is from above, and cometh down from the Father of lights (James 1:17). When God thought to create us, He crafted a unique plan to ensure every aspect of life would be beneficial. Even the unfavorable circumstances that we encounter are a part of His plan. Everyday in His presence develops the attributes He has instilled in each of us. At any point in life, we can call out to God and know He is there. In our darkest hour, God is right there, cheering us on toward the hope of His glory. His promise sits on the other side of the mountains that we have to endure. Through the process, He whispers in our ear not to give up and to keep our eyes on Him. With each step, He instructs our path to line up with our destiny. What He has already thought out will begin to manifest itself to our natural eye, giving way to the authority of God. Everything God has promised to us is already established, it waits on us to reach God's appointed time so we can receive it. Being in right standing with God guarantees we will receive what has already been predestined for us. We are not forsaken, because God has completed the master plan. Our obedience to His commands allows Him to order our steps. Following God's direction will lead us to the land flowing with milk and honey.

**Favor is Yours in abundance!**

Prayer. Lord, You reign in all the earth. At this very moment we praise You for just being God. Lord, You are magnificent and holy. Search us inwardly and remove all manner of flesh. Help us to walk hand and hand with You. You are the guide of our life. Take control of every aspect. Order our steps in Your Word. Control our very response to Your direction; let our response be "yes" at all times. Lord, there is none like You. You created the earth and established us as Your children so that we could share in Your love. Overpower us with Your presence. Let us experience

You in a new way today. Wrap us in Your arms. We are so thrilled to call you Abba Father. We are forever grateful. In Jesus' name we pray, Amen.

# September 23

*Then he called his twelve disciples together, and gave them power and authority over all devils, and to cure diseases.* (Luke 9:1)

God has instilled is us such power and authority that we can trample over devils and cure diseases. Why then are so many of us are not walking in our ability to do these miraculous things? When we initially start school there are core competency subjcts, which we will learn. At the end of each course we are able to align our knowledge with the objectives from the course. In the kingdom of God, we have already been given the power and authority over satan and darkness. God is the one who has equipped us according to our faith in order to operate in our full ability. We have to grow in faith, trusting and believing in the power of God. We operate in God's power and strength to cast out unclean spirits and heal diseases when we make a conscious effort to be used by God. Jesus sent His disciples out with authority and power over all devils and to cure diseases after he prepared them. Victory is already promised to us, we know that. Our preparation is the bridge standing between us receiving it or living hopelessly. Jesus prepared His disciples by teaching them the way of the kingdom. His disciples made a choice to receive all of Him and their faith was expanded as a result. Our fellowship with God prepares us for the work of the kingdom. Functioning in the attributes of God is our way of life. As Christ disciples, it takes, time, dedication, commitment and obedience to function victoriously over every affliction in our lives. Christ already obtained victory for us on the cross; our job is to believe it.

**Operate as a Kingdom Citizen!**

Prayer: Lord God of this earth, exert Your power in this earth right now. Open the eyes of Your children and help us to walk out as Your disciples. Train us and prepare us for the journey ahead. Help us not to retract or to be afraid of anything that may arise in our life. Victory is ours in abundance. Life is ours to live and to be free from the lies of the enemy. Teach us how to stand on the mighty strength of Your power. As we watch the ways of Christ, build our confidence in Your unfailing love. Teach us the ways of the kingdom. Lord, everything we do say and think will be as a result of us seeking Your kingdom and Your righteousness. In all manner of life purify us and instill us with Your wisdom. All power and praise belong to You, in Jesus' name we pray. Amen.

# September 24

*Glory to God in the highest, and on earth peace, good will toward men.* (Luke 2:14)

Have you ever wondered why God instructs us to praise in the midst of suffering and trials? God is teaching us how to respond with a kingdom mindset. In the kingdom of heaven there are multitudes of the heavenly host who continuously praise God 24/7. When we are faced with adversity and decide to ignite praise, we are joining in with the angels in heaven who give God glory. Our praise comes as an assurance of who God is and the strength of His power. We offer praise because we know our God is able to become whatever we need in that moment. His love for us lets us know we no longer have anything to fear or worry about. We are called to be devoted to glorifying God. Exaltations are due to God, since He is the one who created us, watches over us, and promises to be with us at all times. Situations are temporary and constantly change. In God, we know He is the same yesterday, today, and forevermore. Having praise as our continuous response to life empowers us to become familiar with the way things operate in heaven. I once heard someone say the shortest thing we will ever do is live the life we are living. This means our life is short but eternity is forever. We ought to get in the habit of esteeming God for who He is, because when we get to heaven we will join the angels who cry Holy, Holy, Holy is the Lord God Almighty.

**Let Praise be the natural response!**

Prayer: Lord, You are the very air we breathe. Life without You is pointless. Glory, honor, adoration, praise, reverence all belong to You. There would never be enough time to give You the entire honor You desire. We worship You for who You are. Your love embodies the very essence of who we are. One moment in Your presence will change the course of our life. We cry out to You today, asking for an encounter with You like never before. Take us from glory to glory, expand our faith. Help us to be so committed to Your commands that it becomes a natural response to say, “yes” to Your will. Jesus, You are everything, we could go on and on about Your goodness. We do join in with the angels today and bow down at Your feet to acknowledge You as Sovereign. God, we love You. In Jesus’ name we pray, Amen.

# September 25

*For my thoughts are not your thoughts, neither are your ways my ways, saith the Lord.* (Isaiah 55:8)

God's principles are set in place in order for us to operate by a kingdom standard. You see, God is holy, and has given us His commands to show us how to act in accordance with our heritage. This thought process has to be embedded in our spirit, to walk in right standing with God. There are certain events that occur in our life which cause us to react in certain ways. Casting judgment is one of the frequent responses we give when we encounter something outside of ***our*** norm. We have to be extremely careful to take God's attitude when it comes to imparting judgment. God lets us know we shall not judge. I believe God removes this duty from us because we are unable to fully comprehend the extent of other people's motives. Also, we are not in the position to look down our nose at someone else because we too were once called unrighteous. In Isaiah 55:7 it says, *Let the wicked forsake his way, and the unrighteous man his thoughts: and let him return unto the Lord, and he will have mercy upon him; and to our God, for he will abundantly pardon.* God doesn't want us to judge the wicked because He hopes for their return, as He did for us when we were in the world. God shows mercy to the unrighteous when they have a heart of repentance. God's ultimate purpose is for everyone to share in His love. Our response to others is to be uplifting, encouraging, and to speak the truth in love. We do this in hopes of people being able to open their hearts to Christ and get on the right track. With pure motives, God displays His sovereignty to all the earth with a common goal of us spending eternity with Him forever.

**God is not a respecter of persons!**

Prayer: God of mercy, we bless Your name. Look down from heaven and search us inwardly. Remove all manner of judgment, gossiping, backbiting, and evil intents of our heart and replace them with Your peace and joy. Pour out the kingdom of heaven in our lives that we may get acquainted with how we will spend eternity in heaven with You. Lord, teach us Your ways. Grant us a discerning spirit. Keep watch over our tongue. Let our response to others be full of love. Help us to show mercy to others and consider how you accepted us with open arms when we first came into the kingdom. Help us to never forget there is no one without sin, all have fallen short. It is by Your grace alone that we have a new life in Christ. We are forever grateful. We exalt Your name with the highest praise, Hallelujah! In Jesus' name we pray, Amen.

# September 26

*To know the love of Christ which passes knowledge; that you may be filled with all the fullness of God.* (Ephesians 3:19)

Jesus walked the earth as an example to display the fullness of God's love. He had been waiting in the wings since the beginning of time to enter earth to confirm God's love. His compassion for following every command from God enabled Him to do miraculous wonders in the earth. With each healing touch, He visually showed us the power we possess as being joint heirs with Him. His demonstration of God's power was to encourage us in the things of God. It vividly exhibited the depth of God's love. A love that would do anything for us to comprehend the greatness that we have in Him. Jesus physically walked in every attribute given from above. His life was a perfect example, showcasing the heart of God. This display of affection opened the gateway for us to have access to come boldly before the throne of God. We will never be able to fully grasp the magnitude of God's love, because it surpasses knowledge. The little comprehension that we do have is enough to know without a doubt the compassion embedded in God's love; a love so deep that plans of redemption were created before any action on our part was every taken. By grace alone, we are able to join fellowship with the Father and experience His love.

**Jesus loves you!**

Prayer: God, You alone are worthy of all the praise. With an open heart we bow in Your presence to thank You. Open our eyes that we may see the love that You bestow upon Your people each day. Lord, Your love is so deep we can't fully comprehend it. Speak life into the brokenhearted, lost, and those in despair. Help us to know Your love is true and everlasting. It will never lead us astray. You are always there for Your children and desire to help us. Let us bask in Your glory and enjoy the gift of life. We are forever grateful for Jesus, whom You sent as a ransom. There is no greater love than to lay down your own life for friends. Hallelujah! Thank You for redeeming us and considering us as friends. Let

Your love pour over in our lives, that we may love each other and show the world Your power. With every ounce of our being we praise You. In Jesus' name we pray, Amen.

# September 27

*Don't be fooled into thinking that you will never suffer because the Temple is here. It's a lie!* (Jeremiah 7:8 NLT)

The Bible says he who has clean hands and a pure heart are able to stand in the holy place of God (Psalm 24:4). There isn't any other way to get around being obedient to the commands of God. He has created us, as His holy possession, to enjoy the gifts of life. It should bring us great joy to return a heart of gratitude and submission before His throne. God despises nothing more than an ungrateful, disobedient heart. Church attendance alone does not produce the righteousness that God desires from His children. God is searching for a heart that is open to Him, where we have surrendered our entire being to His Holy Spirit. Our way of thinking, coupled with our actions have to be in alignment with His attributes. He examines the intent of our heart and makes judgment according to how we think and respond to life's circumstances. It may seem a bit overwhelming to consider God judging every thought and action. As humans, we feel we deserve a break or some type of leeway for our actions. God is not concerned with giving us some form of validation, He is concerned with righteousness. He has given us the instruments to utilize in order to comply with His commands. His commands are not set in place to dictate or control us as robots. They are there as guidelines to keep us from hurting ourselves and causing unfavorable judgment. We must be careful not to become complacent by thinking our confession of faith is enough to satisfy our commitment to the kingdom. Holiness is a lifestyle, where we have to make a conscious effort to seek God as the head of every aspect of our life.

**God, You Reign Forever!**

Prayer: Lord, You are good and Your mercy endures forever. Lord, search our hearts, examine us inwardly and help us to be obedient to every one of Your commands. Deal with our thought process and help us to cast down every imagination and thought that tries to exalt itself against Your knowledge. Help us to seek Your word and allow Your word to have authority in our inner being. Overpower our flesh to submit to Your Spirit. Enable us with Your strength to be doers of Your word. Let Your word be fulfilling to us. We seek Your face daily for guidance. Teach us how to have clean hands and a pure heart. Dig up every issue from the root that may cause a separation between us. Remove all manner of evil intent from our heart. Let Your statutes bring delight and joy in our lives. We will forever bless Your name. You are righteous; we exalt Your name forever. In Jesus' name we pray, Amen.

# September 28

*I no longer call you slaves, because a master doesn't confide in his slaves. Now you are my friends, since I have told you everything the Father told me.* (John 15:15)

O to be called a friend of God! The sweetness of friendship is built to last a lifetime. So often we find few genuine friends whom we can find no fault in. We long for their fellowship and enjoy laughter, hardships, aspirations, and every part of our existence with them. Jesus came into the world and shared this authentic relationship with His followers. He shared His innermost thoughts with them by opening His heart and pouring out the love of His Father. Everything Jesus received from Heaven He gave to His disciples. He was teaching them the true meaning of love. As Jesus developed a relationship with His followers, He made it clear that He was there for them. Whatever need they had, He was able to help provide it for them. Our relationship with Jesus should not be a mandated routine of us punching the clock, trying to make it into heaven. It should be an authentic relationship that we enjoy. When we come before the throne of grace to speak with our Father, we are able to express our inner thoughts, fears, and dreams. Our communication with God is informal; our love for Him breaks down walls. We shouldn't hesitate during our time with Him. We are able to express whatever is on our mind. As a friend, Jesus tells us that we have access to everything He has. We are able to ask for anything in His name and receive it based on our connection with Him. This relationship is built on our response to His love because there is nothing we can do to deserve His love. He is going to love us forever, through our good and bad times. Our response to His love determines whether or not we walk in obedience to His voice. Love is the instruments that calls us into righteousness. Everything we do with the life that God has given us is based on how we view our love relationship with Him.

**I am a friend of God!**

Prayer: Lord God Almighty, You are an awesome wonder. We magnify Your name today. Thank You for being a friend. Thank You for calling us out of darkness and into Your marvelous light. With all of our strength we will praise You. We lift Your name on high. Lord, open the heart of Your people today that we may experience Your love. Help us to respond to Your love with obedience. With genuine affection, having a grateful heart. Let gratitude be our response to life. Teach us the way to love others that we may be pleasing in Your sight. With all honor we bless Your name. In Jesus' name we pray, Amen.

# September 29

*On the day the Lord gave the Israelites victory over the Amorites, Joshua prayed to the Lord in front of all the people of Israel. He said, "Let the sun stand still over Gibeon, and the moon over the valley of Aijalon." So the sun stood still and the moon stayed in place until the nation of Israel had defeated its enemies.* (Joshua 10:12-13)

Joshua had an intimate relationship with God. He didn't wait until He got into battle to seek the Lord. He sought the Lord first and always kept Him at the forefront of his mind. There, God was in the midst, fighting on His behalf. Joshua looked to God to lead every step of the way. He allowed his faith to function in its full capacity. In his own strength He could not cause the sun and moon to stand still. Joshua developed trust in God through His consistent fellowship. His commitment to God developed His faith.

Making God a priority in our life opens the gateway into a divine connection. Our armor of holiness is never taken off; we always include God in everything. As we include God in everything, everything He has written in the book of life will come to pass. So often God sits in heaven in anticipation, waiting for us to acknowledge Him. When we follow the principles of faith, God is pleased to work on our behalf. God is trilled to fulfill His position as the Almighty. It's in His DNA to exude His virtue in the lives of His people. Faith exercises the power and authority that we have through Jesus Christ. God is waiting to do greater works in the earth. He needs a people who are unashamed to seek His face whole-heartedly. Then, through the Holy Spirit, God will be able to deliver nations through our obedience and commitment to His will.

**Faith that works!**

Prayer: Lord God Almighty, we exalt Your name on this day. Establish the works of our hands. Direct our every path. Open the eyes of Your people. Help us to stop seeking Your throne for selfish ambition, but to come seeking Your will. Lord, You said if we seek You first and Your kingdom that You will add all things unto us. So this day we lay aside what our flesh wants and we come to connect with You in the spirit. Overpower us with Your love. Deposit Your divine plan in us, prepare us and send us out as Your ambassadors in the earth. Ignite the fire within us and stir up the gifts You have placed on the inside of us. Grant us the spirit of boldness and allow us to preach the gospel in love. Lord, we don't want people to perish for a lack of knowledge. Train us in Your ways. Help us to be ready to give an account of Your glory at all times. Jesus, in all that we do we will exalt Your name. You are the God who sits high, but looks low. We are forever under Your subjection. With all praise we say thank You. In Jesus' name we pray, Amen.

# September 30

*For I also am a man [daily] subject to authority, with soldiers under me. And I say to one, Go, and he goes; and to another, Come, and he comes; and to my bond servant, Do this, and he does it.* (Luke 7:8 AMP)

The faith exhibited by the centurion in this scripture is extremely dynamic. I was so authentic that it amazed Jesus to see such faith in a person. The centurion understood kingdom principles and the power God instills in His children. The centurion requested Jesus to come to his home to heal his sick servant. When Jesus agreed and was en route, he sent some friends to stop Jesus, insisting that He only needed to send a word. To a people without faith this would cause confusion. You asked for me to come, and now that I am on the way you stop me. I believe the centurion understood the power of the spirit. When he sent for Jesus to come, knowing the power of God would show up in the supernatural. His mouth called for Jesus in the natural, but His spirit was depending on Jesus to show up in the spirit realm where all miracles take place. We understand the power of God is unseen. We only see the results of His invisible power manifested in the natural. This man understood how faith truly works. It's subject to God's authority. So when Jesus sends His word, the very thing He is speaking has to submit to His authority (the power of God). I dare you to call out to God today in faith. He has given us a plethora of commands that are under our authority in His Word. When we speak God's word into the atmosphere in faith, it has no other choice but to submit to the authority of Christ, which is within us.

**Speak a Word!**

**So shall My word be that goes forth from My mouth; It shall not return to Me void, But it shall accomplish what I please, And it shall prosper *in the thing* for which I sent it. (Isaiah 55:11)**

Prayer: Lord of Heaven, You are the light of this world. All power, majesty and glory are in Your hand. Lord, we cannot begin to thank You enough for the awesome power that You have placed in us by Your Son Jesus. Lord, we open the doors of our heart and invite You in to dwell with us. We utilize the keys to the kingdom and call all things under Your authority. Whatever issues/concerns that plague our heart today we submit to You. We bind up all forces of negativity and loose Your splendor in our lives. God, dispatch Your angels in the earth to minister to our very point of need, that we may be effective servants of the gospel. Help us to proclaim Your glory throughout all the earth. There is none like You, Lord, You are everything. We magnify Your name. In Jesus' name we pray, Amen

# October 1

*O house of Jacob, come ye, and let us walk in the light of the Lord.* (Isaiah 2:5)

God never intended for us to wander this earth alone apart from Him. It is His divine order for us to come before Him every day to receive guidance for our daily tasks. God reveals His plans to us as we commune with Him and we are able to go forth in obedience. Having open fellowship with God teaches us how to walk the narrow path of righteousness in order to stay in perfect fellowship with Him. When we walk with God, we are assured of our expected end. His presence shines light on every dark place in our life, making it noticeable for us to make adjustments. Walking under divine brightness also highlights areas in our life where God wants us to receive revelation. This is made evident where two people can read the same scripture in the Bible and only the one walking in the light of Christ will receive revelation. If we aren't walking with Christ, His word will not penetrate our spirit and cause us to be obedient. The light of Christ is always present, we have to be alert and go seeking after Him for guidance. His light shows us every path of life and keeps us in line with our divine purpose. It allows us to utilize our time on earth effectively. As we wait in expectation for God's leading hand, we are able to enjoy each day. We must understand life is a gift. It should bring us great joy that the Master, Creator of all things wants to dwell with us and teach us all manners of life. This is of great benefit to us. Everything about God and His kingdom is for our advantage to draw us closer to Him to enjoy eternity together.

**In Your Presence is the fullness of joy!**

Prayer: God of the earth, we bow down in total worship before Your throne of grace. Grant us forgiveness today that we may be acceptable in Your sight. Lord, teach us Your ways in order to keep us on the narrow path of righteousness. Let the light of Your glory illuminate the path of our life. Guide every step and decision that we face. We will trust You with all our heart and not lean on our own understanding, but in all of our ways we will acknowledge You. Direct, make straight and plan all of our ways. Everything that we are is because of You, and we are forever grateful. All power belongs to You. In Jesus' name we pray, Amen

# October 2

*So he called every one of his lord's debtors unto him, and said unto the first, How much owest thou unto my lord?* (Luke 16:5)

Life is given to each of us as a gift. Each day is filled with endless opportunities to fulfill our predestined potential by operating in the power of Christ. We are His handiwork, His craftmanship, which He created for His own pleasure. As an extension of Him, we have been given dominion to rule the earth. "The highest heavens belong to the LORD, but the earth he has given to mankind" (Psalm 115:16). We are forever indebted to our Father for the awesome gift of life. We have been chosen as His heirs to take ownership and govern the affairs that we are entrusted with. This includes finances, family, employment, ministry; the list could go on and on. What God is concerned with is how we utilize the precious instruments that He has given to us. At any time, God should be able to see our faithful service playing out in our daily lives. We understand we are incapable of repaying God for the many things He has given to us. Our life is a symbolic representation of our thankfulness; we operate in a fashion that shows care and high regard for everything we received from heaven. Self-control and wisdom are the guiding forces in our lives when we make decisions. They guarantee we show proper care for everything God has placed under our sphere. When we think about a life totally surrendered to God, we have to operate through the Holy Spirit. At the end of each day we should have utilized all of the potential allotted to us, so that when this life is over we have nothing more to give. We are able to come before God and say, "God I did everything you assigned to me." There should be no room for what ifs; we should have a zero balance. Each of us are here for a specific purpose. Refuse every distraction and run this race with endurance.

**I have purpose!**

Prayer: God of mercy, forgive us for our sins this day. Wash us clean, purify our hearts. God, this gift of life is so precious. Open our eyes so that we understand the importance of the life that You have given to each of us. Cause us not to take it for granted, but to come before Your throne of grace every day, asking how we are to please You in our daily task. Each day we give back to You. We want to be found as Your faithful servants. When it's all over, we long to hear, "well done, my good and faithful servant." Teach us how to be good stewards over everything You have placed in our care. Let wisdom and self-control lead us and guide us. Remove all mannerisms of our flesh that we will not fall victim to the tricks of the enemy. We will subdue the earth and have dominion over it. Everything You have placed in this earth belongs to Your people and we are satisfied. With great praise we bless you. In Jesus' name we pray, Amen.

# October 3

*But I will hope continually, and will praise You yet more and more. My mouth shall tell of Your righteous acts and of Your deeds of salvation all the day, for their number is more than I know. I will come in the strength and with the mighty acts of the Lord God; I will mention and praise Your righteousness, even Yours alone.* (Psalm 71:14-16)

I will hope (with great expectation) continually is the prayer of our heart. Our expectation lies in the truth of God's Word. We are confident in His miraculous power. We may never be able to measure the magnitude of His love, but we are able to see it displayed in the nature of our relationship with Him. On a daily basis, when we come before the throne of grace, God meets us with open harms. His love is poured out in abundance as we exalt Him for being Holy. Our response to God's love is that of adoration and honor. As we dwell in His presence, we are able to grow in His strength. We'll never be able to praise God wholeheartedly without a relationship with Him. Praise shows our appreciation and trust in God's ability to work in our lives. When situations arise, our exaltation is translated to God as us saying, "Daddy this one is on you. I will not be moved by what I see. I thank You for the sacrifice Jesus made when He died on the cross for this situation many years ago. I know it is already taken care of. Show me what to do and I will heed to Your command." Praise will change our attitude and perceptions towards life. As we grow in Christ, our praise should be that much more developed. We obtain strength in praise. We have never gained anything by talking about unfavorable circumstances. The only thing our complaints produce is heartache and worry. Praise, on the other hand, has the power to remind us of God's unfailing love. Allowing the Holy Spirit to bring back to our remembrance the many times He has brought us out before. Mediating on scriptures breathes life into our spirit and activates our faith. Our firm foundation in Christ was secured before earth's creation. When we praise, it shows God we accept the sacrificial gift of His Son Jesus. That's reason enough to ALWAYS praise.

**Praise God at all times!**

Prayer: God, You are the Lord of our life. The gifts that You give new each day are magnificent. We are forever grateful for Your lovingkindness towards us. We do not take for granted the things You do for us on a continuous basis. As long as we have breath in our bodies, we will magnify Your name. Your name is higher than any circumstance. Help us not to waste our energy on stress, complaining and doubt, but to exalt Your name. We will stand on Your Word as it pertains to our specific situations. Whatever Your people need, command Your angels to be on post. Our lips will have a continuous praise. Your people are never without counsel. Help us to submit our ways to You and never lean on our own understanding, but in all our ways to acknowledge You. All glory belongs to You. In Jesus' name we pray, Amen.

# October 4

*Let my mouth be filled with thy praise and with thy honour all the day.* (Psalm 71:8)

Asking God to fill our mouth with praise is equivalent to asking God to fill our hearts with joy. Having our hearts filled with joy leaves little room for depression, or for our minds to waiver from the hope of His glory. Continuous praise transforms our inner being and calls our spirit into alignment with the essence of God's beauty. Making a conscious effort to count all things joy and open our mouths to exemplify God's goodness helps to promote a healthy soul. Fear and doubt will not permeate our minds when hardships arise, our praise will teach our minds to stay integrated in God's power of deliverance. As kingdom citizens, we have to take a proactive stance in all things pertaining to life. Praise is instrumental in reminding us of who God is, who we are to Him, and all that we have as a result of being in fellowship with Him. Our praise comes before God like a sweet aroma. It shows our gratitude and thanksgiving for everything He is. It's just like receiving a gift we have been longing for (peace, love, reconciliation, healing, new car, promotion on a job, new baby, etc.). We immediately spread the good news and inform everyone about our new blessing. Feelings of excitement overwhelm our body as we are pleased to share our happiness. Having our mouths filled with continuous praise keeps our mind in constant remembrance of how great God is. We won't be able to keep silent about His goodness.

**I will yet praise Him**

**My mouth shall tell of Your righteous acts and of Your deeds of salvation all the day, for their number is more than I know. (Psalm 71:15)**

Prayer: Lord, You are the air we breathe. Without You life is not worth living. You keep us in perfect peace whose mind is stayed on You. We count all things joy, knowing You are the ruler of everything. Our hearts are open before You this day that You may fill our lips with praise. Cause us to remember Your goodness and think about Your lovingkindness at all times. We cast down depression, fear, doubt, anxiety, low self-esteem, and feelings of loneliness. We loose power, love, joy, gladness, hope, faith, and the willingness to come before Your throne and ask anything in Jesus' name, believing that we will receive what we ask for according to Your will. Direct our footsteps according to Your word, do not allow any iniquity to have dominion over us. All glory belongs to You. In Jesus' name we pray, Amen.

# October 5

*Exalt ye the LORD our God, and worship at his footstool; for he is holy.* (Psalm 99:5)

Have you ever had a friend you could totally rely on? Whenever you called, they were right their by your side. They never cast judgment; they seem to understand all of your circumstances and issue counsel that results in your benefit. You enjoy these types of friends and consider them few and far between. When you find these specials friends you delight yourselves in their presence. You're able to be yourself and not worry about ulterior motives. These are the type of people who grace our lives as a blessing from God. They enter our circle to show us the loving nature of God's relationship with us. He is a perfect friend. One who always has our best interests at the forefront of His mind. "He will ever be mindful of his covenant" (Psalm 111:5). Through our experience with Him, we are able to see his perfect track record first hand. If one is ever searching for a reason why we should exalt (lift up, esteem on high) our God, all we have to do is open His word and see how gracious and full of compassion He is; then begin to think about the goodness of His virtue and allow thoughts of His kindness to permeate our mind. It won't take long for His Spirit to inhabit our praise, while worship exudes from our mouth as we sit at His feet, basking in the glory of His being.

**I will yet praise Him!**

Prayer: God, we exalt Your name on High. We come before Your throne of grace, asking for forgiveness of our sins. We are at Your feet in total adoration. We will not move until we receive everything You have for us. We cast all of our cares at Your feet. We are bare and open before You; search us deep within. Our mouth is filled with praise. God, You are a perfect God. One encounter with You will change the course of our life. Lord, pour out Your spirit upon us this day. We come with a expectation that You will grant the desires of our heart as we delight ourselves in You. Lord, You are worthy of all the praise. With reverence, we give You our heart, mind, and soul. Let Your will be done in earth as it is in heaven. In Jesus' name we pray, Amen.

# October 6

*I will greatly praise the LORD with my mouth; yea, I will praise him among the multitude.* (Psalm 109:30)

Praise is a powerful expression of our reverence for God. Our praise helps us to obtain wisdom. "The fear of the LORD is the beginning of wisdom" (Psalm 111:10). When we fear God, we are honoring Him as Sovereign. Believing God is Supreme ruler of the universe causes us to trust in His principles. Following His principles leads to favorable outcomes. Standing on His covenant and watching the promise manifest in our life makes praise a natural instinct embedded in our behavior. Once we come into the realization of who God is, and how each of His plans are coupled with an expected end, praise will innately flow from our lips, where we are unable to contain ourselves. We live in a society where what we do is constantly under a microscope. So often, outside forces (i.e. circumstances, others opinions) hinder our ability to appreciate God for His awesome power. We fail to remember that we are commanded to praise God no matter what we face, because His mercy endures forever. Circumstances are never the same, what is seen as a hindrance today could be gone tomorrow. We never want to get on the other end of a problem and regret not giving God glory at the onset. Our praise must go beyond our emotions and solely be influenced by God's worth alone. All we have to do is consider the many blessings we receive on a daily basis and contemplate on God's splendor. As a result, we will be able to shout with praise and adoration to an awesome, loving, and perfect God.

**Praise is what I do!**

Prayer: God, we lift Your name up to give You honor. You alone are worthy to be praised. We come before Your throne of grace to thank You for Your lovingkindness. Your mercies are new each morning. How patient You are in loving us. How forgiving You are when we fall short. At all times, praise shall be on our lips. Teach us to never allow circumstances to take the place of our trust in Your unfailing love. Many are the thoughts that You have for us, You consider our needs and set our life in order for Your will to be done. Establish the work of our hands; let Your wisdom guide us through life. With all glory and honor we say, thank You. In Jesus' name we pray, Amen.

# October 7

*For therein is the righteousness of God revealed from faith to faith: as it is written, The just shall live by faith.* (Romans 1:17)

We are incapable of receiving anything from God unless we believe. We have been granted an open invitation into the kingdom of heaven by way of Jesus Christ. Our ability to receive the many blessings He has for us is contingent upon our ability to believe and receive. God is calling us closer to Him by giving us many resources in the earth to stand firm in our faith. As the bible states, the righteousness of God is revealed by our faith in God and our willingness to adhere to his statutes. As we do this, we are more likely to appreciate our spiritual escape from sin and death. Unbelief hinders God from employing His power in our lives. The more we believe by standing on His word, the more His power will be manifested in our lives. Eagerness to believe in the substance of things hoped for and the evidence of things not seen excites God. He looks down from heaven with enthusiasm, saying, "Yes, my child is standing strong relying on the things that I have promised." At the appointed time, He releases that which was already prepared. His power is readily available. We will never be able to see the maximal extent of the fullness of God's power. It's far too great. As we experience more and more of His power, our faith continues to grow. What exists as the greatest miracle to us is a small glimpse of God's power.

**God is bigger!**

Prayer: Lord of mercy, we honor You this day for Your greatness. Thank You for saving us from death. Help us to walk in righteousness today by believing in the gospel of Your Son Jesus Christ. We vow to trust, rely, and stand on Your word in order for Your power to be manifested in our lives to bring glory to Your name. We are Your children. Without You we are hopeless. Watch over us, lead and guide us in the path of righteous living. We surrender our mind, body, and soul to Your governance. All power belongs to You. In Jesus' name we pray, Amen.

# October 8

*But ye gave the Nazarites wine to drink; and commanded the prophets, saying, Prophesy not.* (Amos 2:12)

A Nazarite is one who is consecrated to God by taking a vow not to drink wine, cut their hair or touch dead bodies (Numbers 6). In the Old Testament, God instructed Moses in the way a man or woman could consecrate himself or herself before the Lord by taking a Nazarite vow. This period of time could be as short as 30 days or could last a lifetime. This was a time of separation and dedication to God. The bible says during this time of separation, the person was holy before the Lord (Numbers 6:8). This act of dedication relates to our relationship with God today. As we grow in our relationship with God, there will be times of consecration where we abstain from certain things in order to be completely dedicated to the Lord. We recognize this time of separation and refraining from desires of our flesh will draw us closer to God and help us to mature spiritually. As Christians, it is important for us to set aside times of sanctification in order to receive everything God has for us. In this particular verse, God is describing how the children of Israel were encouraging the Nazarites not to take their vow seriously, and silencing the voice of the prophets. They thought if they could discredit the Nazarites, they would have little influence from God and would be free to carry on as they pleased. As we look around our world today, we can see the very same thing-taking place. People feel that if they take God out of schools and the legislature then they won't be held accountable. God needs His disciples to stand strong in their consecration in order to be a voice to people who are dying from a lack of knowledge. Oftentimes, we fast and consecrate ourselves before God for personal reasons. God requires more from His people. He is looking for a holy generation who will stand in the gap as godly vessels who will receive a word from heaven and are unashamed to spread the gospel.

**Will you be the one?**

Prayer: Lord of mercy, God of grace, what an honor is it to serve You today. I pray that You press upon our heart the very plans that You have for us in this season. Remove all outside forces that may come to take our heart and mind off You. Open our minds to receive the things You have ordained for such a time as this. When You speak, cause our ear to hear and our hearts to obey. We want to be set apart and used for Your most holy work. Prepare us now; show us the path of righteousness. Your Son Jesus paid the price for us to live in You, and we surrender our being to You and allow You to reign in our lives. We bless Your holy name. In Jesus' name we pray, Amen.

# October 9

*For he clave to the Lord, and departed not from following him, but kept his commandments, which the Lord commanded Moses. And the Lord was with him; and he prospered whithersoever he went forth: and he rebelled against the king of Assyria, and served him not.* (2 Kings 18:6-7)

Are you one to take a stance against popular opinion, regardless of the repercussions, in order to stand on your belief in God? Hezekiah was one of many kings during his generation who trusted in the Lord. Even Hezekiah's father was evil in the sight of the Lord. He was raised in an environment that was structured to teach him how to disobey God. Yet, somewhere down the line, Hezekiah made a conscious decision to stand on God's word and decided not to follow the customs of his people. When everyone around him was worshipping false idols and causing God to become angry, Hezekiah stood firm in His faith and remained devoted to God. God is looking for this same moral excellence in you and me today. Although the society we live in today has turned away from God, He should still be able to look at our lives and see our unwavering faith. We have to be willing to be considered outcasts, if we are ever given the choice whether or not to follow God. Many times people fall victim to peer pressure or conform because of temporary acceptance or backlash. The key word is temporary. When we study the bible we see God keeps record of every decision we make. When He has given us opportunity to follow His instructions and we choose to do the opposite, we are in jeopardy of unfavorable consequences. Our concern should not be in pleasing others, when God is the one who has power to cast judgment upon our souls. This promise of judgment is not affirmed to make us live in fear. God sets His commands in place so we have an understanding of what keeps us out of fellowship with Him. He does this in hopes of us choosing the right path in order to receive all of His great benefits. As Hezekiah remained faithful to God and followed all of His statutes, the bibles says, "the LORD was with him; and he prospered whithersoever he went forth" (2 Kings 18:7).

**Obedience is better than sacrifice!**

Prayer: Hallelujah, Hallelujah. Holy, holy, holy, is the Lord of hosts. The whole earth is full of Your glory. Awesome God, we come with our hearts lifted up before You. We come to reverence Your name. God, as Isaiah cried out before You to be sent as a messenger, we come saying, here I am, send me. Prepare us for the journey ahead. Pour out your statutes upon our heart. Wherever You are is where we long to be. We will stand firm in our faith. We put on the whole armor of God, that we may be able to stand against the wiles of the devil. We bind up any negative thought and action that will try to come against Your people. Let Your light shine so brightly within us that darkness cannot hide. We stand as Your followers, we will obey every command that comes from Heaven. Build our confidence in You. Thank You for hearing our prayers. With all praise we glorify Your name. In Jesus' name we pray, Amen.

**For ye were sometimes darkness, but now are ye light in the Lord: walk as children of light: (Galatians 5:8)**

# October 10

*For the scripture saith, Whosoever believeth on him shall not be ashamed.* (Romans 10:11)

When we walked away from the kingdom of darkness and entered into the kingdom of Jesus Christ, His blood consumed our guilt and shame. These attributes were associated with our sinful nature. As we don the spirit of faith and have accepted the gift of salvation, we are no longer living in condemnation. Condemnation is living under strong disapproval. God is not looking at us through the lens of disgust; He is actually very pleased with His creation. He is waiting for us to recognize the greatness He has instilled in us. Understanding our salvation helps us to acknowledge Jesus as our foundation. We no longer have to consider our past mistakes or allow them to keep us in mental bondage. God has forgiven us, and we must forgive ourselves and move forward, trusting Him. Being ashamed stems from embarrassment or guilt from one's actions or attitude. God wants us to embrace the power we now have in Christ. As the Holy Spirit leads us, we no longer engage in behaviors that will bring about shame or guilt. It's important to understand that we cannot depend on our own emotions apart from God. Our emotions quickly react to circumstances and may lead to future feelings of regret. When we believe in the power of God we are able to adhere to His commands, trust His word is true where He tells us how to conduct ourselves, and depend on Jesus as our cornerstone. As we have accepted salvation by confessing with our mouth and believing in our heart, we understand the love God has for us. We must now accept what salvation represents. It has brought us back into right standing with God, opening our eyes to a personal relationship that teaches us He will never let us down. We know God on a personal basis and understand God does not produce shame. As we are in Christ, our life is intertwined in His attributes, so whenever we find ourselves in a state of feeling ashamed, we must surrender our feelings to Him and live free.

**Who the Son sets free is free INDEED!**

Prayer: Lord God of mercy, how awesome it is to soak in Your presence. We bow down before Your throne of grace to honor and reverence You. Lord, look over the hearts and mind of Your people, set us free from shame and guilt. Allow us to walk in right standing with You free from negative thoughts of our past. We bind up negative thoughts and emotions. We silence the lips of people who try to remind us of our past or try to keep us in bondage. Who the Son sets free is free indeed. We are free to love, free to enjoy life, and experience You without limits. God, shower Your love throughout all the earth. Soften the hearts of Your people that those who may not know You will accept Your Son Jesus as their Lord and Savior; believing in their hearts and confessing with their tongues that You are the true and living God. Jesus, we are honored by the perfect example You have given us, help us to live holy, acceptable and pleasing in Your sight. With all praise we say, Thank you. In Jesus' name we pray, Amen.

# October 11

*Hear ye the word of the Lord.* (Jeremiah 2:4)

O to hear from God. How awesome it is. We hear all sorts of sounds in the world we live in. Many of the things we hear come as no benefit to us. If we aren't careful to guard our hearing from certain obscenity (vulgar TV, radio, music, people), we will allow our spirit to be inhabited by harmful forces that come to hinder us, not propel us. If we understand that faith comes by hearing, and hearing by the word of God, we see the power associated with letting words rest in our spirit. Words from God grant us the ability to stand on a firm foundation and have a great expectation for the things we believe in to come to fruition, although we can't see them at the present moment. Our ability to hear goes deeper than just enjoying the sounds of our surroundings. What we hear has the power to change our emotions. When we receive good news, our attitude is filled with joy. Hearing our favorite song on the radio sparks feelings of refreshment. On the other end, hearing can also cause pain. When someone says something hurtful, our emotions change to feelings of being hurt or angry. Our hearing is associated with our hearts, and depending on what we hear, it has the ability to condition our state of being. Thanks are to God, that the words we hear from Him breathe life. Hearing from God is one of the sweetest sounds we will ever hear. Not only do we obtain power, but also we are able to tap into the spirit realm. Our hearing of God's word ignites our faith. After hearing the word, we are willing to confess that faith is the substance of things hoped for, the evidence of things not seen. (Hebrews 11:1). When we hear from God, we obtain instruction, guidance, encouragement, correction, and self-fulfillment. Hearing from God is the only sound we will hear that is consistent in its approach to make us better as individuals. Others may encourage us one time and may even be nice for a while, but God is the only one whose words always come to edify our souls to be in alignment with Him and make us whole.

**I hear the sound.**

Prayer: God, You are amazing. To think about Your attributes would take a lifetime. Thank You for the many things You do in the lives of Your people. Lord, we declare today that Your voice will be the loudest voice of influence in our lives. We will not fall victim to lies and deceit from outside forces. We will believe what Your word says. We confess what Your word says about us and our life in Christ Jesus. We are fearfully and wonderfully made. Your children, whom You have called out of darkness to join in the kingdom of Your Son Jesus Christ. Let the sound of heaven ring loud in our ear. Help us to set aside time to hear from You on a consistent basis. Lord, we don't want to miss what You have already planned for our lives. God, Your love has captivated us; we sit in awe before You, thanking You for Your grace and mercy. Forgive us for any time we have rejected the gift of Life that Jesus died on the cross for us to have. Remove the mindset to even act against Your will. Help us to hear the sweetness of Your voice, which has power to restore. God, You are everything. In Jesus' name we pray, Amen.

# October 12

*Let your conversation be without covetousness; and be content with such things as ye have: for he hath said, I will never leave thee, nor forsake thee.* (Hebrews 13:5)

*Let your character or moral disposition be free from love of money [including greed, avarice, lust, and craving for earthly possessions] and be satisfied with your present [circumstances and with what you have]; for He [God] Himself has said, I will not in any way fail you nor give you up nor leave you without support. [I will] not,[I will] not, [I will] not in any degree leave you helpless nor forsake nor let [you] down relax My hold on you)! Assuredly not!]* (Hebrews 13:5 AMP)

I love God's sense of humor. I believe He sits in heaven, looking down at His people in total awe. When we come into fellowship with Christ and begin to develop a relationship with God, we are able to apply His principles to our life. It displeases God whenever we become upset because we have not received the things we desire. Knowing that when we delight ourselves in the Lord, He will grant the desires of our heart (Psalm 37:4). God is not disappointed by the fact that we desire certain things in life; we fall into error when we feel we haven't received what we deserve. Once we begin to think the world owes us something, we discard our shield of faith and take on a spirit of doubt. Faith will have us to stand on the word, which tells us God will not withhold any good thing from those who walk uprightly (Psalm 84:11). The bible tells us many times how blessed we are when we trust God. God is showing us that at no point in time will He EVER leave us without support. When Christ is our foundation, we can always find the ability to be satisfied with everything God provides. Being content is a learned sense of being; we have to make a conscious effort to trust God at His word. As we experience God and trust in His word, we are able to live satisfied. Our satisfaction comes from knowing God created us to experience a life of abundance. We can never desire more for ourselves than what God has already planned for us. Whenever we find ourselves complaining about the things we desire but have not yet received, we have to do a self- reflection and line our thoughts up with God's promises. We will never find ourselves in a position where we are living uprightly and God has let us down.

**God, I trust you!**

Prayer: Lord, You are awesome. Watch over Your people today. Transform our thought process. Help us to be content with everything we have. We know that as we delight ourselves in You, You will grant the desires of our heart. Thank You for the ability to dream big and be able to trust that all things are possible to him that believes. Shift our focus to be on You that we may store our riches in heaven. Don't allow the world's standards of material gain to distort our image of what righteous living is with You. You own everything. You are our source. Everything we need is in You. Thank You for supplying all of our needs. With honor and praise we bless Your name. In Jesus' name we pray, Amen.

# October 13

*That I may perform the oath which I have sworn unto your fathers, to give them a land flowing with milk and honey, as it is this day. Then answered I, and said, So be it, O Lord.* (Jeremiah 11:5)

Every day, God lays before us a command and free will. Those who choose to obey His commands secure the benefit of reaping from His promises. God is continuously pleading with us to obey His commands. He is trying to get us to understand the principles associated with His covenant. God's covenant is an assured promise He will hold up His end of the bargain. We can't even begin to imagine all of the things God has prepared to release to us if we follow each of His commands on a daily basis. This goes from the smallest command to the commands that require a great deal of faith. Obedience shows reverence to God. It's our expression of love, letting God know we submit to His voice. The covenant is contingent upon our actions. Our daily activities help us understand the fundamentals in fulfilling our obligations. For instance, we have a covenant with our employers. Our agreement is if we work they promise to pay us. We find it easy to obey this command because we receive tangible evidence of the promise being fulfilled when we receive our paycheck. The same principles apply when we hear God's voice and obey it. We are guaranteed to reap every benefit God has promised us. The blessings are readily available; we have to be in a position to receive them. I don't know about you, but I don't want just my basic needs met. I want to dwell in the land flowing with milk and honey, where God has promised to do exceedingly abundantly above all that we ask or think.

**God Your will be done in earth as it is in heaven, Amen!**

Prayer: Lord God of mercy, all power and kindness are in Your hands. With adoration we bow before Your presence to exalt Your name. We come, asking that You search our hearts and remove all manner of sin. Reveal any evil intentions from us, that we may be pleasing and acceptable in Your sight. Let our hearts respond to

Your love. Help us to walk in obedience all the days of our life. When we hear Your word, cause us to be alert and sober minded to obey each of Your commands. Remove anything that may come to steal what You have placed inside of us. Keep the fire burning inside of us to always seek Your face. Let Your words bring joy to our spirit. Your word breathes life and transforms us. We cast down imaginations, and every high thing that exalteth itself against the knowledge of God, and bring into captivity every thought to the obedience of Christ. You reign and rule in us forever. All praise belongs to You. We love You. In Jesus' name we pray, Amen.

# October 14

*And he said unto me, My grace is sufficient for thee: for my strength is made perfect in weakness. Most gladly therefore will I rather glory in my infirmities, that the power of Christ may rest upon me.* (2 Corinthians 12:9)

Paul was brought into paradise and experienced an unspeakable encounter with God. In order to keep Paul humble, God allowed satan's angel to give him a handicap. This handicap was a reminder of Paul's human limitations. God is showing us the constraints we have as humans. Our strength comes only from Him. I would have to believe Paul was at first confused on how one minute He could be in God's presence, and then the next God would allow an affliction to invade his body. Like most people would react, Paul pleaded with God to take his disability away. Instead, God spoke life into Paul saying, "My grace is sufficient." The Amplified Version gives us a better understanding of the revelation Paul received from God. He states "satans' angel did his best to get me down; what he in fact did was push me to my knees." Humility set in once God put the circumstance into perspective. He is saying, life will happen, we will be challenged in every aspect. When challenges do arise, we ought to consider them as gifts sent to us in order to draw us closer to God. The enemy despises nothing more than for his plan of destruction to bring us to a place of worship and praise, instead of fear and depression. Once Paul heard the good news (My grace is sufficient), he quit focusing on the issue and began to celebrate the opportunity to allow God's power to work in his life. Our weakness doesn't come to hinder us; it's a gift from God. It's a set reminder of our need to depend on Him and allow Him to become our strength.

**When I am weak, then I am strong!**

Prayer: Today, I would like to encourage you to pray specifically concerning any areas in your life where you know your human strength cannot get you to prevail. Trust and believe God's grace is sufficient and watch Him work in your life. Bless you!!

# October 15

*Let love for you fellow believer continue and be a fixed practice with you [ never let it fail].* (Hebrews 13:1 AMP)

Love is the very attribute that should guide each of our actions. As we engage in conversations with others, love should be at the forefront of our mind. Love is an action we have to show in the way we express ourselves to others. God commands that we make sure love is our motivation in everything we do, say, and think. This act of kindness may not be favorable when we are faced with difficult people. When we find ourselves in situations where we feel like our love is not appreciated or reciprocated, instead of retracting our love, we can remember the love Christ has for us. When we remember His love, it will help us to recall the many times we have failed to accept Him. Many times in our lives we have been disobedient and not openly embraced His loving kindness. Yet, He never stopped loving us. It is a part of His nature. Love embodies the very essence of who He is. Our actions do not determine whether or not God will love us. His love for us is always the same. This should be our encouragement when we consider our relationships and everyone we come in contact with. The Bible also teaches us to consider how we would like to be treated before we lash out in ungodly behavior. This helps in allowing love to flow more freely. Also, when we take conditions off of our ability to love and just follow God's command, we will be released from a lot of pressure. It's actually harder not to love than it is to love. Love is the only universal language that all people desire. Loving those that God created is our expression of love toward God. God dwells in us, and when we don't love we are denying ourselves fellowship with the Father.

**I will love!**

Prayer: Lord God of mercy, You have given us the opportunity to share in Your love. Those who love are born of God. We thank You for the open fellowship we have with You. Let love be our way of communication with the world. No matter what has taken place in the past, heal our hearts so we are able to receive Your love and show it to others. Let the very essence of Your being work and rule in us. As You abide in us, let all of our actions be pleasing in Your sight. Purify our hearts today not to be selfish. Help us to have a caring heart and give us the ability to love everyone. Whenever we feel challenged in this area we will release it to You. We want to be found doing Your work. You have given us the command to love and we will do it. As far as it depends on us, we will live at peace with everyone. Tear down walls of division and build unity. Help us as the body of Christ to be unified and be the light in this dark world. Let us speak the truth in love and draw all men to Your Son Jesus Christ. Govern our thoughts and our speech, that Your name will be magnified. We give You the glory. In Jesus' name we pray, Amen.

# October 16

*Enter into his gates with thanksgiving, and into his courts with praise: be thankful unto him, and bless his name.* (Psalm 100:4)

I'll praise You

Many ask the question, "how can I enter God's courts with thanksgiving, when my circumstances tell me otherwise?" We have all been at a place where life becomes overwhelming. We feel emotionally depleted and find it hard to find hope in a dire situation. Our emotions have paralyzed our ability to overlook our circumstances, and praising God seems so far out of reach. This is a common mistake we often make. The bible does not say praise God according to circumstances, it says praise God according to His excellent goodness. "Praise him for his mighty acts: praise him according to his excellent greatness" (Psalm 150:2). God's Word has to govern our emotions. His word teaches us to rejoice in hardships and to enter His gates with thanksgiving and into His courts with praise. Verse 3 shows us why we are able to enter His courts with praise. "Know ye that the Lord He is God: it is he that hath made us, and not we ourselves; we are his people, and the sheep of his pasture." Offering praise will become natural when we know that the Lord is our God. He is sovereign and a very present help in trouble. We are His people, His sheep whom He takes excellent care of. Anything that may arise in our lives that has the ability to silence our praise is not from God. Recognizing these tactics at the onset of an issue will set off an alarm in our spirit and cause us to remember how we are supposed to respond. As we enter His gates with thanksgiving, we are reminding ourselves of His greatness and the many times He has delivered us before. The many attributes of God begin to fill our mind and we are able to magnify His name and minimize the problem. Our praise ignites the atmosphere, inviting God to share in our worship. The Bible tells us that a day in God's court is better than a thousand (Psalm 84:10). When we exude God's given principles of praise, we are able to receive His supernatural power. We know when God shows up, He is a consuming fire. His power has the ability to transform every situation, and as His sheep we KNOW He will take care of us. Understanding all of this will allow praise and thanksgiving to become our natural response, a daily function that we prioritize into our intimate time with Him.

**No matter what, I'll praise Him!**

Prayer: Lord, who else is there like You in all the earth? We can search all over and will never be able to find one as great as You. You are everything we could ever ask for; You have made us to be Your very own. You take great care of us. You have given us daily precepts on how to govern our life. You have instilled Your attributes within our spirit. You walk with us on a daily basis. We honor You this day. We offer up our best praise before You. With every breath that is within our body we exalt Your name. We lay before you every concern. There is NO situation You are not aware of. Praise will be our immediate response to life. As Job fell and worshipped before Your feet, we will offer up thanksgiving at all times in all things. You are the true and living God. The King of kings, all power belongs to You. We are forever grateful to be called Your people. We bless Your name today. In Jesus' name we pray, Amen.

# October 17

*"Stand in shock, heavens, at what you see! Throw up your hands in disbelief-this can't be!" God's Decree.* (Jeremiah 2:12)

As God's elect, we should find it very disturbing to see the state our world is in today. Many people have turned away from the decree of God and put their trust in things that produce no profit. We have been called to be ambassadors for Christ. As we look at the news and the things taking place around us, it's our job to stay in constant prayer for our nation and world affairs. We are always called to stand firm in our faith and not to waver from God's decree. Our lives are examples for those who choose not to obey Christ to see the great benefit in serving Him. God is pleading with His people. God is trying to get us to understand the mistakes we make when we deny our value in Him by putting our trust in things that will not last. Many people turn their back on God because of pride. We find it more suitable to fulfill our own desires which produce an artificial satisfaction; when in reality, if one is not walking with Christ they are destroying themselves. Think about it, when we look at the many facets of media, we see how they openly accept and encourage sin. It is very evident how our nation has denied God's presence. Yet, when a catastrophe occurs we call on God, eliciting prayer. As believers, we have to constantly stand in the gap to try to tear down the barrier between conditional righteousness and total commitment. God is a loving, nurturing Father; it hurts Him to even consider the Day of Judgment. With the day approaching, we have a responsibility to teach the gospel and hope people choose life.

**Send me God, I'll be the one!**

Prayer: Lord, You are Alpha and Omega, beginning and end. You know all things; all things came to be by Your decree. We come before You on behalf of every human being that walks this earth. Lord, we pray that in some way You can touch their hearts. As You knock on the door they will willingly open it and let You in to reside. Lord, you desire that no man shall perish. Help those who are lost and confused to choose life today. Send Your disciples in their path to teach and preach the gospel in truth and love. Help others to understand and grab hold of the eternal life that is in Christ Jesus. Help us not to be full of pride. Open the hearts of Your people that they will come to the knowledge of who You are. Send a change in the world that all violence may cease; hurt and pain will not rule the lives of Your people. Help Your people not to be deceived by the lies of the enemy, but to accept Your Word as truth. Thank You that You are everywhere and willing at all times to step in and abide with Your people. Change hearts and deliver souls today. All praise and glory belong to You. In Jesus' name we pray, Amen.

# October 18

*But that the world may know that I love the Father; and as the Father gave me commandment, even so I do. Arise, let us go hence.* (John 14:31)

To love God is to follow all of His commands. Jesus is our perfect example in that He did exactly what the Lord commanded Him to do. He explains the relationship structure as he breaks down the order of operation. Jesus is one with the Father, yet He is subject to the Father. They share the same attributes and abide within each other, but God is the head. Jesus makes this clear by letting us know He was sent to the earth only to accomplish the will of His Father. Jesus received specific instructions on how to operate in in the human form as man. His intimate connection with God paved the way for a committed relationship. Jesus explains to His disciples that it's God who governs His speech and enables Him to do the works He accomplished on earth. Jesus was showing us how our lives were to function as we obey every command from God. Not only is it a display of love, it also makes life meaningful. Believing in the matchless power of God opens the gateway for us to ask whatever we wish in Jesus' name and we are certain to receive it. Our lives have been revitalized; we have been given a fresh start. Life before Christ was bogus. Only when we join with Christ are we able to operate in our true identity. In accepting our authentic self, we are appreciative of our relationship with God and show Him our love by our obedience. Love is an action, a choice we consciously make each day. We decide whether or not we will adhere to God's commands or follow our own judgment. Jesus showed us how to show perfect love, by following every command from the Father. His obedience glorified God in every way; this is testament to kingdom principles and an example of true love.

**As the Father gave me commandment, even so I do!**

Prayer: Lord, You are everything. Life is incomplete without You. We are overjoyed to shout praises before You. We exalt Your name in all the earth. Thank You for Your Word, which breathes life and understanding. Keep us in tune with Your Holy Spirit. Help us to stay committed to our relationship with You. Let the words of our mouth, and the meditation of our heart be acceptable in Your sight. Keep guard over our tongue, control our actions. Let everything we do bring glory to Your name. Let us utter the words of the Bible and remember the example we have in Jesus. Let His way of life shine light on how we are to operate. Open our hearts and ears to receive Your Word as truth. We will delight in following Your commands. Let our acts of love be pure. Help us to relinquish our way of thinking and accept all of Your commands with excitement. Lord, You are amazing and we honor You. In Jesus' name we pray, Amen.

# October 19

*But Naaman was wroth, and went away, and said, Behold, I thought, He will surely come out to me, and stand, and call on the name of the Lord his God, and strike his hand over the place, and recover the leper.* (2 Kings 5:11)

Naaman was stricken with leprosy, a terrible disease of that time. He received word from his wife's maid of a Holy man in Israel by the name of Elisha, who was able to heal him. With hope, Naaman traveled to meet Elisha, only to be greeted by his servant. His servant relayed Elisha's instructions to Naaman, telling him wash in the Jordan seven times and he would be completely healed. Immediately Naaman grew angry. In that brief encounter he lost hope of what he had come to receive. He came for healing, and when he received the remedy he denied it. Naaman came with a perceived idea of how the man of God would heal him. He thought it would be some elaborate heroic act. He couldn't fathom how washing in a dirty river would get the job done. He wanted something with more substance, something more tangible. His perception caused him to miss the very essence of who God is. If our thoughts are not in line with God, we might as well not think. God is everywhere and in everything. When He gives a decree, He is sure to validate His plans. Like Naaman, we often want what our minds have already imagined. When things manifest themselves in a different form from what we perceive, we allow doubt to set in or deny it completely. On the journey to Elisha, Naaman probably imagined the whole ordeal in His head. When God's plans differed from his preconceived notion, He was reluctant to receive the very thing he came for, healing. It's important not to be so self-absorbed that we miss God. Naaman had so much pride; he was willing to risk being a leper all his life instead of having faith in God. It wasn't until his servant put things into perspective that he finally washed himself in the Jordan seven times and was completely healed.

**It only requires faith!**

Prayer: Heavenly Father, we adore You this day. Come into our hearts and saturate us with Your presence. Transform us by the renewal of our minds. Help us to understand Your Word as truth. Expand our faith to trust and believe in everything You say. We have received the gift of Your Holy Spirit and we ask that You continue to pour out Your wisdom. Govern our thought process, help us to be aligned with the things that take place in heaven. Let wisdom govern our thoughts, and actions. Help us to discern all things. There is no greater love in all the earth than what You give. We are forever thankful. Bless Your holy name. In Jesus' name we pray, Amen.

# October 20

*The next day John seeth Jesus coming unto him, and saith, Behold the Lamb of God, which taketh away the sin of the world.* (John 1:29)

Behold the Lamb of God, the light of the world, our Savior Jesus Christ. Behold means to see or to observe a person. When we begin to see and observe Jesus as the Light of the world, He opens our eyes to true life. The very essence of life is understood when we realize the significance of who Jesus is and what He came to earth to accomplish. Before anything came to be, there He was with God, formulating the notion of humans gracing the earth to experience their love. When we gain a high opinion of Christ, we are able to open our hearts to His unfailing love and adore Him for being our redeemer. God's nature alone is deserving of our praise. Constant reminders of how amazing God is will help us renew our mind. Thinking about the love He has for us, and understanding the power of the Trinity (God, Jesus, and the Holy Spirit), develops a thankful spirit within us. Whenever unfavorable situations arise in our life, our first impulse will be to see and observe the Lamb of God. The One whose power took away ALL sin. We will no longer be able to look at circumstances the same. When pressure and anxiety emerge, we can declare, "Behold the Lamb of God." Knowing and believing our God has power and has given us authority to trample over every thing that comes against us and nothing shall harm us. Applying our learned knowledge of Christ is key to a successful life. We know we have the ONE true God who is able and willing to fight on our behalf.

**Behold the Lamb of God!**

Prayer: Now behold the Lamb of God, our Redeemer, Savior of the world, we reverence You for who You are. The King of the earth, the one who is, who was, and is to come. You are everything. Without You we wouldn't exist. We thank You for the sacrifice You made just so we could experience eternal life. We are forever grateful for the love You shower us with each day. We will consider You in all things. You have given us the power to call upon Your name to rule and have dominion over the earth. We will not have fear in the midst of trials, but will call upon Your name. Strengthen us for all that we will endure. Prepare us for the assignment. Equip us for the road of righteousness. Cause us to totally depend upon Your name. Help us to have a constant reminder of who You are. You are the Lamb of God, the Savior of the universe. At the name of Jesus every knee shall bow and every tongue confess. We thank You and adore You willingly. Glory to Your name. In Jesus' name we pray, Amen.

# October 21

*All scripture is given by inspiration of God, and is profitable for doctrine, for reproof, for correction, for instruction in righteousness: That the man of God may be perfect, thoroughly furnished unto all good works.* (2 Timothy 3:16-17)

Daily devotion is a time of coming before God to receive life lessons, instructions, and plans for our assignment. Our time of dedication should entail us sitting at Jesus feet; filled with anticipation and expectation, ready to receive the tools to produce spiritual maturity. As we understand the power incorporated in God's Word, our eyes are open to the limitless potential we are able to possess. God inspired, the Bible is combined with His thoughts and directives on how to live a righteous life. As we journey through life, we should never miss a day of reading His Word. I understand this may be a difficult task, but it can be accomplished with discipline. Reading God's Word prepares us for life. It instills principles in us, which activate the virtue God has already placed on the inside of us. Whatever concerns we have in life can be found in God's Word. Whenever issues arise in our life, we are able to go straight to the Bible and see what God is saying in reference to that very thing. As humans, when problems arise we have been trained to seek counsel from those around us. Our first response to life must be to consider what God says, knowing His word is able to set us on the right course and better our lives. Advice and godly counsel from others should come as a secondary source, only to confirm what God has already instructed. Whenever we are faced with ANY concern, we are able to confirm in His Word how to operate. God's Word is the antidote to Christian living; it empowers, instructs and teaches us how to succeed in life. Without it, we lose our foundation and purpose in life.

**What has God said about it?**

Prayer: Almighty, Savior of the world, we bow down in total reverence to Your name. There is none like You in all the earth.

Lord, you have considered Your servants even before we entered the earth. You have created Your Word as the vessel to give us understanding, truth and insight into righteousness. Lord, let Your Word never depart from our mouth. When we consider life, let us always seek Your counsel. Lord, reading Your Word is the vital necessity in our lives, which we can't live without. There is something special about Your Word and it gives us new life. It's filled with power and able to destroy strongholds. Help us to believe everything you say, without any doubt. Give us the wisdom and knowledge to stand on Your Word and apply it to every aspect of our lives. Don't allow us to miss a day of reading Your Word. Instruct Your Holy Spirit to press upon our hearts whenever we stray away. Keep us close to You, keep us bound together with You forever. God, apart from You is misery. Wherever You are is where we desire to be. Keep us in the palm of Your hand. All glory belongs to You. In Jesus' name we pray, Amen.

# October 22

*Then shall ye call upon me, and ye shall go and pray unto me, and I will hearken unto you.* (Jeremiah 29:12)

The level of our faith can determine the level of emphasis we put into prayer. A wall is created when we allow doubt and unbelief to hinder our ability to trust God. God is trying to get us to open our eyes to the plans He has designed specifically for us. He teaches us the manner in which He operates and shows us the way to freedom and how to enjoy this life. Once we grasp the concept that God has our best interest at heart, we are able to look at life in a new light. We obtain spiritual insight and will even begin to approach life's circumstances with better judgment. God's Spirit helps us to filter through nonsense and discern between good and evil. When we recognize and are able to utilize the keys we have to the kingdom, we are able to come boldly before the throne of grace, asking anything of our Father, believing He will perform it. We have an established covenant with God, where His end of the agreement is always fulfilled. We have to ensure we exercise our faith and come believing every Word God has promised. When we seek His face with our whole heart, He is faithful to give specific plans and manifest EVERYTHING He has guaranteed. Our job is to seek His face on a daily basis. He is waiting for us to communicate with Him. He enjoys our time together as we should as well. In His presence, we receive everything needed for the course of our day. I say it all the time, "it will be a great disappointment to get to heaven and see all of the things God wanted to do for us, but we missed out on it because we failed to ask and spend time with Him." This relationship has to be cultivated and we are excited to spend time with our Daddy!

**Already Guaranteed!**

Prayer: Lord, You are the light of our life. You are the very air we breathe. By Your grace we are able to give Your name glory. Watch over Your people. Help us to understand the truth of Your Word. Let it be the source of all of our actions. Give us all wisdom and understanding. Let Your Word guide our steps in life. Teach us Your commands; let us find delight in trusting in Your Word and not lean on our own understanding. We will mediate on Your Word day and night to be careful to do everything in it, then we will be prosperous and successful. Lord, Your have authority over us, we bless Your holy name. In Jesus' name we pray, Amen.

# October 23

*Beloved, now are we the sons of God, and it doth not yet appear what we shall be: but we know that, when he shall appear, we shall be like him; for we shall see him as he is.* (1 John 3:2)

What an honor to be called children of God. As His children, we have open access to everything in His possession. When we consider the unmerited favor bestowed upon us, we understand that it's through grace that we have obtained such things. Now, as children of God, we receive special favor. Certain things that non-believers are unable to obtain, we are privileged to obtain based upon our connection with the Father. Our life in Christ is extraordinary. This is no comparison to what will be revealed in us when Jesus returns. Our minds don't have the capacity to fathom what this experience will entail. Favor is poured out in our lives in abundance as we follow the example of Christ and receive God's promises. His promises relinquish joy in our lives, as we are able to experience the love of God first hand. "We shall be like Him; for we shall see Him as He is" (1 John 3:2). (Perfect, full of glory, splendor, virtue magnificent, and holy). These attributes will overpower our spirit. When we believe this, it encourages us to commit ourselves to God and follow His commands. which in turns keeps us in right standing with Him, purifying our spirit daily and becoming more like Christ. Every day of our lives is like a bride preparing for her wedding. She spends countless hours in preparation for her special day when she knows her life will change permanently. She anticipates becoming unified with her groom where they can experience joy forever. Each of our days should be spent the same way, pouring all of our energy into becoming more like Christ, and on the day of His return we will see ourselves perfected.

**Get Ready!**

Prayer: Lord, You are everything. There are no words to describe how holy You are. There isn't enough time in the day to give You the entire honor You deserve. Everything about you exudes greatness. Our hearts are overjoyed to be called into the kingdom of Your son Jesus. Thank You for loving us before we even loved ourselves. Thank You for always being that voice of reason and encouragement leading us to the path of righteous living. Thank You for chance after chance. We vow to seek You while You are near. Tomorrow is not promised, so we will praise You today. We magnify Your name in all the earth. Dispatch Your angels to stand guard over our lives. Prepare us for the day's journey. Continue to teach us Your ways, establish the work of our hands. Be the lamp unto our feet and the light to our path. Remove blindness that we may see. Help us to acknowledge You in all things. My Lord, apart from You nothing we do has value, so we invite You in to dwell as the Head of our lives. We totally commit our ways to you. In Jesus' name we pray, Amen.

# October 24

*Wherefore do ye spend money for that which is not bread? And your labour for that which satisfieth not? hearken diligently unto me, and eat ye that which is good, and let your soul delight itself in fatness.* (Isaiah 55:2)

I can only begin to imagine the scene in heaven where God is pondering why we waste so much of our energy on things which are unable to prepare us for eternity. God's bread is the only element able to nourish our spirit. Our spirit is the extension of our being that connects us with God. It is the piece of our being that will rest with God forever in eternity. Our spirit requires proper nourishment in order to produce spiritual growth. When we expend our time and energy on things that are not beneficial, we are unable to obtain the proper nutrients necessary for bearing good fruit. God is pleading with His children to listen earnestly to His commands in order to comprehend the gift He has freely given us. He has declared that we shall eat that which is good. Everything about God produces goodness. His plan for us entails prosperity for every aspect of our life. If we aren't eating good fruit, we have to understand that we are eating bad fruit. Eating bad fruit cannot produce the righteousness that God desires. Everything God is trying to give us is based upon our willingness to be obedient and follow His guidance. In coming to God, we retrieve the essential nourishment needed in order for us to blossom into the vessels He has designed. Our spirit is able to receive satisfaction, and produce heaven's fruit that goes beyond our wildest imagination.

**Imagine That!**

Prayer: O Mighty God, how excellent is Your name in all the earth. With reverence we come into Your presence saying, Hallelujah! Thanking You for Your everlasting grace and mercy. Jesus, teach us to drink from the waters of heaven that we shall never thirst again. Lord, You provide every necessity we could ever think of. Refocus our mind to think about those things that are able to keep us in perfect fellowship with You. Embed Your Word in our hearts; let us speak the Word back to You, knowing it will never return to You void. Open our ears, remove the blinders from our eyes that we may see and hear You. We promise this day to seek Your throne of grace. We find delight in serving You. Help us to understand the truth of Your Word. Let us rely on and trust in Your Word. Help us not to allow life to overwhelm us. We put on Your full armor today and are prepared for the things You have ordained for us. In You we have freedom. We are free to praise and adore You. Nothing can separate us from Your love, and we say thank You, Jehovah. All praise belongs to You. In Jesus' name we pray, Amen.

# October 25

*And it came to pass, as we went to prayer* (Acts 16:16)

God is everywhere and able to be in everything. When we are not in our normal setting, we are still able to seek the face of God. Paul and his companions were on a missionary trip, traveling around spreading the gospel, and everywhere they went they sought the Lord. Even in new towns and unfamiliar places, they went to the place of prayer. They understood the importance of having continuous communion with God. No matter where we find ourselves, be it on a business trip, vacation, etc. there is always an opportunity to pray and seek God. Communication with God is such a vital part of our lives; we can't allow unfamiliar places to throw us off track. Busy schedules are not a viable excuse to miss time with God. Wherever we find ourselves, it's imperative to give God reference. God is not a God of strict routine where you have to stand on one foot and pray for 60 minutes at 4:00am every day or your life will be cursed. All He desires is our best praise. He wants devotion to be special, a secluded time where we come before Him and soak in His presence. It's a time of rejuvenation and restoration, where we are able to experience His glory and receive our daily bread for the journey ahead. There's a major difference in our spiritual alertness when we are faced with unsettling circumstances and we are not secure in the Lord. Not giving God proper reverence makes us vulnerable to the wiles of the enemy. Prayer empowers us to be alert and to be led by His Spirit to accomplish our kingdom assignments.

**I want to be where You are!**

Prayer: Lord, You are so amazing. God, this is the day that You have made, we will rejoice and are glad to be alive today. We want to give You our best praise, a sacrificial offering before Your throne. Shift our focus to know and understand the importance of fellowship with You. In Your presence is the fullness of joy, and at Your right hand are pleasures forevermore. God, you know each day before any of them come to be, help us to seek after You with our whole heart. Nothing in this world is more valuable then our relationship with You. Put life in perspective, we know that only what we do for You will last. We store up our riches in the things above. Renew our mind that we may prove what is good, and acceptable, and Your perfect will. Where You are is where we long to be. Better is one day in Your courts than a thousand elsewhere. Plant our feet by the stream of living water, that we never thirst again. Cause our fruit to come forth in due season. Our delight is in Your word and obeying Your statutes. We are forever at Your service. We exalt You in all the earth. In Jesus' name we pray, Amen.

# October 26

*But thou, O man of God, flee these things; and follow after righteousness, godliness, faith, love, patience, meekness.* (1 Timothy 6:11)

Paul is teaching his son in the faith, Timothy, how to be an effective leader in the church. In this passage specifically, he has instructed Timothy to avoid useless arguments and the strong desire to become rich. Strikingly, Paul calls Timothy what He is, "man of God." As men and women of God, we have to understand who we are in Christ. We are not individuals who lust after earthly desires and engage in unprofitable situations which can draw us away from God. We are the righteousness of God, His chosen heirs. We are set apart to live a life of godliness. Godliness requires that we chase after the things God desires. It is necessary that we be in constant pursuit of things that add value to our character. We have to seek after obtaining faith, righteousness, godliness, love, patience, and meekness. These attributes are built into our biological make-up. They arc only activated when we nurture and develop them through allowing God's characteristics to rule our actions. God is the one who gives us strength to exhibit such character. Determination propels us to walk in godliness. We have to make a conscious effort to model godly behavior to the point where it becomes our natural instinct to respond with such virtue. Self-control is a major component of walking in right standing with God. We know God does not command us to respond to life the way the world responds. This means when we are offended, we are to offer love when we want to retaliate. We are to seek God's perspective in all matters of life. It is easier said than done. Just as Paul was encouraging Timothy, we will need to encourage ourselves. We can do this by having godly friendships, spiritual mentors and feeding our spirit with things that produce bountiful results of good character embedded with moral excellence.

**I want to be more like Jesus!**

Prayer: God of love, grace, peace, kindness, joy, how are you today? We come before Your throne to express our extreme gratitude for choosing us to be Your servants. You could have left us alone to die in our own mess, but because of love, You have shown us mercy. Lord, forgive us for all of our sins. Renew our minds this very moment; cause of to think about the price Jesus paid on Calvary just so we could come back into fellowship with You. The thought alone is enough to draw us to repentance. God, You give us instructions daily on how to live this life with contentment. We put on the fruits of the Spirit today, we will walk in love, joy, peace, longsuffering, goodness, faith, meekness and temperance. Consume every ounce of flesh that tries to rise up against Your Spirit. We give You free reign to rule over our thoughts and actions. Teach us to always consider how our actions will exhibit to the world that we are Your children. When people look at us, let them see You. All glory belongs to You. In Jesus' name we pray, Amen.

**He was oppressed, and he was afflicted, yet he opened not his mouth. (Isaiah 53:7)**

# October 27

*And it shall come to pass, when ye be come to the land which the Lord will give you, according as he hath promised, that ye shall keep this service.* (Exodus 12:25)

God's commitment to fulfill the promises of His word is secure; we are assured He is always reliable. All God asks for in return is for our enthusiasm to remain the same while we are seeking His face, and even after we receive the anticipated promise of His great word. Our praise should not dwindle once God releases that which we have been waiting on. He wants us to be in constant remembrance of His goodness. The intensity level of our praise should always be consistent with the greatness of who we are serving, and not the state of mind we are currently in. When we honor God for who He is, we are able to reverence Him with every ounce of our being. People tend to forget about God after the valley experience. While in turmoil, we often seek the Father, then once He relieves the stress we tend to praise Him a little less. Or it could be the other way around, when we experience great joy we'll bless Him and at the onset of trouble we tend to allow our praise to be hindered by our current state. God's manifestation of the promise is not the ending point of our praise. Our attitudes should exhibit a constant exaltation to the extent that others wonder how we can be so blessed. Our life is a memorial of the goodness of God. We are unable to count the many times God has blessed us. This gives us infinite reasons to always stand in awe of His glory by allowing our mannerism to show others His goodness. In this text, God is forewarning the people that once they experience the promise to keep praising God. Never allow life, whether good or bad, to determine your level of praise. Our praise is ignited and sustained based on our relationship with a Good Good Father!

**God says, "Don't forget me."**

Prayer: Almighty God, we glorify Your name. God, bring back to our remembrance all the blessings You have bestowed upon us. Whenever we think to complain, replace our thoughts with Your lovingkindness. Help us to always be in a state of praise, where we are able to exalt Your name at all times. With every fiber in our being, we will magnify You. Your greatness alone brings joy to our very spirits. We will focus our heart and mind on You. We will praise You according to Your goodness. With great honor we say, Thank you. In Jesus' name we pray, Amen.

# October 28

*I know that there is no good in them, but for a man to rejoice, and to do good in his life.* (Ecclesiastes 3:12)

In the beginning, God formed the earth, planted all forms of nature, crafted the sea and breathed life into man. In the Garden of Eden, God gave His instruction for man to enjoy life by having dominion over all creation. He did all of this for His good pleasure. It wasn't to see who could obtain the most in earthly riches, or who could climb the corporate ladder the fastest. These tools are incapable of measuring success in God's sight. The problem doesn't lie in the material gain associated with success, it differs in the attitude of the successor. Success comes from knowing who you are in Christ and enjoying the life He has given you. Our culture will have us believe that having the largest house and bank account qualifies us as being prominent. How could this possibly esteem us when God deemed us extraordinary at the moment of creation? It's not a status we as believers have to obtain, because it's already in our DNA. Our life reflects our gratitude to God. Our life exhibits our thankfulness for Him giving us such a magnificent platform to enjoy our life. Our enjoyment is solely based upon our will to surrender our plans to God, and allowing Him to govern every aspect of our life. When you think about why and how God created the earth and mankind, you are able to see the true meaning of life. He created us to experience His love and to enjoy the gifts He has given us. Life is a gift from God. Every day is another opportunity to experience His loving joy. Take the time to really contemplate His goodness, I promise it will change your outlook on life.

**Enjoy your gift of life!**

Prayer: Lord, You are so amazing. Just to think about Your goodness brings us joy. Lord, You created us in love, to bestow Your kindness upon us. We are forever grateful. Open the doors of our hearts to enjoy every second that You have given us. Life is in the palm of Your hands. Lord, no matter what we face in the natural, we know the end result and that is victory. Overpower our minds to constantly think about Your goodness. We cast down every negative thought or situation that tries to overwhelm us. You have called us to have dominion in the earth. We have power and authority over every serpent and snake. We utilize the keys to the kingdom today, pour out Your blessings. Give us Your wisdom to face the day ahead. God, what an honor it is to serve You. With all glory and praise we worship You. In Jesus' name we pray, Amen.

# October 29

*Moreover the word of the Lord came to me saying,* (Jeremiah 2:1)

God's Word should be the guiding force in our daily activities. As soon as our feet hit the floor in the morning, we should inquire of the Lord. They did not have the Bible in the Old Testament; knowledge of God was passed down by Word of mouth. God would choose to speak directly to certain people, either personally or through His servants. He gave Moses laws to govern the people in their daily activities, but they did not have the Holy Spirit to guide every step of the way or the Bible to teach them about life. God's direct Word came from heaven to His chosen elect. Those who obeyed God were able to hear from Him. People would seek prophets and priest to obtain a Word from God. Nowadays, we have multiple facets that enable us to hear from God, to include the Bible, Holy Spirit, and our own personal relationship with God. We are able to come boldly before the throne of grace daily to receive a Word from God. God's Word breathes life into our situations and our purpose is manifested through our obedience. God's word is always at hand, but we have to be in a position to receive it. At any moment, we are able to hear from God. He has prepared His Word to cultivate our entire being. We have to ensure we are not bogged down with the issues of life in order to have room for God's Word to reside within us. We never want to be in a place where we have allowed our disappointments to speak louder than the voice of God. Nowhere in scripture does it say magnify our problems. The Bible teaches us to magnify the Lord. Magnifying His greatness shifts our focus and minimizes our problems. We are then able to hear from the Lord concerning our life and the things He has ordained for us to accomplish in the earth.

**What did you say?**

Prayer: God of mercy and grace, we bow down in total reverence. Open our hearts that we may receive a word from heaven. Speak to us concerning Your plan and purpose. Remove any obstacles that stand in our way. Shift our focus to be set on You. You are our foundation. You are the Chief Priest, and our cornerstone. Whatever You say, we will obey. Let Your Word be the strongest force of influence in our lives. Guide us to the scriptures that speak life into our right now situations. Enable us not to be overwhelmed by the miseries of life, but to trust in, and rely on Your Word. All things are made new in Your presence. We will find rest in You. Keep us in the palm of Your hand. We magnify Your name, In Jesus' name we pray, Amen.

# October 30

*Then Peter and the other apostles answered and said, We ought to obey God rather than men.* (Acts 5:29)

Obedience is the key to a loving relationship with God. It is a key asset in gaining intimate fellowship with Him. To love God is to obey God. Without one the other does not exist. Could you obey God if you were in the apostle's shoes? They were tormented, some believers even killed at the mentioning of the name Jesus. Yet, they allowed their agreement with God, Jesus, and the Holy Ghost to fuel their moral obligation to obey everything they heard from heaven. Such determination gives us the willpower to overcome adversity. When God is in a thing it cannot be overthrown (Acts 5:39). Our relationship with Christ should enable us to be bold for the kingdom. When society, friends or family try to dictate what our stance should be toward situations in our lives, we have to seek God's word for the truth. Whatever God says concerning our life should govern our life. Everything He has written in His Word is for our benefit. Every circumstance can be found in the Bible. We have to come into agreement with what God says concerning every one of our situations. When advice doesn't agree with what God says, then we have to check the source. God will not steer us in the wrong direction. He has a plan before Him, where He has carefully thought out every day of our lives. When we make a conscious effort to check with the manufacturer, we are doing ourselves a favor. The foundation of our faith in God is to believe. We can't believe if we aren't in agreement.

**I Agree with God!**

Prayer: Father, we bow down in worship before Your throne. Whatever You say, we vow to obey. Search our hearts, wash us clean as snow. Renew our minds. Let us find delight in obedience. Thank You for Your pleasing and perfect plan. All of creation is in the palm of Your hands. How Holy You are to consider us to bear witness in the earth of Your goodness. Give us a bold spirit today to speak the truth in love. In all situations, cause us to stand on Your Word even if it seems unpopular. We are a peculiar people, a royal priesthood, whom You have ordained and anointed. Mercy and goodness shall follow us all the days of our lives as we speak Your Word to the lost. Cause someone to cross our path that doesn't know You. Give us the opportunity to share the gospel of Your Son Jesus. Open the hearts of those who don't know You, that they are delighted to come into Your kingdom. Forever we are available for Your use. Use us today. All praise belongs to You. In Jesus' name we pray, Amen.

# October 31

*And David said unto Michal, It was before the Lord, which chose me before thy father, and before all his house, to appoint me ruler over the people of the Lord, over Israel: therefore will I play before the Lord. And I will yet be more vile than thus, and will be base in mine own sight: and of the maidservants which thou hast spoken of, of them shall I be had in honour.* (2 Samuel 6:21-22)

David has just brought the Ark of the Lord back into the city and is dancing in adoration before God. His wife Michal sees him and becomes displeased with His behavior. I would have to assume she couldn't imagine the time he spent on the run from Saul, in and out of caves, wondering if he would survive. Or perhaps she couldn't comprehend the intense rise of adrenaline David experienced in the midst of battle as he fought for the children of Israel. I would like to assume Michal could not relate with David's reverence for the Lord. David had experienced drought and almost death, yet if it hadn't been for God's favor upon His life, He would have been defeated. He understood the meaning of totally trusting God. Without God, David was just a mere shepherd boy. God called him into the position of king and gave him victory over every battle. David had a personal relationship with God. His relationship rendered praise and adoration for God. The knowledge of who God is, and what God had done for Him caused Him to dance before the ark of the Lord, withholding nothing. What his wife saw was a dance. What God saw was a thank you. When confronted by Michal, David informed her that it was because of God he was able to sit on the throne as king. David's need to thank God for His mercy birthed authentic worship. No matter what others say, let your worship reflect your gratitude for God. Like David, we must remember who God is to us and what He has called us to, and render praise and thanksgiving however our bodies feel; we can give Him the best praise we have.

**I'm going to Shout!**

Prayer: God, we love you. You have called us to praise You with a shout. We shout Hallelujah to Your holy name. With everything that is within us, we bless You. We are forever grateful of the many things You are doing in our lives. Just the mere thought of You excites our spirit. Without You, our life would be meaningless. We can contemplate the many times You have delivered us before. Being in constant remembrance of Your unfailing love gives us delight each day. We will praise You with all that's within us. In Jesus' name we pray, Amen.

# November 1

*For to be carnally minded is death; but to be spiritually minded is life and peace.* (Romans 8:6)

Choices are always given when it comes to the things of God. He allows us to choose whether or not we will adhere to His perfect plan and fulfill our potential in Him and obtain life and peace. The mind is our strongest weapon when it comes to our success in this world. God has instructed us on how to guard our mind by having us to be led by His Spirit. Our mind has to be reconstructed to comply with God's commands. The attributes of the Holy Spirit are perfect, there is no error found in them. Renewing our minds must become our daily objective. We are in constant agreement with God, by asking Him to reveal Himself within us. As He dwells within us, His way of thinking becomes our nature. It's a constant battle for believers to process the thought of being spiritually minded at ALL times, because outside forces will have us to believe this behavior is abnormal. We are comfortable being spiritual when it's convenient. Yet, God has informed us there is no other way to operate. When we operate by our flesh, we CANNOT please God (Romans 8:8). This command alone should cause each of us to repent daily. It requires extreme self-control, reliance and adherence to the Holy Spirit. We must yield our way of thinking to the Spirit and allow God to fill us with His virtue. Nothing in our flesh adds any value to our lives or to the kingdom of God. The amount of energy we place on preparing our heart and mind to be continuously renewed by God will determine the measure of our ability to withstand our flesh rising up. It is not a game, the devil is on watch; waiting for an opportune time to impute corruption in our lives. "Be alert and of sober mind. Your enemy the devil prowls around like a roaring lion looking for someone to devour" (1 Peter 5:8). We have been called to righteous living in God. In order for us to be spirit-minded we must allow His Spirit to be the driving force of everything we think, say, and do.

**Holy Spirit, have Your way!**

Prayer: God of mercy, we come asking for forgiveness for any way we have not yielded to Your Holy Spirit. Renew our minds today. Let us find joy and delight in being obedient in every aspect of our lives. Lord, apart from You we will fail. Take our hand this day and order our steps. Renew attitudes, refresh the way our mind processes thoughts. Help us to be patient, loving, and kind. Pour out the fruits of the Spirit and let them dwell within our hearts. Be our strongest force of influence. Open our eyes to see life the way you see it. Expand our faith and trust in You. Thank You for freeing us from sin. We repent of everything we have done that is contrary to Your will. We will live our life by the guidance of Your Spirit, always acknowledging Your instructions. You are our peace, and we worship You. In Jesus' name we pray, Amen.

# November 2

*Beware that thou forget not the LORD thy God, in not keeping his commandments, and his judgments, and his statutes, which I command this day.* (Deuteronomy 8:11)

God tells us to beware of forgetting Him as our Lord and His commands, judgments and statutes. This is informing us that at some point we may run the risk of allowing our mind to forget who God is, or what He means to us. Or may even fail to give Him proper position in our lives. You know we'll get too busy for God! When things seem to be going well, it may become easy to push off reading the Word or to attend church. Our mental or emotional state should never interfere with our command to mediate on God's Word day and night. It's imperative for us to hold our relationship with God in the highest regard. Allowing days to pass without spending time with God tricks our mind into becoming comfortable in not seeking God through coming into His presence. One day turns into two days, and before we know it weeks have gone by. God is always present, waiting with expectation for us to turn our heart toward Him. God is sad when we fail to acknowledge Him as the most important aspect in our lives. He is not hurt as though He needs our affection in order to function; He is hurt because of the things He has prepared for us which await our obedience to His commands and fellowship to gain awareness of His awesome plans. We miss out on so much when we disregard His commands and neglect the promises prepared for us when we don't spend time with Him. His commands govern us so we can live our best life. As we heed His judgments, we are guaranteed to reap favorable outcomes. God is finished writing our story, whether or not we receive His promises depends solely on us. Time with God produces so much, clarity, perspective, peace, joy, insight, forgiveness, purpose, and so much more. In remaining close, we experience newness every day. Who wouldn't want to spend time with a God like that?

**It is Written!**

Prayer: Lord, we praise Your holy name. Bless You for saving us. Thank You for calling us as Your own. Keep us in perfect peace as our minds continuously stay on You. Lord, forgive us for any time we have neglected our relationship with You. Press upon our heart for us to come before Your throne of grace daily. Help us to mediate on Your Word day and night, in order to obtain good success. There is great joy and honor in praising You. We are forever grateful for Your promises and the covenant You made with us as Your children. Thank You for the continuous blessings that we receive daily. All honor and praise belong to You. In Jesus' name we pray, Amen.

# November 3

*Jesus answered and said unto them, Go and shew John again those things which ye do hear and see:* (Matthew 11:4)

What miracle are you waiting for to believe God is the true and living God? This reminder should resonate in our mind at all times. Understanding the truth of who God is sets us free. It's easy to verbally express God as the Messiah, but do you truly acknowledge Him as such? When we constantly remind ourselves of who God is, and the power and love He possesses, we are able to enjoy our freedom. As kingdom citizens, we have to remember the works of Christ. At the onset of issues, our lips should formulate words to express who God is. This puts our thought process in proper prospective. God requires us to listen and obey His commands. He has promised to work out any hardships that come our way. When we allow Him to open our spiritual eyes, we are able to see the way He operates. Nothing is new to God. He is always at work, cultivating His purpose in the earth. As Elisha asked God to open His servant's eyes in order for Him to see the manner in which God operates, we too must take our stance and open our eyes (2King 6:17). God's job is always secure; He is fully capable of operating in perfection. Our eyesight cannot be blocked by the trials of life. Every day must be a confession of how we see and hear God. We see the many times He has delivered us before. We see how He operates on our behalf, causing all things to work together for our good. We hear through His Word, prayer, and His disciples, the promises He has set-aside just for us. We know Him; it's just a matter of remembering Him in all things. Wait no long for deliverance, it's already here.

**What are you waiting for?**

Prayer: God of grace, all glory belongs to You. Open our eyes that we may see. We invite You in to reside in our lives at all times. Bring back to our remembrance the nature of Your being. In all circumstances, let us trust in and rely on You. Order our steps in Your Word. Saturate us with Your spirit. Let our eyes look unto the hills, where our help comes from. Be our delight. Enable us to operate as kingdom citizens, how You have ordained for us to be in the world. Allow us to only speak and reiterate what we hear and see you do in heaven. Overpower our thoughts with Your promises, helping us to stand on Your Word. All power belongs to You. In Jesus' name we pray, Amen.

# November 4

*Therefore encourage one another and build one another up, just as you are doing.* (1 Thessalonians 5:11)

Kind gestures have the potential to turn a bad day into a joyful day. When we express the love given to us from Christ, God's love is manifested. Hardships in life are inevitable, uplifting words can possibly change ones outlook on life. Showing kindness to others is self-fulfilling. It enables us to experience the same joy God feels when He is kind to us. One thing I know about God is, He will never discourage His children. No matter what we do or what we fail to do, God will never react with feelings of despair. He cheers us on, to continue in the right path, by teaching us His ways. Most people truly try their best to accomplish their endeavors. It's always rewarding to hear words that will boost confidence. You don't know what it takes for a person to say sorry, or how long someone wrestled with a decision to step out on faith. The mind alone can spark forms of discouragement when it's not firmly fitted in the peace of God. To inform others of how important they are, or how much they mean to you can inspire them to press a little farther. The world can be so cruel, yet we are given the choice every day to spread love. It's our opportunity to shine our light in the world. And guess what? Its Free! That's right, smiling at the cashier or speaking a word of kindness to someone we see in passing can change their mood. It's especially beneficial to display this level of encouragement and uplifting in our own homes. Many times, we get comfortable with those closest to us. We know all of their imperfections and the little things that get under our skin, nevertheless they are still human. They too require love, and who better to display it than us. God is always encouraging us and showing us His kindness. Think about how it feels when someone encourages you, take that same ball of excitement and start a ripple effect and bless your neighbor.

**Bless you!**

Prayer: God, we love you. Thank you for choosing us to share in Your greatness. Wrap Your arms around Your people today. Be near the broken-hearted, and save the crushed in spirit. Bind up all of their wounds. Make us complete in You. Thank You for Your many, many, many blessings. Help us to always remember You. Teach us the art of showing kindness, regardless of our current situation. Let love be the initial reaction towards everyone we come in contact with. Shower us with Your Spirit, fill us with Your virtue that Your love will be manifested in the earth. Your thoughts towards us are innumerable. Make Yourself known to Your people today. Let them feel You in a way they have never felt You before. Make our hearts glad. With all honor and praise we love you. In Jesus' name we pray, Amen.

# November 5

*The heaven, even the heavens, are the LORD's: but the earth hath he given to the children of men.* (Psalm 115:16)

God's domain is in Heaven. He created man to inhabit, subdue and reign in the earth. Everything God wants to do in the earth requires a willing vessel (you and I), in order for this to happen. The earth is our area of dominion. We are rulers of everything God has created. He has equipped us to master the art of survival while we are here on earth. Being in control of a specific area would require one to obtain knowledge and then utilize it. In this manner, we are fulfilling God's intent for human creation. God never intended for us to live in bondage. It's time to erase this manner of thinking from our memory. We have been given authority over everything God created. In order to activate our God-given power, we have to change our way of thinking. God has informed us in His Word of our ability to lose and bind things on earth, and so it will be in Heaven (Matthew 18:18). It is our responsibility to get up every morning and take authority over our day. We must take a proactive stance when it comes to our lives and the things God has placed under our control. He has given us the keys to the kingdom. We are able to call upon the source for whatever need we have in the earth. According to God's will, we will receive it. Don't you believe it's God's will for you to prosper in all of your endeavors? It's just like a Father to want us to be the head and not the tail. A life under the governing of the Father is full of exceeding potential. Not only will you see the vision, you will be able to accomplish unimaginable goals. Jesus tells us in John 10:10, "I came that you may have life and have it abundantly." Abundantly means great increase, and this pertains to every area of our lives. Great peace, Great families, Great careers, Great children, Great ministries, Great purpose, Great marriages, Great finances, Great peace, Great love, Great joy!!!!!

**The earth is our domain, now rule!**

Prayer: God of glory, thank You for this day. We bind up the mind of bondage today. We lose freedom in our thought process right now. Pour out Your wisdom and instill Your promises in us. Help us to know and understand the power that we possess as Your children. You have given us the power to subdue and rule over the earth. We bind up the hand of confusion, low self-esteem, and feelings of being unworthy. Build character in us to know who we are in Christ. Teach us Your ways, so we are not confused in our daily pursuits. Give us a vision, that we may see You in everything we do. In our private time with You, reveal to us Your perfect plan. All glory belongs to You, In Jesus' name, we pray. Amen.

# November 6

*When Christ, who is our life, shall appear, then shall ye also appear with him in glory.* (Colossians 3:4)

Christ is our very being. We carry His DNA. He is in us, and we are in Him. "For ye are dead, and your life is hid with Christ in God" (Colossians 3.3). Our entire image should be a replica of Christ as He is in heaven. What we longed to do apart from God no longer has a opportunity to dwell in our lives. We are now hidden in Christ Jesus. We have taken on His nature. The essence of our being represents His godly character. Everything we do should resemble Christ. It is no longer us calling the shots directing our own lives. Our Father is the one showing/teaching us how to conduct ourselves as His agents in the earth. Jesus is our perfect example. He showed us that it is through fellowship with God that we are able to fulfill our divine purpose in this life. He only did what he saw His Father doing in heaven and only said what God instructed Him to say. As a result, God said, "This is my beloved Son, in whom I am well pleased" (Matthew 3:17), in that Jesus came to earth with a specific purpose, stayed in fellowship with God and completed His kingdom assignment. We represent the kingdom, and are able to accomplish everything God placed inside of us. Our lives are hidden in Christ. This is a promise of hope. We have the King of glory inside of us, and we are with Him seated in heavenly places. This gives us a new perspective and a boost of encouragement to face life with boldness. When people see us they ought to see Jesus. When Christ appears again in the earth, He should be able to look around and see images of Himself through the body of believers. It will be as a mirror reflection of all the saints unified together in one image.

**Look in the mirror!**

Prayer: God of all the earth, we magnify Your holy name. Consume us with Your awesome presence today that we may be able to reflect Your nature in the earth. We die to ourselves today. We mortify our members which are upon the earth; fornication, uncleanness, inordinate affection, evil concupiscence, and covetousness, anger, wrath, malice, blasphemy, filthy communication from our mouth (Colossians 3:5-8). Help us to walk in our new man, having renewed knowledge and displaying Your image. Let every ounce of our being be transformed by Your power. Wash us and make us clean, purify our hearts to live in love. Let our lives be examples and a testament of Your unfailing love. In all of our ways we will acknowledge and consult Your throne. In Jesus' name we pray, Amen.

# November 7

*And we have known and believed the love that God hath to us. God is love; and he that dwelleth in love dwelleth in God, and God in him.* (1 John 4:16)

The features of love help us to understand we were first loved by God. In return, we must develop His loving nature, first by accepting His love, love ourselves, and then loving others. People often associate love with conditions. I'll love you if you do this, or if you treat me a certain way, I'll love you. Agape love requires that we love without conditions. As Jesus loves us without terms, He has called us to exhibit these same characteristic. In our human mind we allow pain, attitudes, and circumstances to condition our ability to love our neighbors. God's love is manifested genuinely with no regard to the recipients actions. In other words, God loves regardless of who accepts it, or who will return love towards Him. Everything He does is triggered by love. Love entails we forgive others even before they offend us. Christ forgave us before we were even born. In love, He shed His blood for us to regain a proper relationship with God. Christ, now being in us, requires us to take on His attributes. We can't walk around claiming we are in Christ and not show love to the world. As Christ is in heaven interceding on our behalf, shielding us from the punishment our behavior warrants, we too must exhibit love on the earth. Love will cause us to turn the other cheek. Love will cause us to be so embedded in the Word that when people offend us, we immediately forgive, because we know offense is inevitable. Love will cause us to pray for others first and consider the reasons for their behavior second. Love keeps us in intimate relationship with God. It shows the world the physical face of God in the earth. God's love should provoke all of our actions and consume every word that forms on our lips. Think about it, Jesus didn't wait for us to get our life in order before He died on the cross. In love, He died on the cross in order for our life to be in order.

**As He is so are we in the world!**

Prayer: God, our Father which art in Heaven, hallowed be thy name. Lord, we come before You asking for forgiveness for not loving the way You have designed us to love. Renew our minds that we may exhibit agape love. Let love flow from our hearts into our actions. Let the world see Your glory through our acts of faith. Love is the essence of our relationship with You. As we dwell in You, help us to master the art of loving our neighbor as ourselves. Let us take on Your nature and truly love without conditions. Help us to love with no regard to how others may feel or react. We will continue to pour out love as You have done with us. Thank You for first loving us. Guide our every thought and action. In all that we do, we will bring glory to Your name. In Jesus' name we pray, Amen.

# November 8

*And he said unto him, Thy prayers and thine alms are come up for a memorial before God.* (Acts 10:4b)

I'm sure everyone has asked the question, "where do my prayers go," or inquired whether or not the Lord hears you when you pray. We are assured that God does indeed hear our prayers and is diligent to answer. Not only does He hear us, but our prayers are on special assignment before Him. The Bible lets us know that our prayers come before God as a memorial. When we pray, we come with an heart of adoration before the Father and offer up thanksgiving. Allowing the Holy Spirit to take charge of our prayers keeps us in right alignment with what is taking place in Heaven. This is the reason why it is so essential that we pray every day. There is so much taking place in the world today that we cannot miss one day of prayer. Hence, the reason we are instructed to pray without ceasing (1 Thessalonians 5:17). Everything that concerns us, concerns God. What better way to get things off of our chest and out of our mind then to lay them before the throne of grace. Not only does this lift a heavy load, it prepares us for the things to come. Our prayers come before God as a reminder of who we are in Him. When He sees our heart turned towards Him, it lets Him know how much we appreciate and adore Him. He is then prompted to pour out His blessing upon His children who are humble and prepared to receive everything He has stored up for us. When we give gifts to our children, we are reminded by their good behavior or their constant presence which brings us joy. God is delighted in the same manner to remember our petitions as a call for His attention. It is not by our works that we receive great blessings from God, but by grace through faith. It is the desire of our heart to attain everything God predestined for us to have. What better way to live our best life than to remain in constant fellowship and ask of the Father.

**Where do my prayers go?**

Prayer: Lord, You are everything. As we come before You today in prayer, we just want to thank You for Your loving kindness. Help us to have such an authentic prayer life that our prayers come before you as a memorial. Help us to build a relationship with You that is built on Your principles. It is sad that the body of believers only come to You when things are going bad. We will come before Your throne daily, seeking after You and Your perfect plan for our lives. God, in You we are able to accomplish anything in this earth. Apart from You we can do no good thing. Keep us in constant fellowship. Remove the scales from our eyes that we may see the light of Your glory. Teach us how to pray, and how to soak in Your presence to hear Your voice. Give us clear and concise directives for our day. Help us not to miss out on hearing Your voice. Help us not to have so much going on in our day that we give you the smallest portion of our day. Help us not to rush in Your presence but to receive everything You are going to reveal in our time alone with You. You make us happy and fill us with joy. All glory belongs to you. In Jesus' name we pray, Amen.

# November 9

*For indeed the gospel was preached to us as well as to them; but the word which they heard did not profit them, not being mixed with faith in those who heard it.* (Hebrews 4:2)

The Word of God is powerful and effective. It possesses the very nature of God to preform that which He has orchestrated since the foundation of the earth. The purpose of God's plan has already been completed. He has laid everything in order, and created all that we need to enjoy a godly life. His Word is full of direction, and is here to guide us on the path of righteousness. When we hear the Word, it should pierce our hearts and ignite something within our spirit. Reading the Bible reveals unknown facts to us about life and our journey in Christ. It must be accompanied with faith in order for it to blossom into it's intended potential. Receiving God's Word without faith is of no effect to His children. Hearing the Word is not enough for it to transform our lives. People hear the Word daily and disregard the power associated with it. When we deny the virtue embedded in God's Word, it hinders us and adds no value to our lives. Our faith enables us to believe in the capabilities of God's miraculous power even before we see them. Our belief then ignites our obedience to His Word and facilitates God's plans in our lives. The Word is alive and active; ready to empower every person who walks this earth to receive revelations daily. God has great plans for us. It is through faith that we receive from heaven. Faith the substance of things hoped for and the evidence of things not seen (Hebrews 11:1). This means we believe God at His Word. Whatever He says, we can rest assured it will happen for us. Our only position is to believe and receive the very promises of God. It requires that we cast down ALL doubt, fear, worry and unbelief. We are confident in God and know He is not a man that He should lie. It is written and so it shall be.

**Get in the Word!**

Prayer: Lord, we honor You this day. Thank You for considering us as Your children. You have created us for such a time as this to walk in righteousness. Life is a gift from above; with great joy will we magnify Your name. Open our hearts to receive Your Word as doctrine for our lives. Let it go forth and complete the work You have ordained for our life. Everything in life that we have to endure is written in Your Word. Nothing is new to You. We accept Your Word and apply faith, and invite You in to govern our lives. You have prepared every season before time began to show Your children the way of life. Christ, we acknowledge Your presence and come boldly before the throne of grace to receive Your help and mercy. In all that we do we will apply Your Word, and believe in Your unfailing love. With a great praise we say thank You. In Jesus' name we pray, Amen.

# November 10

*I praise you because I am fearfully and wonderfully made; your works are wonderful, I know that full well.* (Psalm 139:14)

God went through great lengths when He decided to create us. Every attribute, feature and organ is specifically designed as beauty in His eyes. Formed in the capacity of complete greatness, he called us forth to bless the earth with our presence. Embedded with the very nature of the creator, forced to spend time in a foreign land. Not alone, as God has always been right in the midst. With every passing moment, we never leave His sight. With every step we take He waits to see if we will turn our heart toward heaven and request His guidance. Knowing He is the one who cares for us brings satisfaction to the day's task. As we are filled with knowledge of who we are and how His love has called us out of darkness, we can walk with boldness, shouting how awesome we are. Arrogant, not at all. Simply assurance of who we belong to; the Father, Master, King of Kings, Lord of Lords, God is your praise. Honor flows from our lips as we indulge in the ambiance of His loving touch. Each experience walked through in life was created to draw us closer to God, not to push us away. When we think of the many times we have tried things on our own, there is no comparison to one moment with the Father. Time spent with Him allows us to discover who we are. When the enemy comes with his lies in tow, quickly dismiss the notion of being anything less than who our Father has called us to be, Fearfully and Wonderfully made. Know that full well!

**What do you know?**

Prayer: Father God who is in Heaven, have Your way this day. We come humbly before Your throne of grace, seeking deliverance. Deliver us from the lies of the enemy that tell us we are worthless and don't deserve Your love. Help us to know full well who we are. Renew our minds to understand what Your perfect and pleasing will is for our lives. Build in us a firm foundation based on the truth of Your Word. Let it ignite pure fire in our lives to consume every attribute that was not created in heaven. Destroy all power of evil which comes to steal, kill and destroy the beautiful creation you have predestined. You remind us daily of Your lovingkindness by Your grace and mercy. Help us to take time to acknowledge Your presence and not take for granted time spent with You. Let the light of Your glory shine brightly upon our hearts that we may know without a doubt who You have called us to be. All glory and praise belong to you, in Jesus' name we pray, Amen.

# November 11

*Then Peter said unto them, Repent, and be baptized every one of you in the name of Jesus Christ for the remission of sins, and ye shall receive the gift of the Holy Ghost.* (Acts 2:38)

Everyone who accepts the invitation of Christ takes on the role of a disciple. As a follower of Christ, we should be so filled with the Holy Ghost that when God sends us on assignment to minister to people, His word in us pricks their heart. There is no room for shyness or feelings of doubt when we are concerned with the Father's business. If we deal with such concerns, it is important to bring them before the Father in prayer. Ask Him to prepare our heart for kingdom work. The work of the ministry goes beyond pastors and leaders in the church. Each one of us has been called to be God's ambassadors in the earth. When we look around at the evil taking place in the world, it should ignite our passion to desire to spread the gospel, the message of hope. When we come to Christ we must first repent, ask for forgiveness of our sins and turn away from ungodly behavior. The Bible says then to be baptized in the name of Jesus for the remission (cancellation of charge) of our sins, and we will receive the Holy Ghost. The Holy Ghost is God's Spirit working through us. We are then able to surrender ALL of our plans to God. Being led by the Spirit will prepare us for a life of ministry. We are all ministers (servants of God). Our testimony will brings others to Christ if we allow the Lord to use us.

**I'm ready to work!**

Prayer: God of all wisdom, power and glory, we surrender our lives before Your throne of Grace. How awesome it is to dwell with You. In total adoration we lift up our hearts to You. Thank You for your new mercies that we received just this morning. Keep us in the palm of Your hands. Forgive us for all manner of sin. Anywhere we have been unfaithful to You, reveal it to us today. Help us not to be separated from You due to our own negligence. Open our hearts and minds to be in constant prayer and dedication to our relationship with You. Whatever concerns Your people have today, we lay them at Your feet. We come before You empty that You may fill us with the Holy Ghost. Ignite Your fire within us. Use us for the divine plan and purpose You have created us for. The promises is for Your people, we sit in expectation of Your goodness. With every ounce of our being we magnify Your name. In Jesus' name we pray, Amen.

# November 12

*The Lord bless thee, and keep thee.* (Numbers 6:24)

Early on in my relationship with Christ, I didn't fully understand His virtue. I hadn't quite grasped the concept of intercessory prayer or its power. In my time of petitioning the Lord, my heart would become overwhelmed with the concerns of those around me. In prayer, I would call out to God and say, "Give them one of my blessings, I know I've been good, let them use one of mine, because I know they need it." My heart's intent was right; I just hadn't obtained wisdom concerning God and His grace. God is the one who blesses, He has unlimited opportunities to bestow His goodness upon us. There is no number associated with our name to control how many times we can be blessed. Oftentimes in our mind, we think once we receive a good thing we have to wait a certain amount of time before God will bless again. God is the creator of blessings and wants to bless every person that walks this earth. It is His nature to grant unusual favor, we are the ones who stand in His way by limiting Him in this regard. There should never be a time in our lives when we feel ashamed to come before our Father to ask for anything in prayer, either for ourselves or those we know. It is His great pleasure to give us the kingdom of heaven. He is the source of all things. He has an ordained time for us to receive all of His blessings. What God gives will never be retracted. When He decides to bless, it will come forth in that manner.

**Blessings come forth!**

**Prayer**: Lord of grace and kindness, we honor You this day. Remove all form of doubt from our hearts and minds. Take the shield off of our heart that we may let You in to reside. We desire Your love to keep us in perfect fellowship with You. Thank You for continuing to bless us daily. Waking us up this morning was a blessing. Allowing us to breathe in air is because of You. Everything that we are is because You love us. Help us to comprehend that Your love is not based on anything we could have ever done, but is given strictly because of Your compassion for us. As Your children, help us to be a blessing to those around us. Open our eyes and enlighten our hearts to show compassion to those in need. We take the limits off of You this day. We invite You in to do all the things You have created us for. This life is not our own, we give it back to You. Use us for the uplifting of Your kingdom. We will forever shout glory. In Jesus' name we pray, Amen.

## November 13

*And they shall put my name upon the children of Israel; and I will bless them.* (Numbers 6:27)

One day my daughter ran into my room and informed me that everything she owned was made in China. She said, "Mom my dolls, clothes, toys, covers were all made in China." She was inquisitive as to why one country took such great ownership in the creation of so many things. Her little mind continued to wonder every time she came across a new item she would check the tag and reply, "MADE IN CHINA." For a couple of days she would inform everyone who crossed her path that most things were made in China. When people see us it should spark the same enthusiasm, as we are MADE IN THE KINGDOM. God has put His name on us, and everywhere we go should exemplify how magnificent we are. Being that God created all things, all things should resemble His nature. Unfortunately, many deny heaven's design and take ownership in the false nature of the flesh. For those who are proud to be MADE IN THE KINGDOM, it should leave an imprint on the minds of those we cross paths with. Thoughts should linger in their minds of how distinct kingdom citizens behave and carry themselves. When we pass by, they will be able to say they were MADE IN THE KINGDOM. God has created us to be SET APART, not to fit in and be like the people in the world. God has put His name on us, He has secured us in the palm of His hands. Living for Him is a two-fold gift, we walk out our purpose and He in turn blesses us. As individuals, when we vouch for someone and put our name on the line, we expect the person to hold our gratitude with high regard. The same is true with God. His name is always on us. God is in the midst where ever we go, cheering us on and exclaiming how proud He is of His beautiful creation. Don't ever forget God has His name on you; you are MADE IN THE KINGDOM.

**MADE IN THE KINGDOM!**

Prayer: God, we love You. Thank You for pouring out Your love upon us daily. With great honor, we take full ownership of who we are in Christ Jesus. We give access to You to fill us to the brim until it overflows with Your Spirit. Your plans are perfect and pleasing. Show us the path that You have so carefully thought out for us. Let our minds be at ease as we come continuously in Your presence to dwell with You. Let this day be a day of remembering How much You love us. Lord, make Your face to shine upon us and be gracious to us. Give us Your attitude and mannerism, so people can see YOU through us. God, we thank You for all You do. In Jesus' name we pray, Amen.

# November 14

*Then will I cause you to dwell in this place, in the land that I gave to your fathers, for ever and ever.* (Jeremiah 7:7)

With every promise there is a command from God. Our part is tremendously easy if we would hide the Word of God in our heart. When the Word is hidden in our heart, it becomes active in every circumstance and enables us to be led by Christ. Our destiny has been written, it stands still, waiting for us to catch up to our appointed time. There is nothing worse than missing out on God-given opportunities. Everything in our life must line up with the Word of God. This includes our thought process, attitudes, and actions. God will not conform to the manner of man, we are the ones who must be molded around God's characteristics. His Word is able to transform us into the holy creatures He has predestined. It is a necessity to get into the Word daily and apply it to our lives. There is a (scripture) Word from God pertaining to every situation we will ever encounter in life. Consistency through faith is the only way we are going to remember God's commands and receive every promise He has for us. God orders our steps by His Word (Psalm 119:133), giving us the ability to be in perfect fellowship with Him. Yes, it takes true commitment and dedication to constantly come before the throne, but it is well worth it. When you have placed before you luxury or doom, most people are sure to pick luxury. This is what we have as Christ heirs. We have access to everything in the Kingdom. Allow the Word to transform and enlighten you to every good and perfect gift waiting on your arrival.

**He Promised!**

Prayer: God of grace, mercy and honor, we come before Your throne in total adoration. Who could love us the way You do? No one could ever take Your place as Most High. What a privilege to be called Your child. We acknowledge the sacrifice You have made for us to have right relationship with You. We shall never take it for granted. Help us to believe in the truth of Your Word.

Let it govern our mind, body and soul. Enable us to hear and obey all of Your commands. Let us not hinder ourselves from obtaining the promise. Help us to be slow to speak and quick to listen. Ignite the fire within our spirit to constantly seek after Your plans for our lives. Order our steps in Your Word: and let **no iniquity** have dominion over us. Hallelujah, we bless Your name, in Jesus' name we pray, Amen.

## November 15

*But Micaiah said, "As surely as God lives, what God says, I'll say."* (1 King 22:14)

For the word of God is quick, and powerful, and sharper than any two-edged sword (Hebrews 4:12). God's word possesses such power that it is able to instantly transform our lives. When God speaks, thing happen. By His Word the earth was formed and all things came into existence. His Word has been tried and proven perfect. The most significant thing about His Word is it is full of benefits for His children. God, being Sovereign, has created such a system for His people to have truth and understanding. Without God's Word being active in our lives we are unable to be effective for the kingdom. Many people hear the Word and are not transformed because they fail to perform what the Word says or possess underdeveloped faith. Letting the Word fall on deaf ears only hinders us from fulfilling our predestined purpose in the earth. We obtain favor as we adhere to the Word and perform God's commands. God speaks clearly to those who seek after Him diligently and consistently with an open heart. We understand each day we attain new mercies; we are able to hear a fresh Word from the throne of grace. God opens the gateway to fellowship daily. When we turn our hearts to God, He is able to deposit into us His divine truth. His truth (His Word) keeps us safe, and is able capture our circumstances and make them come into submission and obey Christ. Prayer, fasting and reading the Bible will cause the Word to grow in our lives. Maturing in Christ will cause us to say only what we hear God say. No value is added to our lives when we speak words without truth. When we have a relationship with Christ, His Word transforms us and it becomes our nature to exhibit His attributes in everything we do.

**Your Word is power and truth!**

Prayer: God, You are everything. We come before Your throne of grace, asking that You fill us with Your Holy Spirit. Let the words that we speak be pleasing in Your sight. Whatever comes out of our mouth let it be what we have heard from You in heaven. Transform us, renew our mind, and keep us in perfect fellowship with You. Let us speak the Word in truth. We cast down imaginations and every high thing that exalteth itself against the knowledge of God, and bring into captivity every thought to the obedience of Christ (2 Corinthians 10:5). All praise we give to You. In Jesus' name we pray, Amen.

# November 16

*For he shall give his angels charge over thee, to keep thee in all thy ways.* (Psalm 91:11)

Angels are spiritual beings, created by God to fulfill His purpose. When God places them on assignment they give precedence to His commands and do exactly what is requested of them (Psalm 103:20). God has employed His angels to minister to those who will inherit salvation (Luke 22:43). They are sent into the earth to serve you and me. Angels are innumerable and are always on post. We have security in God's protection, knowing that we have specific angels assigned to us (Matthew 18:10). The Bible gives numerous examples of how angels ministered to His people throughout history. Angels shut the mouth of lions for Daniel (Daniel 6:22). They were on the battlefield with Elijah to engage in combat (2 Kings 6:17). They even ministered to Jesus in the wilderness (Mark 1:13). Angels are agents of God, and their sole purpose is to obey His voice and render praise. When we choose to find rest in God, He is sure to command His angels concerning us. Every time you read scripture, put Your name in the passage and rely on God's servants to keep us in all our ways.

*"For he shall give his angels*
*charge over* ***Nicole****, to keep her in all her ways."*

**Employ your angels.**

Prayer: Lord, You are great. Everything You do is set up to draw us closer to You. We come before Your throne of grace with an open heart, mind and spirit, inviting You in to take up permanent residence. You created the earth and all things belong to You. We are forever grateful to be considered Your ambassadors. Help us to dwell in the secret place of the Most High and find rest under Your shadow. Thank You for being our refuge and fortress, all trust belongs to You. Enable us to trust You, even when we are not able to comprehend what is taking place. We know and understand You are in control and are fighting on our behalf. You have employed innumerable angels to minister to us and enable us to securely function in the earth. We say, thank You. Command Your angels to be on post and guard our every footstep. We bless Your holy name, in Jesus' name we pray, Amen.

# November 17

*Jesus wept* (John 11:35)

The depth of God's love goes beyond the scope of our intellect. If you have ever experienced deep compassion or feelings of love for another person, you are able to obtain a glimpse of how God yearns for us. From the Master's view, He creates the gift of love, moment by moment, to be poured out among the people He loves. Love ignites thoughts of joy. When in love, you contemplate ways of being together, thoughts fill your heart with joy. Images of time spent together are on constant replay in your mind. Love in it's purest form can produce no wrong. The love of God is just that, perfect. His thoughts for us are too many to be numbered (Psalm 40:5). God experiences pain in the same instance that we do. By our connection, He is able to endure right along with us. In Christ, we have a friend who can shine light on our dark situations and keep us connected to the vine. Our connection reassures His Sovereignty. We are free to fall into the arms of our Lord and embrace His love. Here in scripture we find Jesus' friend Lazarus has just died. In fact, he has been dead for four days. Jesus was met by Lazarus' sisters and his friends who were all weeping and mourning his death. At the sight of their sorrow and the love Jesus had for His friend, Jesus too wept. This displays His great love and compassion for mankind. Although a few scriptures earlier, Jesus declared "this sickness is not unto death, but for the glory of God" (John 11:4), He was still able to relate to our human emotions and experienced the pain of grief with his beloved creation.

**Behold how He loved him!**

Prayer: Many are the thoughts and plans that You have concerning Your people. In love, You created us to be in connection with You. When we open our eyes, we can see the magnitude of Your love. Help us to embrace Your love. Let it be engrafted in us, that we may show the world Your face through our words and actions. Wrap Your loving arms around those who are in despair. Be a comforter to those in need. Bring to our remembrance the deep compassion that You have for each of us. Help us to remember we are not forgotten. You never sleep nor slumber, and are always concerned with Your people. We are forever grateful. We honor and bless Your name. In Jesus' name we pray, Amen.

# November 18

*Give therefore thy servant an understanding heart to judge thy people, that I may discern between good and bad: for who is able to judge this thy so great a people?* (1 Kings 3:9)

The majority of contentions in the earth are caused by lack of understanding. Understanding gives us the ability to comprehend the perceived intent of one's actions. God's wisdom gives us a clear vision of how/why things take place in the earth. When we are able to discern between good and evil, it takes away the anxiety and frustration of not understanding. God never intended for us to walk the earth hopeless, without an understanding. Everything that takes place in the earth has a purpose and a designed season. When we obtain godly wisdom, we become satisfied with knowing how his creation operates. We are able to display wisdom from above and develop as individuals who show compassion and love as a reflection of God being in us. With His help, we are able to see, analyze, deal with, and overcome issues that arise in our lives and the lives of others without becoming paralyzed by darkness. His light will shine upon our circumstances and enable us to believe in His perfect plan. It is impossible for God to make a mistake. Wisdom opens the eyes of our heart to envision and receive the things God has prepared for us.

**But the wisdom from above is first pure, then peaceable, gentle, open to reason, full of mercy and good fruits, impartial and sincere. And a harvest of righteousness is sown in peace by those who make peace. (James 3:17-18)**

**Wisdom is a free gift!**

Prayer: Lord of mercy, we pray this day for a heart of understanding. Help us to discern between good and evil. Let your intent be revealed to us. Remove the initial response from us to cast judgment on our neighbors. Give us a heart of compassion, joy, understanding, peace and long-suffering. Let us be able to understand the things taking place in this earth. Fill us with godly wisdom. Let us seek You in all things. Let Your Word enlighten the eyes of our heart that we don't roam earth without a purpose. Prepare us as Your servants to hear Your voice at all times. All glory and honor belong to You, In Jesus' name we pray, Amen.

# November 19

*The world cannot hate you; but me it hateth, because I testify of it, that the works thereof are evil.* (John 7:7)

Jesus explains the nature of hate to be an attitude of discomfort and dislike for another person. He tells us some people in the world came to hate Him only because He caused them to look in the mirror and realize their way of thinking and actions were not instituted by the Father. Isn't it interesting that people will love you so long as you are in agreement with them. They will like you while you go along with the way they conduct themselves and take on the same mannerisms they possess. Jesus forced people to own up to their behavior and recognize God's way of operating is for our benefit and produces righteous living. People don't just wake up hating others. Somewhere along the line, they have experienced some form of discomfort, tension or confusion which led to these feelings of disgust. Jesus came to the world to call us out of our mess and sinful nature. In doing so, people were resistant because they could not fathom being wrong. As children of God, we will encounter such resistance as well. Jesus has prepared us for such passionate dislike and instructs us not to be offended. We are not to be concerned with people not being able to face the reality of being shown their disconnection with God. Hatred is brought on by pride and one's choice not to accept the peace of God. When people hate you because of your relationship with Christ, be encouraged as it is not you they hate, but merely the relationship you have with the Father that they have yet to accept. Be encouraged.

**Hate is a choice, love is real.**

Prayer: Lord, we honor You this day. We understand that we live in an evil world filled with hate and ungodly attitudes. We loose love in the atmosphere. Wherever there lies an attitude of hate, contention, or confusion, replace it with Your unfailing love. As we know, love covers a multitude of sin. Pour out Your Holy Spirit to comfort those who are experiencing hate and rejection because of their relationship with You. Help them not to grow weary in well doing as they will reap a bountiful harvest in due season. Open the eyes of our heart to understand as they hated Jesus, they will also hate us. Let us not be offended by the world's evil intent. Build us up with Your strength that we may spread the gospel with boldness, covered with love. Have Your perfect work in us. All glory belongs to you. In Jesus' name we pray, Amen.

## November 20

*I say unto you, that likewise joy shall be in heaven over one sinner that repenteth, more than over ninety and nine just persons, which need no repentance.* (Luke 15:7)

Judgment does not belong to the saints of God. God alone is the only one who can cast judgment on our brothers and sisters in Christ. Like the angels, we too should rejoice when people come into the kingdom of God. Often, we try to keep each other bound to circumstances and decisions that we see others make. Instead of offering encouragement we offer judgment. Our stance should be that of our citizenship, which the Bible tells us in the Kingdom they rejoice when people repent and give theirs lives to Christ. If we could look in the mirror more often and reminisce on the many things God has forgiven us for, we would be able to love people to Christ. Salvation is a gift given by the Father to all who walk the earth. We all are the promise of God, the children of Abraham. It should grieve us deeply when others are not living in a godly manner. Our continuous prayer should be for our brothers and sisters to desire a closer relationship with Christ, and for those who don't know Him to come to have revelation of who He really is. We should be spurring each other in the grace of God, so that we all may function as the body of Christ. It is with great honor that we ourselves have come to repentance and are able to sup at the Father's table. Love and encouragement must become our daily nature. To show the world the love of Christ by speaking the Word in truth embedded with the power of God will draw men to repentance and ignite a party in heaven.

**I am my brother's keeper!**

Prayer: God, You are the lover of our soul. It is a privilege to dwell in Your presence. We call all who may not know You to come before You with a heart of repentance, asking for Your Son to dwell in them. God, forgive us of our ungodly behavior and wherever we have missed the mark. Overpower us with Your Word that it becomes our nature. Shield us with Your Holy Spirit that we may have Your heart. Instead of casting judgement based on other's circumstances and decisions, let our first response be that of love. Help us to encourage our neighbor and understand that we all live under grace. Let Your love work through us and be the universal language. Fill us with Your Spirit. With a great praise we say thank You. In Jesus' name we pray. Amen.

## November 21

*Wherefore I will yet plead with you, saith the LORD, and with your children's children will I plead.* (Jeremiah 2:9)

The mere fact that we were born is an implication of God's love. He has forever longed for us to dwell in the midst of His presence. In each passing moment, He waits in delight for us to embrace His generosity and soak up the gift of His love. It not only breaks His heart when His creation has a hardened heart, it changes the official destiny that He has prepared for us. He is not thrilled with the promise of judgment day when those who have denied His name will be forever separated. He uses each opportunity to make an emotional appeal for us to enjoy a relationship with Him. His request comes daily for us to walk in righteousness. Everything within His plan points to us spending eternity with Him. We are able to fully understand the truth in His ways being higher than our ways, as He gestures for us to be excused from our sins and dwell in open fellowship with Him. With a request for forgiveness and turning away from our sins through the acceptance of Jesus, God willingly receives us in as His own. Every day that we live, we receive an invitation to the most exquisite event of our lifetime, in the arms of our Daddy. Where we are the guest of honor being drawn in to partake in our kingdom citizenship.

**He's calling you!**

Prayer: Lord God of glory, thank You, thank You, thank You for requesting us to be a part of Your eternal family where You have prepared for us great things that our minds can't even begin to comprehend. Lord, let us hear the call each day and follow after You. Help us not to get in our own way. Open the eyes of our heart to understand the love and compassion You have toward us. Let us enjoy open fellowship with You. Show us how to come boldly before Your throne of grace with praise, adoration, and thanksgiving. With all honor we love you. In Jesus' name we pray Amen.

# November 22

*Glory to God in the highest, and on earth peace, good will toward men.* (Luke 2:14)

Glory to God in the highest was the shout of praise that echoed from the multitude of the heavenly host. They exuded a mighty praise before the Shepherds as they were full of excitement at the birth of Christ. Their praise exemplified the magnitude of God's greatness that they experience on a continuous basis in the heavenly realm. As they appeared to the wise men in the natural, they were inviting them to join in on the worship experience. They encouraged them by showing them how to praise God for who He is. I can hear them now, saying to the wise men, "You don't even know what You have in Christ Jesus, but by our worship you can see how awesome He is." I believe their worship was an attempt to show the wise men how awesome of a gift they were receiving in the birth of the Messiah. At this point in history, the children of Israel had only heard about the coming of a Savior. The multitude of the heavenly host not only exhibited the great praise that God deserves, but also decreed a blessing of peace and good will toward men. The Hebrew word for peace is Shalom, which stems from the root word Shalam which means to make restitution, and to make whole or complete. It's usage is in relation to causing someone to have deficiency in some way. It was the responsibility of the person who caused the deficiency to restore that which was lost. The noun Shalom means state of being, whole or complete, or without deficiency. The multitude of the heavenly host came to tell the world everything they were receiving in Christ. We caused our own loss of kingdom position (separation from God) due to disobedience. Without Christ, it would be left up to us to try to restore proper relationship with God, which is impossible in our own ability. God said, I will send my Son who makes all things whole and complete without deficiency. What we couldn't redeem in our human nature, Christ did for all.

**Lord, thou wilt ordain (order, decree, make official) peace for us: for thou also hast wrought (beaten out or shaped by**

**hammering) all our works in us. (Isaiah 26:12)**

**Christ Did it all!**

Prayer: Lord of mercy, God of hope, all power and life are in Your hands. We will never know how much it cost to see our sins upon that cross. We bow down in total reverence at the thought of You coming to this earth with the specific assignment of being our Savior. What we couldn't do for ourselves, You did in love. God, we are forever thankful. Bring this to our remembrance anytime we form our lips to complain. Help us to remember the peace (wholeness, without deficiency) that You have given to each of us who love You. It is official that we are redeemed by the blood of Your Son Jesus. We shout "Hallelujah". We will be glad in the Lord and rejoice, because You are righteous we will shout for joy. All glory and honor are Yours in abundance, saturate our hearts with Your presence. In Jesus' name we pray, Amen.

# November 23

*Then Jesus went with them. And when he was now not far from the house, the Centurion sent friends to him, saying unto him, Lord, trouble not thyself: for I am not worthy that thou shouldest enter under my roof.* (Luke 7:6)

When we come before God we must consider our attitude. As kingdom citizens, we have been promised many blessings from our dear Father. When we begin to consider how blessed we are, it may cause an attitude of being boastful. This means we consider ourselves worthy of the calling. Don't get me wrong, we are redeemed. We have been predestined by God, but our sinful nature deems us unworthy. "None is righteous, no, not one" (Romans 3:10). It is by grace, a mere gift from God, that we were not consumed the very first time we failed to obey Him. Our attitude has to be one of meek characteristics and be evident when we approach the throne of grace. Often, we feel we deserve the blessings of God because we have accepted Jesus as Lord and feel entitled. We must acknowledge God as sovereign and understand our position as the lower vessel in His kingdom. This Centurion considered Himself unworthy to even come to Jesus or allow Him to enter His home, so he sent friends to speak with Jesus on his behalf. This portrays a humble attitude. He heard Jesus was the man with all power. He then considered himself unworthy of such majesty to even grace His presence. Instead, he had faith enough to believe in His power and respected His authority and asked Jesus to just say a word and his servant would be healed. We learn many things from this passage, including that God requires we know our position and honor His. Faith in Jesus produces a right standing with God and enables us to come boldly before His throne of grace. We must also understand the power associated with God's Word. His Word can go to the farthest corner of the earth to perform it's intended purpose.

**At Your Word Jesus!**

Prayer: God of mercy, love, kindness and all manner of good, we honor You this day. We relinquish our hearts, minds, and spirit unto Your authority. Help us to understand our position in Your kingdom. We understand You have called us in as Your own due to Your loving kindness and by no power of our own. Let us consider how we approach You. Show us the condition of our heart and how we are to render thanksgiving before Your throne. Teach us the proper way to acknowledge You as Lord. Let our exaltation be pleasing in Your sight. Thank You for considering us as Your servants and embedding Your Holy Spirit within us. Forgive us if we ever boasted in ourselves and have not given You proper reverence. Establish the divine connection with us. Teach us how to bless You in all that we think, say, and do. We glorify Your name. In Jesus' name we pray. Amen.

# November 24

*Let your light so shine before men, that they may see your good works, and glorify your Father which is in heaven.* (Matthew 5:16)

One particular day, I was parking at the library when the Holy Spirit instructed me to park away from the door on the other side of the parking lot. Initially I wondered why, then I consensually said "I know God enough to trust Him, nothing He does is for granted." I parked in the unusual spot and immediately my vision was blurred due to the sun beaming down from the sky when it hit me. The light of Christ should beam so brightly from our being that we consume the area around us. No matter how I maneuver, the sun will still shine brightly and consume everything in its presence. If I choose to move or take shade that is my choice, but the functions of the sun remain the same. When we allow the light of Jesus to illuminate out of us, we are able to shine in the midst of the evil that is taking place in this world. When we step into a room, instead of being timid Christians, scared to offend people, things will fall into place and become blinded by our light and bow down to the power of God. We have to walk in the disposition of who God called us to be. He has embedded us with His Son Jesus Christ. When Jesus walked the earth, the demons knew who he was and asked Him not to torment them. He instructed His disciples to do the same work when He left, and that they would also do greater things as well because He was going to the Father, and anything we ask in His name He would do for us so that His Father might be glorified (John 14:12-14). Are you allowing God to do greater things through You that His name might be glorified? Your light will shine before men as you allow Christ to operate through you. It is not in our own power, but through our obedience we are able to step on the scene, and all things are consumed by God working through us and Him being glorified.

**Be glorified through me!**

Prayer: God of Abraham, Isaac and Jacob, we come before Your throne with a great praise. We are thrilled to call you Master. Abba Father, we adore You. Create in us a clean heart and right spirit that You are able to use us for Your glory. Let the magnitude of Your power shine so brightly through us that everything we do will be brought into captivity to the obedience of Christ. Let obedience be our nature. Enable us to hear Your voice louder than anything else in this world. When people look at us, let them see You. Show us the issues within us that we need to remove that You may have enough room to operate in our heart. Consume our heart, mind and soul with Your glory that You will be exalted. Transform us by renewing our minds that we may prove what is the good, acceptable, and perfect will of God. Relinquish us from the lies of the devil and allow us to function in total freedom in Christ Jesus. What an honor it is to praise You. In Jesus' name we pray, Amen.

# November 25

*Become the kind of container God can use to present any and every kind of gift to his guests for their blessing.* (2 Timothy 2:21 MSG)

In today's world, we are constantly being influenced and influencing others. Every decision we make can either add value to our existence or hinder our ability to mature. God created each of us with the ability to obtain His nature and utilize our gifts and talents to help encourage those whom we come into contact with. He has chosen us as His special vessels who are able to contain the power to absorb attributes from heaven and exude them in the earth. When we choose to use the gifts and talents He has given us towards things that don't add any value to our lives, we are not benefiting from God's grace. We have been given the ability to subdue the earth and utilize everything to fulfill our purpose. If we choose to deny the greatness God has prepared for us, we are being filled with things that will hinder us. If we aren't being filled with godly attributes, we are being filled with the things of this world which add no positive effect to our walk with Christ. It is a command from God that we meditate on His Word day and night. When we are in constant meditation, we are able to become molded in our original design. What we put in our spirit will come out of our spirit and determine how we affect the world around us. If you have ever learned a lesson by trial and error, I am certain you are sure to warn someone else before they err in the same manner. This is the very reason why it is important to be the kind of gift God can use to empower others in order to accomplish the work of the kingdom.

**What type of gift are you?**

Prayer: Lord, Your mercy is awesome. You are the greatest gift to us. We honor You this day. Lord, establish the work of our hands. Show us how to operate in the gifts You have enabled us to have. Teach us how to be filled with Your Spirit and walk after You. Remove the desire from our hearts to do anything contrary to

Your will. Enable us to be the vessels of fine pottery so You are able to trust us. As you search our hearts, remove any impure motives that are there to hinder our progression and maturity in the faith. Let our hearts be pure that we may see You. All praise belongs to You. In Jesus' name we pray, Amen.

## November 26

*And the grace of our Lord was exceeding abundant with faith and love which is in Christ Jesus.* (1 Timothy 1:14)

God will not require anything from His children that he hasn't first performed. Paul, an apostle of God, was not always the brilliant preacher of the gospel that we know. He was first an accuser of those who preached the gospel. Here, Paul speaks about the grace, coupled with love and faith, that saved His life. It was not until He experienced an encounter with Jesus that he come to realize His true identity and calling in life. In the midst of persecuting God's people, Paul was able to become a recipient of God's mercy. God's mercy goes far beyond what we see with the natural eye, day-to-day with the favor that He bestows upon us. He indulges it with faith, and as we know, faith is the substance of things hoped for and the evidence of things not seen. In the midst of Paul persecuting the church, he did not see himself as a convert and future writer of most of the New Testament, but God did. He exhibited faith to call Paul out of his disobedience into a life with Him because of love.

The same is true for us today, as God shows us how to have faith. It was by His faith that we were called out of darkness and into the kingdom of Jesus Christ. He first grants us mercy for the many times we have not followed after Him and done things according to our flesh. Love enables Him to see past our mistakes and remember the reason why we were created. That is faith to have the evidence of the things that are not seen. When we were in our mess, we could not see the hope of God's calling upon our lives. Yet, He said if you trust me, I will show you your purpose and reveal to you the things I have prepared for you. It is the substance of things hoped for. God hopes we will all walk in our calling and allow the scales to fall off our eyes in order to exhibit the great faith that He has instilled in us. God is the very foundation of love and calls us daily to recognize His goodness and mercy.

**God's Grace is exceeding, and abundant with faith and love!**

Prayer: Lord, You are the great "I AM," author and finisher of our faith. In everything that we do, we will acknowledge You. Thank You for forgiving us for our sins and calling us out of darkness. Continue to consume us daily that we may walk in righteousness with You. By Your love alone are we saved from the evil of this world. Before we knew You, You had faith enough to keep us on this earth in order to have an opportunity to accept Your Son Jesus in our life as our LORD. In our nonsense, You still covered us with Your grace and mercy. We thank You for always thinking of us. Remove the scales from our eyes today, that we are able and willing to accept You and Your purpose for our lives. Help us not to take Your kindness for granted, but to show the world Your love. With great honor we say Hallelujah, all glory and praise belong to You. In Jesus' name we pray, Amen.

# November 27

*But seek ye first the kingdom of God, and his righteousness; and all these things shall be added unto you.* (Matthew 6:33)

During our devotion with God, our first act of communication should be reverence, followed by asking God for His will to be done in our lives. God has a specific plan for His children every day. He commands that we inquire about His divine plan for our lives in order to fulfill our purpose. When He says *seek first His kingdom,* He is trying to get us to open our eyes to the truth of our inheritance. When we were called into His kingdom, we inherited everything under the Father's possession. When we look at the world from our eyes, we are unable to understand all of the surrounding circumstances that make things as they are. Coming to God first, inquiring of His virtue puts us in right position for Him to deposit the very thing we need for each of our days. Seeking God first will bypass all of the unnecessary things that will not add any value to our lives. Requiring God to speak first into our lives gives us an inside look at the things He has already ordained since before the beginning of time. We are able to obtain a mindset of freedom and ability to pray for the things that are on the heart of God. When we consider God's business, He is already working out the matters of our heart that concern us. Seeking a right standing with God first shows God that we understand His position in our lives. We acknowledge Him as God and recognize His power. We surrender our concerns to His authority, knowing that He cares for us and will not withhold any good thing from us. We are not bound to problems, but are free to walk in our divine purpose understanding our citizenship is in heaven. We are kingdom citizens, called to righteousness, able to walk in our purpose with kingdom guidance.

**I have a plan!**

Prayer: Lord, You are good and Your mercy endures forever. God, we come giving You honor and praise. This day, we ask for Your will to be revealed in us. We put aside every ounce of our being and submit to You. Work in us according to Your perfect plan. Help us overcome obstacles, and allow us to accept the narrow path of righteousness with great joy. Let us find fulfillment in laying down our will for Yours. Fill us with all knowledge and spiritual understanding. Let us walk in our inheritance, knowing the power and virtue that You give to those who love You. Give us this day our daily bread. We will not be concerned with worry or any issues that comes to take our mind off of You. We believe and know You are Alpha and Omega. You have an expected end for those who love you. With all praise we say thank You, in Jesus' name we pray, Amen.

# November 28

*And Elijah said unto Ahab, Get thee up, eat and drink; for there is a sound of abundance of rain.* (1 Kings 18:41)

Ahab was the king of Israel who the Bible says did more evil in the sight of God than any other king who came before him. During his reign, he built altars and worshipped the idol god Baal. Baal was supposed to be the god of rain, which was a necessity for sustainment of the people during this time. God instructed Elijah to inform Ahab that there would be no dew or rain unless the word came from him. Israel went several years without rain until God revealed the sound through the prophet Elijah.

Even in Ahab's disobedience, God wanted to show him how much he cared by providing something he could not produce himself. The rain came as a way to allow Ahab and the disobedient children to see there is only one God. Neither Baal or Ahab could harvest rain. God is crazy in love with His people. He will use His servants who are in constant fellowship with Him to bring forth a divine word to change our life and call us to repentance. If we, like Elijah, are obedient and faithful to God, we too can hear the sound of heaven. Intimate relationship with God will produce everything we need. “Thy kingdom come. Thy will be done in earth, as it is in heaven” (Matthew 6:10).

Not only did God show Elijah there would be rain in the midst of drought, he heard abundant rain. They were about to receive everything they needed and then some, just so they would know the power of God. When God does something, He does it exceedingly, abundantly above all that we could ever ask or think.

**Get Ready!**

Prayer: God of mercy, God of love, all power and might are in Your hands. We come humbly before Your throne, asking that You prepare us for abundant living in all areas of our life. Transform our minds to be in a position to hear the sound of heaven. Let us hear what the angels hear as they sit at Your feet. Empower us with Your Word that we are able to abound more and more in knowledge, and in all wisdom. Fill us with the fruits of righteousness to enable us to please You. With all glory and praise we honor You, in Jesus' name we pray, Amen.

## November 29

*Have not I commanded thee? Be strong and of a good courage; be not afraid, neither be thou dismayed: for the LORD thy God is with thee withersoever thou goest.* (Joshua 1:9)

It is a command to be strong and courageous. Our outlook on life must be inspired by our determination to accomplish everything we put our mind to. When we fail to walk in our God-given attributes such as having an attitude of a conqueror, we are actually being disobedient to God's original intent for our behavior. Instead of always thinking about the things that are against us, we should consider the very essence of who God called us to be. Since He commands us to be strong, we know our strength is found in Him. Comprehension of the power of God will release fear in our lives. If God can cause a sea to split in half and raise Jesus from the dead, surely He is capable of guiding us. We obtain courage in knowing God is in control. His very presences says, *"Nicole I wrote the course of your life before any day came to be, just walk in my direction with assurance of me leading you."* Fear sets in because we are scared of the unknown. Our mind plays tricks on us; causing us to think about the possible negative outcomes, when the exact opposite should be taking place. It would be more fearful if we were to actually see the attacks the enemy has prepared to use against us. God, as our refuge, intercedes the enemy's plans by shielding us. This allows us to focus on our primary purpose in Him. He commands that we not be afraid because He has already defeated any plans that would keep us from our destiny. Rest assured of the confidence that we have in Christ Jesus, knowing all things are well in the kingdom.

**It is well!**

Prayer: Lord God Almighty, You are the great God, ruler of the universe. All power belongs to You. With great pleasure do we exalt Your name. We come before Your throne of grace, boldly professing You as Our refuge. You are the one who keeps us from hurt, harm and danger. Where the enemy plans to destroy us, replace it with Your loving purpose. Remove fear, anxiety, and the spirit of laziness that would come to hinder Your children. Build a stature of divine courage and confidence, that we know without any doubt the power we possess in this earth. You have given us the power to trample over every serpent and snake, and over the enemy where nothing should harm us. Encourage the hearts of Your people to walk hand-in-hand with You, focused on our kingdom assignment. With our whole heart we will follow after You in everything we do. With all honor and praise we magnify Your name, in Jesus' name we pray, Amen.

# November 30

*I will bless the LORD at all times: his praise shall continually be in my mouth.* (Psalm 34:1)

Worship is a way of showing God respect. It's an attitude of thanksgiving and complete surrender to His Spirit. Our worship should be so authentic that it draws others in. Bystanders should see our worship and desire to join in. When we worship, we are not concerned with the matters of life, but with the perfect God we serve. If constant reminders of issues plague our thoughts, we are to make a conscious effort to override them with God's promises. Start quoting His promises (scripture), give Him praise, and allow His Spirit to bring to our remembrance His faithful track record. Most importantly, call those things which be not as though they were (Romans 4:17). In the midst of our worship, by the Spirit of the LORD we surrender to the presence of the Holy Spirit and allow Him to take control. God's praise will be on our tongue, allowing us to join in with the angels who cry out holy, holy, holy, in a continuous praise. As we allow the Holy Spirit to embody our worship, His praise will continuously be in our mouth. His standards and attributes will fill our heart and soul. We will enjoy worshipping a God who is loving/kind and whose nature consumes our very being and fills us with exuberant praise.

**I have a reason to praise!**

Prayer: Lord, You are so amazing, honor and glory are who You are. It would take a lifetime to show our gratitude for Your marvelous works. Praise is the very nature of thanksgiving that we will give You every day of our lives. When we think about how You've kept us every day, our hearts are filled with joy. Your plans and purpose are for our very benefit. We are more than thrilled to be called Your children. In everything that we do, we will boast about Your love. Fill us to the rim until it overflows with Your praise. Show us how to worship, let us not be consumed with anything else in life that tries to take Your place in our heart, but let us always have a heart to adore, reverence, fear, and honor You for being El Shaddai. In Jesus' name we pray, Amen.

# December 1

*O taste and see that the LORD is good.* (Psalm 34:8)

When you have experienced something good, you yearn for more. God, being the best thing one can experience, satisfies us beyond our wildest imagination. To come into fellowship with God is like an out of body experience. Our heart is filled with gladness as we experience an unexplainable, euphoric encounter with God. Everything else in the world is diminished by His presence, and pure satisfaction sets in. When we see a good thing we wish, hope, and dream of obtaining it. Those who have ambition set out to achieve those things most desirable. When you taste a delicious meal, your taste buds are filled with delight, you lavish in the moment and long to repeat the occurrence. Our mind has a record of being satisfied and promotes ways to feel this way again. On a continuous basis, can we taste and see the goodness of the LORD. Our mind too has a record of the exceeding power God possesses and how He can turn our darkest day into a ray of sunshine. How He can turn bad into good and release the pressure of life. In turn, we indulge in pure peace. God is the good thing which has been tried and proven to satisfy and cause His children to yearn for more. Each day spent with Him kindles the aspiration for more time in His presence. We desire Him as we have found pure satisfaction and fresh well of living water to sustain us. The more we experience His goodness, we are enlightened to His greatness and it keeps the fire burning within, never to let Him go. On a daily basis, we can and will taste and see that the Lord is good.

**Hungry for Your Presence!**

Prayer: For a day in thy courts is better than a thousand. Where you are is where we desire to be. Replenish our hearts today that we may have room to indulge in Your sweet pleasure. Our refuge is in You. You are the great thing; nothing else shall be desired above You. Thank You for allowing us to experience You daily. Bring us into continuous fellowship with You. Teach us ways we can fall deeper in love with You. Allow our worship to kindle a burning desire for Your presence. Let us sit in silence and allow Your Spirit to consume us. Lead us on the path of righteousness for Your name's sake. Be satisfied with our praise. We will bless the LORD at all times, and Your praise shall continually be in our mouth. In Jesus' name we pray, Amen!

# December 2

*Now we have received, not the spirit of the world, but the spirit which is of God; that we might know the things that are freely given to us of God.* (1 Corinthians 2:12)

The Spirit of God is a gift given to us to reveal God's heart. By the power of His Spirit we are able to discern between good and evil. Our ability to truly comprehend the life we have been given is only revealed when we allow the Holy Spirit to direct our path. The Spirit given to us is not concerned with the ideas of how man desires to experience life in the flesh. The Holy Spirit is an extension of God, who is given to us as an advocate to reveal our great purpose. Things that are not understood by our human intellect, God makes plain through His Spirit. When God's Spirit is in a thing, there is nothing that our flesh can do to help aid His works. The Holy Spirit is our avenue to receiving from God the necessary tools we need to overcome life. When we consider God's Spirit, we must understand the power embedded within the Spirit's nature. The Spirit is an entity of God who searches His heart in the Spirit realm (God is Spirit). In return, the Spirit then reveals the plans and purposes to those who have a relationship with God. We often don't have to speak a Word when the Spirit of God enters the room. When we surrender, we are able to hear a sweet sound from heaven pouring out the very nature of God.

**I still have many things to say to you, but you cannot bear them now. When the Spirit of truth comes, he will guide you into all the truth, for he will not speak on his own authority, but whatever he hears he will speak, and he will declare to you the things that are to come. He will glorify me, for he will take what is mine and declare it to you. All that the Father has is mine; therefore I said that he will take what is mine and declare it to you. (John 16: 12-15)**

**Spirit Dwell in Me!**

Prayer: Yahweh! We surrender our lives before You. What a gift You have given us in Your Holy Spirit. Where the Spirit of the Lord is there is Freedom. We will walk in liberty today. We are free to love, free to explore, free to fulfill our destiny. By the strength of Your hand we are able to speak boldly the things of Christ. We do not boast in ourselves but only in You. Thank you for the comforter, healer, wisdom, knowledge and power of Your Spirit. Pour out Your Spirit upon Your people that we may receive Your heart. Your plans and desires are what we long for. We come seeking deeper relationship with You. Purify our hearts that we may have room for Your Spirit to dwell. Reveal to us the great and marvelous things in Your plans. Encourage our souls to delight in Your glory. In all things we will give thanks. In Jesus' name we pray, Amen.

# December 3

*I remember the days of old; I meditate on all thy works; I muse on the works of thy hands.* (Psalm 143:5)

Who you are and what you believe is evidently displayed in the midst of adversity. When feelings of sadness arise, it is often easy to soak in our own self-pity. We find it to be a natural response to replay the events of discord over and over in our head. We tell friends and family about our situation, prompting our sadness to grow into a much bigger issue such as depression, anxiety, fear or anger. Depression is a very common state of emotions. Everyone at some point has experienced feeling sadness, being unhappy, or like your life is about to come crashing down. Depression sets in when these feelings are uncontrolled for a specific period of time. God, in His uniqueness, knew the trials of life would ignite such feelings of despair and provides a way of escape from the trap of deteriorating emotions. Instead of giving constant energy into the situations, we have to determine the truth of the matter. The reality is, maybe bad things have happened to us that warrant such feelings, but they shouldn't cause us to be paralyzed. It should be a constant prayer for God to renew our minds. In renewing our mind, we must remember the God we serve and mediate (mutter- speak; make a sound with one's voice) on His Word. Speaking His Word will cause our mind to shift off the issue and onto the promise. Reflecting on the many times He has delivered us before will allow us to maintain joy. When you experience life there will be periods of emotional pain. Once you get to the other side, you can often look back and say, "Lord, that wasn't that hard." This should be the stance at the onset of the problem. When reality states issues have arose, truth will show us that being shielded under the shadow of the Almighty enables our thoughts to be absorbed in the power of His strength. Then we are able to fully cast our cares at His feet, allowing Him to build in us the character He predestined. Situations are not the issue, as they are guaranteed in life; our ability to choose the truth (God) or the lie (devil) will determine how we allow our emotions to be shifted.

**Remember who you are!**

**Finally, brothers and sisters, whatever is true, whatever is noble, whatever is right, whatever is pure, whatever is lovely, whatever is admirable—if anything is excellent or praiseworthy—think about such things. (Philippians 4:8)**

**Prayer:** Lord, You are Good and Your mercy endureth forever. We know depression is not one of the promises You have given to Your children. We bind up all negative thoughts, to include feelings of giving up. Suicide will not be an option in the kingdom of Your people. Cause your people to be glad and to think about the goodness of Your glory. Step down in every situation and provide a way of escape. Remove thoughts of despair and replace them with Your loving kindness. In all things, let us think about the truth of who we are in Christ Jesus. You have called us to be conquerors and to have victory in all aspects of life. Send Your angels to serve the needs of Your people. We love you, in Jesus' name we pray, Amen.

**If anyone is dealing with depression please seek help. I am also available for prayer. Jesus is a healer!!!**

# December 4

*He that hath no rule over his own spirit is like a city that is broken down, and without walls.* (Proverbs 25:28)

Self-control is very important to God, as it is listed as one of the fruits of the Spirit. This fruit is among the eight others that indicate we are being led by the Holy Spirit, which is the only way to please God. These attributes set us apart from those who choose to follow after the lust of the flesh and are contrary to the Will of God. It is my guess, as one striving after Christ, we do not want anything to hinder our relationship. We often try to put labels on the different types of sin where we consider one to carry more weight than the other. When God looks at sin (breaking His law), He considers them all to be disobedience. Our attitude speaks volumes to those around us. When we render anything less than the heart of God, we must repent and seek God for help. Self-control pertains to all aspects of our life. It should be our prayer every day for the Holy Spirit to help us. The decision to allow our flesh to be crucified is a choice we make daily. God will send help and reason in all circumstances. It's our job to choose either to walk in our flesh or His Spirit. There's power in self control. If we are really saved, which I know we are; the Holy Spirit will convict us and show us the areas of our life where we need to apply self-control. God is so awesome in the wisdom that He bestows. He is actually warning us against our own destruction. "Do they not provoke themselves to the confusion of their own faces?" (Jeremiah 7:19b) You see, without self-control we leave ourselves open for destruction to set in. When we say no to the Spirit, we are saying, "God I don't need you to cover me, I can handle life on my own," which is not the case, being that God knows all, it is of benefit for us to allow Him to be in control.

**Who controls you?**

Prayer: God, You are everything. We are in complete awe of You. Thank You for considering Your servants this day. This is the day that the Lord has made, let us rejoice and be glad in it. Forgive us for all acts of unrighteousness where we have failed to control ourselves. Lord, we come before You, asking, seeking, knocking, and desiring a better way. Touch every area of our lives and allow self-control to become our nature. Let us be so in tune with Your Spirit that we ask You before we do anything. Pour out Your spirit in our minds, hearts, and attitudes. Release us from the need to be right and cause us to desire to be righteous. Where man has caused anger, let us return love. Where there is hurt, let us return peace. As far as it depends on us, let us seek to live at peace with everyone in this earth. Restore families and relationships to bring glory to Your name. Let us be the peculiar people you have ordained for such as time as this. In everything that we do, we are pleading for Your Spirit to consume us. Hallelujah Yahweh! It is with great privilege that we surrender our being to You. In Jesus' name we pray, Amen.

# December 5

*Seek ye the LORD while he may be found, call ye upon him while he is near.* (Isaiah 55:6)

The Bible tells us several times to SEEK the Lord. The word seek has a very profound meaning. It implies more than a one-time event of searching for a specific thing. Seek means to look in order to find, keep trying to obtain, and inquire or search carefully. It is important to seek in order to find the Lord because of the many difficulties we will face in life. We are constantly aiming to hear from God in order to prepare us for the journey ahead. When you consider a battle during war, the opponents do not wait until they are in the midst of combat to seek direction on how to engage the enemy. They have been trained and given instruction before they even make it to the battlefield. They often conduct exercises (simulated battles) to prepare for real enemy engagement. This has to be an God-inspired practice, as He longs for us to be in constant aim of His preparation. When we know God as our Lord, we are able to sit before Him in daily devotion, receiving our training. This training prepares us for the many obstacles of life. They enable us to walk in the midst of the flood on high water. When unimaginable turmoil sets in, God's peace will be our response. This behavior does not exist on it's own. It comes from searching for God, who promised to be near for all who call upon His name. Preparation allows us to build a reliance and loving relationship with God. Now, in the middle of circumstances, when we call upon His name we know He is near; ready to help us.

**These things add up. Every one of us needs to pray; when all hell breaks loose and the dam bursts we'll be on high ground, untouched. (Psalm 32:6 MSG)**

**Be Prepared!**

Prayer: Great God, You reign with all power in Your hands. It is with great honor that we come before Your throne of grace, seeking You in prayer. Lord, let this be the constant desire of our heart to seek after You. Let us aim at hearing from You daily. A day out of touch with You is far too long. Life without You will only bring about our demise. This we know is not Your plan for Your people. We thank You that Your thoughts are of peace for us and not of evil, You have crafted a perfect way of living for us. Give us Your plans as we keep striving towards You. Our desire is to please You. Transform our minds not to consider our own way, but in all our ways to acknowledge You. Grateful are we to know You have called us to be Your own. Lead us through the path of righteousness for Your name's sake. All glory and honor belong to you, In Jesus' name we pray, Amen.

# December 6

*According as he hath chosen us in him before the foundation of the world, that we should be holy and without blame before him in love.* (Ephesians 1:4)

When we consider our day's journey, it is imperative to remember the promise. God promised that we are were whole and holy and without blame in His sight. The image others paint of us to include our own harsh self-criticism does not compare with God's vision of His people. In the planning process of the creation of earth and its beings, God crafted us in His love. He has poured upon us His divine nature and we are able to walk free from negative thoughts about who we are and what we are to Him. Man's view of us cannot begin to validate the greatness that God has put on the inside of us. First we were created in love to be the focal point of God's love. Then we were crafted with every good and perfect gift needed to enjoy life immensely. God's love is free and it draws us near to His being. It encompasses the purity of His nature as we see His gifts of mercy and grace bestowed upon us daily. It is not enough to assume we are great, we have to know- be convinced it is in our DNA. We were created with the power of the Almighty's hand. There are no bounds to the things we can accomplish and do in this earth. Limits don't exist in the plans God has for His children. We were created to do the extraordinary. If the things we are doing are not blowing our mind, it may be time to seek God for the supernatural. When God is in a thing, our minds are unable to fathom how He is accomplishing such great tasks. Everything He does is marvelous (Miraculous; supernatural). It's NOW time for us to be who God called us to be, and nothing less.. greatness awaits.

**So thank God for his marvelous love, for his miracle mercy to the children he loves. He poured great draughts of water down parched throats; the starved and hungry got plenty to eat. (Psalm 107:9)**

**Be You!**

Prayer: God of the earth, we bow down and worship You. You are excellent. Lord, show us who we are in Your Son Jesus Christ. Give us the spirit of wisdom and revelation to know You as our Lord. Draw us close to You. We desire a intimate relationship with our Creator. In love, you created Your people that we should know You as our friend. Renew relationships today. Cause us to find freedom in communion with You. Open our hearts to receive the many blessings You have stored for us in heaven. Before the foundation of the earth was formed You knew us. Ignite Your love on the inside of us, let us receive You with our hands stretched toward heaven. We are who You said we are, we are Your children, filled with Your power to subdue the earth. With all praise we glorify Your name. In Jesus' name we pray, Amen.

# December 7

*And Joshua said, Alas, O Lord God, wherefore hast thou at all brought this people over Jordan, to deliver us into the hand of the Amorites, to destroy us? would to God we had been content, and dwelt on the other side Jordan!* (Joshua 7:7)

A life filled with God's purpose must be coupled with a life of obedience. God gives clear concise direction of how to live life in abundance. Let's remove from our conscious library the image of abundance being only material gain. God's idea of abundance goes far beyond what money can buy. Our peace of mind, power to destroy the plans of the enemy, strength to endure the trials of life, and how to encourage others to follow Christ are among the ways God wants to pour into our lives until it overflows. When walking with God, we should always be in a constant state of maturing. With each passing day, our faith has the opportunity to be expanded. Our knowledge goes a little deeper and our wisdom contains more virtue. The unfamiliar usually creates barricades, hindering our ability to move forward. Opposition renders fear and can develop paralyzing reactions to our growth. God's promises are easy to accept. We always want them to appear out of thin air, not knowing there is a process that must first take place in order to receive them. On the journey to the promised land, we will face contention. During these times it is important not to underestimate God. His plans are well thought out, error-proof and guaranteed to produce favorable outcomes. During conflict, it always seems more opportune to wish things back the way they used to be, not knowing our past could hinder us or even destroy the path God has prepared for us. We should never fear challenge or hardships. It is in the midst of such things where the power of God is revealed. Whenever struggles arise, ask God "How can I grow from this and bring You glory," then simply proceed forward.

**Everything God does has purpose!**

Prayer: Lord God Almighty, our love for You goes beyond the depths of the sea. We love You with an everlasting love, for Your greatness is revealed to us day by day. Lord, remove fear, confusion, and disappointment from among Your people. When obstacles arise, let our stance be to fall on our knees and seek Your face. Understanding belongs to You, grant us with overflowing wisdom to endure every obstacle in life. Fear will not reside in us. Power and strength belongs to those who love You. Replace anxiety with patience and trust in Your Word. Let our lips boldly speak Your promises of righteous living. Circumstances will not hinder us any longer from getting to the promises You have prepared for Your people. Everyone of Your children will receive every spiritual blessings in heavenly places in Christ. Let Your glory go before us. Be a lamp unto our feet and a light unto our path. We will follow You forward. With all honor and praise we say thank You, in Jesus' name we pray, Amen.

# December 8

*Heal me O LORD, and I shall be healed, save me, and I shall be saved; for thou art my praise.* (Jeremiah 17:14)

Truth be told, all power belongs to God. He renders the time when we are to be born and has prepared for the time for us to meet Him again. These facts should help us in our understanding of who God is to us individually. He is the one who considers our circumstances and says no, that's too much, or they can endure a little more in order for my purification process to prevail. God determines what we can handle and how we should develop in the life He has graciously given to us. Our life is a gift from above, manufactured to exhibit the gratitude of the one who created us. Whatever hand we have been dealt in life can be lived joyfully in the presence of God. When we consider the path of our life, we have to consider the thought and planning that has already taken place in the heavenly realm concerning us. Every choice, before it presents itself in our lives, has been considered by our Father. As we trust in, and rely on Him, we can appreciate Him as our approving official. We may think we have control of our lives because we live under the grace of free will, but it is God who renders the results based on the choices we make. It is of great benefit to us if we admire Him for being our foundation. Allowing God to be God gives us peace, as we know everything He does is brilliant. When we surrender to His plans and adhere to His commands, we have confidence in our future and are able to celebrate God during every phase of our life.

**Who is God to you?**

Prayer: Lord, You are good and Your mercy endures forever. Look down from heaven and search the hearts of Your people. Show us the ways of righteousness. We thank you that our job is easy, as all power belongs to You. Help us to walk in our purpose, following Your every command. We will extol You with great exaltation. We celebrate You today for being our joy, peace, foundation, our everything. We surrender to the plans You desire for us as Your children. Prepare us for life in order for Your plans to go forth. Move us out of the way. Our hearts are set on pleasing You. It is with great honor that we think about Your goodness and praise You, in Jesus' name we pray, Amen.

# December 9

*And he said unto me, Son of man, stand upon thy feet, and I will speak unto thee. And the spirit entered into me when he spake unto me, and set me upon my feet,* ***that I heard*** *him that spake unto me.* (Ezekiel 2:1-2)

God spoke to Ezekiel while he, along with the children of Israel, were in exile. He came to Ezekiel in a vision during a time when the people thought God had forgotten about them. It was a time of severe discomfort. In this vision, Ezekiel is given His purpose to be God's voice to the children of Israel. When the Lord appeared, Ezekiel is consumed by God's splendor and falls to his face in reverence or fear, the Bible doesn't say. Then the Lord speaks to him, calling him Son of man. This shows us the connection Ezekiel had with the Lord. God trusted Him enough to call Him into His presence to give him His purpose. He instructs Him to stand on His feet. Surely, God could have spoken to him with his face to the ground, but He wanted all of His attention. He needed him to be in position to receive his assignment. When we stand, we are able to focus our attention. It's far easier to get distracted sitting down or laying on the ground. He didn't need anything hindering what He was about to say. The Spirit of God then entered Ezekiel and he was able to hear the Lord speak. The Spirit is so significant in our ability to operate and function in God. The Spirit is the only one who knows the deep things of God. "Even so the things of God ***knoweth no man***, but the Spirit of God" (1 Corinthians 2:11b). The Spirit had to enter into Ezekiel to reveal the things of God. We as humans cannot in our own wisdom discern the plans of God. It is by His Spirit alone that we receive truth and revelation. Like Ezekiel, we have to be trustworthy. Can God trust you with His purpose? Surely we all have a divine purpose and all fall into God's great plan. The dividing poll comes when it's time for God to send us out on assignment. Does He constantly have to save you from yourself, or are you ready to receive the plan and carry them out with a boldness for His kingdom? See, the plan is ready for God's people, it's us who often hold up the process. If we look around, time is not standing still. We must exhibit a desire to walk in our purpose. God will not force Himself upon us. He will go where He is welcomed. I want to be empty when Christ returns, knowing that I accomplished everything God sent me to the earth to fulfill. This may sound like a cliché, but it is possible to go before God DAILY and ask how we can serve Him.

**Will you serve Me?**

Prayer: Our Father which art in heaven, Hallowed be thy name. Thy kingdom come. Thy will be done in earth, as it is in heaven. Give us this day our daily bread. And forgive us our debts, as we forgive our debtors. And lead us not into temptation, but deliver us from evil: For thine is the kingdom, and the power and the glory forever, Amen.

# December 10

*God is in the midst of her; she shall not be moved: God shall help her* ***and that right early.*** (Psalm 46:5)

God hears the cry of the humble and the heartbreak of the righteous. Be assured there is nothing you will ever endure that God is not aware of. In His awareness, He sustains us with the strength of life. He provides for each and every one of our needs. What then causes so much despair especially among His children who are called into close fellowship with Him? The mere fact of unbelief causes our focus to shift off of the power of God. He sits in heaven with His hand stretched out, saying, "**I AM** here to help you." Believing in His power is a required stance that we as Christians must take. It is especially important for us to secure our foundation in Christ in order to prepare for the storms of life. In one instant everything could be going well, then in a blink of the eye, turmoil can erupt in our lives. When this occurs we are confident to see God's promises of being our refuge and strong tower manifest. It feels good to shout glory during Sunday service when the preacher prompts us to thank God for being El Shaddai (Lord God Almighty; All-sufficient one), but what about in the midst of the storm when you can't pay your bills, when your marriage brings more destruction than joy, or your health is failing, or when depression sets in. Who do you call? Often we as humans find it easy to wallow in our own self-pity. This is not the way for the saints of God. He has commanded us to fear not, and to know Him as our Very Present Help in trouble. God stands in the midst of EVERYTHING we go through, looking to see if we are going to sink or swim. We sink when we take our eyes off of Christ. We swim when we look adversity in the face and declare God is in control, He is my Help, when I call upon Him He will answer.

**It's time to swim!**

Prayer: Lord God Almighty, *"There is a river, the streams whereof shall make glad the city of God, the holy place of the tabernacles of the Most High" (Psalm 46:4).* This place, O Lord is where we will dwell with You forever. Every aspect of our lives are sustained in You. You are the ruler of this earth, all power belongs to You. Thank You for setting our pathway straight. There is no confusion in our lives. Remove all obstacles as we trust and rely on You. Ignite the fire You have placed on the inside of us to walk in our purpose. Life will not cause us to stray from You. Hurt, pain, despair, and heartache, will not deter us from our purpose in You. Everyone of Your children will be secure in Christ Jesus, knowing who they are in You. We look to you as our very present help in trouble. When the world feels likes its caving in, we will trust You. When the odds are stacked against us, we will declare, "Yea, though I walk through the valley of the shadow of death I WILL FEAR NO EVIL" (Psalm 23:4). God, You reign and for that we shout Glory! All is well with the saints of God. Look down from heaven and pour out Your love. We lift up our hearts in total adoration to You. We bless You, in Jesus' name we pray, Amen.

# December 11

*Thou shalt not be afraid for the terror by night; nor the arrow that flieth by day; Nor for the pestilence that walketh in darkness; nor for the destruction that wasteth at noonday.* (Psalm 91:5-6)

The Bible makes it very clear of the enemy's presence in the earth. If you haven't figured it out by now, if you're living for Christ you are a threat to the kingdom of darkness. Satan searches the earth, looking for people to destroy. he has devised plans, tricks, and lies to confuse God's people. It is his job to cause confusion and lead people in disarray. The difference between the enemy and God is the enemy's only power comes from what we relinquish to him. The truth is, we have power over the enemy. "I have given you authority to trample on snakes and scorpions and to overcome all the power of the enemy; nothing will harm you" (Luke 10:19). God is the ruler of the universe and has power over everything. He has promised to keep us under the shadow of His wings, in His presence, where nothing can harm us. The way to a life of protection from the tricks of the enemy is to dwell in the secret place of the Most High. You can't outsmart the plans of the enemy without the wisdom of God. What the devil presents to us looks good, feels good, and is often not revealed as evil until it is far too late. Having daily fellowship with God reveals the secret plans of the enemy and allows us to grow in the knowledge of who we are in Christ. Knowledge is half the battle. Many Christians are living defeated lives due to a lack of knowledge. If we are unaware of the power we posses in God, or fail to believe, trust in, and rely on His power, we will continue to be defeated. That's not God's plan for any of His children. Our faith should be so evident that the enemy flees from us in terror, knowing God is our weapon. We should be so girded in the truth of God's Word that the tricks of the enemy are defeated by our faith every time. Our concern should not be with the plans of the enemy, but with the plans of God. Fear and confusion are not from God. It is His desire to enable us for the trials of life as our refuge and protection. He needs us to have so much trust in Him that nothing should cause our faith to waiver.

## There's no fear in God!

Prayer: Lord, we honor You as King of our lives. We thank You for allowing us to live this day. God, we understand the tricks of the enemy are ever present in this world. It is his desire to destroy all that you have created. This day we stand against the plans of the enemy over our lives and the lives of our loved ones. We declare in the name of Jesus that every plan of the enemy will be revealed and destroyed. Give us a mind to discern between good and evil. Gird us in your Word, that we know who we are in Christ Jesus. Remove every ounce of doubt and fear, replace it with true assurance that You fight on our behalf. Help us to mature in our faith, knowing the many things You have proven in our lives already. As the obstacles seem more advanced, give us more grace to endure the journey. Lord, in You we shall fear nothing in this earth. We are forever grateful for the long life full of mercy that you haven given each of Your children who love You. It is with great pleasure that we bless Your holy name, in Jesus' name we pray it is so, Amen.

**The Lord *is* my light and my salvation; Whom shall I fear? The Lord *is* the strength of my life, Of whom shall I be afraid? (Psalm 27:1)**

# December 12

*For I earnestly protested unto your fathers in the day that I brought them up out of the land of Egypt, even unto this day, rising early and protesting, saying,* ***Obey*** *my voice.* (Jeremiah 11:7)

Often, the biggest struggles in our lives are birthed from small situations we didn't tend to. We refused the warning signs and brushed the problems off as minor, when in reality, had we dealt with the minor issues, our bigger issues wouldn't have flourished. God makes it simple when He created the earth and called the people of Israel, He said, "Obey my voice, you will be mine and I will be yours." How awesome is that, to have God as your own. This is the covenant God so thoughtfully prepared for those who obey His voice. Obedience is a very important attribute of our Christian life. Obedience pleases God as it shows Him how we reverence Him above our own desires. God doesn't require us to obey Him as an act of harsh authority, but totally out of love. He is actually saving us from ourselves. We alone cannot produce the righteousness that God desires. By obedience, we are able to be guided by the Holy Spirit every single day of our lives. God has prepared every day for each of His children. If we seek His face daily, we will receive everything for the days journey. A relationship with God includes commitment, diligence, and consistency. God uses many facets to reach His people, including books, preachers, prophets, testimony, and the list goes on. He is overly concerned with us and desires for us to walk in holy communion. Not so He can control our lives, but that we may have eternal life. The warnings are ever present in this world of the things to come to those who disregard His voice. We don't want to be on the wrong side of the fence when Jesus returns. We want to be ready, it should be our nature to adhere to God. In doing so, we enjoy great relationship, fully satisfying with our Friend, Father, Lord and Savior, our God.

**God wants the best for You!**

Prayer: Lord, You are good and Your mercies endure forever.

There is none like You in all the earth. What a privilege to be called into Your kingdom. Lord, we cry out to You this day. Order our steps in Your Word. Let not iniquity have dominion over us. Help us be doers of Your Word and not only hearers, deceiving ourselves. As Your sheep, help us to know Your voice. Convict our spirit when we stray away from You. A day out of Your presence is far too long. Lord, some people have lost communication with You, or may not know how to come before You. Teach us this day how to love to be in Your presence. Give us the words to pray. Teach us how to have unrestricted fellowship with You. Cause us to take the limits off the time we spend with You. Let our worship be authentic. When we come into Your place of holiness, remove every ounce of our flesh and cleans our minds so we can focus totally on You. We surrender our will to You this day. We long to fall in love with You daily. God, there are no boundaries to Your glory, your splendor cannot be contained. God, we worship You in Spirit and truth. Have Your way in our lives. We honor You, in the name of Jesus we do pray, Amen, Amen, Amen.

# December 13

*Trust in him at all times, you people; pour out your hearts to him, for God is our refuge.* (Psalm 62:8)

Trust is assured, reliance on something and total dependence on something. The Bible instructs us to trust ***in*** God at ALL times. The breakdown in our communion with God becomes evident when our trust (total dependence) shifts. Our human minds find it easy to rely on God when things are going our way, when our emotions are what we call stable. God doesn't think or operate in the way we do. When we have a kingdom mindset, we must take on a new way of operating. Our lives are now in line with His predestined plan. God requires our trust (total dependence) to lead us through life's many obstacles. Trust is not an attribute we can turn on and off based on our current circumstances. It is a vital necessity, required for an effective life with Christ. God knows all, has considered all, and wants to reveal all that we need to obtain full satisfaction in our true identity in Christ. Trust is an action that must be exercised. He not only gives us the opportunity to trust (assured reliance) in His unfailing Word, He says pour out your heart to Me. This invitation is for our benefit. He understands every aspect of life, the good and the bad. He allows us to come into His presence and present our concerns as an avenue of release. We are able to express our hurt, pain, expectation, joy, and our entire being to the Master of the universe, knowing He cares for us and will provide whatever we need in that moment. It is not enough to trust Him when things go according to our comfort level. It is a command to trust ***in*** Him at ALL times in order to receive full enjoyment in the plans He created us for.

**Will you trust Him?**

Prayer: God of great mercy, we bow down in Your presence. We honor You this day for Your greatness. All power belongs to You. We long to be where You are. This day we ask for a new mindset, a kingdom mindset. Show us how to trust You when things don't go our way. Enable us to rely on You when everything within us is pulling us in the opposite direction. Let the communication with You be the very thing we desire throughout our day. You are the one who knows our purpose. We thank You for Your plan to prosper us and that you have an expected end for us. Give us hope this day to trust in Your unfailing love. As we pour out our hearts, command Your angels to be on post in every area of our lives. We submit our relationships, careers, family, finances, health, mind and soul to You; do what you see fit. Mature us to our rightful place in Your kingdom. Thank You for being our Refuge, Redeemer, Provider, Healer and very present help in trouble. We know in You we cannot be shaken. It is with great honor and praise that we bless you, in Jesus' name we pray, Amen

# December 14

*For there are three that bear record in heaven, the Father, the Word, and the Holy Ghost: and these three are one.* (1 John 5:7)

One of the most important aspects in our relationship with God is our ability to believe. Our relationship starts with us first believing that He is who the Word proclaims Him to be. Not only believing in God, the Creator, but also in His Son Jesus and the comforter the Holy Ghost. The three persons known as the Trinity are the very foundation of our faith. Our faith causes us to believe in the unseen, trust the unimaginable, and rely on testimony of our forefathers. Let's face it, with everything going on in the world, if we are not firmly grounded in faith we could easily have doubt in God. What we see with the natural eye can take our focus off of the truth of who God is. The Spirit is truth. The Spirit is the one who searches the heart of God and reveals Him to us. Belief requires us to deny ourselves. We can't try to make sense of the nature of God because He is unexplainable. His wisdom far surpasses what our intellect can possibly comprehend. What our belief does is birth total reliance in the power of God.

Believing in the power of God is a choice we as individuals have to make daily. Belief brings about freedom. The Trinity desires a relationship with us in order for us to dwell in our proper position under their safety. When we believe in the power they possess, we are able to truly submit our ways to God, giving Him free reign in our lives. Belief produces a connection with the Son of God. When we believe in the Son of God, we join in agreement with the three who bear witness in heaven. The three who assemble together on behalf of all creation are secure in Their power and nature. They send the Holy Ghost to confirm and validate the things to come and what takes place in heaven. All of these things come from a relationship and believing in who they are. Knowing the truth of who God is and the Power He possess frees us from doubt and lies from the enemy.

**Connect with the Trinity!**

Prayer: God, you are the King of the earth, the lover of our soul. Thank You for allowing us to see another day. Your grace and mercy keeps us and gives us new strength. Lord, we are honored to be called Your children. We ask for forgiveness this day for any ounce of doubt or unbelief. Lord, You see the things we have to endure in the earth and have promised to never leave nor forsake us. Build in us a faith that cannot be broken. Thank You that in Your Kingdom we find fresh anointing, power and liberty. God, you said if we believe in Your Son that we have overcome the world. Help us to subdue it. Let us work in the earth, doing everything You have ordained for us to accomplish. Send Your Spirit to bear witness in the earth of Your greatness. We deny ourselves today and take on Your way of thinking. Transform us this day to be the very thing You have predestined. Let us walk in righteousness all the days of our lives. It is with great honor that we bless You as Lord of our lives. In Jesus' name we pray, Amen.

# December 15

*Praise him for his mighty acts: praise him* ***according to HIS*** *excellent greatness.* (Psalm 150:2)

**Saint**: God, I don't feel like praising You. My life is messed up, I'm hurt and alone. Nothing I try to do ever works out. When I seek your face it seems like you take forever to answer. Life is real, its hard for me to keep a smile on my face when the pressure is weighing me down. I know the Bible says that You will never leave me nor forsake me, but I can't feel You. When I look around at my life, I just feel like giving up.

**God:** I'm sorry you feel this way my child. Just to be clear, I am always near. I never promised you the road would be easy, but what I did promise is that My Spirit would always be with you. If you have breath in your body you have a reason to praise Me. Life is not always what it seems. I have called you to praise me according to My greatness, not according to what your eyes can see. If you really take a look around, your role is easy. It's me that shields you from the grasp of the enemy. I allow a little pressure in your life at times to mold you into my perfect image. If you could only see the many things I have protected you from, your praise would be different. In My kingdom the end is already written and I gave you a glimpse into your future. You know without a shadow of a doubt in Me you reign victorious. If you could take your eyes off of the problems in your life and really praise me according to My greatness, worry, doubt, fear, disappointments, anger, anxiety and pressure wouldn't rule in your life. Instead you would experience My great peace and be totally satisfied in My presence. Praise releases pressure and shifts your energy towards the very thing you were created to be concerned with, and that's Me. So the next time you feel overwhelmed, shout Hallelujah, give thanks for the many things I have done and continue to do in your life and watch the atmosphere change in that very instance.

**Saint**: God, You are so right. You promised there was nothing in this world that could harm me or overwhelm me. When I think about Your greatness, I have nothing to complain about. Lord, please forgive me for ever complaining. Thank you for allowing me to cast my cares upon Your throne, knowing that You care and hear every prayer. Lord, I love You!!

**Prayer:** God, You are amazing. There is nothing in this earth that could compare to Your greatness. Forgive us this day for ever complaining or having doubt or fear. Your Word has promised us a life of hopeful living. In Your Presences is the fullness of joy and at Your right hand are pleasures FOREVER more (Psalm 16:11). There is nothing happening in the earth that You are not aware of. You know our day before we even rise. Help us to mediate on Your Word day and night. Let it build in us a unbreakable trust and dependence on you. Lord, we thank You for all of Your great wisdom and glory. In Jesus' name we pray, Amen.

# December 16

*Do not be afraid, little flock, for your Father has been pleased to give you the kingdom.* (Luke 12:32)

Who likes free gifts? "I do, I do...." God sits in heaven in an array of bountiful possessions, waiting to bestow them upon His children. As a child of God, we have knowledge of the kingdom treasure God has given us access to. Our Father, Ruler of the universe has everything we could ever need. Not only does He possess it, He wants to give it to us. He wants us to know that it's okay to seek Him for all of our needs. We were created for this very reason, we are designed to be dependent upon Him. He didn't design us to worry about anything, but in all things to seek (to look for, to ask, go in search, strive) for His Kingdom. What is His Kingdom, you ask? His Kingdom is His dwelling place where the fullness of joy lives and where at His right hand are pleasures forevermore (Psalm 16:11). His Kingdom possess all manner of need and desire. We are incapable of fulfilling our own purpose in life without Jesus. Every person, regardless of their level of success, will ultimately have to answer to God. Thankfully, He is not far away. He gives open access to those who are willing and obedient; those who long to walk in their destiny. He invites us in to dwell at His table with open arms. Giving us permission to approach, enter, and use the great things in His kingdom.

**Are you ready to receive?**

Prayer: Lord, we honor you. We are so grateful for your grace and mercy. In all your goodness you have included us in Your great plans. We thank You for your great kindness. Keep us close to your unchanging hand. Remove worry and doubt from our minds, renew it with the truth of your Word. Give us all wisdom and spiritual understanding to live a life free in Your presence. We render all glory before You this day. In Jesus' name we pray. Amen.

# December 17

*But I say unto you, That every idle word that men shall speak, they shall give account thereof in the day of judgment. For by thy words thou shalt be justified, and by thy words thou shalt be condemned.* (Matthew 12:36-37)

The Bible teaches us that our words have the power of life and death, and those who love it will eat its fruits (Proverbs 18:21). Our tongue has the potential to damage and to bless, depending on how we use it. This instrument requires a lot of self-control. Our relationship with Christ requires us to examine ourselves and take caution how we use our freedom. The words coming out of our mouths have the potential to either justify our heart's motives or condemn us. We are justified in our speech when we allow the Holy Spirit to work within us, birthing the fruits of the Spirit in which there is no law against it. Being in connection with the Spirit gives you a calm, patient, loving, and humble attitude. When the time comes where you are presented with an opportunity to use your words as a weapon, the spirit of self-control should overpower any negativity and contrary behaviors. I get we are not perfect, but striving for perfection; which means we take every step necessary to walk in the image of God. When we are not in tune with God and His Spirit, we leave room for evil to flow from our lips. We understand the scriptures as it states: out of the abundance of the heart our mouth speaks (Luke 6:45). We must ask ourselves what are we allowing into our heart. Only those things of positive influence should be allowed in the secret chambers of our heart; those things that will draw us closer to God and are of benefit to us. Each day we have to make a conscious effort to guard our spirit and feed it with admirable enhancers that are pleasing to God. When faced in certain situations, our words can shoot off into the atmosphere and remain permanent before we are even conscious of what we said. God is clear when He states we will give account for every idle word we speak.

**Watch over your tongue!**

Prayer: God, we come before your throne with a humble spirit to worship at your feet. We ask that you would keep a watch over our tongue that the words we speak are pleasing in your sight. Keep us from grieving your Spirit with any work that is not pleasing to you. Let us be filled with things that produce righteous fruit. Help us to store our riches in heaven. Where you are is where we desire to be. Keep our tongues from deceiving others and ourselves. Let the words of our lips be uplifting and full of love. By your grace and mercy are we alive and give you thanks. We will praise you according to your greatness. In Jesus' name we pray, Amen.

**As a good man out of the good treasure of his heart brings forth good: and an evil man out of the evil treasure of his heart brings forth evil. For out of the abundance of the heart his mouth speaks. (Luke 6:45)**

# December 18

*The twenty-four elders (the members of the heavenly Sanhedrin) fall prostrate before Him Who is sitting on the throne, and they worship Him Who lives forever and ever; and they throw down their crowns before the throne, crying out, 11 Worthy are You, our Lord and God, to receive the glory and the honor and dominion, for You created all things; by Your will they were [brought into being] and were created.* (Revelation 4:10-11)

How is it that many see the sun, moon and the stars and still refuse to believe there is a God? A God who sits in heaven upon a throne were He is worshiped day and night. The members of His heavenly assembly see the marvelous works of His hands and count it as pure honor to fall down before His face in total worship. They grasp the importance of who He is, What He is, and what He desires to be to each of us. In heaven, they experience every ounce of His bountiful nature and enjoy His presence with reverence. They understand the truth of creation, the fact of God creating all things for His glory. Revelation gives us a strategy of how we are to worship Christ in our daily pursuits. As the twenty-four elders came before God casting their crowns, we too must come before God, humble and rendering our best praise. When we come into His presence, our minds must be clear, we must come with a heart of adoration. Our worship should exude our sole dependence upon His great power. Laying down our entire being in His presence opens our hearts to focus solely on His greatness. Once we push ourselves to the side, we can be filled with His nature allowing His Spirit to control the atmosphere. Everything God requires to build on the inside of us comes through in our worship. Worship shows God we surrender to and accept His love and acknowledge Him as Lord forever and ever.

**Will you worship?**

Prayer: Lord of Heaven, God of the earth, we bow down in total adoration in Your presence. We invite you in our hearts this day as our Father. Overpower our entire being. Be the God in us that we can't be to ourselves. Show us the work of Your hands. Help us to know that it is by Your loving-kindness that we were created. It is by Your will that we exist. We count it as pure joy to esteem your praise. Give us more of You. Help us to worship you in the splendor of Your holiness. God, you desire all the praise and we will give it to you. Thank you for allowing us into Your grace. We honor You with every ounce of our being. In Jesus' name we pray, Amen.

# December 19

*As a son honors his father, and a servant his master. If then I am a Father, where is My honor? And if I am a master, where is the [reverent] fear due Me? Says the Lord of hosts to you, O priest, who despise My name. You say, how and in what way have we despised Your name?* (Malachi 1:6)

The last thing we as believers want to do is grieve the Spirit of God. It is our heart's desire to honor God with our very being. In order to honor God, we must understand the difference in what pleases God and what is contrary to His Will. God looks down from heaven at every action we take. He not only sees our behavior, He understands the motives behind every thought, every word we speak, and then how we carry out our behaviors. In order to give God the proper respect due to Him as our Father we must know Him as our Father. A relationship between a father and a child is one based upon love, respect, and total adoration. Many times, we can see in our natural relationships with our parents that no matter how they make us feel, there is always a level of respect for them. We are apprehensive in the words we speak around them and we strive to please them. God, as the ultimate Father and Master delights in these same things. We can't assume He is pleased with everything we offer. We have to take pleasure in serving God. Everything we give God should be our best. Everything we do for Him should be authentic. There should be nothing on this earth we give more respect to than our Awesome Father. We must constantly do a self-evaluation in our relationship with Christ. Asking these questions, am I giving Him the best that I have to offer? Is He pleased with me? What can I do to better my relationship with Christ? All of these things will help keep us in proper relationship with God. Being conscious of our behavior will open our hearts to hear from Heaven to see how to properly please our Father.

**Do I please You?**

Prayer: God, you are our King, Our Father and Great Redeemer.

We count this day as a blessing. We ask for forgiveness in any area of our lives where you are not in the proper position. Reveal your ways to us; help us to be pleasing in your sight. Convict our spirit when we fall short and we will repent. God, we honor you as the love of our lives it is our duty to worship you and praise you in Spirit and truth. In Jesus' name we pray, Amen.

# December 20

*For a thousand years in thy sight are but as yesterday when it is past, and as a watch in the night.* (Psalm 90:4)

Patience is one of the attributes God requires every believer to obtain. We often lose hope and become discouraged when we have to wait long periods of time for His promises. Let's be honest, waiting isn't fun. We live in a generation where we want the end result before we accomplish the work needed to get things done. This is not the way God operates. Time is not an issue for God. He cannot be limited by the constraints of time, or by anything for that matter. He created time as a boundary for us. We couldn't bear to see everything God has prepared for us all at once. So if you find yourself waiting for specific things in life, be assured God is in control. What seems like days, months, or years are only seconds in the sight of God. What you need, God already has prepared for you, and you will receive it at the appointed time. God's ways are perfect and pleasing. It pleases God to give you the Kingdom of Heaven. Knowing His timing has no limits; I encourage you to wait with a cheerful heart. What we have to understand is God has already completed every day of our lives. He has a storehouse in heaven with our blessings, which we have access to. The fastest way to accept and receive the treasures of heaven is to be obedient to God through prayer, fasting, and reading and studying His Word, then applying it to our lives. God is for us, He and heaven are rooting for us. They are yearning for us to succeed. Be excited about your future, His promises are Yea and Amen!!

**God's timing is Perfect.**

Prayer: God of mercy, God of grace, we bow down in Your presence and say thank you. We honor you this day for being concerned with us. In your timing, you capture every day of our lives. The things we are seeking you for, you already have a set time of manifestation. We have hope in your unfailing love. Encourage your people today to wait upon the Lord as you renew our strength. Help us to have a joyful heart as we stand on your promises. In Jesus' name we pray, Amen.

# December 21

*So likewise ye, when ye shall have done all those things which are commanded you, say, We are unprofitable servants: we have done that which was our duty to do.* (Luke 17:10)

A life fully devoted to God requires self-less service. We are positioned at the feet of the cross in full awareness of our commitment to the commands of God. What He commands us to do, we will accomplish with a heart of adoration. We listen with an attentive ear and move at the request of His holiness. We can not boast in the work that He has called us to this earth to do, after all, it is by His mercy that we are able to enjoy life. A life of committed service in God gives us fulfillment, as we know this is our purpose. God has commanded each of us to live holy and acceptable in His sight. Each of us has a unique purpose and He gives assignments according to His plan for our lives. It shall be with great honor that we esteem Christ in all that we do, and not look for God to reward us for doing those things He created us for. I know this may not sound fun, yet if we look at the nature of God, we will find joy in self-denial. Joy comes from knowing our service in Christ is not in vain. He has promised to bless us beyond our wildest imagination. He requires that we leave the blessing part up to Him, as His ways are perfect and we are incapable of rewarding ourselves in a God-like manner. It brings pleasure to God when we serve with our heart towards Him and not seeking after self-gain (Matthew 6:33).

**It's my duty to serve.**

Prayer: God in Heaven, we come before your throne of grace to give You honor and praise. Bless us this day to seek to do Your will above all else in this earth. Let Your name receive the honor in all that we do and say. Speak to us that we may know Your voice. Remove self-seeking recognition; shift our focus to be on You. Let us walk in purpose, esteeming you in all that we do. In Jesus' name we pray. Amen.

# December 22

*The Lord is my strength and song, and is become my salvation.* (Psalm 118:14)

Remember during recess when it was time to pick teams for kick ball. The captain from each team would seek out the most athletic, strong, and ambitious players. The players they knew had the most potential of leading their team to victory. Life is no different. When faced with many obstacles and daily decisions, we have the opportunity to pick the best defensive/offensive player, and that is our Lord and Savior. He waits on the sidelines to be exalted by our trust in Him. His track record is perfect, being undefeated every time. He is endowed with power, stronger than any force in the heaven and earth. We exist so that His strength can be acclaimed and utilized for our well being.

God never misleads in making us think our lives would be problem free. What He did promise is that He is faithful to perform Mighty deeds in our lives. In the midst of everything we encounter, He stands as our deliverer against all forces of evil and anything that is not like Him. In knowing that He has become our salvation, we have confidence and understanding of His power and greatness. He can only become what we allow Him to be in our lives. If we desire to be fully enthroned in His grace, we must allow ourselves to be controlled by His Spirit. He then becomes everything we need in all situations. Deliverance in every level of our existence.

**God is near!**

Prayer: Lord, we exalt your name in all the earth, no one is greater than you. Your love embodies our heart and gives us a reason to praise. You encourage us by your grace and patience with all mankind. Forgive us this day that we may be free from sin in every area. You have become our salvation; our hope and trust are found in your hands. Show us the true meaning of our existence that we may be all that you designed us to be for your glory. With every breath we will praise you. Thank you for your loving kindness which you give each day. Pour your wisdom upon us like never before, let us be found in the splendor of your glory. We cry out for all of you in abundance. Consume us this day with your love and power. Renew our hearts, build new trust in our being today. Let our hearts be overwhelmed with your greatness. All honor and praise belong to you. In Jesus' name we pray, Amen.

# December 23

*The Lord replied, "My Presence will go with you, and I will give you rest."* (Exodus 33:14)

A shadow is a replica of the original object cast in the background and reflects exactly what the object is doing. God wants us to find rest in His shadow and do what He does. He calls out for us to act like Him and respond like Him as if we were a mere reflection in the mirror. Wherever He desires for us to go, we are assured that He has travelled that route before and has perfected the entire course just so we can end at our destination, which is victory. Be bold and full of excitement, there is nothing that can take God by surprise . He gives clear warning signs and directions on what He requires of His children. Not only does He give us direction, He says follow me, let me lead you and then you can copy what you see me doing. In God's presence He gives you the letter of what He has already accomplished. His Presence goes before us to clear the path, prepare the way, and set all things in motion. Just like a shadow is a mere reflection of the image it is imitating, we are to be under God's shadow. Jesus was in divine connection with the Father; He could not operate apart from God. In all of His doings, He followed the example of what God was showing Him. "I tell you the truth, the Son can do nothing by himself; he can do only what he sees his Father doing, because whatever the Father does the Son also" (John 5:19).

God sets the course then turns around and carries us through what He has already completed to take us to our finished mark. Have you ever thought about why God requires that we trust Him? It's because all of His plans are already completed. We are given the opportunity to share in His glory and gain intimate connection with Him by walking out His plan. He desires to spread His love on us, so we may embrace our divine inheritance. God never intended for us to do anything alone. He is waiting for us to call on Him and walk in our sacred purpose.

**Where you lead I will follow!**

Prayer: God of glory, King of all things, where ever you are is where we long to be. If your glory isn't there God, take the desire away from us. With this gracious time you have given us on this earth to be used for the uplifting of your glory and your magnificent plan, we come before your throne to worship at your feet. With all power and glory in your hands, we bow at your feet. We come that your name may be exalted. The thoughts and the plans that you have for your people go beyond anything we could ever imagine. So we say, thank you for first loving us. Thank you for your time and patience with us all of the days we have fallen short of your glory. Touch our hearts with your Spirit that we may return back to our first love, the original intent that you created us for. Let your favor fall among us. Build our confidence that we may be bold for your kingdom and excited about our life in Christ. This day and forever we give you praise. In Jesus' name we pray, Amen.

# December 24

*Woe is me because of my hurt!* (Jeremiah 10:19)

How do you feel when you turn on the TV and see a dying nation? You see senseless acts of people killing each other. We don't even have to turn on the television to see the destruction in the earth. We can look in our own families and sees lives that are being lived below their full potential. We often encounter many facets of our society where God is not present in the lives of His people. What is our reaction? Is it to laugh at the woman on the reality show who, for a little bit of money, is selling her soul to the world to be laughed at because she never had anyone speak the Word of God into her life. Do we stand idly by and talk about the woman who has multiple children by different men and still no ring. Do we turn our nose up at the man who prances around with jeans tighter than spandex and a switches harder than women. Or do we seek the throne on their behalf and carry the burden they are obviously struggling with as well. God has given us wisdom to know the truth of His Word. By the blood of Jesus we are set free. Free from the lies of this world, free from the sin that try to plague the lives of our generation.

Now is the time to feel the burden of our nation and stand in faith. Go forth into the throne of grace and petition God for those who don't know Him. Those who were never told they were important. Many people who are lost in this world are a product of their environment and misinterpretation of who God truly is, and how much He actually loves them. If people would take the time to show them the magnitude of Christ's love, things would be a lot different. It is our God-given duty to intercede for those who don't know Christ, who have fallen away from Him and desire more of Him. We have to take a stand and truly feel the pain of this nation and encourage them in the Lord. The nations are depending on us to show them the God we proclaim. It isn't enough to be satisfied with self-growth in the Lord. God is pleased with us going deeper in Him, but He requires that we reach back and bring along everyone in our path to know the truth of His word. God created

His people to live in Him. In our own being, we are not living to merely exist. “O' Lord, I know that the way of man is not in himself: it is not in man that walked to direct his steps” ( Jeremiah 10:23). We don't possess the knowledge to fully grasp all of the concepts of life without God. In God alone, are we able to walk in true diligence and freedom. He desires this for every person walking this earth. Expand your heart and lift up the nation, that all may know Christ, adore Him and have opportunity to receive Him.

**I am my brothers keeper!**

Prayer: God, We come that Your name may be glorified in all the earth. We pray for every stronghold to be lifted off of Your children. Deliver the alcoholic, release the abused, heal the hurt, and renew the weak. We call all the saints to join together in prayer to lift up all things that are not pleasing in Your sight. God, we will pray for those who don't know You. Every need is supplied in Jesus’ name. Your people will not have to turn to drugs or violence to receive attention or to numb pain, but in You they will receive total freedom and deliverance. They will live a life full of peace and happiness according to Your perfect plan. The plans of the enemy will not overpower the love that You have for them. We encourage Your people this day to chose life and walk in Your grace. By our faith, we believe You will change the hearts of Your people and this nation will walk in love. Your name is glorious. In Jesus’ name we pray, Amen.

# December 25

*But the Lord is faithful, and He will strengthen you and protect you from the evil one.* (2 Thessalonians 2:3)

The Lord has a protection around us. As we journey through life, we will encounter those who don't adhere to the commands of God to shun all evil. They will try to cause us harm, either in words or by actions. It is inevitable for us to encounter some type of harsh treatment. At times it may even come from those close to us, and even fellow believers. In those hard times we are able to lean on God. Our trust in His faithfulness will encourage our hearts to pray for those who deliberately try to harm us. God commands that we display His principles in every situation. No matter how difficult it may be, we are to act like Christ in favorable and unfavorable times. There is no excuse for us to display anything less than the love of Christ through our behavior. This may not be an easy task, for some of us it may be a natural reaction to defend ourselves when we have been wronged. Notice it is a natural reaction, not a spiritual one, and we aim to allow God's Spirit to work through us at all times. It is very beneficial for us to rely on God's Spiritual characteristics to empower us to overcome all of the evil in this world. The key is we have to exemplify Christ at all times. Our reactions must be controlled in order to show how Christ resides in us. The reason we are able to react Christ-like is based on our trust in God as our protector and shield His promised Word. When people do harsh and hurtful things to us, we ought to pray for God's mercy, knowing that God is just and protects His children.

**And I also say to you that you are Peter, and on this rock I will build My church, and the gates of Hades shall not prevail against it. (Matthew 16:18)**

**Come away from your emotions!**

Prayer: Lord, this is Your day of glory. Filled with Your grace and mercy, we come before Your throne to say thank You for all

You have done and continue to do for Your beloved children. Encourage Your people to continue on in faith with our eyes and hearts focused on Your principles. Let Your glory be exalted in this earth. As Your obedient vessels, help us to have self-control in all situations. When evil tries to come against us, we know You will stand in as our shield and protection. Renew our minds to see the power of the enemy over those who don't believe in you, and encourage us to stand in the gap for people who don't know You. In all things we acknowledge you as King, in Jesus' name we pray, Amen.

# December 26

*I want to know Christ—yes, to know the power of his resurrection and participation in his sufferings, becoming like him in his death, [11] and so, somehow, attaining to the resurrection from the dead.* (Philippians 3:10-11)

Paul desired Christ himself. He did not seek after the rituals of religion or want a facade of Christianity; he longed to experience Christ for Himself. Paul knew the power associated with Christ from the Kingdom of Heaven, and he longed to be used by God. Not only to be used by God, but to partake in the enjoyment given in allowing God to reveal Himself. As ambassadors for Christ, we have access to all of our inheritance in the Kingdom of heaven. We are able to experience the transformation of our earthly being into the purpose for which God created us and operate as spiritual creatures. We are able to exalt His name in the earth in attempts to draw all men to Christ, that they may accept their inheritance as well. Not only did Paul want to know Christ, he was willing to go through everything Christ went through just to experience the glory of God. He was not moved by the idea of suffering or the ridicule he endured as a servant. Whatever the cost, He desired Christ, as he knew the satisfaction he would obtain through being in Christ forever. This testimony of Christ's life gave Paul insight into the magnificence of God's awesome power. The short years we have on earth are but a testament of God's glory. What a joy to be used by an extraordinary ruler for the uplifting of His Kingdom. In our existence and obedience to God's control, we are able to experience Christ and share in His glory. Jesus knew who He was in God and trusted God's plan. We too know the power of God. Although we may not know the exact outcome of how God will operate His perfect plan in our lives, we have hope and security in knowing our outcome is victorious. We are promised a great future in Christ.

**I owe You my life!**

Prayer: God our Father, which art in Heaven, we exalt You. We love You, thank you for first loving us. There is great joy in being able to experience your awesome power. Lord, this day we lay down our will for Your perfect plan in our lives. God, we ask for the opportunity to be used by You as your servants to bring glory to Your name. In all the earth, Your name will be exalted. Give us a heart to seek after You, transform our thinking to know and love Your commands. Ignite in us the desires that You have had for us since the beginning of creation. Show us Your plan and strategy for godly living, so we don't miss anything You have ordained for us. Just to be where You are is what we desire. No matter if we have to experience suffering in order to be like You, we take the full armor of Your being and walk in faith. Knowing that You are in control of our being, we trust You will keep us safe from harm. Reveal Yourself to us in a new way, expand our faith, renew our strength and expose us to Your glory. God, we honor You. It is a pure pleasure to be in Christ. In Jesus' name we pray, Amen.

# December 27

*If ye then being evil, know how to give good gifts unto your children; how much more shall your heavenly Father give the Holy Spirit to them that ask Him?* (Luke 11:13)

We have the ability to do great works here on earth. Kind-hearted people tend to go out of their way to care for others, especially those they love. Jesus correlates our relationship with God to a parent with a child. He shows us how man is imperfect in his ways, yet we are able to still give good gifts to those we love. God, being All-Powerful and loving, has a greater responsibility to give to those who ask as well. We don't ask God for things just so we can hear ourselves speak, because we know that God knows what we need before we ask. We are challenged to be persistent in our request in order to build our reliance on the Father. It enables us to build our communication with Him and experience the manifestation of His glory as HE provides for us according to our faith. When we are in need, we have to be persistent and ask God for His provision for our situation; having the mindset to know our God will answer and give to His children. This is confirmation of His characteristics. God is capable of doing anything we could possibly think we have a need for. He requires us to pray and seek Him in order to build our dependence on the Holy Spirit. The Holy Spirit is available to supply all of our needs. All we have to do is ask, and God is faithful to give us more of Himself in the attributes flowing through His Spirit. We are promised a line of necessities from our Father. The Holy Spirit is our guide, our peace, and our comforter. Everything we require is given to us in God. He is faithful and hears the request of His servants. He sends His Spirit to turn our desires into His plans. Retroactively, what we are asking God for is really already what he planned for us. He was waiting on us to tune into our citizenship in His kingdom and walk in our inheritance.

**Everything you need, God has!**

Prayer: Sing to the Lord a new song; sing to the Lord, all the earth. Sing to the Lord, praise His name; proclaim His salvation day after day. Declare His glory among the nations, His marvelous deeds among all peoples. For great is the Lord and most worthy of praise; he is to be feared above all God's. For all the gods of the nations are idols, but the Lord made the heavens. Splendor and majesty are before him; strength and glory are in his sanctuary. Ascribe to the Lord, all you families of nations, ascribe to the Lord glory and strength. Ascribe to the Lord the glory due his name; bring an offering and come into his courts. Worship the Lord in the splendor of his holiness; tremble before him, all the earth. Say among the nations, "The Lord reigns." The world is firmly established, it cannot be moved; he will judge the peoples with equity. Let the heavens rejoice, let the earth be glad; let the sea resound, and all that is in it. Let the fields be jubilant, and everything in them; let all the trees of the forest sing for joy. Let all creation rejoice before the Lord, for he comes, he comes to judge the earth. He will judge the world in righteousness and the peoples in his faithfulness. (Psalm 96)

# December 28

*Ascribe to the Lord the glory due His name; bring an offering and come before Him. Worship the Lord in the splendor of His holiness.* (1 Chronicles 16:29)

When we come before the Lord to worship it should be an act of honor. We should be ecstatic to come into God's presence with a joyful praise. It is an opportunity to think of the great and mighty works of His Kingdom. It gives us the ability to show God that we are truly grateful for all that He is, and all that He provides for us. Worship can take place in any moment, at any place. It doesn't have to be in a church atmosphere. When we worship God, we are giving back to God what He has so graciously given to us. Worship allows us to praise God according to His splendor. Praise requires that we meditate on the holiness of God. All of His glory which allows us to see each day. We are able to think about the many times God has been our fortress. Our praise represents our heart's acknowledgment of how much we truly love God. To think about the goodness of God should prompt our spirit to rejoice. Everything associated with God deserves our praise. It is by His grace alone that we are able to be in connection with such majesty. He seeks those who will respond to His love by giving themselves over to Him in worship. Worship is coming before the Lord with our hearts lifted to Him bare and open, requiring His Spirit to take control and bring us into His presence. In God's presence there is strength and joy. Every need we have, and every desire are in the dwelling place of the Most High. He longs that we come to Him and give the proper appreciation due to His name. He does not ask us to worship Him according to our standards or how we feel. We are to worship Him in the splendor of His holiness, according to who He is. This requires that we lay down our emotions and our human thought processes and free ourselves to think about His holiness, His word, His promises, and all that He has done and continues to do. When we are in a place of total surrender to God, we have no other choice but to be filled with His Spirit and experience His loving nature

**Your worship must engage your spirit in the pursuit of truth. That's the kind of people the Father is out looking for: those who are simply and honestly themselves before him in their worship. God is sheer being itself—Spirit. Those who worship him must do it out of their very being, their spirits, their true selves, in adoration. (John 4:23-24 MSG)**

**Worship is a gift!**

Prayer: God, we love you. We thank you for first loving us and choosing us to be your children. Father, this day we pray that our worship will be for real. Clear our minds and our conscience, let us put every thought on the back burner and come into Your presence with a clear mind, waiting in expectation for Your Spirit to overpower us. Renew our minds, create in us a clean heart that our worship may bring glory to Your name. Let us praise according to Your holiness. Every need is met and every heart is made whole in Your dwelling place. Teach Your people how to worship, let our worship be accepted in Your sight. We worship you in our finances, our speech, our character, our careers, our relationships, and in all that we do. Lord, I bind up everything that is not like you, all things that come to throw us off track in Jesus' name. Let us be inspired today to think of your glory and splendor at all times and give your name praise. In Jesus' name we pray, Amen.

# December 29

*Simon Peter answered and said, "You are the Christ, the Son of the living God."* (Matthew 16:16)

Who is Christ to you? Jesus asked the disciples in expectation, to see who they proclaimed Him to be. The reply Peter gave was an indication that Peter believed in his heart that Jesus was Christ, the Son of the living God. His willingness to be open to the voice of God enabled Him to give the correct answer. In His time with Jesus, Peter was able to see the work of the living God firsthand. His heart was in connection with God, and it enabled Him to know who Christ was. He was able to give account of Christ being the true and living Messiah. God wants us to truly believe in our heart that Jesus is our Savior and the Son of the living God. Once our hearts are able to accept Jesus as He is, God will reveal His mysteries to us. This is an individual proclamation that we have to profess on our own. Believing in our heart is one thing, but to profess it in our lifestyle is a lifetime experience. Knowing Christ is the Son of God should manifest our faith in our lifestyles. We should be so entwined in kingdom business that God is able to reveal Himself to us; just as He alone revealed to Peter that Jesus was Christ, the Son of the living God. We have to know Christ to be our Lord and Savior, the living Messiah. Having knowledge of who Christ is makes it easier for us to deal with the stresses of everyday life as we are able to stand firm in the power of Christ. Our thought process has the power to dictate every situation that we encounter in life. If our minds are set on the fact that Christ is in us and nothing can come against Him as He is our shield, we are able to be grounded by our faith. Christ told Peter that He was blessed in receiving the revelation from God. We are blessed just in believing the report of the Lord. Not only are we blessed, but our faith entitles us to embody the plans of the kingdom. When we believe nothing can come against us, we are actually inheriting great powers in God by our faith. As Jesus said, we have the keys to the kingdom of Heaven. All of God's power is within us, to be used according to our faith. Power and all forms of godliness are given to those who profess Jesus as Lord and operate in the knowledge of His strength.

**Who do you say I am!**

Prayer: God, you alone are the King of glory, the one who sits high and looks low. Nothing is hidden from Your presence, You know the heart and mind of all of creation, yet You love us the same. Your love is not built on conditional circumstances, but solely on Your being. Just because of who You are, we are thankful. With You on our side we can accomplish anything. We owe our life to Jesus for His awesome sacrifice. In His dying on the cross, He made sure that we were able to live. By His obedience, we are drawn into Your presence and walk in Your favor. By the work of Your hands, we are able to speak life into the atmosphere and stand on Your Word. The keys to the kingdom of Heaven are placed in the hands of those who believe in Your Son Jesus. Guide us in our assignment, that we will bind all things that are not from You here on earth and loose those things that You desire to bring Your name glory. We lay down our will for Your perfect will. In Jesus' name we pray, Amen.

# December 30

*Yet, you desired faithfulness even in the womb; you taught me wisdom in that secret place.* (Psalm 51:6)

God created us with the need to function with total dependence upon Him. He designed us with the necessity of always needing to depend on Him. Not that He requires a boost in ego, He desires for us to rely on Him that we may be able to know how to function and operate in the earth to our fullest potential. In order for our purpose to flourish in its fullest potential, we need to trust and depend on God. In His infinite wisdom, we are able to live to our maximum ability. We are not able to comprehend everything that takes place in the earth. We may try to make justification for our being, but they are mere opinions. God is the only one who knows the true meaning of life. We are able to obtain insight into our existence and gain knowledge to endure our days from the love God has for us. He longs to pour His Spirit upon us, that we may know the mysteries of His heart. God didn't create us with the intention for us to walk this life blindfolded. He requires that we abide in Him, join in perfect fellowship with Him, and obtain clear instructions on a daily basis.

God is so awesome. If we truly seek after His wisdom on a consistent basis, He will reveal great things that will enable us to make not only wise choices, but the best choices possible. What God requires of us is faithfulness. Faithfulness to our relationship with Him. In our communication with Him, we are able to be directed in the path of righteousness. God's required faithfulness from us even before we were separated from our mother's womb. He controlled us, even in our mother's womb and required our organs to be obedient to His command. By His wisdom, the embryo grows at the command of God and develops into a fetus. The heart begins to beat and the limbs begin to form. This is the beginning of God's teaching, as it shows us all things are under God's control. By faithfulness to the process God designed for reproduction, a baby is born. Faithfulness to God's commands always results in us developing wisdom. As seen in the baby, our body is subject to God's voice. He is the only one who can tell our organs when to stop functioning.

**God is in control of us, if we really think about!**

**And teaching them to obey everything I have commanded you. And surely I am with you always to the very end of the age. (Matthew 28:20)**

Prayer: Thank you for being our God, thank you for being our refuge, our peace, our joy, our entire being. All things are subject to your voice. When you speak, all things fall into place. Let your Word saturate our hearts in such a way that our minds are open to your wisdom. Employ your Spirit to bring all things back to our remembrance as we carry out each day in a manner that is pleasing to you. God, we offer up our minds to you, our heart, our soul, that we may be obedient with a grateful heart. In Jesus' name we pray, Amen.

# December 31

*This vision-message is a witness, pointing to what's coming.* (Habakkuk 2:2)

When God gives a fresh revelation, it is us tapping into our purpose for living, as it is a clear declaration of what is to come. The vision is a message from God, telling us what He had planned for us before we thought to seek Him. His plan was already thought out and ordained "Before I formed you in the womb I knew you; and before you came forth out of the womb I sanctified you, and I ordained you a prophet unto the nations" (Jeremiah 1:5). He planned each course of our life, that we may seek Him and ask what's next. The vision given by God points to what's coming next. It is the very instinct of God being birthed through us. The message comes as a strategy from the Spirit, to be birthed in the earth for the fulfillment of God's perfect plan.

Everything that God speaks will come to pass. He cannot lie. His plans and visions for His people wait in expectation for us to be in a position to hear from Him. We often think we are waiting for God, when He is actually waiting on us. He waits on us to be open to His master plan and receive His instructions, then carry them out. Every day that we are alive on earth coincides with the next. What you did yesterday effects today and what you do today will effect tomorrow. This is why God desires for us to be in constant fellowship with Him. That we may learn His plan, write His plan, and be prepared for the execution of His plan. God is always working and in connection with us. We are the one's who turn Him on and off. God sends His message to the earth for His children to grab hold of, and better themselves in His wisdom. Sadly, some will acknowledge His glory and others will let it pass them by. Whatever choice you make, His word will go forth and accomplish what He ordained it to do.

**So is my word that goes out from my mouth: It will not return to me empty, but will accomplish what I desire and achieve the purpose for which I sent it. (Isaiah 55:11)**

**Purpose is why you are here!**

Prayer: God of honor and God of grace, let Your Spirit fill our hearts that we may be empty in Your presence. Burn everything off of us that is not like You. In your presence is the fullness of joy. We come this day to hear Your plan, we lay down our plan that Your will may take precedence in our lives. Encourages our hearts to be about Kingdom work, that Your purpose will flow through us. Whatever You desire, let it be our desire. Teach us how to encourage others through Your wisdom. We thank You that we are able to obtain wisdom. Thank You that Your grace gives us new revelations each morning. Guard our hearts from the tricks of the enemy. We lift up our hearts, minds, and souls to You today, that we may prosper in Your Spirit and subdue the earth. Let Your word be in us to speak into the atmosphere and charge everything to be under Your control. We pray for Your plan and purpose to saturate our lives. Lord, we trust You. In Jesus' name we pray, AMEN.